On Progress and Prosperity

Essays 2019-2024

Laurence B. Siegel

Edited by Wayne H. Wagner

Foreword by Theodore R. Aronson

Montesquieu
Press

Copyright © 2024 by Laurence B. Siegel
Published by Montesquieu Press
Del Mar, CA 92014

MontesquieuPress.com

First Edition: October 2024
Hardcover ISBN 978-1-7361484-3-3
ebook ISBN 978-1-7361484-1-9

Library of Congress Cataloging-in-Publication Data
Names: Siegel, Laurence B., 1954-, author. Wagner, Wayne H., 1938-, editor
Title: On Progress and Prosperity: essays 2019-2024 / Laurence Siegel.
Description: First edition. | Del Mar, CA: Montesquieu Press [2024]
Includes foreword by Theodore R. Aronson and index.
Library of Congress Control Number: 2024918008

Cover image: Public domain Cover design by Klazina Stanwick
Print book interior design by Amanda Cohen
Chapters marked CC BY-NC-ND 4.0 (at the end of the chapter) may be freely copied, forwarded, and reposted, with attribution, for noncommercial use. They may not be modified, incorporated into another work, or used for commercial purposes without the express written permission of the author. To ask for permission, please write to **lbsiegel@uchicago.edu**.

Chapters containing a copyright notice are subject to the usual restrictions attendant to copyrighted material. For permission, contact the copyright holder. The Foreword is copyrighted © 2024 by Theodore R. Aronson. The Preface is copyrighted © 2024 by Wayne H. Wagner. All other front- and backmatter and the cover design are copyrighted © 2024 by Laurence B. Siegel

Interested in bulk copies? Email **lbsiegel@uchicago.edu**
The author is available for speaking events. He is a CFA Institute Voice of Influence.
See https://rpc.cfainstitute.org/en/voices-of-influence

10 9 8 7 6 5 4 3 2 1

About the Cover Painting

Trade, specialization, the division of labor – these are the building blocks of an economy, of progress, of human betterment. They are the path away from subsistence living toward a productive community. And trade with people far away – people one doesn't even know – is how you begin to transform a primitive economy into a modern one.

The cover painting by Jan Breughel the Elder, entitled "Harbor Scene with St. Paul's Departure from Caesarea," is featured not for its religious content (about which I have no opinion) but for its startling beauty and, most importantly, its depiction of a trading society two thousand years before our own. We don't know if Breughel, painting in The Netherlands in 1596, created a historically accurate scene or if, instead, he was extrapolating from the prosperous trading milieu in which he lived. In either case the painting brings to life the intimate relation between trade and good fortune. The large ships are not mere fishing vessels – although they bring sustenance, the most basic human need – but vessels of commerce, bringing goods from afar and sending the products made by those in the painting to markets in distant lands. That is how the economy grows and people thrive.

The painting hangs in the North Carolina Museum of Art, Raleigh, North Carolina.

On Progress and Prosperity explores the relationships between production, exchange, capital, the freedom to pursue one's enlightened self-interest, and the progress we can hope to achieve in the future. It is composed of book reviews and other essays written between 2020 and 2024 for investors and the general public. Deep thanks are due to Ted Aronson (AJO Vista), Lara Crigger and Heather Bell (Advisor Perspectives), and Bob Huebscher (now retired from Advisor Perspectives) for the sponsorship and publication of most of these articles, and to my co-authors, other publishers, and many friends who gave advice and criticism. Happy reading.

ii

Also by Laurence B. Siegel

As author

Fewer, Richer, Greener (Wiley, 2019)

Unknown Knowns (Montesquieu Press, 2021)

Puzzles of Money, Inflation, and Debt, with Thomas S. Coleman and Bryan Oliver (CFA Institute Research Foundation, 2021)

Benchmarks and Investment Management (CFA Institute Research Foundation, 2003)

As editor

Revisiting the Equity Risk Premium, with Paul McCaffrey (CFA Institute Research Foundation, 2023)

Robert C. Merton and the Science of Finance, with Luis Garcia-Feijóo and Timothy R. Kohn (CFA Institute Research Foundation, 2020)

The Productivity Puzzle, with David E. Adler (CFA Institute Research Foundation, 2019)

Rethinking the Equity Risk Premium, with P. Brett Hammond and Martin L. Leibowitz (CFA Institute Research Foundation, 2011).

Insights into the Global Financial Crisis (CFA Institute Research Foundation, 2009).

The Future of Life-Cycle Saving and Investing (in three volumes), with Zvi Bodie, Dennis McLeavey, Rodney N. Sullivan, and Lisa Stanton (CFA Institute Research Foundation, 2007, 2009, and 2012)

Stocks, Bonds, Bills, and Inflation Yearbook (annual), Ibbotson Associates, Inc., Chicago, 1984-1994

Also by Wayne H. Wagner

Investment Management: Meeting the Noble Challenges of Funding Pensions, Deficits and Growth, with Ralph A. Rieves (Wiley, 2009)

Millionaire, with Al Winnikoff (Renaissance, 2001)

The Complete Guide to Securities Transactions (Wiley, 1989).

FREE COLOR PDF OF THIS BOOK
FOR BOOK PURCHASERS

This hardbound book contains only black-and-white illustrations, including many that are much more dramatic and beautiful in color. For a free PDF of this book containing the color versions of the illustrations, please send proof of purchase of the book (Amazon screenshot or equivalent) to the author at lbsiegel@uchicago.edu.

Table of Contents

Foreword by Theodore R. Aronson ix
Preface by Wayne H. Wagner: The More You Read, The More You Know xi

Progress

1. Deirdre McCloskey and Art Carden Explain How the Modern World Came to Be 3
2. Matt Ridley Uncovers the Mystery Behind Innovation 17
3. Doing More with Less: Andrew McAfee on Dematerialization 29
4: Why Brad DeLong Thinks the Long Boom Is Over 45
5. "Fewer, Richer, Greener!" 57

Investing

6: The Price of Time 91
7: Harry Markowitz and the Philosopher's Stone 107
8. Would Charles Darwin Have Been a Good Investor? 129
9. How Venture Capital Thrives by Betting on Weirdness 143
10. Financial Folly, Religious Frenzy and the Delusions of Crowds 157

Technology

11. Henry Kissinger on the Promise and Threats of AI 175
12. Cloudy with a Chance of Technological Breakthrough 189
13. Mark Mills on the Cloud, the Robot Revolution, and Machines That Think 203
14. Why Are Elephants So Smart and Buildings So Short? 221

Political Economy

15. Johan Norberg's Plan to Save the World Through Capitalism 237
16. Paul Samuelson and Milton Friedman, The Frenemies Who Defined 20th Century Economics 251
17. Friedman's Bulldog? Edward Yardeni Presents a Brief for Capitalism 267
18. Why Joel Kotkin's Fear of American Neo-Feudalism Is Unfounded 277

Provocative

19. How to Think: Steven Pinker's Instruction Manual for Your Brain 293
20. Twenty Rules for Life: Morgan Housel's Antidote to Chaos 305
21. Home, Home on the *Range:* The Advantage of Generalists over Specialists 317
22. "Money Changes Everything": The Many-Faceted Mind of Will Goetzmann 331
23. Michael Lewis on the Unlikely Trio That Defeated the Pandemic 343
24. Malcolm Gladwell's "Talking to Strangers": On Preventing Financial Fraud and Worse 357

Index 371
About the Author 386
About the Editor 387

On Progress

That the better self shall prevail and each generation introduce its successor to a higher plane of life. – *John Lancaster Spalding; motto of Hawken School*

Progress began to retrogress when Wilbur and Orville started tinkering around in Dayton and at Kitty Hawk, because I believe that two Wrights made a wrong. – *Ogden Nash*

No one should be discouraged, Theaetetus, who can make constant progress, even though it be slow. – *Plato*[1]

On Prosperity

I've been poor and I've been rich. Rich is better. – *Beatrice Kaufman*

The consequences for human welfare involved in questions like [how to make less developed economies grow] are simply staggering: Once one starts to think about them, it is hard to think about anything else – *Nobel Prize winner Robert Lucas*

It is the great multiplication of the productions of all the different arts, in consequence of the division of labour, which occasions, in a well-governed society, that universal opulence which extends itself to the lowest ranks of the people. – *Adam Smith*[2]

TO JOSH, ASHLEIGH, AND ELIZABETH

And to friends of progress, freedom, and enterprise everywhere.

---

[1] The Sophist, http://www.perseus.tufts.edu/hopper/text?doc=Perseus%3Atext%3A1999.01.0172%3Atext%3DSoph.%3Apage%3D261

[2] The Wealth of Nations, Book I, Chapter I, p. 22, para. 10.

Foreword by Theodore R. Aronson

Spend enough time in our business, and you will meet everyone. At least everyone worth meeting. And so it was, my meeting Larry.

Over the course of many years, a friend, Liz Hilpman, shared snippets of a dude she knew who shuttled between New York City (job) and Chicago (home). She always described him as really intelligent...and "different." Of course, lots of Wall Streeters are really intelligent, but I assumed she also meant he was not your typical Wall Street guy. Fortunately for me, I would come to know "different" meant so much more than not typical.

My curiosity eventually got the best of me, and I wrangled a meeting with Larry at his perch at the Ford Foundation. My first impression of Larry was that of a gentleman — literally, a *gentle man*. He was so interested in what I had to say, I immediately felt important in his presence and almost forgot *I* had asked for the meeting with *him*. Over the next quarter century, I learned what lies beneath his gentle exterior — a powerful wit, a hilarious sense of humor, and a muscular intelligence that feeds on a curiosity and interest for everything he encounters.

In fact, the diversity of Larry's interests is only surpassed by the copiousness of his output — the reviews, articles, books, and monographs he produces far exceed the material he consumes, if not in quantity, certainly in caliber. Eventually, I volunteered my firm, AJO Vista, to serve as a distributor of Larry's materials. That may sound generous, but I must admit, my motives were a bit more selfish...

AJO Vista's mailing list was established from 40 years of industry relationships. It includes clients, prospects, reporters, and FOAJOVs (friends of AJO Vista). In fact, 40 years in the world of investing is actually enough time to both meet everyone and have them included on your mailing list — even the thought-leaders in the investment world. The selfish part of using our publishing partnership? Not only did AJO Vista receive his work hot-off-the-press, but the reaction of our recipients from the anticipation and excitement he created only redounded to our benefit.

AJO Vista will eagerly continue to be one of the vessels delivering anything Larry produces. Of course, Larry doesn't lack venues to publish — key among them are his own website (https://larrysiegel.org/), a Substack currently being developed, and his perch as Research Director of the CFA Institute's Research Foundation. This book is yet another!

In the able hands of Wayne Wagner, many pieces from the AJO Vista/Siegel collaboration (Larry's work, AJO Vista's delivery) grace the following pages.

I'm sure you'll find Larry's writing as I've often described it — insightful, erudite, articulate, and opinionated — with the added advantage of being right! And when he isn't, he's interesting anyway.

Theodore R. Aronson
Philadelphia, Pennsylvania
August 2024

Ted Aronson is founder of AJO Vista and AJO, a trustee of Spelman College, and past chair of the CFA Institute and the CFA Institute's Research Foundation.

Preface

The More You Read, The More You Know

Wayne H. Wagner

Oscar Wilde wrote,

> "In old days books were written by men of letters and read by the public. Nowadays books are written by the public and read by nobody."

As you read this book, you will challenge Oscar Wilde's clever assertion. In these pages you will find sparkling reviews of serious books.

Larry Siegel's gift to you, the reader, is a shortcut to understanding important new ideas.

Larry reads significant books written by serious thinkers. Authors who have something important to say will require much more reading time and comprehension time than most readers can afford. Larry has an uncanny ability to extract the most important and insightful information and make that available to you with style, sophistication, and (rarest of all) humor.

If you've read this far into this introduction, you have already revealed that you are a person who enjoys seeking knowledge. Read on.

> The more you read, the more you know.
> The more you learn, the more places you'll go.
>
> —Dr. Seuss

Let me tell you a little more about the author. Larry's jobs as director of research for three different investment organizations have led him to read dozens of books on finance and related topics. His interests have always extended beyond finance into the realms explored in this book, but only in recent years has he begun to write about them.

Larry's books present ideas that are *known* by distinguished writers, but often *unknown* by people who might benefit from them. Larry titled his first book of collected readings *Unknown Knowns* for that reason.

Unknown Knowns gathered essays Larry had privately circulated or that had appeared in that excellent publication for financial advisors, *Advisor Perspectives*. That book featured twenty-five essays on investing, finance, retirement, money, governance, and a catch-all section called Provocative. The book was well received, including by a reviewer who said that it

> ...will reward the reader with many an "aha" moment, as you realize [Siegel] has turned the rock around to a different side than the one we usually look at and noticed something both important and new.

This is Larry's second book of essays. It follows the same pattern: twenty-four articles in sections headed Progress, Investing, Technology, Political Economy, and the further-ranging Provocative collection.

Where does Larry get his ideas? Many are suggested by friends and colleagues, while others might be picked off a bookshop shelf.

Leading authors worldwide are enhancing our understanding of science, economics, social issues, and other fields of knowledge. We all want to know the essence of new thinking, but we don't have the time to delve into the lengthy tomes written by these authors. The books are often too long and detailed for general use, yet we readers want to know about the most significant ideas each author presents.

Larry enables us to do that by:

- **Reading a book**, then summarizing the key thoughts in a review.
- **Interviewing**. Larry is constantly seeking interesting thinkers and getting them to share their wisdom.
- **Co-authoring**. Larry can't do it all alone, and he engages other authors in cooperative writing.

Larry's challenge is to summarize a multi-hundred-page treatise in a consistent ten to twenty pages. What a tough assignment!

Larry then goes beyond the usual confines of a book review to include concepts and speculations outside the domain of the original author. He integrates the author's thoughts into his broad knowledge base, which he then shares with the reader.

So, enjoy your reading. As Larry reminds us, each chapter is a magazine article, so you can read the book in manageable bites – delicious ones, if you ask me.

—W. H. W.
Larkspur, California
June 2024

Progress

The future will look like the past in many ways – it always does. In other aspects, it will reflect changes that arrive gradually until they suddenly arrive at warp speed. When we're in a rapidly changing environment, as we seem to be now, the ideas of forward-looking individuals are needed to influence the direction and speed of that path. Here are the thoughts of some brilliant minds reflecting on how we got to where we are in today's world, and where we might be headed.

Wayne's favorite: Deirdre McCloskey and Art Carden Explain How the Modern World Came to Be.

(It would be too fawning to select Larry Siegel's Fewer, Richer, Greener.)

—W.H.W.

Chapter 1. Deirdre McCloskey and Art Carden Explain How the Modern World Came to Be

Laurence B. Siegel
September 2021

How Did the World Go from Poor to Rich?

After tens of thousands of years of living at a subsistence level, how did the world suddenly become so rich?

By "suddenly" I mean in the last 250 years (I'm a long-term investor). However, even if you think in shorter time frames, the rise of China in the last 40 years, and of the United States, Europe, and Japan in the century before that, would have come as a big surprise to a caveman or a medieval peasant. In their new book, *Leave Me Alone and I'll Make You Rich*, Deirdre McCloskey and Art Carden set forth a new and provocative answer to this question.

It was not capitalism, capital accumulation, education, pure science, technology, political freedom, or the rule of law allowing people to keep the fruits of their labors. Those were all necessary but not sufficient conditions. Other civilizations had those virtues but no Industrial Revolution resulted.

It was a sudden increase, in northwestern Europe in the 1700s, in the *respect and dignity accorded the bourgeoisie*. The missing ingredient was *Bourgeois Dignity*, as McCloskey titled one of her books.

While this line of thinking might sound like a purely academic exercise, it's not. Getting the right answer is key to the future of global economic growth, as each country tries to find the best path forward. And the success or failure of these efforts is key to long-run future rates of return for investors today.

Laissez faire

McCloskey and Carden leave no doubt as to their basic philosophy: The book's title is an amended translation of the familiar French phrase *laissez faire*, meaning, roughly, "leave me alone." (A French government minister in the 1700s asked a businessman how he could help the business community, and *laissez faire* was the businessman's answer. It caught on.) The authors' amendment, "...and I'll make you rich," reflects their passionately held view that a thriving commercial society is good for everyone, not just for the business owner.

Deirdre Nansen McCloskey
Source:
https://www.deirdremccloskey.com/books/

They also believe that a commercial republic — Hamilton's phrase[1] — is morally good and offers a milieu in which people can best realize their spiritual as well as their material potential.

About the authors

But McCloskey is no doctrinaire libertarian or conservative. Far from it. She describes herself as:

> a literary, quantitative, postmodern, free-market, progressive-Episcopalian, ex-marxoid, Midwestern woman from Boston who was once a man. Not "conservative"! I'm a Christian classical liberal.[2]

---

[1] Apparently. Writing collectively as "Publius," Alexander Hamilton, James Madison, and John Jay seem to have coined the felicitous phrase, describing what we might now call liberal capitalism. The Federalist Papers #6, in which the phrase first appears, is usually attributed to Hamilton.

[2] Source: https://www.deirdremccloskey.com. Carden is a more conventional conservative, but the book's ideas are mostly McCloskey's.

Talk about eclectic!

She's also a graphomane, a person who can't stop writing. She's written 24 books, some of them very long, and 400 articles. She needed Art Carden, an economics professor and popular Forbes.com contributor, to help her condense her three tomes, *The Bourgeois Virtues*, *Bourgeois Dignity*, and *Bourgeois Equality* (collectively called the Bourgeois Trilogy and weighing in at 1700 pages), into the one reasonably short, and very good, book that is the subject of this review. While I'd only recommend the entire trilogy to the fully retired and intellectually voracious, *Leave Me Alone and I'll Make You Rich* is Sunday reading, accessible to everyone. It conveys very effectively the message that McCloskey has spent the last 15 years of her life honing.

Some wrong answers to the "great question"

Art Carden
Source: https://www.econlib.org/ archives/2014/06/ evidence_that_e.htm

A large and highly informative proportion of *Leave Me Alone* is devoted to discussing conventional reasons why the world started to become rich since the Industrial Revolution, and why they were necessary but not sufficient conditions. The authors show respect for the various explanations I listed above — it is not quite a debunking — and then demonstrate that these conditions, while necessary, were not enough.

They then transition to the "One True Explanation" (I'm not mocking McCloskey; I'm quoting her own self-mocking phrase). This review follows the same outline: the conditions that the authors think are necessary but not sufficient, and why they are not sufficient; then bourgeois dignity, the secret sauce.

A Quick Summary of the Conventional Explanation

McCloskey and Carden take the explanation set forth by the historian Niall Ferguson, whose most recent book, *Doom*, I reviewed somewhat favorably in *Advisor Perspectives*,[3] as the conventional starting point that they seek to replace or modify:

> Our friends on the moderate right...extol the "Killer Apps," as...Ferguson calls them. His list is: "better property rights, a work ethic, a consumer society, competition, modern medicine, and science." We agree that any decent society should want more of these. But we disagree that they are the "killer apps" explaining why people in some places are very rich while people in other places are very poor.[4]

Let's now consider the killer apps, including some not listed by Ferguson, one at a time.

It Wasn't "Resources or Railways or Property Rights"

It certainly wasn't natural resources. In the aftermath of World War II, Burma (Myanmar) and the Philippines were regarded as the most promising Asian economies because of their natural resources. Burma's per capita income in 1950 was higher than that of Hong Kong, Korea, Malaysia, and Thailand.[5] Today it's one of the poorest countries in the world outside Africa, with a PPP GDP per capita one-twelfth that of Hong Kong, the richest of that bunch, and one-fourth that of Thailand, the poorest. The Philippines have also done badly, although not "Myanmar badly."

The countries with the most abundant resources are in Africa, South America, and Central Asia. These are among the poorest, not the richest, parts of the world.

It wasn't railways. The railroad was a world-changing invention, yet it lowered the price of corn coming from Iowa by only 50%; meanwhile,

---

[3] https://www.advisorperspectives.com/articles/2021/08/09/niall-ferguson-says-were-getting-worse-at-dealing-with-catastrophes-but-hes-wrong

[4] Echoing the late Harvard professor David Landes, whose classic book on this topic is titled *The Wealth and Poverty of Nations: Why Some are So Rich and Some So Poor*. Landes, sometimes called an institutionalist, says the key variables are "institutions and culture first; money next; but from the beginning and increasingly, the payoff was to knowledge." Landes' lively book is a delight to read, filled with historical facts and insights. It is the book that started me on the path to being an amateur (very amateur) development economist.

[5] Wong, John. 1997. "Why Has Myanmar Not Developed Like East Asia?" *ASEAN Economic Bulletin*, Vol. 13, No. 3 (March), pp. 344-358.

transportation by barge became less costly too. "To this day, a good deal of the corn crop leaves the Midwest by barge," write the authors. Without railways, we'd have a small Chicago and a giant Saint Louis, and cars would have been developed earlier. The authors estimate, using a low-tech analysis called the Harberger triangle, that the net gain to the United States from the coming of the railways was 2.5% of GDP, about one year's growth. Who would have guessed it?

Property rights are a different story. They *have* to matter, don't they? They do matter, up to a point: If you can't be sure of getting and keeping the profit from an activity or enterprise, why bother? Societies with few or no private property rights, such as the former Soviet Union, usually fail quickly and dramatically.

McCloskey and Carden respond:

> [Property rights are] again necessary, but nothing like sufficient... English common law [which strongly guarantees property rights] was in place hundreds of years before the Enrichment... The...historian Alan MacFarlane notes that "England was as 'capitalist' in 1250 as it was in 1550 or 1750." It relied on property rights and the rule of law.

But no Great Enrichment in England until well after 1700.

Trade? Same answer. "Trade...is ancient... Amber from the shores of the Baltic and lapis lazuli from Afghanistan turn up in Egyptian grave goods. European grain prices moved together *by arbitrage* in the late Middle Ages."[6]

It Wasn't Capital Accumulation

The idea that saving and investment are vital for economic growth is so deeply ingrained (a five-year old with a piggy bank can understand it) that many readers will think that it just has to be right. Again, the iconoclastic authors say, "No, it isn't." They argue that "accumulation was necessary, as were sunlight and the presence of a labor force, but it raised income sharply only when it embodied brilliant new ideas, such as containerization." The authors emphasize their belief that *only new ideas*,

---

[6] My italics.

implemented through commerce made possible by a profit motive, make growth not only plausible but inevitable. McCloskey and Carden call this hypothesis "innovism," a clunky word for a brilliant concept, and one to which I'll return.

I find some fault with the "innovation is everything" position. Let's start with this hypothetical: If you do everything tomorrow in the exact same way that you did it today, the economy won't have grown. You have to do it a little better tomorrow for the output of your little economy to increase.

Here's the rub: Let's say that a machinist in Cleveland finds a better way to manufacture a ball bearing. The GDP of Cleveland rises by the amount of the improvement. A few days later, a machinist in Cincinnati hears about the improvement and imitates it. No new idea has been created in this second step, but the GDP of Cincinnati has increased by just as much as the GDP of Cleveland. Democratization of existing ideas, through trade, transportation, and communication, is almost as important as the creative impulse that produced the new idea in the first place. McCloskey and Carden don't address this.

It Wasn't Education and Science

Here, McCloskey and Carden go against basic intuition (including mine) once again:

> ...[A]s sources of the Great Enrichment, the wonderful schooling and glorious science were limited in scope. The Great Enrichment got going without much schooling and without much in the way of "high" science...until 1900 or so.

The authors go on to show that literacy rates were low until late in the Great Enrichment, and that tinkering and commercially motivated invention were more important to economic growth than advanced math, nuclear physics, or even biology until the last century or so. That is a reasonable assertion – although I'd want to ask some other economic historian whether "high science," which began with Isaac Newton (1643-1727), was really that distant from material progress for the two and half centuries before 1900.

But I object to the conclusion! You do not need mass literacy to make technological progress — you need a community of highly literate experts on various subjects. Three percent of the population with advanced literacy ought to make a huge difference. A society in which only three percent were competent in John Adams' famous list,

> mathematics and philosophy, geography, natural history and naval architecture, navigation, commerce and agriculture, [which one pursues] in order to give their children a right to study painting, poetry, music, architecture, statuary, tapestry and porcelain

might be considered a pathetic failure in spiritual or aesthetic terms. But it could be quite prosperous because of the achievements of those three percent. Look at the United States in 1900, a hundred years after Adams, when only 6.7% of young men and women (and a much smaller percentage of the total adult population) had completed high school. It was a very rich country by the standards of the time.

It Wasn't Imperialism, Slavery, or "Wage Slavery"

I'd like to dismiss these with a wave of the hand. They are all variations on "taking that which doesn't belong to you." This has been tried by kings, priests, and generals since the beginning of historical time. It always results in the appearance, but not the reality, of prosperity. It's a zero-sum game: My prosperity comes at the expense of your poverty. Many people still believe that is the case with business and capitalism, but if McCloskey and Carden cannot convince you otherwise, nobody can.

Are Rich People Bad?

The idea that prosperity is a zero-sum game set me off on a digression that passes through first-century Israel. Jesus said, "It is easier for a camel to pass through the eye of a needle than for a rich man to enter the kingdom of God."[7] Why? What did Jesus have against rich people?

In those times, rich people ordinarily got that way by seizing other people's resources. Jesus had a good reason not to like them. But with

---

[7] King James Version, Matthew 19:24

economic freedom, one can get rich in a non-exploitative way: just produce something other people value, and keep the profits. Whole countries could increase their prosperity by industrializing, instead of by plundering other countries. As a result, with the dawn of capitalism, wars over territory and resources began to diminish, as documented in Steven Pinker's best-seller, *Enlightenment Now*, which I reviewed in 2018.[8] (Pinker provides evidence that the paroxysm of wars in the first half of the twentieth century was an exception to the secular decline in violence, not the rule.)

And the respect and dignity accorded businesspeople grew as people began to experience the benefits of a commercial society. Which was the cause and which the effect? McCloskey and Carden clearly say that the new respect accorded the bourgeoisie was the cause, and prosperity and the success of commercial society the effect, but it is not clear. An argument can be made either way.

At any rate, in the biblical passage referenced above, we see a vivid example of the anti-business position that the Greeks, Romans, Catholics, and many others held and carried forward until the Enlightenment and, in modified form, to the present time. McCloskey's Bourgeois Trilogy, and the book reviewed here, persuade us to at least consider the possibility that a shift from anti-business to pro-business attitudes was the key to the Great Enrichment, the 30-fold increase (100-fold in the advanced countries) in the standard of living over the last 250 years.[9] But it is always hard to distinguish cause from effect in historical speculations.

---

[8] https://larrysiegeldotorg.files.wordpress.com/2018/05/ajo-siegel-pinker.pdf

[9] These multiples reflect not only the "time price" of goods and services – the number of hours of labor needed to procure them – but also my assessment of what I call the "effort price," the amount of misery experienced in each of those hours. Backbreaking work that puts the worker in an early grave has largely been replaced by what our forebears would call easy work. That's a very important part of the improvement in living standards that is often overlooked. (The pure time price of goods and services declined by a smaller but still very impressive amount; see Tupy, Marian, and Gale Pooley. 2023. *Superabundance*. Washington, DC: CATO Institute.)

Is Capitalism the Secret Sauce?

We get to the fun part. Yes, it's capitalism. No, McCloskey and Carden don't call it capitalism — they hate the word. As you recall, their name for the secret sauce is the "respect and dignity accorded the bourgeoisie." How can these two very different-sounding ideas represent the same secret ingredient?

I link the two as follows: Reduced to its essentials, capitalism means economic freedom. In the words of Mark Kritzman, a celebrated investment analyst, economic freedom is "the idea that, if you produce a resource, it's yours to do what you want with it."[10]

The dignity accorded businesspeople by the larger society also means economic freedom, the ability to act in one's own interest without becoming a pariah. You are only free if you can practice your craft without social or religious disapproval or worse.

This is one reason why the Jews became the business class in medieval and Renaissance Europe. Non-Jews couldn't be soiled by the taint of commerce — their religion (sort of) forbade it.[11] Also, Jews, chased from country to country, knew they had to carry their human capital, the ability to earn money, wherever they went. They developed skills that could be practiced anywhere. These included business skills.

The secret sauce for self-sustained growth, according to both McCloskey-Carden and me, then, is *economic freedom*. The newfound dignity of the bourgeoisie is a cultural expression of that underlying idea. Which came first is a question I cannot answer. McCloskey and Carden have, of course, made their position clear — it was bourgeois dignity that brought about the flourishing of economic freedom. But other theories abound, and I wouldn't dismiss them quite yet.

---

[10] Personal communication.

[11] This didn't stop the Medicis, Fuggers, and other trading families that became very rich in those times.

And finally, since the word "capitalism" is misleading (economic freedom has very little to do with capital) and has come to mean whatever a given speaker likes or doesn't like, let's retire it as McCloskey and Carden suggest.

One-and-a-Half Cheers for Innovism

But what word shall we replace it with? McCloskey and Carden have suggested "innovism," the system that both produces and rewards innovation. It will do — but it will not do well. It focuses most readers' minds too narrowly on growth through better engineering, rather than through any of the other channels — salesmanship, distribution, financing, business organization, and so forth — that contribute to betterment over time. The authors would counter, correctly, that innovation can take place along any of these channels, and that only an unimaginative reader will equate the word with mere clever tinkering. But I still think "innovism" is tin-eared, especially if it's supposed to proxy for economic freedom supported by liberal democracy.

Three Cheers for the Commercial Republic

To sum up, "economic freedom with liberal democracy" and "respect and dignity accorded the bourgeoisie" are so closely related that they come down to the same thing: liberty. A society conveys what it values by choosing whom it elevates to a position of respect: the ancient Greeks, philosophers, athletes, and dramatists; the Romans, lawyers, orators, and builders; medieval Europeans, saints and religious leaders.

Starting around 1600 in the Low Countries and 1700 in Britain, men (and they were almost all men) of a practical bent gained admiration: scientists, engineers, architects, writers, painters. The most practical were businessmen, buying and selling tangible goods all day. When this new bourgeois class became heroes instead of goats, an ambitious person could achieve respectability by joining the Commercial Republic instead of the kingdom of God or the military or the royal court. And that is how capitalism, or more properly a society dominated by people freely engaging in commerce and trade, came to be.

Today, McCloskey and Carden's bourgeoisie doesn't just consist of entrepreneurs, those celebrated heroes of today. It also includes engineers, salesmen, accountants, assistant managers, software developers, and medical, financial, and legal professionals of all stripes. It is the dominant class in every advanced society in the world.

What do We Get for All This Bourgeois Dignity?

Whatever the reasons for the Great Enrichment, I've been talking about it at length without putting it in pictures. A graph is the best way to visualize growth over time, so look at Exhibit 1 — a reconstruction of per capita GDP in England, in today's money, over the last 750 years. (I choose England because it has the best very long-term data, chiefly records of wages and prices, from which modern economists can make rough estimates of per capita GDP.)

The line in Exhibit 1 shows the stages of the Great Enrichment as experienced in that country, which led the way during the critical seventeenth through nineteenth centuries. There is a point of inflection around 1660, when the English Civil War and Glorious Revolution brought more economic freedom to the island. There's another around 1820, when the Industrial Revolution was in full flower, and a bigger one around 1920, when the country became fully modern. (I use a log scale so that the earlier inflection points don't become invisible.)

Exhibit 1 — The Great Enrichment is not a figure of speech or a misinterpretation of history. It really happened.

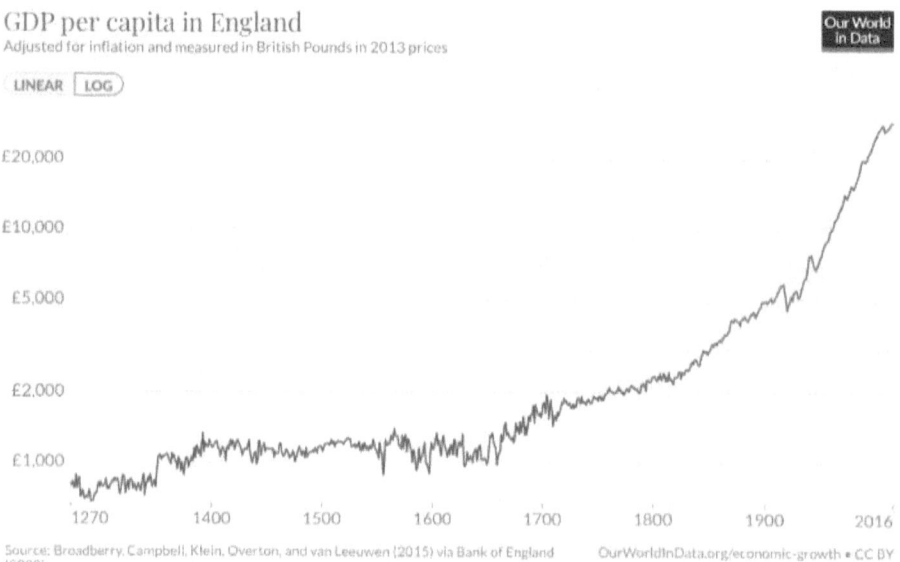

But what about the rest of the world? We all know that the United States, much of Europe, and Japan (the "West") thrived since 1700, but there are still a lot of poor people in the "rest." How much has bourgeois dignity helped them?

A great deal, but later in the "rest" than in the west. Look at Exhibit 2. The blue line, representing the entire world, lags the United States by about 80 years. Thus, the world lives – on average, with wide variation – at a standard the U.S. reached around 1940-1950. The compound growth rate of per capita GDP has been a remarkably consistent 1.8% per year, in the U.S. and the U.K. for 200 years and for the world for at least 150, a rate that compounds up to huge increases over long periods of time.

Exhibit 2 — The amazing tenacity of the global economic growth rate

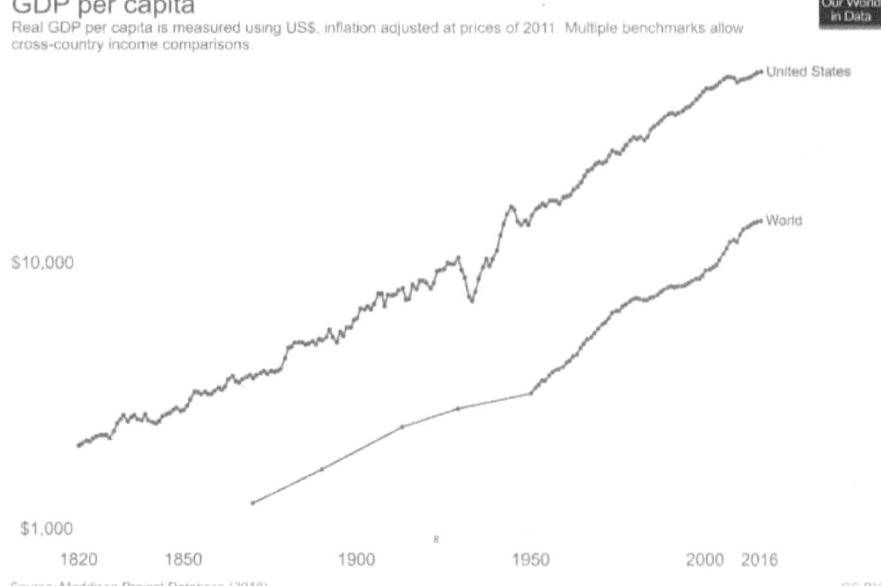

Source: https://ourworldindata.org/economic-growth

This is a tremendous accomplishment. But it's not good enough. We need more bourgeois dignity and economic freedom.

Recommendations for Readers

There are a lot of classical liberal books. What makes this one special?

The authors have an unconventional answer to the question of how the world got rich in the last quarter of a millennium. Unless you're already familiar with Deirdre McCloskey's books, articles, and videos, you probably haven't thought of the dignity newly afforded the bourgeoisie in the 1600s and 1700s as a factor — much less the dispositive factor — in explaining the world as it is today.

The book presents details exposing the inner workings of McCloskey's astonishingly fertile mind. Just about anyone else writing 1700 pages (the trilogy, not this book!) about the bourgeoisie would have accomplished little other than a surefire formula for putting people to sleep. McCloskey and Carden's writing is lively and easy to read.

They've compressed their ideas into fewer than 250 pages of accessible storytelling. Those who do economic research rarely recast it in popularized form. Those who write popular books on economics are rarely capable of doing original research. McCloskey and Carden are excellent at both endeavors.

I enthusiastically recommend this book.

Chapter 2. Matt Ridley Uncovers the Mystery Behind Innovation

Laurence B. Siegel
October 2020

Ever wonder why the world enjoys a substantially higher standard of living than ever before? According to Matt Ridley, it is because liberal democracy, nurtured over the last 250 years in the countries on the technological frontier, is the essential catalyst for fostering innovation.

Why do we care about innovation? Because economic growth, the magical-seeming process that has brought prosperity to much of the world, relies on it. The economy grows not just through putting more people, resources, and capital to work; that's the easy part and it explains a little.[1] But the 30-to-1 (or 100-to-1, depending on whose data you believe) increase in well-being since the Industrial Revolution comes from *innovation* — the ingredient that enables you to do more with less: more production using fewer materials, more results achieved in less time, more satisfaction with less effort.

Matt Ridley
Source: http://www.mattridley.co.uk/

In *How Innovation Works*, Matt Ridley, the author of *The Red Queen*, *The Rational Optimist*, and many other works on biology, evolution, the economy, and progress, turns his attention to the anatomy of

---

[1] The capital accumulation explanation for growth, which is valid for small improvements, fails at a large scale because of diminishing marginal returns to capital (you have plenty of capital but nothing profitable to invest in).

technological advancement. (Ridley, properly the 5th Viscount Ridley, is a hereditary peer of the House of Lords and was trained as a biologist.)

Even more than the esteemed Stephen Jay Gould, Ridley has been the inspiration for my writing. The first paragraph of *How Innovation Works* is a fine example of how Ridley's mind functions:

> An idea pops into my head as I [photograph a duck]: a riff on the second law of thermodynamics... The idea is this: the electricity in my iPhone's battery and the warmth in the eider duck's body are doing roughly the same thing: making improbable order (photographs, ducklings) by expending or converting energy.
>
> And then I think that the idea I've just had itself, like the eider duck and the iPhone, is also an improbable arrangement of synaptic activity in my brain, also fueled by energy from...food...but made possible by the underlying order of the brain, itself the evolved product of millennia of natural selection acting on individuals, each of whose own improbabilities were sustained by energy conversion.

Ridley concludes: "Improbable arrangements of the world, crystallized consequences of energy generation, are what both life and technology are all about." Whew! That's quite a string of connections, all sparked by a photograph of a *bird*.

How Innovation Works isn't consistently that good, but it's pretty close. Much of it is a retelling of familiar stories about invention and innovation. But it is a compelling, short, and easy-to-read book because, tucked into the vignettes and reflections that make it up, we find "Ridleyisms" — surprising connections like the one about the bird — on almost every page.

There are two parts to the book. The first consists of Ridley's vignettes, short tales averaging five pages, recounting how a particular innovation came to be. They are classified into seven categories: energy, public health, transport, food, low-tech innovations, communication and computing, and prehistoric innovation. (Yes – a very long time ago, human beings invented the dog. More about that later.) I found low-tech innovations to be the most fun of the categories, because I knew the least about them.

Where Innovation Comes From

The second part is more philosophical. Ridley asks where innovation comes from, why it sometimes blossoms or fades, and how we can get more of it. The book's subtitle, "and Why it Flourishes in Freedom," is telling.[2] He outlines a vision of innovation that he describes thus (I condense somewhat): "Innovation is gradual... different from invention... often serendipitous... recombinant... involves trial and error... is a team sport... is inexorable... [involves] a hype cycle... prefers fragmented government... [and] increasingly means using fewer resources rather than more."

This list is very powerful and comes close to being a complete theory of human progress. It is, of course, only a theory, which means that it could be tested and found wanting. I am fascinated by "prefers fragmented government," because Joel Mokyr, an economic historian of great renown, also favors this as an explanation for the rise of Europe in early modern times, a concept I cover in my book, *Fewer, Richer, Greener*.[3]

Ridley's vision of technological improvement, then, goes something like this:

- Teamwork and parallel efforts, not heroic individual achievement, are the principal source of innovation;

- Incremental innovation is the ingredient that, when accumulated over time, results in profound change;[4] and

- The democratization of technological benefits, not invention or scientific discovery *per se*, is what drives the growth of the economy.

---

[2] The book's original subtitle, "Serendipity, Energy, and the Saving of Time," probably aimed at British readers, is actually more revealing of the book's contents.

[3] Page 294 in chapter 17 of Siegel, Laurence B. 2019. Fewer, Richer, Greener: Prospects for Humanity in an Age of Abundance. Hoboken, NJ: John Wiley & Sons.

[4] See the excellent article on incremental and process innovation, "Reviving America's Forgotten Innovation System: Fostering US Growth through Incremental Product and Process Innovation," by Dan Breznitz and Peter Cowhey, in Adler, David E., and Laurence B. Siegel, editors, *The Productivity Puzzle: Restoring Economic Dynamism*, Charlottesville, VA: CFA Institute Research Foundation, 2019. The authors demonstrate that such innovation is largely brought about by line workers and rank-and-file engineers.

This point of view echoes those of Sir Isaac Newton, who said that if he has seen farther it was because he stood on the shoulders of giants; and Thomas Edison, who (Ridley emphasizes) benefited from the incremental innovations of forebears going back centuries. Edison famously summed up the process as "Genius: one percent inspiration and 99 percent perspiration."

Let there be (much cheaper) light

To give a flavor of Ridley's vision of innovation as a process, rather than the more widely told tale of heroic invention, let's look at the most familiar invention story ever told: Thomas Edison and the light bulb.

Sir Joseph Swan
Source: https://en.wikipedia.org/wiki/%20Joseph_Swan

Electric lighting began not in 1879 with Edison's tungsten-filament, incandescent bulb but in 1802, when Sir Humphry Davy ran current from a battery of batteries [5] (see Exhibit 1) through a device consisting, originally, of two carbon electrodes separated by air. The continuous spark between the electrodes produced a bright light. This "carbon arc lamp," later familiar to moviegoers as a source of very intense light for projectors, was also the forerunner of the fluorescent bulb, which works on the same spark principle but uses metal electrodes and mercury vapor instead of air.

The usefulness of electricity for lighting was obvious to everyone by the 1870s. Tinkerers as well as organized teams of researchers worked on a myriad of ways to replace the arc, or spark, with a tangible filament that would use less electricity per unit of light produced and be durable enough for practical use. The outlines of a

---

[5] The etymology of the word "battery" for an electrical cell is Davy's design that hooked together multiple cells in a battery, like a battery of armaments.

solution were obvious to Edison and his many competitors; the exact specifications were not.

At least 21 people made contributions to the light-bulb design significant enough to justify the claim of light-bulb inventor. Other than Edison, Joseph Swan had the strongest claim. Twenty years Edison's senior, and sporting a luxuriant beard and a knighthood, Swan was quite a contrast to the faux-humble country boy from Ohio who just happened to be an electrical engineer.

And, of the 21 inventors, Ridley writes, "Swan was the only one whose work was thorough enough and whose patents were good enough to force Edison to go into business with him." The two men's joint venture, called Edison & Swan or Ediswan for short, prospered in Britain. Amazingly, the firm still exists: "Ediswan still survives as a manufacturer of valves (located in Bromsgrove, England)," reports Wikipedia.[6]

Yet I'll bet not one American schoolchild in 1000 has heard of Joseph Swan.

Better, Easier, Cheaper

Of course, the whole point of innovation is not to demonstrate one's cleverness, but to help other people (and make money thereby). The incandescent light bulb really bent the curve of lighting cost downward, although it had been headed lower for a long time. The decline in cost accelerated further after the light bulb became commercially successful near the end of the 19th century.[7] The Ediswanian miracle bulb is a shining example (sorry) of doing more with less, in this case producing more light with less energy and, more importantly, less labor to pay for the energy. Ultimately, that is what innovation is for: to make life easier.

The Ediswanian Rule

The many-fathered light bulb is, Ridley argues, not the exception but the rule: "Six different people invented or discovered the thermometer, five

---

[6] https://en.wikipedia.org/wiki/Edison_and_Swan_Electric_Light_Company, accessed on September 23, 2020.

[7] The lighting cost curve over time is shown in my book, *Fewer, Richer, Greener*, on page 150. The cost per lumen-hour fell by a factor of about 10,000 between the year 1300 and today.

the electric telegraph, four decimal fractions, three the hypodermic needle, two natural selection." The science writer Logan Chipkin notes that "even Einstein's theory of relativity... may have been discovered shortly thereafter by Hendrik Lorenz."[8] Henri Poincaré was also hot on the trail of relativity at the same time, and there were many other participants in the story.

Importantly, critics and skeptics of relativity theory did not hurt the cause: they helped by showing where the blind alleys were, just as with the lightbulb developers who failed to find a usable filament material, and (this is important) documented their work.

Computers

Ridley's little vignettes have a family resemblance, all pointing to the idea that innovations are a "team sport" and achieve worthiness only when they become democratized: cheap and widespread. The electronic computer is a case in point. The computer was the result of so much collaboration, achieved over two centuries (Lady Ada Lovelace, the first coder, was born in 1815), that no specific person can be said to have invented it. Charles Babbage's mechanical (not electronic) "difference engine," designed but probably never built, dates from his collaborator Lady Lovelace's time, but it took another century before Alan Turing, Claude Shannon, and John von Neumann, working independently but at about the same time in the 1930s and 1940s, realized that an electronic machine could be taught to compute.

John Horgan, a science writer, explains:

> Shannon showed how an algebra invented by the British mathematician George Boole in the mid-1800s — which deals with such concepts as, "if X or Y happens but not Z, then Q results" — could represent the workings of switches and relays in electronic circuits.[9]

---

[8] https://quillette.com/2020/05/29/how-innovation-works-a-review/

[9] Horgan, John. 2016. "Claude Shannon: Tinkerer, Prankster, and Father of Information Theory." *IEEE Spectrum*, (April 27), https://spectrum.ieee.org/claude-shannon-tinkerer-

In a November 2017 review of Jimmy Soni and Rob Goodman's biography of Shannon,[10] I said Shannon's insight meant that, "if you wanted to construct a machine that could perform operations involving Boolean logic, you could build it out of electronic circuits. That is what a computer is. Consequently, Shannon's paper has been described as the most influential master's thesis ever written."

Add that to the myriad of innovations in electronics, math, and code-writing taking place around that time and you eventually got — in 1945 — a team-built and hand-assembled monstrosity called ENIAC. It weighed 30 tons, was the size of two buses parked end to end, and contained 18,000 vacuum tubes and five million hand-soldered joints.

Computers have since gotten smaller and more powerful (but you knew that). The one in your iPhone, taking up but a small fraction of the device's volume, has more computing power than a $30 million Cray-2 supercomputer from the 1980s, and 100,000 times the power of the computer in the Apollo 11 moon landing craft. Now that's democratization! And it was all done one step at a time, mostly by people who were trying to make marginal improvements to some aspect of it, not by heroic inventors jumping out of the bathtub and, like Archimedes, shouting "Eureka" when they made their discovery. Computers are the best example of incrementalism in innovation: "There is no day when you can say: computers did not exist the day before and did the day after, any more than you can say that one ape-person was an ape and her daughter was a person," writes Ridley, ever the evolutionist.

Man Invents Dog.
Dog Domesticates Man

Low-tech innovation, one of Ridley's specialties, is fun to study because we perceive it as background noise. The sanitary disposal of human waste is a story of gradual innovation and democratization. The ancient Romans

---

prankster-and-father-of-information-theory.

[10] Siegel, Laurence B. "The Unicycling Genius Who Invented Information Theory," in my 2021 book, *Unknown Knowns*, Del Mar, CA: Montesquieu Press.

had toilets and one Sir John Harington, the godson of Queen Elizabeth I and an amateurish poet,[11] invented the flush toilet in 1596 but made only one of them (for the Queen). Almost 250 years later, Thomas Crapper made flush toilets commercially practical and thus widespread.[12] Slow, incremental progress, not heroic achievement.

You think toilets are low-tech? Let's go back farther in time...about 30,000 years. Humans sitting around a campfire, eating the catch of the day. Wolves approach the camp, hungry for leftovers but wary of the humans, who have been known to attack wolves with spears.

One wolf dares to approach the camp closely enough to actually snare some leftovers and finds the humans not entirely hostile. Over time, a population of wolves becomes associated with such camps, and fairly quickly (in evolutionary time) they become "dogs," domesticated wolves shaped by selection pressure from humans to be friendlier, more docile, and more helpful in tasks like hunting than wild wolves. A new species, *Canis familiaris*, has become genetically, behaviorally, and physically distinct from the wolf, *Canis lupus*. It is the first large-scale (bigger than a bacterium) organism that has been genetically modified by humans, and the first one modified intentionally.[13]

The genetic engineering of dogs by humans did not always work out well. A proud and beautiful wolf of 30,000 years ago would be embarrassed to admit that the "thing" in Exhibit 2 is a direct descendant.

Amazingly, as Ridley reports, research by the Russian geneticist Dmitry Belyaev (1917-1985) showed that foxes can also be turned into "dogs" in just a few generations through selection pressure from humans, by breeding for friendliness and docility. While the fox-dogs do not closely resemble wolf-dogs genetically, they do behaviorally and even physically, with floppy ears,

---

[11] Harington is responsible for the familiar bit of doggerel, "Treason doth never prosper/ What's the reason?/ For if it prosper/ None dare call it treason." It's not Shakespeare, but there is some wisdom in it.

[12] Wallace Reyburn's 1969 biography of Crapper is entitled *Flushed with Pride*.

[13] Prey animals may also have been genetically modified by humans through selection pressure, but it is harder to tell. Bacteria are continuously genetically modified, by humans and other animals, to be helpful servants in our guts.

curly tails, foreshortened faces, and pleasant dispositions.[14] Who knew that genetically modifying an organism could be so easy?

Ridley also points out — although he is not the first to do so — that dogs also modified the behavior, if not the genetics and physical bodies, of people. They trained us to tolerate their presence, feed them, and protect them from harm. If an alien species visited us, they would think that people are slaves to dogs and horses. We pick up their scat and we feed them out of our own food supply.

Exhibit 2

Wolf genetically modified by humans, 30,000 years after first contact

That is no mean accomplishment on their part! Of course, it is a fair trade. We get companionship, help with hunting, and, in the case of horses, rides. Why should the economics of exchange apply only to people?

Thinking About Innovation

The second, philosophical section of the book merits a separate review. Like the first section, it is composed of vignettes, but they are of altogether a different character. They are what Blaise Pascal called *pensées*, thought bites.

Democratization

Ridley's single most important thought-bite is that invention is only worth the time and trouble if it leads to an improvement in the lives of many people. A recurring theme in Ridley's books is that technology makes it

---

[14] See also Goldman, Jason G. 2010. "Man's new best friend? A forgotten Russian experiment in fox domestication." *Scientific American* guest blog (September 6), https://blogs.scientificamerican.com/guest-blog/mans-new-best-friend-a-forgotten-russian-experiment-in-fox-domestication/

possible for ordinary people to enjoy benefits and luxuries that only the rich could previously afford. Even in ancient times, the wealthy could afford enough candles to provide adequate light, and could pay servants to light and extinguish them; today almost everyone can afford electric lighting. A rich Roman could have servants warm up water for bathing; today, hot and cold running water are ubiquitous. In Mozart's Vienna, live music was available to the fortunate; today the same music can be heard on a very cheap radio. In *How Innovation Works*, Ridley fully develops this theme, noting, "it is the people who drive down the costs and simplify the product who make the biggest difference."

Yet there are limits to what even a rich person can do without modern technology. Until the late 1800s, a king or a president couldn't call his mother unless she was in the next room. Nobody could take penicillin if they got sick; they either died or got better naturally. Technology does bring truly new products and services to the marketplace.

Does science lead to technology, or the other way around?

One of Ridley's more heterodox ideas is that basic scientific research is not the fount from which technology springs; it more often works in the opposite direction. Practical people tinker with real-life problems, and then scientists try to figure out why the solution works and only then make more general discoveries.

For example, variolation (deliberate infection with a small amount of the pathogen) was practiced for smallpox as early as 1700 and was promoted by Lady Mary Wortley Montagu, a young mother who was herself a smallpox victim early in the 18th century. Yet the reason for it working was not known until Louis Pasteur, in the 1860s, proved the germ theory of disease correct. Moreover, smallpox was caused not by a bacterium (which was visible in Pasteur's microscopes) but by a virus, which is much smaller and not known to exist until 1892. Technology — variolation, which evolved into the more general practice of immunization — led science, in this case by more than a century.

Likewise, nobody knew what an electron was when Edison (and many others) ran trillions of them through wires to produce light and heat, and to power every gadget imaginable. Electrons were discovered in 1897 by a scientist who was curious to understand why electricity "worked." The same story can be told about many other pairings of science and technology — or, should we say, technology and science?

Why innovation flourishes in freedom

Innovation occurs whenever people use resources (including their own human capital) more fruitfully today than they did yesterday, which is always and everywhere. But when does innovation *flourish*, with one advance quickly building on another and materially increasing well-being? Ridley argues:

> [T]he secret sauce...is freedom. Freedom to exchange, experiment, imagine, invest, and fail; freedom from expropriation or restriction by chiefs, priests, and thieves; freedom on the part of consumers to reward the innovations they like and reject the ones they do not.
>
> Liberals have argued since at least the eighteenth century that freedom leads to prosperity, but...they have never...found the mechanism, the drive chain, by which one causes the other. Innovation, the infinite improbability drive, is that drive chain, that missing link.

This is the punch line of the book. Ridley started out by Climbing Mount Improbable (Richard Dawkins' memorable phrase):[15] the duck, the iPhone, his own brain, our lives as we know them — all arrangements of elementary particles that shouldn't be organized that way but are. He finishes by claiming that innovation is the reason these improbable arrangements do exist. Ridley even claims that life itself is an innovation, albeit unintended (like many other, more humble and human innovations):

---

[15] Dawkins, Richard. 1996. *Climbing Mount Improbable.* New York: W. W. Norton & Co.

That it happened four billion years ago, when there were no living creatures, let alone intelligent ones, and that we don't know very much about where and how it happened, does not detract from its status as an innovation. We do know that it was all about energy and improbability, both of which are crucial to innovation today. And the fact that nobody planned the origin of life is also a key lesson.

Advice for investors and general readers

Investors rely on innovation for that most basic factor in determining asset returns: economic growth. The growth model is this: Output equals the amount each worker produces per hour (called productivity) times the number of hours worked. Since one can work only so hard, and we don't directly control the size of the population or the fraction that is working, increasing productivity is the most natural way to increase the quantity of goods and services produced and available for consumption.

Innovation is definitionally the principal source of growth in productivity. If you find a way to do more with less, you've innovated — and that is how people and economies become more productive. Thus, investors need to be keenly aware of the sources of, and obstacles to, innovation in their search for prospective returns.

Unlike some of Ridley's other books, *How Innovation Works* is a quick, easy read — 396 pages of large print. It does not provide the liberal arts version of a technical education in a new field, as his books *Genome* (about human genetics) or *The Red Queen* (about sexual selection) do. It is not, as Ridley claims, his best book — I'd give that honor to *The Rational Optimist*, which sets out the case for human progress in both the past and the future. But Ridley's third or fourth best book, explaining the mechanics of said progress, is a more enriching experience than most authors' very best. Read it.

Chapter 3. Doing More with Less: Andrew McAfee on Dematerialization[1]

Laurence B. Siegel
October 2019

"Live long and prosper." – Mr. Spock (Leonard Nimoy)

Does a prosperous global society need access to energy supplies that grow faster than the population? In other words, does energy use per capita need to grow for productivity and wealth to increase? Conventional wisdom says yes, and historically energy use has proceeded in tandem with economic growth. But a new book tackles this question and reaches the surprising and optimistic conclusion that we can live better while consuming *less* energy and *fewer* material resources.

To appreciate the importance of this issue, start by considering the following puzzles. Why has your record collection been replaced by a weightless assemblage of bits and bytes? Why do you use a third as much gasoline as your grandfather, even though you drive many more miles? Why is the long-term trend of real (inflation-adjusted) commodity prices down?

Because of *dematerialization*, argues MIT professor Andrew McAfee in his new book, *More from Less*.[2] Every organism on Earth tries to economize, that is, to get more output from fewer inputs. But until recently mankind

---

[1] Some of the ideas and a little of the wording of this article appear in my book, *Fewer, Richer, Greener* (John Wiley & Sons, 2019).

[2] It's rare that a subtitle is so long that it requires a footnote, but the full title of the book is *More from Less: The Surprising Story of How We Learned to Prosper Using Fewer Resources – and What Happens Next*. In coming up with a title, McAfee could have well afforded to implement some of the economizing forces that he loves so much.

bucked the trend, consuming more and more and never getting to the "less" part.

That is partly an illusion, though.

We've been getting more from less for as long as we've been in existence — that's an important part of what economic growth *is!* But we have also just been consuming (and producing) *more* – more stuff, more energy, more of everything. Both increases in population and increases in per capita consumption have contributed to this growth. Recently, however, we've begun to tip into *actually using fewer resources*, without suffering any loss in utility. This trend will continue and intensify, and that's what McAfee's book is about.

The idea of dematerialization is not new. In his book *Nine Chains to the Moon*, the visionary architect and inventor R. Buckminster Fuller described "ephemeralization" almost a century ago.[3] (The Greek-derived word "ephemeralization" sounds fancier than Latin "dematerialization," but they're the same thing.) Fuller wrote,

> Do more and more with less and less until eventually you can do everything with nothing.

That's hyperbole, typical of Fuller's overwrought prose. You cannot make something out of nothing. But, as McAfee ably demonstrates, making more out of less is what much of the human enterprise is about, and is how we progress from poverty to prosperity.

The Parable of the Smartphone

Please join me in the following thought experiment. It is 1985, only 34 years ago, well within the modern era of advanced technology. Assemble a roomful of gadgets that will provide the same services as the apps that

---

[3] Fuller, R. Buckminster. 1938. *Nine Chains to the Moon: An Adventure Story of Thought.* Philadelphia: J.B. Lippincott & Co. "Nine chains" refers to the idea that if you made a chain out of all the people on Earth at the time (a little over two billion) by having each stand on the next one's head, it would stretch from the Earth to the Moon nine times over. Bucky Fuller was a little weird.

are now (in 2019) on your smartphone. While you're doing so, keep track of the prices:

Exhibit 1 — Cost of replicating the functions of a smartphone using devices available in 1985

Function	1985 device	1985 cost (in today's dollars)
Mobile telephone	Motorola DynaTAC	$9,000
Text and image messaging	Generic fax machine	1,105
GPS	Magellan	6,650
Voice recorder	Realistic CTR-70	110
Digital watch	Casio DBC-600	45
Portable music player	Sony Discman	400
Encyclopedia	Britannica	2,210
Radio	Sony CFD-444 boom box	640
Video game console	Nintendo	440
Portable color TV	Casio Mini Color TV	665
Camera	Casio SPRINT	295
Video camera	Sony CCD-V8	3,745
Video player	Generic VCR	1,105
Video conferencing system	Future Systems Inc.	110,520*
Processing power	Cray-2 supercomputer	32,000,000

*Plus substantial user fees

Source: https://www.webfx.com/blog/internet/how-much-did-the-stuff-on-your-smartphone-cost-30-years-ago/. Money amounts in 2015 dollars.

The room needed to accommodate all this would have to be quite large, and the total cost is $32,136,910. Drop the supercomputer (which has the same processing power, 1.9 gigaflops, as a good smartphone) and it's $136,910.[4] Drop the video conferencing system, too, and it's a still princely $26,390.

---

[4] A gigaflop is a billion floating-point operations ("flops") per second.

For comparison, the best smartphone, capable of all these functions and many more, costs about $1,000 and fits in your pocket.

All right, I'm gilding the lily. Nobody would have bought 1.9 gigaflops of processing power in 1985 to obtain all the functions of the not-yet-invented smartphone. But that's the power your phone now has,[5] and it helps with complex apps like Waze, which merges three advanced technologies (a detailed street map with live-updated traffic information; a way of ascertaining the driver's position, speed, and direction; and a social network for warning the driver about police and other inconveniences).

Andrew McAfee
Source: https://commons.wikimedia.org/wiki/File:Andrew_McAfee_FT-McKinsey_BBYA_2014 (LowerContrast).jpg

The exhibit also leaves out functions that were unimaginable in 1985, such as ride sharing software that not only matches drivers and riders but (this is the fun part) changes prices continuously so that the supply of drivers and demand from riders both adjust, resulting in almost every driver getting a customer and almost every rider getting a ride. We are, indeed, doing more with less. (A smartphone is not quite "nothing," Buckminster Fuller notwithstanding.)

And I've also cherry picked by discussing the most dramatic example of dematerialization I can find. Most things are not disappearing as quickly as the 1985 pile of gadgets. But, as McAfee shows, dematerialization is happening in many spheres of activity, including energy usage (very important), and is accelerating.

---

[5] 2024 update: the most powerful iPhone, the A17 Pro, has 2,150 gigaflops of computing power – an 1,131-fold increase in about five years. It is impossible to write about information technology without updating the numbers very frequently.

The Second Machine Age

McAfee, an MIT Sloan School professor and co-director of the MIT Initiative on the Digital Economy, is best known for his book co-authored with Erik Brynjolfsson, *The Second Machine Age*. That 2014 book expressed the concern that the current wave of robotic automation makes workers and machines into substitutes for each other, rather than complements as was the case in the first machine age (the Industrial Revolution). The prospect of mass unemployment and extreme inequality troubled them, even as they foresaw large increases in overall productivity and wealth that would result from "brilliant technologies."

The current volume, a solo effort by McAfee, is more optimistic. In his conclusion, he writes that we now have the opportunity to replenish that which we've taken from the Earth, and that:

> [a]mazingly enough, doing...this won't require radical course changes in our economies or societies. We just need to let the four horsemen of the optimist— capitalism, technological progress, public awareness, and responsive government — do more of what they do. Which is, as we've seen, to let us and our planet flourish.

My four horsemen of optimism are capitalism, cumulative learning, good governance, and a culture that favors innovation and enterprise – McAfee and I are not that far apart. Put these together and technological progress will come.

Did the environmental movement start off on a wrong track?

McAfee begins by recalling that the modern environmental movement adopted a formula proposed in 1971 by the biologist Paul Ehrlich and the physicist John Holdren to measure "society's total negative impact on the environment."⁶ The formula, as modified slightly in later work, is known as the IPAT model:

$$I = P \times A \times T$$

where I is impact (defined as always negative), P is population, A is affluence (proxied by GDP per capita), and T is technology. Thus, affluence is always bad; but, backpedaling a bit, Ehrlich and Holdren admit that "technology could be either good (such as solar power) or bad (more coal plants), but when it was good, it 'tend[ed] to be slow, costly, and insufficient in scale.'"⁷

This kind of thinking led to what I call a "poverty strategy" for saving the Earth. It is one of the worst ideas ever foisted by scientists on an uninformed and gullible public.

Subsistence living is environmentally destructive, and early industrial life, while more economically rewarding, was polluting and poisonous. Only advanced technological societies can be environmentally clean — or can afford to. To get green, get rich.

This principle is formalized in the environmental Kuznets curve (EKC), or clean-dirty-clean curve, which says that societies first pollute more as they industrialize, then pollute less as they approach a post-industrial status. Two celebrated economists, Gene Grossman and Alan Krueger, set forth the EKC theory in the 1990s, and there is much evidence supporting it.⁸

CRIB Notes

Yet the poverty strategy – now called "degrowth" – grew in popularity, evolving into a recipe for environmental salvation that McAfee calls CRIB: *C*onsume less, *R*ecycle, *I*mpose limits, *B*ack to the land. All, he says, are

---

⁶ The quote is from McAfee, summarizing Ehrlich and Holdren's work.

⁷ Again, the quote is McAfee's. Double nested quotes are bad enough, but putting this attribution in the text would have required triple nested quotes.

⁸ Grossman, Gene M., and Alan B. Krueger. 1995. "Economic Growth and the Environment." *Quarterly Journal of Economics*, vol. 110, no. 2 (February), pp. 353-377. They circulated a related, unpublished paper in 1991.

terrible ideas when executed naively or thoughtlessly. Some are terrible ideas no matter what you do. I'll consider each, but not exactly in the order in which they appear in the acronym.

Consuming less is fine for the comfortable. You don't really need a 4,000 square foot house or that third car. Many of us are overweight. But, of the 8 billion people now living, fewer than two billion enjoy a first-world living standard.[9] The rest are hoping for their chance, and many are now getting it. We don't want that to stop – it would be the cruelest trick ever played by the rich on the poor.

Recycling, McAfee says, is "big business...yet...irrelevant for dematerialization. Why? Because recycling is about where resource-producing factories get their *inputs*, while dematerialization is about what's happened to total demand for their *outputs*."

"*Back to the land* is bad for the land," McAfee advises. Back to the land is kind of cute; the image of self-sufficient agriculturalists, whether the stone-faced Iowa farmer and his daughter in Grant Wood's famous painting or a group of hippies in modern Vermont, is appealing.

But McAfee writes that

> homesteaders use more land, water, and fertilizer than do "factory farmers"...[and] rural life is less environmentally friendly than urban...dwelling [which is very energy-efficient]...As economist Edward Glaeser summarizes, "If you want to be good to the environment, stay away from it."

Now that's an aphorism worth remembering!

---

[9] The total population of countries considered high-income by the World Bank is about 1.1 billion, but high-income people in middle-income countries, such as Mexico and China, are experiencing a first-world living standard. However, some people in high-income countries do not experience a first-world living standard.

Imposing Limits: The Best and the Worst Ideas

McAfee reserves his strongest words — and biggest page budget — for *Imposing limits*. It is "the worst idea, and the best one," he says.

China's One-Child Policy

He regards the one-child policy imposed by China in 1979 as the most destructive population control effort ever attempted. In fact, he goes a little overboard, quoting approvingly a group of Chinese demographers who write,

> While [the Cultural Revolution and the Great Leap Forward were] grave mistakes [that] cost tens of millions of lives, the harms done were relatively short-lived and were corrected quickly afterward. The one-child policy, in contrast, will surpass them in impact by its role in creating a society with a seriously undermined family and kin structure.[10]

One can debate whether the benefits outweighed the costs of the one-child policy. They probably didn't. But to say that it was more damaging than the Great Leap Forward and the Cultural Revolution is, well, a great leap backward. In an article on the value of trust in societies, Yuyu Chen of Peking University and David Yang of Harvard reminded us that the "man-made disaster" of the Great Leap Forward resulted in the worst famine in human history, killing 30 million people in 1958-1961.[11]

It is hard to feel sorrier for people never born than for those who were starved to death by an incredibly barbaric set of policies. And it is hard to "correct quickly afterward" the physical, mental, and economic damage done to the survivors. Famine is the cruelest of the four horsemen of the apocalypse. It is especially cruel when it could have been completely avoided.

---

[10] Feng, Wang, Yong Cai, and Baochang Gu. 2012. "Population, Policy, and Politics: How Will History Judge China's One-Child Policy?" *Population and Development Review*, vol. 38, pp. 115-129.

[11] Chen Yuyu, and David Y. Yang. 2019. "Historical Traumas and the Roots of Political Distrust: Political Inference from the Great Chinese Famine." Working paper, http://davidyyang.com/pdfs/famine_draft.pdf.

By the way, a footnote of McAfee's reminds us that a fanatic, in Winston Churchill's memorable phrase, "can't change his mind and won't change the subject." McAfee notes that "when China announced the formal end of the one-child policy in late 2015, [the 83-year-old] Paul Ehrlich responded with a tweet...'GIBBERING INSANITY - THE GROWTH-FOREVER GANG.'" We'll leave it to the reader to decide who's insane.

Preserving nature and natural resources

While imposing limits on childbirth meets with McAfee's strong disapproval, imposing limits on exploitation of the environment elicits in him the opposite reaction. National parks, according to writer Wallace Stegner "America's best idea," are a wonderfully effective way of preserving scenic natural wonders forever. We can protect wolves and bears and elephants and whales. We can make it criminal or exorbitantly costly to fill the air and water with poisons.

Only government can do these things, and as societies become more affluent they demand that their governments divert some resources, formerly dedicated to immediate survival, toward these higher goods. We saw this force at work in the United States in the last century and we are beginning to see it in China. Responsive government is an asset as important as natural resources, labor, capital, or social trust.

Inside Dematerialization: Decoupling Energy Use from Affluence

Let's take a closer look at an aspect of dematerialization with which McAfee is deeply concerned: energy efficiency. The terrifying diagram in Exhibit 2, with its familiar hockey-stick shape, shows the tight link between the growth of global GDP (the blue line) and energy use (green and red dots) over a very long period of time — 2,000 years. Energy use grew at about the same rate as aggregate global GDP, that is, GDP per capita multiplied by world population. Both started rising rapidly around 1800, when the Industrial Revolution began.

Exhibit 2 — Two thousand years of global GDP and energy use

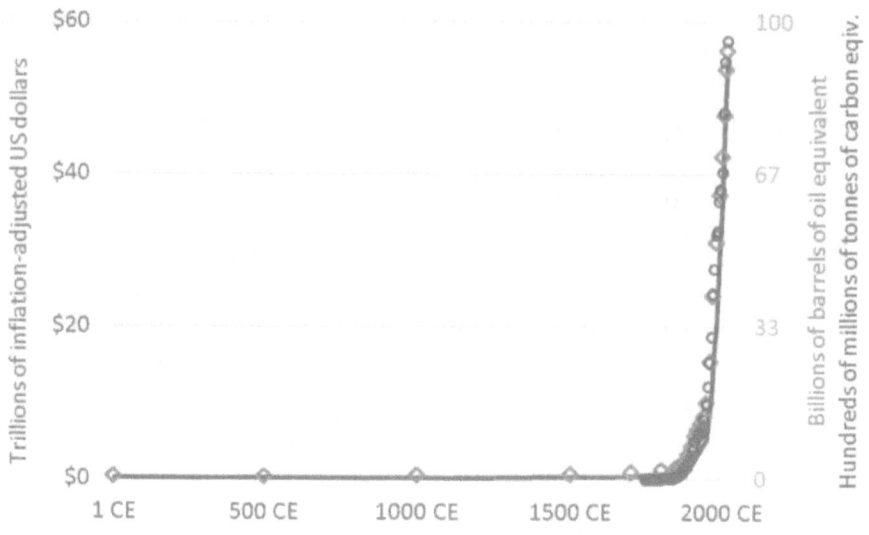

Line: Global GDP in inflation-adjusted dollars (left axis). Diamond: Billions of barrels of oil equivalent (right axis). Circle: Hundreds of millions of tonnes of carbon equivalent (right axis).
Source: https://www.darrinqualman.com

The diagram ends in the year 2000, so what about the current millennium? World population is continuing to grow — albeit at a much reduced pace, with "peak population" expected to be between 9.5 and 11 billion sometime later in this century, followed by a decline. Moreover, continued growth in GDP per capita is not just desirable but necessary for those parts of the world that are not already rich. Thus, aggregate world GDP is going to grow a lot.

Energy and other resources must "decouple" from global GDP. Fortunately, as McAfee shows, and as Exhibit 3 makes clear, decoupling of energy use from GDP growth started almost a half-century ago, and continues to this day. We need to find, and are finding, ways to make this decoupling accelerate. (Energy is particularly important to the decoupling argument because it is the "master resource," the resource that makes all other resources valuable because it "enables us to convert one material into another," wrote the late Julian Simon a generation ago.)

Exhibit 3 — Energy and real GDP per capita, aggregate figures for g7 countries

Source: Created by Reddit user usrname42 using data from the World Bank, http://databank.worldbank.org, series 'GDP (Constant 2005 US$)', 'Energy Use'

Although the diagram is a little old, the trends have continued and accelerated.

What causes this decoupling? McAfee credits both the supply-demand-price system of classical economics and the role of responsive government referred to earlier. The price system makes scarce resources expensive and causes users to economize or find cheaper and better substitutes. We can see this in Exhibit 3 where, in the 1970s, huge increases in oil prices caused consumers and industry to use less oil. Governments, for their part, do things like imposing corporate average fuel economy (CAFE) standards on cars and rewarding taxpayers for installing energy-saving devices in their houses.

Over long periods of time, the resource savings made possible by decoupling (or, in simpler terms, increased efficiency) adds up meaningfully. At the 1.5% annual rate of improvement observed for both the U.S. and the world over the last quarter century,[12] energy use per unit of GDP will decrease 37% by 2050 and 57% by 2075. These forecasts

---

[12] https://yearbook.enerdata.net/total-energy/world-energy-intensity-gdp-data.html

assume no radical change in the energy mix, such as fusion reactors or a yet undiscovered way of storing and transporting solar power — but such innovations can be expected over such a long period, especially when motivated by the prospect of large profits.

As a result, the actual improvement in energy efficiency will be quite a bit larger.

Capitalism and Progress

Reacting to the anti-capitalist mood of the moment, McAfee places considerable emphasis on the importance of free markets in achieving the dematerialization he's celebrating. "More from less" is embedded in the very nature of capitalism: capitalists may want to sell more and more, but they don't want to *buy* more. So they are powerfully motivated to find ways to economize on inputs.

Here is a powerful example of *More from Less* that is decades old. In 1979, the Staggers Act was passed under the watch of President Carter. The law deregulated transportation. What happened? Innovation and capital investment boomed in freight transportation, driven by the efficient use of capital and the adoption of hyper-efficient shipping containers that fit on ships, trains, and trucks. U.S. freight railroads became the most efficient in the world.

We also got a green new deal out of this: The amount of energy used to move a ton of freight one mile fell by 65% between 1979 and 2010

How Government Helps

But environmental remediation is not all about deregulation. Regulation helps too, as McAfee reminds us (beating some sense into the hard-core libertarians in the crowd). In January 2020, a global regulation known as IMO 2020 will prohibit all ocean-going ships from using fuels with a sulfur content above 0.5%, compared with 3.5% now. Only ships fitted with sulfur-cleaning devices called scrubbers will be allowed to continue burning high-sulfur fuel. Every country must follow these rules if they want their cargo unloaded, and the rule eliminates a terrible source of pollution — as did the Clean Air and Clean Water Acts in the U.S. a half-century ago.

Rich, efficient, and growing economies do this. McAfee identifies the twin factors of public awareness and responsive government as two of the four horsemen of the optimist. Everybody wants a clean environment, but poor people want other things more — eating, for example. It is hard to raise public awareness of environmental issues among people who have a very high time-discount rate because they don't know where their next meal is coming from.

As people become more prosperous, they not only demand more environmental protection from their government but have the ability to pay taxes to support the demand. And, of course, only a government that cares about the will of the people (and that is competent) will respond appropriately by regulating and deregulating, taxing and subsidizing, so as to produce the maximum environmental benefit *while taking cost into consideration.*

Disconnection

McAfee writes that *personal disconnection* is a threat to our well-being, right alongside climate change (which he says is real and bad), war, terrorism, and a pandemic. The wave of populism that is enveloping the world may be a reaction to that, with people perceiving a need to belong to something larger than a family and smaller than the human race. A nation-state or race fills that need. It's irrational, but perhaps hard-wired into our collective behavior.

Disconnection is, of course, a real phenomenon, and McAfee is right to include it in the litany of problems that need to be solved. The sociologist Robert Putnam, in *Bowling Alone* (2000), argued that what he called "social capital" — the web of personal connections that builds trust in a community and lowers crime, loneliness, and transaction costs — is declining. It has declined further since 2000. The percentage of adults in the U.S. who are married is at an all-time low: 50%.[13] These are signs of

---

[13] https://www.pewresearch.org/fact-tank/2017/09/14/as-u-s-marriage-rate-hovers-at-50-

declining social health. And social capital is a vital ingredient, along with financial capital, human capital, and other traditional forms of wealth, for society to thrive and grow. I will leave it to the sociologists and others who have studied this topic more closely to comment further on McAfee's views, but he is onto something.

Recommendations for Readers

More from Less is a fairly easy read, and is modestly sized. However, it is about one narrow aspect of technological progress — dematerialization — and readers seeking a broader perspective on the future should check out McAfee's previous book (with Erik Brynjolfsson), *The Second Machine Age*, instead. Peter Diamandis and Steven Kotler's *Abundance* also hits many of the same notes, with a slightly different perspective. Both of those older volumes are basic reading for those interested in the literature of the new optimism.

But readers seeking the details of the dematerialization revolution should definitely read *More from Less*. It is the first modern popular book on this topic. All the other work is dryly academic.

At the risk of sounding mercenary, my own book, *Fewer, Richer, Greener*, covers these topics broadly and has a chapter on dematerialization, influenced by (and quoting admiringly) both of the books mentioned above.[14]

Advice to Investors

If the continued dematerialization that McAfee is forecasting takes place, it's good for equities because, having been partly freed from resource-cost constraints, we will get a lot of economic growth. *But it will not be good for all*

---

education-gap-in-marital-status-widens/

[14] Feeding my ego even more, I appear (as an unnamed character) in *More from Less*. McAfee recounts the story that, almost a half-century ago, Milton Friedman autographed a Monopoly™ board, adding the phrase "Down with Monopoly." I was the student who invited Professor Friedman to the sherry hour at the University of Chicago dorm where he did this.

equities. Some companies and industries will be hurt while others will be helped immensely. Actively managed portfolios can benefit from this insight.

Natural resources firms might suffer while technology companies advance. Energy companies will have varied results depending on which energy sources turn out to be the most economical and plentiful. Thus, fundamental analysis by farsighted and well-informed analysts will help to generate returns superior to those produced by cap-weighted indices.

The rub is that most analysts think they're farsighted and well informed. Those who have modest opinions of their own ability drop out of the active management game and buy index funds. Index funds today ensure that you benefit from the innovation and extraordinary growth in Apple and Amazon while Toys 'R' Us and J. C. Penney fade away; the same will happen with winners and losers from dematerialization, so index funds should not be considered *verboten*.

As always with active management, then, the toughest job is picking managers who will win, on a risk-adjusted basis, over the long term. They all say they will, but mathematics dictates that a little fewer than half can actually do so.

Last Word

No physical quantity can grow at 3%, or 1%, or even 0.1% per year, forever. But the good news is that "utility," the economists' catch-all term for whatever is good and valuable to people, need not be delivered in physical form. Economic growth – that is, growth in utility – will continue long past the time that the use of physical resources has peaked and begun to decline.

The author thanks Stephen C. Sexauer, chief investment officer of the San Diego County Employees Retirement Association, for his substantial contributions to this article. –W.H.W.

Chapter 4: Why Brad DeLong Thinks the Long Boom Is Over

Laurence B. Siegel
October 2022

> "Everything is amazing and nobody is happy."
> — popular saying

There are two kinds of economists: those who labor in the fields trying to understand the economy better, and those who propose bold sweeping solutions to universally acknowledged problems. (I oversimplify, but not much.)

I usually find the first kind fascinating and the latter kind annoying — except when a lively writer and polemicist like Brad DeLong tries to be both. His *Slouching Toward Utopia* is both a masterly history of the twentieth-century American economy and an iffy prescription for fixing it.

J. Bradford ("Brad") DeLong
Source: https://substack.com/
@delongonsubstack

Having studied economic history — the most important specialty in economics — for most of his adult life, DeLong knows how to tell a tale using detail rather than broad generalities, and words rather than mathematics. It's a compelling read.

But, as the great curmudgeon of the last century, H. L. Mencken, said, "There is always a well-known solution to every human problem—neat, plausible, and wrong."[1] In its policy prescriptions and grim forecast of the future, DeLong's book is Menckenesque: elegant, convincing, and incorrect. I recommend it with half a heart. You will learn a lot of economic history. Just don't try to create a society along the lines he prescribes.

Was 1870-2010 a very special time?

DeLong's "grand narrative" resembles that of the economic historian Robert Gordon, whose 2015 book I reviewed a decade ago.[2] The narrative is that the Second Industrial Revolution, which started in 1870 and brought us the automobile, the telephone, the airplane, the electrification of everything, and so on — was the most important one. Unlike the first Industrial Revolution a century earlier, it propelled human existence from near-universal misery to (on average) modest affluence today. On this point DeLong is right. But he argues that we'll be lucky to hold onto the gains; actually, we'd be unforgivably stupid not to.

The book's title, *Slouching Toward Utopia*, references the phrase "slouching toward Bethlehem" in William Butler Yeats' beloved poem "The Second Coming," which itself is a riff on Percy Bysshe Shelley's "Ozymandias." Both poems are parables about destruction. We can see where this is going.

One of DeLong's many arguments is that the Long Boom (my term, not his) that began around 1870 ended a few years ago — in 2010 by his reckoning. Before questioning this thesis, let's first understand it.

---

[1] Often misquoted and/or attributed to other writers, this quote is from Mencken's *The Divine Afflatus*, in Prejudices: Second Series (1920), London: Jonathan Cape; full text online at https://www.gutenberg.org/files/53467/53467-h/53467-h.htm. An afflatus (Mencken loved fancy words) is a breath or wind, which when "divine" produces creative inspiration.

[2] Siegel, Laurence B. 2015. "Robert Gordon, the Special Century, and the Prospects for Economic Growth." Advisor Perspectives (December 22), https://larrysiegeldotorg.wordpress.com/wp-content/uploads/2016/01/siegel_gordon_prospects-for-economic-growth_2015_12_28.pdf.

Why 1870? "Inventing Invention"

What happened around 1870, DeLong contends, is that we set up institutions that systematically promoted new ways of doing things. Before that, we invented things, but there were no organized and well-funded efforts to do so. He claims that, around that time, we "invented invention."

DeLong also believes that our philosophy or attitude toward invention changed. We acquired "a burgeoning understanding that there is a broad and deep range of new technologies to be discovered, developed, and deployed." This philosophy replaced the earlier admiration of "great amateurs" who made scientific or engineering discoveries out of curiosity, the desire to better mankind, or the need to make a profit.[3]

I'll unpack the phrase, "invented invention," in a moment. First, let's look at the difference between the pre-1870 and the post-1870 invention ecosystem. During the first Industrial Revolution, individual craftsmen and experimenters did most of the creative work; because the effort was not organized on anything like a large scale, inventions dribbled out of these great amateurs gradually, over a century. But the Second Industrial Revolution was a burst of change that came almost all at once. As the celebrated economic historian Robert Gordon wrote, "every aspect of life experienced a revolution."

The years from 1870 to 1914 saw one radical innovation after another in quick succession. Considering how long it took humans to come up with a practical bicycle, the airplane came awfully soon afterward. When flying in an airplane we are sitting in a chair in the sky. Only 18 years before the Wright Brothers' first flight, there were no cars, and bicycles were primitive gadgets that only interested thrill-seekers.

---

[3] "Great amateurs": Isaiah Berlin's phrase, as far as I know, which DeLong does not use. The era of great amateurs (when amateur scientists could make important discoveries because science was not very advanced and sophisticated lab equipment was not required) was roughly 1700-1870.

The Secret Sauce

So, what specifically did we do to invent invention? DeLong writes,

> I think the answers lie in the coming of the industrial research laboratory, the large modern corporation, and globalization, which made the world one global market economy

Big science, big business, and global trade. For a man associated with the center-left (DeLong was in the Clinton administration), that's a brave take — it's rare for an academic, outside of a business or engineering school, to say something nice about big business. And he's right about globalization; I worry that the current trend of deglobalization will hurt us considerably. Wake me up when re-globalization starts.

Why 2010? This argument is weaker

So far, I'm with DeLong on the history. I said earlier that the book was elegant, convincing, and wrong. What part is wrong?

The long boom is not over

There are two areas where I strongly disagree with DeLong. One is his assertion that the Long Boom ended in 2010. It didn't. While the current geopolitical scene is turbulent and dangerous, technological progress has not stopped and actually seems to be accelerating. We are living through six technological revolutions at once: AI and robotics, biotech and medicine, energy, space, materials science, and agritech. Because agritech is probably the least familiar of these fields, I've reproduced some material from McKinsey describing some recent advances in it. Next time you eat a steak, thank the cow as usual, but also thank the Supervisory Control and Data Acquisition (SCADA) team at UC Davis!

Exhibit 1 — The Agritech Revolution

Smart crop monitoring	Drone-assisted farming	Smart livestock monitoring	Autonomous farming machinery	Smart property and equipment management

Irrigation and nutrient distribution is monitored using sensors and image analysis to optimize water and fertilizer use and plant growth through precise adjustments in real time.	Drones collect data using imaging and other sensing techniques. The data are then analyzed in real time to enable remote actions to increase yield and reduce losses from insects and other pests.	Each animal receives care and feeding based on body-sensor data and movement tracking. Illnesses can be detected early and the animal can be medicated remotely through the feeding system.	Robots and other machinery perform targeted actions based on sensor data, GPS data, and image analysis to minimize waste of resources and labor, thereby boosting crop yield.	Preventive and corrective maintenance improve equipment performance and reduce costs of downtime and repairs, as well as reducing risk of fires and other loss events.

The period since 2010 was also not so bad economically, with global production growing from a per capita PPP GDP of $13,965 in 2010 to $17,081 in 2021. (These are in constant dollars.[4]) That's 22% in 11 years or a compound growth rate of 1.85% — *almost exactly the long-run rate of global per capita growth for more than a century*. Despite DeLong's pronouncement that 2010 marked the end of an era of innovation, the pace of innovation was the same before and after that date.

The market is neither human nor inhuman

My other disagreement is with DeLong's attempt to meld the free-market economics of Friedrich Hayek with the communitarian socialism of the anthropologist Karl Polanyi. This desire is based on DeLong's observation that the current system is "not human." I'll get to this later, after I've cooled down a bit.

---

[4] These data are in 2017 dollars and are from https://data.worldbank.org/indicator/NY.GDP.PCAP.PP.KD. PPP means purchasing power parity (that is, the numbers adjust for differences in the cost of living between countries).

The Water Buffalo Man

DeLong contends that the large amount of economic inequality in the world is a harbinger of slower growth, or no growth. Not only is that idea wrong, but DeLong himself presents the best possible argument against it: most of the world still needs to play catch-up with the advanced economies.

"There's someone in Bangladesh who would almost surely be a better economics professor than I am and is now behind a water buffalo," DeLong told Annie Lowrey at *The Atlantic*.

He continued, "The market economy gives me and my preferences 200 times the voice and weight of his. If that isn't the biggest market failure of all, I don't know what your definition of market failure could possibly be."

It's true that DeLong currently has more economic power than the water buffalo man by a factor of 200, but this exchange reveals exactly what is wrong with DeLong's reasoning.

If everyone in the world had already realized their full potential — if, following along with DeLong's cute example, everyone who *should* be an economics professor were *already* an economics professor, then future increases in well-being would be limited to increases in human potential itself, a tough order. (Improvements in technology and the volume of accumulated knowledge will help a little but will not produce the great leap forward that Mr. Water Buffalo needs.) Human potential, as opposed to human achievement, is relatively fixed; we get smarter or more creative or more moral at glacially slow rates, if at all.

But because, as DeLong correctly says, only a few people have realized their full potential, future economic growth will involve the rest of the world moving in that direction as quickly as they're able. The granddaughter of the man walking behind a water buffalo in Bangladesh may, in fact, become an economics professor. (By then we will have too many of them, and I'd advise her to pursue something else.) In fact, Bangladesh has one of the highest economic growth rates in the world precisely for this reason: it is easier to imitate a pioneer than to be one.

The Miracle is Not Over

Lowery's *Atlantic* article about DeLong is titled "The Economist Who Knows the Miracle Is Over," with the subtitle, "An era of remarkable prosperity has ended." This statement of Lowery's, purporting to explain DeLong's thinking, makes the bonehead undergraduate error of confusing levels with rates of change.

If no more economic growth ever occurred (a rate of change of zero), and the economy remained in a steady state indefinitely (at the current high level), an era of remarkable prosperity would nevertheless *have just begun*. Human beings were on the planet for tens of thousands of years and were overwhelmingly very poor, with short lives, before DeLong's magical year of 1870.[5] Now the world is, by historical standards, rich. If nothing ever improved from this point forward — which is preposterous, but let's accept it for a moment — then the prosperity of "all future people" will be many times larger than the meager prosperity of "all past people." That's the miracle.

Everyone reading this was born into a world in which the basic ingredients of a decent life have already been invented. We should contemplate our amazing good fortune, lest we squander it because we take it for granted.

Slouching away from Utopia

While reminding us that attempts at utopias always come to a bad end, DeLong has a utopia of his own, a blend of the free-market economist Friedrich Hayek and the communitarian socialist philosopher Karl

---

[5] I can make the case for September 2018 (not 1870) being the date the world became "rich." More precisely, it is the date when the Brookings Institution reported that half the world's population was middle class (by their own modest standards — it is not the definition of middle class that an American or European would use). See https://www.brookings.edu/articles/a-global-tipping-point-half-the-world-is-now-middle-class-or-wealthier/. The Economist reported the same development earlier, in February 2009; see https://www.economist.com/special-report/2009/02/14/burgeoning-bourgeoisie. Remember, however, that despite this incredible progress, the other half of the world's population is still poor.

Polanyi as noted earlier. Both men were original and creative thinkers. Hayek, not the young whippersnapper Milton Friedman, was the principal spokesman for free markets in the Age of Keynes.[6] Polanyi, lesser known but a major figure in the social sciences, "believe[d] that life can only flourish when markets are properly embedded within social relations and subjugated to non-economic norms."[7]

While the mix of Hayek and Polanyi suggests he'd be in favor of a mixed economy, we already have one — and a lot of people are unhappy, especially DeLong, who describes what we have now as "not human."

The world does have inhuman aspects, but they are a failure of governance or of human nature, not of the capitalism that DeLong abhors (when he is not praising it). Venezuela and Sri Lanka, onetime success stories, are collapsing because of abysmal political leadership, not because capitalists are allowed to keep the return they generate on the capital they've deployed.[8] Taiwan, South Korea, and today's Vietnam show how capitalism, melded with high-quality governance, can produce results that are more human and humane than anything these countries have ever experienced before.

Can we return to a folk society?

DeLong calls for a restructuring of society. He imagines his restructuring proposal is liberal but it is deeply reactionary, throwing sand in the gears of mobility and ambition to achieve what Kurt Vonnegut, building on the ideas of the anthropologist Robert Redfield, called a "folk society."

DeLong seems not to understand that his desired blend is unattainable. It's unattainable because the benefits of modernity would have to be

---

[6] A highly entertaining 2010 rap video, found at https://www.youtube.com/watch?v=donERTFo-Sk, features cartoon versions of John Maynard Keynes and Friedrich Hayek arguing the basics of macroeconomics. Watch it; it beats going to class.

[7] https://philarchive.org/archive/FARTDM, p. 330.

[8] The Sri Lankan economy has perked up since I first wrote this, due to recission of a highly inadvisable ban, in 2021, on synthetic fertilizers.

almost entirely sacrificed to feed the desire for a folk society.[9] Vonnegut *did* understand:

> [P]rimitive societies...were all so small that everybody knew everybody well, and associations lasted for life. The members communicated intimately with one another, and very little with anybody else...

> There was no access to the experience and thought of the past, except through memory. The [few who lived to be] old were treasured for their memories. There was little change. What one man knew and believed was the same as what all men knew and believed. There wasn't much of a division of labor. What one person did was pretty much what another person did.[10]

Vonnegut describes — knowingly or otherwise — a world where per capita income is three dollars a day. *That* is what is not human. Three dollars a day was the level of living that almost all of humanity experienced until the 1700s in northwestern Europe and eastern North America, and until 1870 or more recently in the rest of the world. Under those circumstances we would often starve; we would die, on average, in our thirties; and women would have to bear a dozen children in order that three survive to adulthood.

In the good-hearted pursuit of an imaginary Arcadia, then (see Exhibit 2), the human race would have destroyed everything it has built over the last 200 years and most of what it has built over the last three thousand years. (Greece, Rome, and Renaissance Italy were not folk societies; returning to Arcadia would not mean accepting the living standards of those successful civilizations, but something much worse.)

---

[9] Redfield (1897-1958) originated the term and was the first to describe what he called a folk society; Vonnegut just gave it much more visibility by discussing it in his best-selling book, *Wampeters, Foma & Granfalloons* (1974) and saying that a folk society was the (often unspoken) goal of the hippie culture.

[10] Found at https://claremontreviewofbooks.com/folk-tales/. In this article by Patrick Deneen, Vonnegut is quoted as saying that "we are full of chemicals which require us to belong to folk societies, or failing that, to feel lousy all the time...[but] and there aren't any folk societies for us anymore." That is why many people pursue the impossible dream of creating one.

Exhibit 2 — Some young Americans discover that a folk society is a vacation, not a livelihood

Source: https://www.messynessychic.com/2019/04/23/the-last-great-california-hippie-commune-is-still-going-strong/

The rational side of DeLong knows this: "Only a fool," he says, "would wittingly or ignorantly slouch or gallop backward to near-universal dire global poverty."

The emotional side of DeLong does not: "...Polanyi saw that Hayek's vision of a market-bestowed utopia was unsustainable by *dint of being inhuman.*"[11]

F. Scott Fitzgerald famously wrote, "The test of a first-rate intelligence is the ability to hold two opposing ideas in mind at the same time and still retain the ability to function." DeLong passes that test: he is for markets, and he is against them. His ambivalence suggests he wants a compromise, but it is not clear what that compromise would involve. Implementing his vision of the good society would result in a very bad one. That conundrum embodies the tragic vision of which thinkers have spoken since Aristotle.

---

[11] My italics. Those are harsh words.

People who imagine they have the secret formula for making everyone happy should write provocative books, but not rule.

Everything is amazing and nobody is happy

DeLong reminds us repeatedly that, despite his admiration for much that the market accomplishes ("Hayek was a genius"), a market economy is "not human" because it does not achieve Polanyi's communitarian goals. It does not make us happy.

That is because it's not supposed to! The market is an economic system, not (*pace* Ayn Rand) a moral system. The market determines prices, how much is produced, and how the fruits of production are allocated among the various claimants. A market economy consists of everyone doing what they think is best for themselves. The only possible alternative to a market economy, then, is everyone *not* doing what they think is best for themselves! The only way to make people act against their own perceived interest is to use force. We would live in a tyranny.

Non-market economics has been tried at varying levels of enforcement ("democratic socialism" and all that), and it has failed to produce either prosperity or human satisfaction. The very pleasant economies of Nordic Europe are not socialist at all; nobody but the market sets prices or directs production. They are capitalist with a large welfare state, a world of difference.

Meanwhile, the pursuit of happiness is a problem for philosophers, painters, clergymen, and poets. Possibly psychiatrists. Definitely musicians.

Conclusion

Returning to the epigraph that opens this article, if everything is amazing, why is nobody happy?

We are asking too much of economics if we expect it to make us happy, to solve all moral or existential problems. Economics probes how we organize our efforts at making a living and improving our well-being each generation.[12] In asking economic growth to be a cure-all and then finding it wanting, DeLong shunts the discussion onto a wrong line. What I wish DeLong had asked, and what many development economists do ask, is: having discovered, around 1870, how we can make a much larger proportion of us rich, how do we bring the benefits of that discovery to the rest of us?

DeLong is a young man by economists' standards (he's 62) and possesses considerable gifts. I hope he writes that book next.

The author deeply appreciates the contributions of Stephen C. Sexauer and Lee A. Kaplan. –W.H.W.

---

[12] In the wake of Gary Becker's extraordinarily productive life, economics now does more than that, applying economic reasoning to "issues such as crime, discrimination, and the economics of the family" (according to the University of Chicago's Nobel laureate website). But most economists, most of the time, study people in their roles as producers and consumers – not the entirety of human existence.

Chapter 5. "Fewer, Richer, Greener!"

Larry Siegel's Highly Contrary, Surprisingly Practical Future Vision

Interview by Kathryn M. Welling

Reprinted with permission from Welling on Wall Street, September 10, 2021

There's no getting around it. For all his financial acumen, intellectual firepower, and years of experience in trying to meld the minds of Wall Street to scholarly research, Larry Siegel remains both highly rational and a dogged optimist. Amazing.

Larry is also a familiar face to faithful WOWS readers, having shared his insights in numerous interviews and articles over the years. This time he's back for the wholly optimistic purpose of explaining why, despite all indications to the contrary, we're not going to hell in a handbasket. (We did the interview in late June, before anyone knew the "Delta variant," as infectious as chickenpox, would have even us fully vaccinated types digging out our masks again. But Larry's optimism is unwavering.)

More specifically, Larry wrote a great book, Fewer, Richer, Greener, which he had the unmitigated bad luck to release just before COVID-19 sucked all the oxygen out of the world. But, in his iconoclastic and contrary take on how to cure our climate woes and build a prosperous world for generations to come, Larry remains a true believer. In fact, he's out to relaunch his book. Listen in.

— KMW

Kate Welling: Welcome, Larry. Congratulations on being able to put together a relaunch of *Fewer, Richer, Greener*. I can't imagine unluckier timing than coming out with that title on the cusp of the pandemic lockdowns.

Larry Siegel: It was pretty bad. The book sold very well for a few weeks after it was released. Especially after Jason Zweig wrote a great review of it in the *Wall Street Journal*. It went to No. 1 on Amazon in economics and also No. 1 in history. But once the pandemic hit, nobody was in the mood to want to read about progress.

Kate: It did seem incredibly counterintuitive in the moment.

Larry: It took two years to write the book and get it published. In that amount of time, things can change but I didn't think they would change *that* much. Anyway, this interview is the booster-rocket phase of the relaunch. I'm also accepting every speaking engagement and podcast appearance that I can get, and posting on Twitter and LinkedIn. That's the rest of the relaunch.

Kate: Alas, social media is the key these days, if you can stand to stick with it.

Larry: Well, I'm going to certainly highlight this interview, because it was an interview you did with me very early in 2013 that got me thinking I should explore the topic more deeply in a book. Prior to that, I had only written an article about it, published in the *Financial Analysts Journal*.

Kate: I claim no credit. Your ideas were provocative even before we started getting to "Fewer" people in a way no one expected or wanted.

Larry: Yes, I certainly didn't mean a pandemic.

But I also have indirectly influenced a woman in her early twenties who asked Jason, "Why should I invest in a retirement plan when, forty-some years in the future when I should have access to that money, the Earth will be a rotating cinder? And we're all gonna die."

Kate: Talk about bleak!

Larry: Well, yes, we're all going to die — but not all at once. Jason had to explain to her, using my book, that her future and that of her possible children — if they choose not to kill themselves in the mistaken belief they'll die at a terribly young age — is actually very bright.

They'll be able to take advantage of all the technology that we have, all the economic progress that we've made — plus a lot more, including medical progress in controlling viruses that we couldn't even imagine until earlier this year. Instead of terrifying kids with apocalyptic thinking, we should be teaching them how to identify and solve problems, how to distinguish the real ones from illusions and chimeras.

What's more, we need to teach them that we do have ways of solving our environmental problems, and tell them that they'll likely figure out even better solutions.

Kate: Your ecological optimism is undoubtedly the most controversial part of the book.

Larry: Right. I've even been accused of being a global warming denier. My response is, "Well, if I'm a climate change denier, why did I write five chapters on how to fix it?"

Kate: My guess is that your accusers haven't read beyond your book's title.

Larry: Clearly not.

Kate: Just reading your chapter headings would give them more than an inkling — long before they'd get to your final chapter, on "Ecomodernism," where you lay out in admirable detail the rational environmental solutions you think we should be pursuing posthaste — urbanism, nuclear energy, genetic engineering, and what you call ecosystem engineering.

Larry: Right, the first thing I explain is "Why Poor Is Brown and Rich Is Green." Subsistence living and rapid industrialization can cause profound environmental degradation. But then, when a certain level of wealth is reached, there comes a tipping point. Environmental protection becomes both desirable and increasingly affordable — and societies become better stewards of our natural surroundings. Richer means greener.

Kate: What do you go into in your other three chapters on a greener future?

Larry: Well, "A Skeptical Environmentalist," referring to the author Bjorn Lomborg, explores the current state of the environment, how it got this way, what its prospects are — and how all of that relates to what's known as the environmental Kuznets curve.

The next chapter, called "Where Did My Record Collection Go?", explores what's called "dematerialization."

Kate: That sounds like science fiction —

Larry: Not quite. It's a trend in some advanced economies (and even a few not-so-advanced) toward trying to do more with fewer resources. Prioritizing experiences over physical possessions.

From there, the next green chapter uses the example of the extraordinary career and mind of *Whole Earth Catalog* author and pioneering environmentalist Stewart Brand to explore practical strategies for improving the future — ones that seem to turn today's environmental orthodoxies on their heads.

I think those five chapters are pretty strong evidence of my green bona fides, however contrarian some of my ideas may seem. I believe, in fact, that many of our problems can be solved through technology and engineering. But some are social — and so tougher nuts to crack.

I didn't really address this in the book, but if I write a second book I may feel compelled to. We've become horribly divided as a society, and that division keeps us from getting much of anything really constructive done because we need a large majority of people to agree on what to do.

Here's just one example: We absolutely, positively need nuclear power to replace much of the fossil fuel energy powering today's world. But try getting a majority to vote for that! Part of the mutual hostility we see all around us is manufactured by the media and by people trying to advance their own causes, but part of it is real.

An article came out recently showing that working class incomes have declined over the last 40 years. But the number of people in the working class also has gone down. So we're more prosperous on average by a considerable amount, but this improvement hasn't included everybody.

Kate: Which is the rub —

Larry: That is part of the source of the division, and I don't know what to do about that. But the world has been going to hell in a handbasket for as long as anyone can remember — and it never quite seems to get there. Instead, we're going in the opposite direction. Measured by just about any objective measure you choose, the health and wealth of the human race have been improving rapidly and, major wars excepted, almost continuously for at least the last 200 years. And there is every reason to expect this trend to continue — most dramatically in the developing world, but also in the developed world, more slowly because we're starting from a higher base.

Kate: Your book serves up a lot of examples of economic and social divides in history —

Larry: That's right. Athens and Sparta, the Optimates and the Populares in Rome, the various conflicts in the Middle Ages between the church and nascent states. The Cavaliers and Roundheads. The North and South in the U.S. Civil War. You can find social divides in every history book, yet we act as though this has never happened before.

Kate: What's never happened, for far too many people, is any real exposure to history's lessons. And that ignorance isn't bliss.

Larry: That could be the problem. If human nature doesn't change very fast, but the circumstances in which we live our lives do, you might want to learn about both — and that understanding can be found in the history books.

Kate: School has changed a lot since our days in grammar school —

Larry: Right, the No. 2 Eberhard Faber pencil is no longer the pinnacle of the technology. You've read, "I, Pencil," right? The classic economics essay about how no single human knows how a pencil was made.

Kate: Refresh my very dim recollection.

Larry: Different people contributed different pieces of knowhow and materials, but the essay's conceit was that no one in the world knew how to do all of it. That article, by Leonard Read, was published in the *Freeman* in 1957. He was trying to demonstrate to, I guess, school children that our capitalist system organizes cooperation between people who don't know each other, don't even know that each other exists, and live in different countries — the rubber tree guy in Malaysia and the lumberjack in Canada. The little bronze thing that holds the eraser on, which is called a ferrule, comes from yet a third place. Then somebody else puts it together.

Kate: Don't forget the graphite.

Larry: Right, and don't forget the marketing and distribution. Pencils don't just magically appear in your drugstore.

Kate: They don't? I'm so disappointed. But that's the kind of enlightening diversion you sprinkle throughout *Fewer, Richer, Greener*— **making it an unpredictably fun read.**

Larry: That's because I'm unable to focus on any one topic for long.

Kate: You had a good editor, then.

Larry: It was Dave Stanwick, who is also my research assistant. Although he edited the book, he let me be me, which is always risky.

Kate: I know you too well to ask you to elaborate. Instead, let me ask why you're trying to rekindle excitement over your relentlessly optimistic book now, with climate issues and miserable vaccination rates jockeying with fraught politics in the headlines, globally as well as nationally?

Larry: I think this is the right time and that it is what people need — to be reminded of the powerful long-term upward trends that are working in their favor. The mood of the country, if not the whole world, has turned sharply upward with the arrival of the vaccines. I'm not sure how things are where you live, but here in San Diego, and to some extent in Chicago, you cannot get a table in a restaurant. Last night I couldn't park within four blocks of downtown Del Mar, which is a sleepy town of 5,000 people. The pent-up need for social interaction has manifested itself in people just going crazy. And they've got tons of money to fuel it, because they had nothing to do but save it for 15 or 18 months.

So yes, it's the right time to relaunch an optimistic book. But I'm going to propose a second edition to my publisher, with two chapters on COVID-19. [2024 *update: It will be a sequel, not a second edition.—LBS*] One chapter will say that things can go terribly wrong and a society can move backwards a long way, very fast. It's happened before. We had World War I and the Great Depression, then World War II. We had another Pretty-

Bad Depression in the 1970s and then again in the 2000s. So progress isn't linear. Then too, we've had plagues before — most of them much worse than COVID. But *in the very long run*, the growth line is so close to being linear that you can't tell it apart from a straight line on a chart when you are comparing incomes or other measures of prosperity over time.

Kate: If you take a long-enough perspective, almost any disaster gets washed out.

Larry: Not really. From the earliest times of recorded history to somewhere in the 1700s human progress was so slow on average that you could barely measure it at all. Something like 98% of the people in the world in the 1700s were living on the same $3 a day that people were making — that's in today's money — in the times of the ancient Greeks and Romans. But when you look more microscopically within that period, there were great, localized, flourishings of civilizations — Greek, Roman, Islamic, and the High Middle Ages in Europe, plus the Renaissance, obviously.

Kate: Which all flamed out —

Larry: Yes, they all ended in some sort of disaster. It was usually caused by war, sometimes disease or famine. War is the easiest one to control. When the only way to expand your wealth is to take someone else's, you're going to get a lot of wars. But in a free society, that is, one with markets and capitalism, the best way to expand your wealth is to produce things more efficiently or produce more of them with the same resources or else discover more resources. In the modern free world there are several channels for getting ahead in an economic sense. So we shouldn't have as much war.

Though I have to concede that one of the bloodiest periods in human history was less than a century ago. So it's a not a foregone conclusion.

Kate: Unfortunately, better technology enables deadlier weapons.

Larry: Right. Steven Pinker wrote *The Better Angels of Our Nature* about that. He showed what he called the Hemoclysm of 1914 to 1945 —

Kate: That's an ugly term.

Larry: It's terrible, but descriptive. Pinker is a real artist with words. What he argued in his book was that, awful as it was, that period was consistent with the amount of violence that had existed at earlier times in human history. It wasn't a new high.

Kate: That's not much consolation, a sobering realization, really.

Larry: Yes, that's right. But then that spasm of great violence went away. Except that Pinker would actually expand the Hemoclysm to include the Chinese Revolution, because about as many people died in the Chinese Revolution as died in Europe in WWII.

Kate: It was also a horribly bloody thing.

Larry: Yes, and all because one man, Mao, convinced the Chinese people that communism was the way to prosperity, though it's not. What a son of a bitch.

Kate: To say the least. But Pinker's overriding message wasn't entirely grim. He actually argued — what we see on the nightly news notwithstanding — that mankind is getting less violent. And your thesis is likewise optimistic. You say modern society is somehow compounding progress, instead of letting it flame out —

Larry: Yes. Eventually what happened was the Enlightenment and the Industrial Revolution, and what Deirdre McCloskey calls the Great Betterment. Innovations began building on each other. Pinker writes more about the Enlightenment, because he's talking about intellectual enlightenment, while McCloskey focuses more on "economic betterment," with the emergence of the bourgeoisie. These historians are all in sympathy with one another, despite the differing nuances in their explanations of what has changed for humanity, beginning, basically, in the 17th Century. Everyone talks about it slightly differently, including me. But I tend to be a McCloskeyite.

Kate: Funny, how that works, with University of Chicago folks.

Larry: I was one of her students.

Kate: You're saying we entered a virtuous circle of development starting around the Industrial Revolution?

Larry: That's right. Building on the work of Larry Smarr, I call this piling on of innovation "linked exponentials," and I might write an article or even a book with that title someday.

Kate: I don't follow.

Larry: The idea is that nothing can grow exponentially forever; growth levels out. But in the leveling out phase, seeds are planted of something else that will start growing exponentially from there. That is why long-term economic progress is possible.

And I think what makes progress self-sustaining are trade, low-cost communications and transportation, *and peace.* If you lived in China or India or Africa during the time of the Italian Renaissance, word of those Italians' inventions didn't reach you, or at least not in time to be of any use in your life. Likewise, most Italians of the Renaissance had never heard of the inventions of the Islamic Golden Age in the 800s.

Kate: Different cultures, in essence, had to reinvent the wheel throughout history.

Larry: They had to reinvent the wheel because books are the way that knowledge is transmitted over time, and most cultures didn't have books — or didn't preserve them.

Kate: Explaining the sorry lot of most people.

Larry: That's right. Only a few monks had books — and many of those didn't even understand what they were copying. Or, if they could read it, the news didn't get out. That activity, interestingly, was centered in Ireland.

Exhibit 1 — Child mortality rate for selected countries, 1800-2015

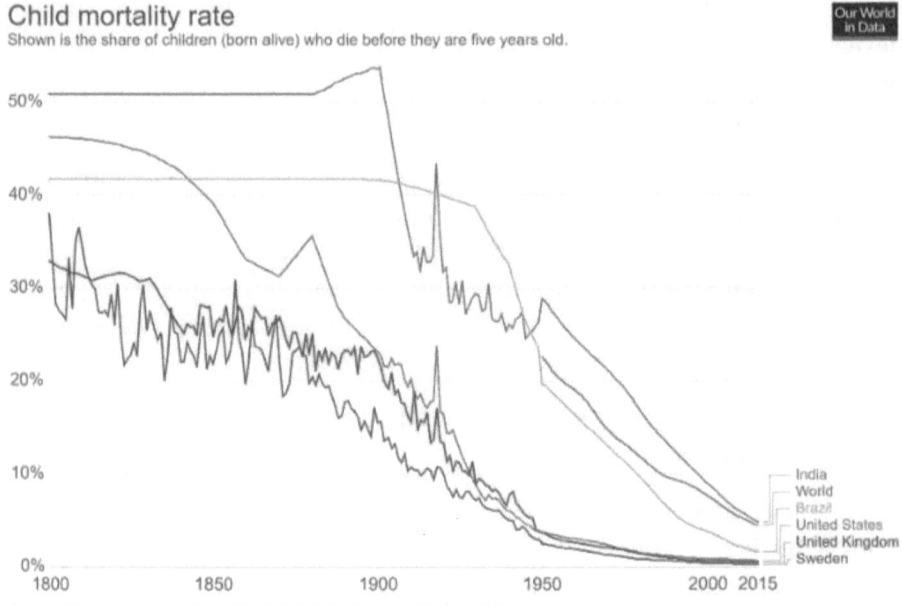

Source: Max Roser (Gapminder estimates up until 1949 and UN Population Division from 1950 to today), Our World in Data, *http://ourworldindata.org*. License under CC BY. Underlying sources shown in the figure.

Kate: Literally, an island off the Continent's shore, where "foreign" ideas could be guarded and cross-fertilization most likely prevented.

Larry: Well, it's still an island in a somewhat remote location, but it's now wealthy and well-educated because of low transportation and communication costs that have evolved in the last 150 years — although Ireland didn't really flourish until the last 50 years —

Kate: Well after many of my ancestors left in search of better lives.

Larry: That's why you're here and not in a thatched roof cottage in the west of Ireland. And that's why I'm married to someone whose father's family came from the same place. They would have stayed put if things in Ireland had been better.

Kate: That's what prompts almost all population migrations.

Larry: That's right. And it will probably continue, although there are a lot of people migrating now, not to avoid starving to death, but because they have gotten an education but have poor job prospects. So their reason to leave is on the next level up of the hierarchy of needs. They could stay put, and — if they were satisfied with their situations — they could live somewhat reasonable lives in the poorer countries. But they can turn on the TV or their cell phones and see how life is lived in France or Japan or Canada or eastern Long Island or San Diego. So if they can get here, they come. I don't blame them one bit for trying. But we can't literally take in everyone who wants to come, because there would be 4 billion people in America — but my heart is with them.

Kate: But we could take in a lot more immigrants than we've been admitting lately. Actually, this economy could use the population growth.

Larry: Yes, we could.

Kate: And we could maybe live up to founding principles.

Larry: I agree, and I think that we will.

Kate: Okay, let's circle back to the reason for this chat — "Fewer, Richer, Greener." You clearly weren't thinking a pandemic when you penned "Fewer." But you are saying fewer people is good news?

Larry: Right, I acknowledge that the global population is large and it's continuing to grow — but at the slowest rates since the 19th or 18th century. See Exhibit 2.

Exhibit 2 — World population growth, 1750 to 2015, with projections to 2100

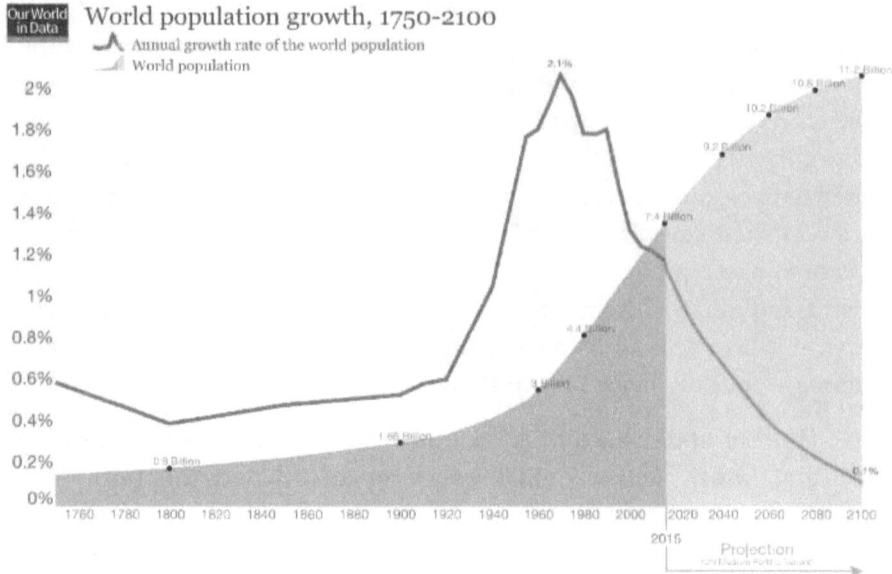

Data sources: Up to 2015, OurWorldInData series are based on UN and HYDE. Projections for 2015-2100: UN Population Division (2015) – Medium Variant. The data visualization is taken from OurWorldInData.org. There you find the raw data and more visualizations on this topic. Licensed under CC-BY-SA by the author Max Roser.

Even so, just because of the laws of large numbers, and the population momentum stemming from the fact that we now have a lot of young people who haven't had their one or two kids yet, demographers' projections are that we're going to add another 3 billion people to global population in this century. But then it will taper off and stop.

Exhibit 3 shows the total fertility rates in each country. They are close to replacement rate in most of the world as of a few years ago (because those are the most recent data for which I have a nice map). Fertility rates are even lower now.

Exhibit 3 — Total fertility rates by country as of 2024

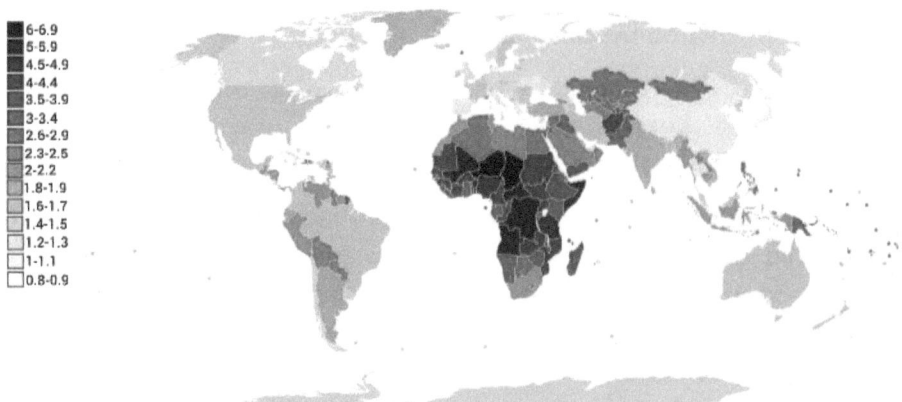

Note: I chose this graphic because the TFR gradations are finer than in most other available graphics. The differences between 0.8-0.9, 1.0-1.1, etc. are very important.
Source: Created using data from the World Bank,
https://www.reddit.com/r/MapPorn/comments/1bmna2e/fertility_rate_map_2024/#lightbox

Kate: Humans don't typically interpret growth stopping, anywhere, as good news —

Larry: But the biggest contributor to my optimism is the too-little appreciated fact that the population explosion is close to ending. Permitting a world of fewer and richer people to also be greener.

Kate: Whoa — that projection is for an additional 3-plus billion people on a planet that's already telling us it's pretty overstressed —

Larry: My analysis is based on the idea that environmental quality is an economic good like any other. Subsistence living is about the most environmentally destructive lifestyle imaginable, but it's hard to see the destruction because the population is small and the destruction is just beginning; the environment looks pretty.

As an economy begins to develop, it gets dirtier. Heavy industry is the way out of abject poverty. But eventually, as a society gets richer, it can afford to pay for large helpings of environmental quality. The whole point of getting rich is to buy things one wants. Of course, nearly everyone wants a beautiful, clean and safe natural environment, but people also have other priorities — eating, for example. When calories are scarce, future benefits are discounted at very high rates — all people care about is the present. When there's abundance, people can invest in the future, including in environmental quality.

This is all well-documented and represents what economists call the "environmental Kuznets curve" — the tendency of societies to become environmentally cleaner as they pass a certain threshold of affluence.

Kate: So your vision of a greener world leans heavily on rational economic decision making leading to healthier choices for the planet — a pretty big ask. Long-term thinking and incorporating full cost accounting for "externalities" scarcely seems to come naturally these days.

Larry: I believe that the externalities are best dealt with through pricing them and making people pay the full price — including the externalities — for what they do. So we do want to have markets for things like carbon and noise pollution. Light pollution, too.

We've more or less gotten rid of poisoned rivers issues in this country, but not in India. We actually haven't gotten rid of polluted air and water in China yet — although they're doing something about it earlier in their development than we did in ours. And in Mexico, there's a lot of pollution going into the Tijuana River, which then flows across the border into the United States and out into the Pacific Ocean — where we have to clean it up. Obviously we could make a deal which would eliminate that problem by charging Mexico the cost of cleaning it up, but enforcing it could be a problem.

Kate: You think? Especially when at least some of that pollution is coming from factories set up to export stuff to the U.S.

Larry: Right. It's possible that Mexican leaders will say we don't care about your deal; we just want the revenue from the factories. These are social engineering problems and I'm not very good at social engineering.

Kate: I'm not sure anyone really is. Are there even any well-functioning markets in externalities —

Larry: Emissions control markets are already working very well in the United States and Europe; less well in the rest of the world, but they are catching up. The air in American cities has become dramatically cleaner in the last 50 years, and you can drink the water. A lot of this improvement is due to emissions markets, sometimes called cap-and-trade. In developing countries, the markets are less well developed but they are moving faster in the right direction than we ever did.

Kate: Then you assume a continuing role for government in your greener future?

Larry: Yes, I do. You need a government to monitor compliance and enforce the rules. Isn't that why we established governments in the first place?

In any event, I'm acutely aware that my *Fewer, Richer, Greener* thesis is at odds with what mostly passes as received wisdom these days — that overpopulation and natural resources constraints will result in a future that's crowded, poor and dirty.

Kate: And slower population growth, you're saying, is the first step in that better direction?

Larry: It's already in place in most of the world. Almost all of the population increase that demographers expect, up to the peak at the end of this century, will occur in Africa. Already, India, Mexico, Iran, Brazil, Turkey — some very surprising places — and, obviously China, have reduced their population growth rates to first-world levels. Not quite as low as we are — we would actually be losing population if we didn't have immigrants — but to sustainable levels. It is two to two and a half children per family in some of those countries. Iran, I believe, is at one and a half to two. I believe that Brazil has now gone below two, too. *[2024 update: China's population growth rate has gone negative.]*

Kate: By sustainable, you mean?

Larry: A couple merely replacing itself has two children; that's the sustainable rate. The experts believe that the world will reach peak population late in this century at around 10 to 11 billion.

Kate: And those numbers are based on —

Larry: The United Nations Population Division's reports. I don't do my own demographic research. I rely on the experts, in fields where there really are experts. Nassim Nicholas Taleb, whom we all know and many of us love, says that there are two kinds of experts: Real ones who are experts in things like hydraulic engineering, medieval Portuguese, and how to fix a tooth that has a cavity. And phony experts such as those on politics, religion, morality, and so forth.

Kate: Where we are plagued by oversupply.

Larry: We have an oversupply of phony experts. But the people who study population dynamics are closer to dentists and hydraulic engineers than to talking heads. They observe the ways that people are making family planning choices in different environments, different societies. What they've found is that — except in Sub-Saharan Africa and parts of the Muslim Middle East — we have now passed the point of economic development where people want to trade in the benefits of having more children for the benefits of having fewer children. (See Exhibit 4 for economic growth rates over the very long run in the U.S. and the world.) That's exactly what's going on. People are responding to incentives they may not even know exist.

Exhibit 4 — Income per capita, 1820 to 2018 (US) and 1870 to 2018 (world) in today's dollars.

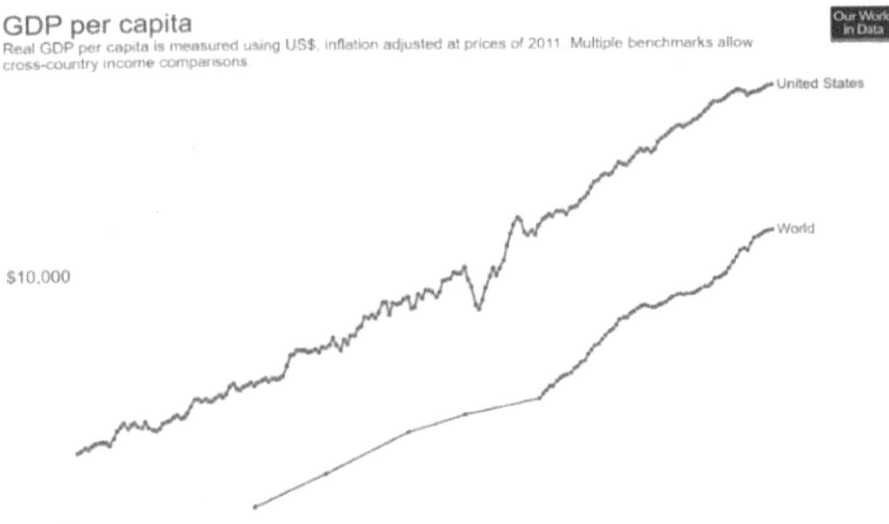

Note: Income and GDP are not the same, but the growth rates of the two variables are very similar. "Today's" dollars are 2011 dollars. To convert to 2024 dollars, multiply by 1.39.
Source: http://ourworldindata.org/economic-growth.2, Maddison Project Database, 2018. Our World in Data. Licensed under CC BY 4.0.

When my wife's grandfather — and grandmother, who I guess had the tougher job — had 15 children, they were in an environment where only 7 or 8 of them were expected to survive to work on the farm. In fact, they were healthier than average, and I believe 13 survived to adulthood. So we got fast population growth. But the U.S. has now gone through a demographic transition from being probably (on average) a 6-or-8 children per family country to a 1-or-2 child country. And now most of the rest of the world has likewise gone through that transition.

Kate: Except Africa.

Larry: Yes, but it isn't even all of Africa. The part of North Africa that's in the Muslim Middle East has mostly gone through a demographic transition — but not entirely. In temperate Southern Africa, by which I mean South Africa, Namibia, and Botswana — they already have their population growth rates down to the upper range of having it under control. And — if they didn't have terrible governance — you also could include Zimbabwe and maybe a couple of other southern African countries with temperate climates in that group. It's a very different part of Africa than Central and West Africa. It's much more prosperous and the population growth is much slower.

Now, the UN's demographers say that we're going to have 4 billion Africans out of a total of 10 or 11 billion people on the globe when population peaks. Their forecast sounds too high to me. Still, they are the experts and I should take their forecast somewhat seriously. So I'm going to take the under on 4 billion, but it's not going to be less than 3 billion.

What Deirdre McCloskey makes of this black population boom — and I love this quote so much, it's in my book in two different places — is that, just because of the very wide standard deviation of outcomes, especially among Africans (who have tremendous genetic diversity within that continent), a large proportion of the geniuses in science, technology, and the arts are going to be black by 2100.

We didn't see it coming, but it's coming, and they'll be as dominant as the English were in 1890 —

Kate: Careful, you're going to scare folks —

Larry: Or the Jews were in 1955. There are not a lot of Jews in the world, but Jews in the '50s pretty much ran the world of universities, research labs, symphony orchestras, the medical and legal professions — you name it. If it took a lot of intellectual firepower, the Jews were there.

Now, not all Africans are going to be capable of doing that — but not all Jews are, either. Still, work the math. If there are 3 billion Africans in 2100, and you just take just the top 5% of them, you're talking about 150 million African geniuses. Compare that to the Jews, where the total population is only 18 million — a lot of whom aren't in the top 5% of anything. I love playing around with numbers and with ideas like this — thinking as a futurist. Besides, I'm going to scare whom, exactly? White supremacists? I don't care.

Kate: Can I take it that part of your optimism is because you think education will be sufficiently globalized and improved over this century that all of those African geniuses will be nurtured into full flower?

Larry: I don't know. It's obviously technologically possible. Is it socially and politically possible? Probably. People are going to demand it. If they can't get that education in, say, Nigeria, they're going to get it in England — or whatever other country they can get to for an education. Because now you can fly intercontinentally for a price that people can save up for. Something like that has been possible for a long time. Look at all the Italians in New York whose ancestors came between 1870 and 1920. Sitting on those boats for a week wasn't free. But you only had to save up for that once. Then, when you got here and were more prosperous, you'd bring grandma over and so forth.

On the other hand, I'm very bothered by what's going on in our educational system in this country. It is getting worse.

Kate: The pandemic definitely hasn't helped —

Larry: No, but education's problems predate COVID. They have been getting worse for two reasons. One is that it has become too politicized. But the more profound reason is that we're trying to impart an education that was designed in the nineteenth century for the English, French, and German élites — for the top 5% to 20% of their students — to *everybody* now, regardless of whether all of our students today can — or want to — benefit from it.

What's more, realizing that this "education" program has failed at the high school level, we're sending our students on to community colleges and to remedial courses in local branches of state universities. There, they encounter professors who are often very capable — I've been quite impressed with the caliber of the people teaching at that level — but these kids are not prepared. We have to teach them *how* to learn before we can teach them *what* to learn. But many of them simply don't care enough to put in the effort. They want to get out of there.

Kate: It's hard to blame many them for just wanting their tickets punched by that point. They need jobs and want to get on with their lives. All schools have succeeded in teaching them, too often, is failure.

Larry: Right, there's no question our schools really are not sparking a lot of desire to become educated men and women. But the trouble with this situation is partly economic. Frankly, there just isn't much opportunity in today's U.S. economy for people with only traditional labor skills. Even with good high school educations. For several decades after World War II, we were in a monopoly position in manufacturing in the United States. Factory work and other low-skilled or unskilled jobs paid fairly well because no one else in the world was in a position to do that work.

Kate: Those circumstances are long gone —

Larry: Exactly. China and Indonesia and Brazil — places we call the middle-income countries — can not only do it cheaper than we do, but also tend to do it better. Manufacturing work is a big step up for their workers, not a big step down. They're very happy to be making, in our money, $15,000 or $30,000 a year as factory workers. They were lining up around the block to get those jobs when they were paying $5,000. Now, these are PPP (purchasing-power parity) numbers. The figures are lower in their own currencies. But this competition means that it's hard to find something for Americans of less-than-average academic or technical ability to do.

Kate: So we throw up our hands? Or work to get educators and business to find innovative remedies? Reimagine work, as they say?

Larry: Yes, reimagine work. I think we will work through this in the same way that we worked through getting tens of millions of farmers off the farm — when they were not needed there anymore because of increased agricultural productivity — and into the cities.

Kate: Into the factories, you mean? Didn't that essentially take the Depression, WWII, and the postwar economic boom?

Larry: Yes, into the factories, but it started much earlier. It was a diffuse and gradual transition. Farming and factory work, rural and urban living — those things involve very different skill sets. But people eventually adapted. It was a big step to go from working 15 or 16 hours a day in the fields during the good weather season — and hoping you'd grow enough food to survive the winter — to working an 8 or 9-hour shift, year round, and getting paid weekly or whatever. Or to go from living with no neighbors for miles to crowding into an apartment. But people muddle through.

Kate: Okay, so we're headed into a world with much slower population growth, but many more African geniuses. That's your "Fewer." How do we get to "Richer"? The pandemic has done much to accentuate the gulf between the haves and everyone else.

Larry: Well, there's a certain kind of have-not that has more than most people in the world. If you're making $17 an hour in a stable job, you're better off than 80% of the people in the world. But you're still way behind the median U.S. standard of living.

Kate: And your buying power in a third world slum is not the relevant comparison. Not to mention that you probably have zero health insurance, little safety net.

Larry: Obviously all Americans would like to "live like Americans," and we need to make that possible for everyone. However, comparing the living standards of the American poor to those of the Mexican or Chinese or African poor is not wrong. Everyone in those countries who decides to immigrate or not immigrate to the U.S. makes that comparison.

Globalization raises very complex questions. For example, while inequality is rising within countries it is decreasing dramatically across countries. Is this good or bad? Should an American call center operator be happy she is now competing with an Indian call center operator? Of course not, but the Indian is probably very happy. There is a net gain from this trade but not a gain for both parties, and we haven't figured out how to make this process fair or smooth. Protecting workers and companies from competition is not the way, though.

In my ideal world, everyone would have the opportunity to become middle class. If you only care about people in the United States, you get a very different ideal world than if you have a broader view.

Kate: Then again, you repeatedly point out in your book how much better off everybody is, today, because of progress, than even the most powerful men in the world were, even in the nineteenth century. What's your story about one of the Rothschilds?

Larry: Nathan Mayer Rothschild was the world's richest man in 1836, with a fortune expressed in today's dollars that approximated those of Jeff Bezos and Warren Buffett *added together*. Yet he died at age 58 of an infection that, a century later, could have been cured with a dollar's worth of penicillin.

Kate: Timing is everything! But richer is almost always better —

Larry: Yes, back to "Richer." The global economy is growing at about 1.5 to 1.8% a year per capita which adds up to a lot of money over long periods of time.

Kate: Thank you, miracle of compounding.

Larry: So China's per capita GDP is about what ours was in the 1920s — when we thought we were a first-world country by any standard.

Kate: True that.

Larry: China's GDP per capita today is actually higher than ours was then, but not much. Mexico is about where we were in 1952, when we thought we were an even more advanced first-world country and so on. This is the Great Convergence in global economic development since 1948. (It's called that because it followed the Great Divergence, which started in the 1800s with developed-country standards of living pulling farther and farther ahead of the rest of the world.) See Exhibit 5.

Exhibit 5 — The Great Convergence

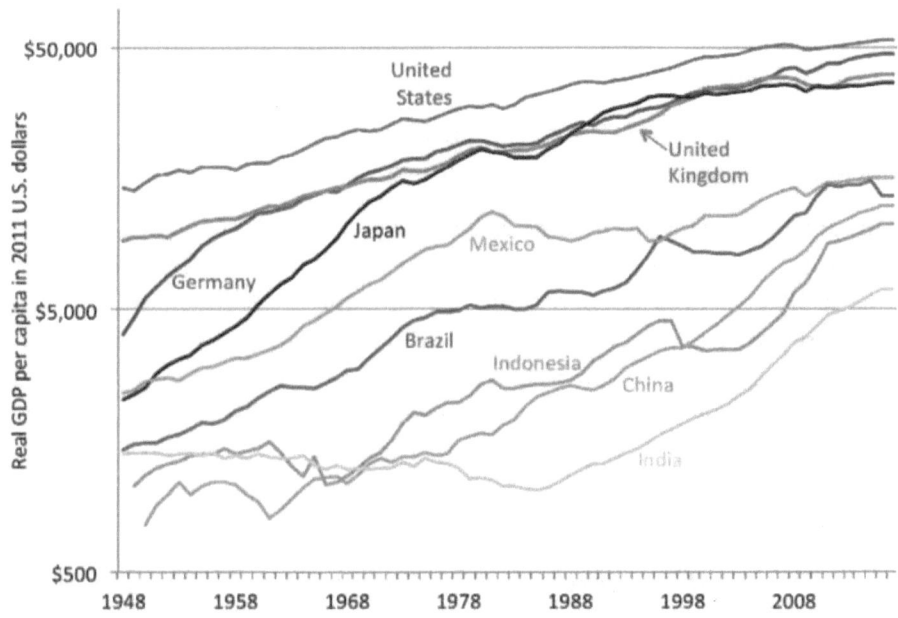

Source: Constructed by the author using data from The Maddison Project.

This convergence is not going to stop. Recently, we reached a milestone: according to the World Bank, half of the world's population is now middle class — not what we think of as middle class in America, but not living in hardship. What it means in this context is that people have enough money to cover basic needs — food, clothing, shelter, with enough left over for a few luxuries, like fancy food, a TV, motorbike, home improvements, higher education. The progression I see is that Ethiopia is going to become more like Peru and Peru is going to become more like Southern Brazil and Southern Brazil is going to become more like Germany — it will be a long time from now, but it will happen.

Kate: All boats will be lifted?

Larry: No, inevitably, some will fall through the cracks. It'll be countries with bad governments, bad institutions. Not bad people.

Kate: Just very unlucky.

Larry: Yes. Anyway, my point is that we are getting richer despite our own worst impulses to impose bad government and to do things that stop economic and technical progress in its tracks.

Kate: In part, because we forget how much better off we are than our ancestors were?

Larry: Yes, even if your income today is only in the 50th percentile, you're better off than a one percenter was in 1900. You have a car, an air conditioner, access to penicillin, all of which, in 1900, didn't exist. Granted, that top dog, back then, could hire an army of servants to cater to his whims. But if he got sick, the only pills available were cod liver oil, which did absolutely nothing. There are lots of ways to show that the amount of progress we've made is tremendous and that, basically, economic growth means that people of ordinary means can enjoy benefits or services that only the rich could afford in earlier ages.

Kate: The chart in *Fewer, Richer, Greener* of cell phone users in Africa, Exhibit 6 below, is probably your most dramatic illustration of the life-changing potential of innovations —

Exhibit 6 — Cell phone ownership surging in Africa

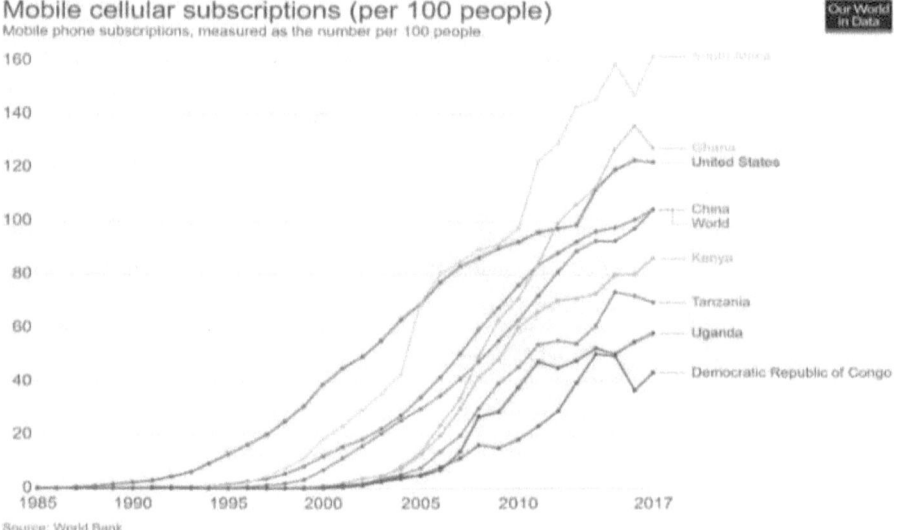

Source: http://ourworldindata.org/technology-adoption. Licensed under CC BY

Larry: Demand for affordable and accessible cell phones in Africa is practically insatiable, with the mobile devices connecting and empowering their users in countless ways formerly out of reach to ordinary Africans at any price. In *Fewer, Richer, Greener*, I described very affordable private schooling in Kenya paid for by the parents using apps on a phone. Even better known in East Africa is a cell-phone based financial service started by Vodafone, called M-PESA. (Pesa is Swahili for money.) Designed for "unbanked" Africans, it allows them to receive and store money, make payments, get cash from an ATM — do everything they could do with a bank account, without dealing with bankers or buildings, so not needing to travel to a bank branch — all on their smart phones. There are tens of millions of users, in many African nations, and the enterprise is profitable. Its benefits to consumers are spectacular. Banking services provided to the poor in Africa — before M-PESA — scarcely existed. And those that could be found were awful, with exorbitant fees and unreliable service.

Kate: Small wonder cell phone usage there is supercharged.

Larry: And that revolution has just begun. That progress comes about because people's desire to have tomorrow be better than today is incredibly strong, driving them to innovate.

This is Deirdre McCloskey's key idea: Increases in prosperity can only come from innovation because we're already doing the best we can with what we've got. In order to do any better, you have to do something more efficiently, invent something entirely new, or, more likely, make tiny improvements in what we have today.

So the computer I'm using today has a better chip than the five-year-old one that I recently retired. Chips aren't a new invention. The improvement is just Apple deciding that if they're going to sell you a new computer every few years, it will have to be a little better than the last one — or you're not going to buy it.

Kate: At least until the thing's planned obsolescence kicks in —

Larry: They do that, too. It's really annoying. But the improvements add up. Compare a 2021 car to a 1981 model. They both do the same thing. Allow you to drive somewhere. But the quality of the 2021 car is incomparably higher.

Kate: The superior fuel efficiency of the 2021 model brings up the "Greener" aspect of your book. Optimism about the environment is definitely contrary to the zeitgeist. The pushback must be fun.

Larry: Perversely fun. Mostly because people have simply convinced themselves, first of all, that any kind of economic progress or advancement destroys the natural environment. It doesn't. It could, if you did not care about the natural environment and made no provisions, made no effort to control the pollution, control carbon usage and so on.

But again, with enough money, you can do all this. And, when you look at how long people have been working to, for instance, eliminate pollution, you can see that some things, at least are getting better, not worse. Exhibit 7 is a very long-term chart of the evolution of sulfur dioxide and smoke pollution in London from Shakespeare's day to, essentially, now.

Exhibit 7 — Sulfur dioxide and smoke concentration in London, 1585-2000

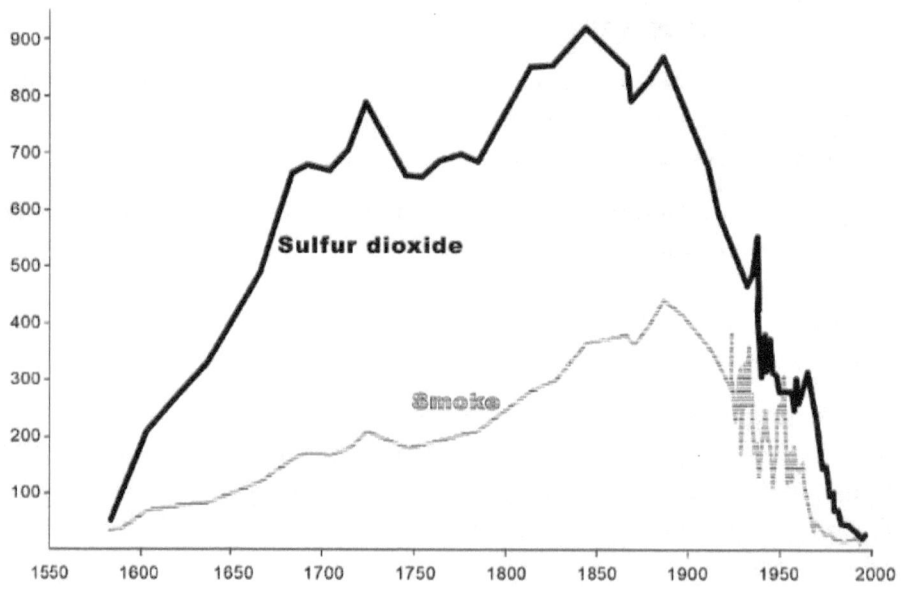

Source: Adapted from Lomborg (2001).

Kate: Where does the data come from? I doubt that the Bard's cronies were measuring sulfur dioxide emissions.

Larry: These are estimates by a British environmental scientist, based on records of coal imports into the city. The chart shows that smoke pollution increased sharply for 300 years before starting to drop even faster starting in the last nineteenth century — so that by the 1980s, London's smoke pollution fell below the levels of the late sixteenth century. Even though the city's last severe smog emergency killed about 4,000 residents in 1952, London's air today is clearer than it's been since the Middle Ages — and has been getting better for over 100 years.

Kate: That's very good for Londoners, Larry. But that city was pretty much the capital of the first world for all of that time. I don't know how germane its experience is to very much less privileged places on the globe.

Larry: Countries don't have to have the resources of the British monarchy, or Switzerland, to engage in meaningful environmental preservation. The Dominican Republic is not exactly rich. With a PPP GDP per capita of $19,228, it's close to the world average, and about on par with China. But it's about more than six times as wealthy as Haiti, the poorest nation in the Americas — with which it shares the island of Hispaniola. Haiti, wracked with political turmoil and dominated by criminal gangs, has a per capita PPP GDP of $3,054.

Exhibit 8 – Border between Haiti (left) and Dominican Republic

Source: https://wedocs.unep.org/bitstream/handle/20.500.11822/17680/UNEP_Haiti-DomRep_border_zone_EN.pdf

This photo shows the border between the two countries. Haiti is denuded, the Dominican Republic, richly forested. The richer you are, the more of the environment you can protect. In part, the countries' divergent paths are tied to cultural factors. The Dominican Republic has absorbed far more European commercial influences; Haiti, seemingly every downside of the slave trade, rebellions and wars with France and Spain. But mainly, one country is dirt poor and the other is an emerging middle-income economy. A starker difference in environmental quality could scarcely be imagined.

Kate: No argument. On a lighter note, I didn't notice much about Wall Street's favorite green venture, Tesla, in your book.

Larry: I am encouraged by the development of electric cars — if their batteries are charged with electricity generated by nuclear power. There won't be enough solar and wind power in the world to keep everybody's cars going unless you're willing to devote a massive and environmentally destructive amount of resources to solar and wind. And even then, there wouldn't be enough power at the right time and the right place.

Kate: Building more nuclear capacity is a big sticking point for a lot of people.

Larry: I hope not — or that they get over it — because nuclear is not only our safest power source, it's the only one, other than fossil fuels, that we have in any great abundance now. We don't have to discover a new technology. It's old technology.

Kate: Given the potential for nuclear accidents, that's not particularly comforting —

Larry: Well, I do believe that the traditional model of giant nuclear plants, each one custom-built, is outdated. They should be as interchangeable as the "327" engines in a General Motors truck. You could have 10,000 nuclear generators scattered around the world — and they could generate all the power the planet is ever going to need. They could be built with interchangeable parts, staffed with interchangeable personnel.

Kate: The thing is, the Earth isn't interchangeable if something goes wrong.

Larry: Look, because fuels have been so cheap, for so long, we haven't seriously tried to develop new sources of relatively cheap energy, at least until fairly recently. Wind and solar have roles to play, but because of intermittency and other issues, they simply can't replace all fossil fuels at any time in the foreseeable future. But how long do you think it would take to develop a truly safe nuclear reactor? One that doesn't fall apart in an earthquake? Melt down in a tsunami? That's impervious to terrorism? And that has multiple back-up systems in case something goes wrong? Is that within the power of human imagination?

Kate: Probably, especially if money is no object. But what to do with spent radioactive fuel might still be a dealbreaker.

Larry: There are various technologies for dealing with spent radioactive fuel, a topic on which I am not an expert. The French seem to be on the leading edge of this. I'm a techno-optimist. I think we will figure out what is the best technology and use it. We'd better, because the world needs a lot more electric power.

Kate: It's a TINA situation?

Larry: There is no alternative. In today's world, we're generating about 30 petawatt-hours of electricity per year. Yet many of the people in the world don't have enough energy to do the basics of life. There are still people — as you read in my book — in Kenya who have to walk four hours a day to gather sticks to start cooking fires in their fireplaces — which don't have vents and turn the insides of their houses into carbon monoxide hells. Do you want to take energy away from these people?

Kate: No, an upgrade would be much better.

Larry: Well, I want to sell them kilowatts — cheaply — they need more energy. In this country, we don't really need more energy, but we do need a way of getting it that doesn't involve burning coal or gas or cutting down forests. Nuclear is the easy answer. Jeff Bezos is funding the development of a fusion reactor in England.

Kate: Promises, promises — remember that oldie?

Larry: Yes. I'll grant that there's never been a feasible commercial fusion reactor built. So it takes somebody with $100 billion, who isn't answerable to the taxpayers or the voters, to try to do it. *[2024 update: it's still quite some time away.]*

Kate: The idea has never been demonstrated on any scale. Other than over Hiroshima.

Larry: Yes, but that was fission, the H-bomb is fusion.

Kate: Right. Duh. Uncontrolled fusion is "perfect" for a bomb, but not a power plant.

Larry: Okay, but a working steam engine had not been demonstrated in 1600 — nor had a working electric motor been demonstrated in 1750. Energy transitions take a long time, a lot of money, and a lot of people, and it still might not be possible.

Kate: Aren't you concerned about sea level rise as a result of global warming?

Larry: I'm concerned but, again, I don't foresee a catastrophe. The Ganges Delta, the Mekong Delta, the Mississippi Delta in Louisiana, Bangkok, and Manila, maybe even some low-lying places in the United States may get wet. People may have to move uphill. The best estimate I've seen is that 200 million people will have to move uphill in *this century*.

Kate: How are 200 million people going to move uphill in this century?

Larry: If 200 million out of, let's call it, 10 billion, or 2% of the world lives in low-lying areas that are going to be physically threatened by rising sea levels, they'll have to move to survive. And governments — all of us — are going to have to pay for it. Because the affected populations mostly can't afford it. But we have some advantages that our forebears didn't have — airplanes, weather forecasts, radio, television, the internet. People are not all going to drown the way that the Dutch did when a dike failed way back when. If you compare that 200 million to the number of people who move internationally every year, which is 180 million, it's not that daunting. What's daunting is the social aspect.

Kate: You think it's hard to convince people to get vaccinated? Try to get them to move.

Larry: Exactly. People hate change, and avoid doing the right thing until it's almost too late. But how do we get 180 million people to move internationally every year? "We" don't. Incentives work their magic. There is a pull and a push. The pull is a better life somewhere else in the world. An example of the push is the threat of a slaughter in Afghanistan. Usually the incentives are economic, but sometimes they are life-or-death. At any rate, people do move when they have to or want to.

Kate: Extrapolating current trends far into the future — as investors often do with corporate earnings — can lead to horrible forecast errors, you're implying?

Larry: It sure can! My point is, a lot of the alarmism we're hearing is based on projecting compound rates of change out forever — when that's an absurd thing to do. When people projected the 1970s' rate of population growth out forever, they come up with estimates of like 3 trillion people on earth by 2300.

Kate: Sure, that's how the Club of Rome came up with its infamously dire predictions.

Larry: Right. So you've got to think, okay, none of their predictions have come true except one, which was that their members would do very well on the speaking circuit.

Kate: Prophets of doom always seem to sell more books than optimists.

Larry: They do. The prophet of doom sounds smarter — and sounds like he's trying to help you. By contrast, the optimist sounds like he is trying to sell you something. I wrote that in my book — and I intend to fix that. With *Fewer, Richer, Greener*, I'm going to make money by saying what's right about the world as well as what's wrong with it.

Kate: Godspeed with that, Larry. Thanks.

Investing

I'll take the easy way out and use the same introduction I wrote for *Unknown Knowns*. Careful spotters might notice that I did change one word. I changed "provocative thinking" to "provocative wisdom."

> This is home turf to Larry.
>
> Larry didn't start college or graduate school thinking about a career in finance, but research assistant positions and coursework pulled him toward economics and investment management. Decades later, he is well known for his provocative wisdom and understanding of these subjects.

Wayne's favorite: Edward Chancellor's *The Price of Time*. Here's Amazon's introduction:

> "A comprehensive and profoundly relevant history of interest from one of the world's leading financial writers, *The Price of Time* explains our current global financial position and how we got here."

People think of interest rates, when they think of them at all, as the price of money, but Edward Chancellor, a prominent financial historian, argues that they're the price of time. Larry explains what Chancellor means by that and discusses how the history of interest rates is relevant to today's investment problems.

—W.H.W.

Chapter 6: The Price of Time

Laurence B. Siegel
August 2022

I'm a sucker for a good read. I'm also a sucker for a good book with fine art on the cover (magnificent example below from 1514). But I am the biggest sucker for a good review of a good and pretty book!

What follows is Larry Siegel at his best — charged up, witty, engaged, and critical. His review of Edward Chancellor's latest, *The Price of Time*, is titled the same. Why? As Larry says, "It's such a great title — short and provocative!"

—Theodore R. Aronson

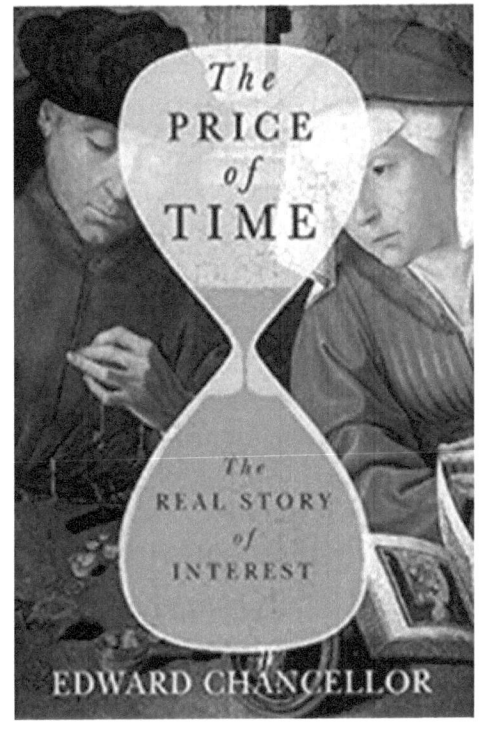

> "I returned, and saw under the sun, that the race is not to the swift, nor the battle to the strong, neither yet bread to the wise, nor yet riches to men of understanding, nor yet favour to men of skill; but time and chance happeneth to them all."
>
> — Koheleth[1]

My favorite of the many brilliant verses in the Wisdom books of the Old Testament frames the problem faced by finance. Finance, said Roger Ibbotson, is the branch of economics that deals with time and uncertainty. While finance appears extraordinarily complicated, when simplified to its barest essentials it relies on two prices: the price of risk (chance) and the price of time.

We see attempts to discern the price of risk all over the place. The equity risk premium is the price of business risk — yet we can't measure it, only give wide estimates. Insurance premiums measure the price of mortality risk, medical risk, and property risk. Betting markets can price just about any risk you can think of.

But what is the price of time? In what sense does time have a price? Why is it, of all these prices, the only one you can look up each day in the newspaper? (The price of time is the interest rate, in case you haven't guessed by now.) And what can we learn from an intensive study of that price, across history and the extent of the globe?

Edward Chancellor, one of the finest writers ever to turn his attention to financial markets, tackles both the deep history of interest rates and the current controversies surrounding them in his new book, *The Price of Time*. If an investor were somehow only allowed to have a dozen investment-related books (let's say he was in prison), this would be one of them. The others would include Peter Bernstein's *Against the Gods*, Matt Ridley's *The Rational Optimist*, and Nassim Taleb's *Fooled by Randomness*.[2]

---

[1] Ecclesiastes 9:11, King James Version (1611). Koheleth means "the preacher" or "the teacher" and that is all we know of the identity of the author of Ecclesiastes (which is itself a rough Greek translation of the Hebrew word Koheleth). The Wisdom books were traditionally thought to be written by King Solomon, but probably were not.

[2] *The Price of Time* might not make my top 4, but only because of the narrowness of its subject matter. It's as well written as the other three I mentioned. Bernstein's *Capital Ideas* and 2 *Capital Ideas Evolving* are more directly relevant to the practice of investment management,

You can finish the list. Tastes vary, but my list is biased toward history and long-term thinking, and I'm sure Chancellor's list would be too.

This essay mixes an assessment of *The Price of Time* with a more general inquiry about interest rates, their role in the economy, why they're so low, and whether they should be higher (Chancellor says yes).

Purpose and structure of the book

"This book," Chancellor writes,

> was...inspired by a Bastiat-like conviction that ultra-low interest rates were contributing to many of our current woes, whether the collapse of productivity growth, unaffordable housing, rising inequality, the loss of market competition or financial fragility. Ultra-low rates also seemed to play some role in the resurgence of populism as Sumner's Forgotten Man started to lose patience.

(Frédéric Bastiat was a nineteenth-century French economist and legislator who championed Adam Smith's free-market ideas on the Continent. William Graham Sumner, a 19th-century Yale professor, coined the phrase "the forgotten man" to refer to the party called "C" in a political — not market — transaction where A and B decide what C will give to D. Nice fellows, those A and B.)

The Price of Time begins with a history of the interaction between interest rates and, well, everything else in the world. Describing how interest and capitalism are inseparable, Chancellor writes, "We trace

Edward Chancellor
Source: https://www.idler.co.uk/
product/investment-with-edward-chancellor/

---

but *Against the Gods* (about risk) should be required reading for anyone who takes risk — and that's all of us. Taleb's book, likewise, should be required reading for anyone who deals with statistics and numbers — again, that's all of us.

the origins of interest to the Ancient Near East...and follow its story through the Middle Ages to the birth of capitalism in Europe..." Exhibit 1 shows 5000 years of interest rates on best credits (mostly sovereigns) — we really are experiencing the lowest rates in history![3]

Exhibit 1 — 5000 Years of Interest Rates

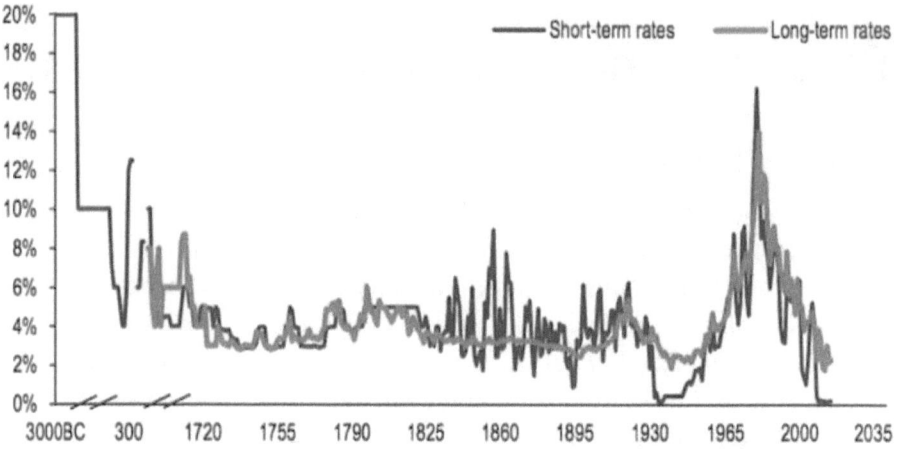

Source: https://www.businessinsider.com/chart-5000-years-of-interest-rates-history-2016-6. Underlying sources: Bank of England; Global Financial Data; Homer, Sidney, and Richard Sylla, *A History of Interest Rates*, 4th ed., Hoboken, NJ: Wiley Finance.

Low interest rates have historically been observed in low-risk, mature societies and have thus usually been regarded as a good thing. The relationship flips around, however, when administered interest rates — in this case, achieved through the Fed's open market operations— become so low as to discourage savings, promote wild speculation, and keep "zombie" enterprises alive that should die as part of the process that Joseph Schumpeter called "creative destruction."

Part Two explores these latter themes. Chancellor writes,

> [W]e examine in greater detail [Claudio] Borio's thesis that "low rates beget lower rates." These chapters are arranged around the various functions of interest, namely its influence

---

[3] How quickly an essay like this can become out of date! Interest rates in early 2024, less than a year and a half after it was written, are far from being the lowest in history.

on the *allocation* of capital, the *financing* of companies, the *capitalization* of wealth, the level of *savings*, the *distribution* of wealth, the measurement of *risk* and the regulation of *international capital flows*.[4]

It's a rich pageant of macroeconomic thought, told from Chancellor's contrarian, some might say Victorian, point of view.

Why this book is controversial

The Price of Time is controversial because much of current thinking, and almost all of current practice, in monetary economics is the exact opposite of Bastiat's and Chancellor's. Low interest rates are widely thought to be an unalloyed good. Keynesian economists, who are in charge of most of the world's central banks, advocate lowering interest rates when the economy slows, because (they argue) low borrowing costs encourage investment, for example by making big purchases by consumers and businesses more affordable. In emergencies, interest rates could be lowered — by central-bank open market operations, not by free-market forces — almost to zero.

The effectiveness of this approach is still being evaluated, but the basic concept has guided monetary policy since the end of World War II. Since the Global Financial Crisis of 2007-2009, however, central bankers acted as if it is always an emergency. Earlier this year, Stephen Sexauer and I wrote,

> When you're a fireman, you benefit from an abundance of fires. When you're a central banker, you are unseen doing the work that keeps our money and banking systems up and running, except in economic emergencies. In emergencies...you become a rock star...[T]his does not make for good policy.[5]

---

[4] Emphasis in the original. Borio is head of the Monetary and Economic Department of the Bank for International Settlements (Basel, Switzerland).

[5] Siegel, Laurence B., and Stephen C. Sexauer. 2022. "Debunking 7-1/2 Myths of Investing." *Journal of Investing*, 30th Anniversary Special Issue, p. 97.

Chancellor picks up on the fire theme. The Fed has been accused of creating, using super-easy money, a series of asset bubbles that then had to be corrected through a policy of tight money. The resulting seesaw is disruptive and expensive (the S&P 500 declined 49% in 2000-2002 and an incredible 57% in 2007-2009, comprising a "lost decade"). Chancellor agrees with this critique of the Fed. Noting that firemen have been known to set fires to guarantee their importance, he writes, "[O]ne is drawn to James Grant's conclusion that the Fed's "functional dual mandate has become that of arsonist and fireman." Ouch.

The "Fall" of 2008

In the fall of 2008, two things happened in the monetary system.[6] First, central banks became the lenders of last resort when the bank runs started to occur—they lent against good assets and made a tidy profit doing so. In the U.S., the Fed's balance sheet went from about $900 billion to $2 trillion as they purchased the panic-driven avalanche of assets out of money market funds and investment banks. The Fed made about $100 billion per year doing this.[7] Within two years, those additional $1 trillion in assets left Fed and went back into the financial markets.

Second, in an attempt to actively support the economic recovery, the Fed and central banks worldwide pushed trillions upon trillions of dollars in government bonds (called quantitative easing, QE) to push short-term interest rates down to zero in the United States and negative numbers in Europe and Japan — and they kept them there for ten of the last thirteen years. As shown in Exhibit 1, nothing like this had ever happened before, except briefly in the 1930s, in the 5000 years of history documented by Sidney Homer and Richard Sylla in their masterpiece, *A History of Interest*

---

[6] Thanks to Edwin Burton (University of Virginia) for this inexcusable pun about the crash in the fall of that year. *The Fall of 2008* is the title of his book on the topic.

[7] The Fed followed closely, but not exactly, Walter Bagehot's famous 1873 recommendation, summarized by Paul Tucker, for central banks to "to...lend early and freely (i.e., without limit), to solvent firms, against good collateral, and at 'high rates'" to stave off financial panics. What the Fed did not do was to lend at high rates. (Bagehot was the revered editor of *The Economist* and a popular writer on finance; the recommendation is in his *Lombard Street: A Description of the Money Market*. Sir Paul Tucker is a British central banker.)

Rates, on which Chancellor and the rest of us rely for our long-term historical information.

Near the end of this extended period of ultra-low and negative administered rates, a strange new philosophy called "modern monetary theory" (MMT) by its proponents, and inflationism by its opponents, took hold. MMT held that a sovereign government had no limits on the creation of debt in an attempt to boost its GDP, and that rates would still remain low. For a short while, that's what happened: massive fiscal deficits, extraordinary levels of government spending, and what Fed chair Jerome Powell called "stubbornly" low interest rates. But, even after the 2020-2021 COVID pandemic with its supply shocks and massive $5 trillion fiscal helicopter drop of serial relief programs, we didn't get much inflation.

In 2022, that changed quickly and dramatically. Now we are in an inflationary spasm that is causing savers (especially retirees) to panic and causing economists to reconsider their Keynesian dogma and any favorable view of MMT they might have had.

Chancellor vs. Bernanke

I've gone through all this background to show that Chancellor's hard-money advocacy, powerfully supported in the second section of *The Price of Time*, is deeply contrarian. It is a swim upstream in the spring floods. Nobody wants to hear that the monetary policies of the last two decades, and possibly much longer, were no good and could lead to our eventual ruin. That is pretty much what Chancellor is saying — and he goes farther. He argues that, in our modern history, interest rates kept too low by a sovereign have always led to chaos, and potentially economic collapse, as eventually market forces, risk, and the natural price time win out. Chancellor, channeling Friedrich Hayek, calls this "the new *Road to Serfdom*."[8]

---

[8] Chancellor is referring to Hayek, Friedrich. 1944. *The Road to Serfdom*. Abingdon, UK: Routledge Press.

The Economist, never shying away from controversy, has argued in a double book review, of Ben Bernanke's *21st Century Monetary Policy* as well as Chancellor's volume, that while Chancellor is by far the more elegant writer and better debater, he is wrong and Bernanke is right:[9]

> Mr Bernanke's framework is more compelling than Mr Chancellor's, as low or even negative interest rates can co-exist with humanity's natural short-termism. Suppose someone has a wage income of 100 in their working life and zero in retirement. Though they may not target a 50/50 split, they will save to avoid penury. Lots of people building up a nest-egg — even one that is small relative to their working incomes — creates an imbalance that can, as a result of market forces, push rates lower than their discount rates. "Justice is violated when lenders receive little or nothing," Mr Chancellor writes. He might as well rage against a population pyramid.

The Economist concludes by saying that "when the time comes to appoint a central banker, choose someone like Mr. Bernanke."[10]

This debate is not new. In 1900, L. Frank Baum, in a best-selling book, lampooned authorities who claimed the ability to control everything and fix whatever's broken in the economy.

Exhibit 2 is a scene from a later dramatization of his book.

---

[9] August 13, 2022.

[10] The case for low rates deserves a hearing too, but space constraints require me to punt. The references in this footnote will help. Although it's a dull read, Bernanke's *21st Century Monetary Policy* is the go-to source, the author having shepherded us through the most difficult economic circumstances in at least 40 years. Growth rates in the recovery after the crisis were seriously subpar, a result that some blame on central bank policy. That, however, is not a satisfying explanation; other forces are at work. Tom Coleman's and my summary of the case for low rates (which we opposed) is in Siegel and Coleman (2015), pp. 6-7, https://larrysiegeldotorg.files.wordpress.com/2015/10/siegel_coleman_phooey-on-financial-repression.pdf.

Exhibit 2 — Skeptical citizens try not to be fooled by a pompous central banker

Yes, The Wizard of Oz was a political screed for adults as well as a wonderful drama and allegory for children.[11]

A stellar group of academics weighs in

I might dismiss *The Economist*'s comments (except the one about the population pyramid, which is very clever) with a wave of the hand, attributing them to that magazine's incorrigible establishmentarianism. Given their self-image as The Voice of Reason and Responsibility, how could they come to any other conclusion?

It turns out that the *Economist*'s view has support in surprising places. At the request of the CFA Institute Research Foundation, I recently convened an 11-participant, all-day discussion on the equity risk premium, which was published by that organization as a book and in other formats in 2023.[12]

---

[11] See https://en.wikipedia.org/wiki/Political_interpretations_of_The_Wonderful_Wizard_of_Oz, accessed on August 29, 2022.

[12] The book, *Revisiting the Equity Risk Premium*, is available online as a free public download at https://rpc.cfainstitute.org/research/foundation/2023/revisiting-equity-risk-premium-2021 and in print at https://www.amazon.com/Revisiting-Equity-Premium-Laurence-Siegel/dp/1952927358/. The participants were Rob Arnott, Cliff Asness, Mary Ida Compton, Elroy Dimson, Will Goetzmann, Roger Ibbotson, Antti Ilmanen, Marty Leibowitz, Rajnish Mehra, Tom Philips, and Jeremy Siegel. I was the organizer and moderator, and I co-edited the book with Paul

The topic turned to negative interest rates, and Jeremy Siegel, the author of *Stocks for the Long Run* and possessor of a notably sunny disposition about the markets, said:

> An insurance asset, as you know, will very often give you a negative return...When everything is priced in money, and the concern is about another financial crisis or a pandemic...or whatever, prices of goods and services and real assets decline, and bonds — nominal fixed assets — do extremely well. They take on a sharply negative beta, which gives them a tremendous hedging ability. I think trillions of dollars' worth of demand are generated to hold that asset.

When an asset faces massive unexpected demand, and the supply is relatively fixed in the short run as with bonds, the price rises and the yield falls. Negative interest rates.

The conversation went further into the rabbit hole:

Rajnish Mehra: If there is a famine tomorrow — if times are good today and times are really bad tomorrow — then I would give up a lot of stuff today to get something guaranteed tomorrow in a very, very bad state of the world where the marginal utility is very high. Then I will get negative rates. But that's not a world I want to live in.

Laurence Siegel: That's a declining economy. You can get negative rates in equilibrium in a declining economy, but not in any other state...We got...positive real rates from thousands of years in the past until 13 years ago. Which is the rule and which is the exception?

Jeremy Siegel: You can get a negative risk-free rate of interest in a growing economy. I'm not saying that it will happen. But it can be an equilibrium in a growing economy.

Roger Ibbotson: I agree with Jeremy because most of your investments involve risk, and have positive payoffs. It is just the risk-free rates— the

---

McCaffrey. A series of blog posts about the discussion are at
https://blogs.cfainstitute.org/investor/tag/equity-risk-premium/; explore the blog back through time to read all the parts. The first blog post based this event was on April 8, 2022. Videos of the discussion are at
https://players.brightcove.net/1183701590001/experience_6480b09578652c0025f77ae8/share.html.

real risk-free rates — that are negative. I don't see any reason why they couldn't continue...indefinitely.

I didn't ask the participants to explain their position in detail. We didn't have time, and it wouldn't have been fair to put them on the spot like that. But when two out of three of the most distinguished finance professors in the world say that you can have negative real interest rates in equilibrium in a growing economy, we have to listen. ("In equilibrium" means that the negative real rate is a market-derived rate, a fair price for time, not a mistake imposed by authorities.)

A more immediate concern: Government budgets and nominal debt service

Of course, one can only take this kind of argument so far. In real life, governments and other economic agents owe a *lot* of money. All debt is floating-rate in the long run (because even the longest bonds mature and the issuer has to roll them over at the new rate).[13] So, while higher interest rates might be desirable from a growth point of view, you can't raise rates so much that they would bankrupt the government. There is an extensive literature on this which I won't get into, but it suffices to say that the Taylor-rule Fed Funds rate of 6.83%, using the Atlanta Fed's Taylor rule calculator and their own default assumptions, is too high given the fiscal status of the U.S. government.[14]

---

[13] There's an exception: Investors used to be able to buy perpetual debt, which never matures but instead pays interest "forever." The British government began to issue such bonds, called consols, in 1751 and they remained in circulation until the government redeemed them (bought them back) in 2016. Other than a few very exotic issues, no perpetual bonds remain on the market.

[14] https://www.atlantafed.org/cqer/research/taylor-rule?panel=1, "Alternative 1" default assumptions as of August 26, While governments should be and are more concerned with intermediate-and long-term interest rates, the Fed Funds short-term rate is indicative of the general level of interest rates and is the only rate that the Fed controls, thus my emphasis on it.

Moreover, such a high rate would still produce a fairly large negative real rate if inflation continues at its current 9% pace! Clearly we are in a bit of a box due to the size of government debt. (Debt hawks, including Chancellor, have seen this coming for a long time.)

The Grumpy Economist gets the last word

Chancellor is not the only economist who thinks interest rates are too low to be consistent with robust growth. In his blog, "The Grumpy Economist," John Cochrane, an impeccably pedigreed macroeconomist and financial economist who has written authoritative books on asset pricing and the fiscal theory of the price level, states:

> All current macroeconomic theories start with the same basic story: when interest rates are higher, people consume less today, save, and then consume more in the future. Higher real interest rates mean higher consumption growth.[15]

For those who care about the future beyond the next few quarters, then, higher real interest rates are to be desired. Rather than trying to maximize current consumption or production, as measured by quarterly GDP data, we should be trying to maximize wealth, which is (by simple accounting identities) the present value of all future consumption.

Too much doom and gloom?

Like any scholar of markets, Chancellor does not get everything right. For more than a decade he was an investment strategist with Jeremy Grantham's prestigious asset management firm, GMO, and he's been influenced by Grantham's thinking (which is often a good thing — but not

---

[15] "Three views of consumption and the slow economy," blog post on Sunday, February 3, 2013, *The Grumpy Economist*, https://johnhcochrane.blogspot.com/2013/02/three-views-of-consumption-and-slow.html.

always). He approvingly quotes Grantham as having said, in 2011, that the "days of abundant resources and falling [real] prices [of natural resources] are over forever."[16]

The CRB commodity price index responded by promptly falling in half, from 320 at the 2011 top to 162 at the 2016 bottom. More recently, commodities soared again because of the COVID crisis and concomitant monetary stimulus but, notably, did not surpass the 2011 high — and, just this summer, the bellwether gasoline and copper prices plunged. Forever is a long time, and the long-term trend of real raw materials prices has always been down.[17]

I'm as concerned about the impact of low interest rates and an unremitting easy-money policy as anyone. But the real economy has a way of shaking off burdens like these — in the horrific 1930s, real U.S. GDP grew 1% a year; in the stagflationary 1970s, an impressive 3.2% per year. We are in trouble but not enough trouble to justify some of Chancellor's chapter titles, which have a *National Lampoon* tinge: "A Big Fat Ugly Bubble," "Your Mother Needs to Die" (about unfunded pension liabilities and inadequate retirement savings), and the clear winner — "The Mother and Father of All Evil" (Recep Tayyip Erdoğan's opinion of rising interest rates). While Chancellor's intent is to amuse, his underlying thoughts are serious.

The Price of Time is brilliant and provocative, but it's just too one-sided — too much like the insightful but usually wrong doomsday forecasts that have peppered the financial pages since the pronouncements of Henry "Dr. Doom" Kaufman's in the 1970s, David "Rosie" Rosenberg more recently, and Marc Faber all the time. Over the period Chancellor has been participating in markets — about 30 years, so let's use 1990 as the starting date:

---

[16] Grantham, R. Jeremy. 2011. "Time to wake up: Days of abundant resources and falling prices are over forever." *Resilience*, April 29, https://www.resilience.org/stories/2011-04-29/time-wake-days-abundant-resources-and- falling-prices-are-over-forever/..

[17] In January 2022, in "Generational Differences Are Less Important Than You Think," https://larrysiegel.org/generational-differences-are-less-important-than-you-think/, I wrote, "the Thomson Reuters/CoreCommodity CRB Index, a reflection of resource scarcity, has been falling since 2008 and (linking indices) is lower in real terms than it was in 1913." See https://www.jstor.org/stable/3872481 for the data. I have not updated the estimate to reflect the recent rise in that index.

- Global real GDP has doubled (from $38 trillion to $80 trillion);[18]

- The percentage of the world's population living in extreme poverty as defined by the World Bank has fallen from 36% to 9%; and

- The real (inflation-adjusted) S&P 500 with dividends is up 425%, or 5.2% per year

There's a species of Wall Street pundit known as the permabear.[19] You know you've encountered one when they say, no matter when you ask them, that this is the moment that these favorable trends will turn around and run the other way *forever*.

But the downdrafts never last forever. Chancellor could have been more careful not to sound the permabear alarm, because the information he presents does not justify it.

Conclusion

"...[I]nterest is a fundamental part of human society, a bridge between the present and the future," writes Kevin Coldiron, a *Forbes* columnist and retired fund manager.[20] "Given the long list of potentially negative effects [of zero or negative rates] documented by Chancellor," he continues, "prudence suggests we should avoid setting rates at [those levels], lest that bridge be weakened or washed away. After all, as Chancellor says in his book — capital consists of a stream of future income discounted to its present value using interest rates."

---

[18] Global real GDP *per capita* has grown more slowly because the world's population has increased.

[19] I was tempted to finger Chancellor's former employer, Jeremy Grantham, as yet another permabear but he is way too nice and a personal friend, so I won't. I'd just note that on December 9, 2023 he said that the S&P 500, then at 4700, could fall to 2200. Of course it could, because anything can happen.

[20] Coldiron now teaches at Haas Business School of UC Berkeley. We worked together when I was a consultant to Barclays Global Investors.

Let's dig a little deeper. Interest is the way we balance the claims of the future against those of the present, an important task if ever there was one. The future is long (it might as well be infinitely long) and it has become fashionable to talk about what we, in the present, owe to the future including the very distant future.[21] To begin to solve that riddle, we need a financial link between the present and the future. That function has been served by interest rates, which do double duty as discount rates, for some 5000 years. If that link becomes corrupted through bad policy or for other reasons, as it has periodically in the past, we won't be able to do much to help future generations. We will become focused only on our own welfare, and that's not good.

"Without [positive real] interest, therefore, there can be no capital," continues Coldiron. "Without capital, no capitalism."

And we need capital and capitalism. Lots of it. And we always will.

The author thanks Stephen C. Sexauer, CIO of the San Diego County Employees Retirement Association, and Kevin Coldiron, lecturer in finance at the University of California, Berkeley, Haas School of Business, for their helpful comments and assistance. –W.H.W.

---

[21] See Cowen, Tyler M. 2018. *Stubborn Attachments: A Vision for a Society of Free, Prosperous, and Responsible Individuals.* South San Francisco, CA: Stripe Press; and MacAskill, William. 2022. *What We Owe the Future.* New York: Basic Books. The latter has been described as the most highly publicized-in-advance philosophy book of all time.

Chapter 7: Harry Markowitz and the Philosopher's Stone

Stephen C. Sexauer and Laurence B. Siegel

***Financial Analysts Journal*, 14 December 2023. Reprinted with permission.**

"I know some things," he said. "I can, you know, do math and stuff."

— Harry Potter, in *Harry Potter and the Philosopher's Stone*, by J. K. Rowling

Most investors believe we "know some things" – and that we can do some "math and stuff." But the question is: Do we know what we need to know? Do we know all the pieces?

The late Harry Markowitz could certainly do math and stuff – he majored in mathematics as an undergraduate at the University of Chicago. He always considered himself first and foremost a philosopher, and that's how he lived his academic life.

He gave us a portfolio philosophy: a systematic way to define and measure investment risk, and then the insight that risk should be balanced against our desire for returns. He also gave us the mathematical method to optimally combine securities to form a portfolio, one that achieves the balance just described.

The two stages of portfolio selection

Harry's philosophy and math were unsurpassed and have been the foundation for portfolio construction and asset allocation for seventy-one years. But his contribution was incomplete, and Harry told us so back in 1952: The optimal portfolio calculation, now known widely as mean-variance optimization (MVO), requires decision makers to enter their estimates of expected return and risk for each security or asset class.¹ What Harry did not do is tell us how to find reasonable estimates of risk and return. The opening lines of his dissertation, which eventually led to a Nobel Prize, frame this division of labor when building a mean-variance optimal portfolio:

> The process of selecting a portfolio may be divided into two stages. The first stage starts with observation and experience and ends with beliefs about the future performances of available securities. The second stage starts with the relevant beliefs about future performances and ends with the choice of portfolio. *This paper is concerned with the second stage.*²

He was silent on what the inputs should be! And, in case we didn't "get" it the first time, Markowitz added,

> [P]rocedures for finding reasonable [means] and [covariances] ... should combine statistical techniques *and the judgment of practical men.*³

In this essay, we make the case that, while Markowitz adeptly solved for an optimal portfolio of stocks given *accurate inputs*, its extensive use today is incomplete, because almost every user – from pension and endowment boards to investment consultants and advisors all the way down to individual users – ignores or assumes away the question of whether the inputs are any good.

Moreover, even if you have good inputs and are very mathematically capable, most decision makers – pension trustees, consultants, and portfolio managers – are not aware of the tendency of MVO to magnify the errors of the input assumptions, or, as Richard Michaud and Robert

---

[1] There exists today an entire family of MVO algorithms tailored to the specific circumstance of the investment decision being made. Also, because Markowitz designed his algorithm to construct a portfolio of individual stocks, we will keep that frame of reference in this essay, but what we say also applies to asset classes.

[2] Markowitz (1952). Our italics.

[3] Our italics.

Litterman said independently in 1989 and 1990 papers, to be an error maximizer.⁴ More about that later.

Hence, the title of this essay, "Harry Markowitz and the Philosopher's Stone," confirms that the gem Harry gave us, with a nod to the brilliant (and very unfairly maligned) J. K. Rowling, still needs a philosopher's stone to transform an endless supply of data and uncertain forecasts into sensible and defensible inputs to MVO, with sound portfolio decisions as the outcome.⁵

"That's your job, not mine."

Harry was a philosopher and scholar to the end. He remained on the faculty at the University of California San Diego in La Jolla, California, until his death in June 2023 at age 95. It was common for Harry to be at Bruegger's Bagels in Pacific Beach many mornings working on the fourth volume of his book on optimization and decision making. Locals, who include the authors of this article and fellow faculty member Michael Melvin, would arrange to meet Harry late mornings to talk about his work and then go off to lunch. At those lunches, we would prod Harry about when he would finish his 1952 work, letting us know how to do stage one of an MVO optimization, choosing the expected risk and return inputs. Harry's response was always gracious, but mischievous: "That's your job, not mine."

MVO is now used everywhere in portfolio decision-making, especially in the $9 trillion of defined-benefit pensions plans in the U.S. and $7 trillion in the defined-contribution retirement funds. Overall, it's accepted as the gold standard for portfolio construction for much of another $26 trillion of corporate equities and mutual fund shares held by investors outside of retirement plans.⁶ Its outputs are regarded by many decision makers, who typically have limited skills in advanced mathematics or capital market risk

---

⁴ We cover in detail later. Richard Michaud (1989) famously argued that unavoidable estimation errors in optimization lead to a "fuzzy" solution – a cloud of near-optimal portfolios not statistically distinguishable from another – rather than a unique "optimal" portfolio.

⁵ Rowling's *Harry Potter and the Philosopher's Stone* (1997) was released in the U.S. under the title *Harry Potter and the Sorcerer's Stone*. "Very unfairly maligned" refers to a controversy discussed here (off topic).

⁶ Fed Z1, 8 June 2023

and return estimation, as the *scientifically correct* – "optimal" – portfolio weights in the asset allocation decisions they confidently approve.

Our goal in writing this article is to say, "Until we complete Stage 1 and do what Harry said is our job, the MVO technology is an incomplete vessel."

We really do need to develop solutions to Stage 1, "combining statistical techniques with the judgments of practical men," that are worthy of what Markowitz's Stage 2 (MVO) is today: a theoretically and computationally sound method, conceptually understood by everyday practitioners and widely accepted and used.

Roadmap

We pursue two goals in this article. First, we simply want to honor Harry Markowitz by describing his remarkable discovery and the context in which it was made, and then telling the story of how a group of researchers – we'd call them giants – built on it over the last three-quarters of a century to create, in Galileo's words, "a new science."

Second, we want to improve the quality of the estimates used in Step 1, because there is always the danger that uninformed and overconfident people will misuse MVO and produce bad results, which end-user investors will nonetheless have to live with.

Third, we present a philosophical or methodological framework for thinking about, and (if our readers apply the framework) arriving at, optimizer inputs. We call this, somewhat lightheartedly, the "philosopher's triangle" because it involves three sets of capital market assumptions. You'll be relieved to find that we do not provide "the answer" – and we could not if we wanted to, because *there's no such thing as a philosopher's stone*.

Markowitz's central insight

Seventy-one years ago in the *Journal of Finance*, in his classic paper "Portfolio Selection,"[7] a very young Harry Markowitz connected the obscure mathematics of the emerging field of operations research with the problem of building an efficient portfolio of securities. Portfolio efficiency is a foundational concept – what mix of securities maximizes expected return at each given level of risk? – and involves the elegant and exacting calculation that Markowitz devised. Now known as mean-variance optimization (MVO) or Markowitz optimization,[8] this method – as we noted earlier – is seen as the scientific gold standard for guiding portfolio decisions about the many trillions of dollars invested across all asset classes in pension, endowment, insurance, and individual portfolios.

"Welcome to the faculty"

When Markowitz was searching for a dissertation topic at the University of Chicago in the early 1950s, he was waiting outside his advisor's office where he met a stockbroker who suggested he look into the stock market. At that time, the stock market was not being studied in any serious quantitative way,[9] and it was not obvious how Markowitz might proceed – but, he recalled, "It occurred to me investors should be concerned with risk as well as return and I went to the library and pulled a statistics book out of the stacks."[10] The rest is history.

Later, to get his Ph.D., Markowitz had to defend his dissertation before a group of senior professors. He recalled,

---

[7] Markowitz (1952), pp. 77-91.

[8] MVO is also sometimes called modern portfolio theory (MPT), but the term MPT is best used to refer to a much broader body of knowledge, embracing not only MVO but also the capital asset pricing model, dividend and capital structure indifference, the no-arbitrage condition, and other -post-Markowitz finance concepts. Moreover, "modern" does not quite fit a set of concepts that are between 71 and 50 years old; let's just call this body of knowledge "portfolio theory."

[9] In the 1930s, the Cowles Commission collected stock and bond data starting in 1871, providing the foundation for later research by Markowitz, Fisher and Lorie, Ibbotson and Sinquefield, and many others. See Dimand (2009).

[10] Personal communication with Stephen Sexauer in 2019.

> When I defended my dissertation as a student in the Economics Department of the University of Chicago, Professor Milton Friedman argued that portfolio theory was not Economics, and that they could not award me a Ph.D. degree in Economics for a dissertation which was not in Economics." (Markowitz 1990)

Legend has it that Friedman then immediately said, "Welcome to the faculty, *Doctor* Markowitz."

A bolt from the blue

Like John Napier's 1614 discovery of logarithms, Markowitz's invention came unexpected and unheralded. Lord Moulton, describing Napier three centuries later, wrote:

> The invention of logarithms came on the world as a bolt from the blue. No previous work had led up to it, foreshadowed it, or heralded its arrival. It stands isolated, breaking in upon human thought abruptly without borrowing from the work of other intellects or following known lines of mathematical thought.[11]

We can say the same of Markowitz optimization.[12]

A science of investing emerges, 1952–1972

In the seven decades since Markowitz's discovery, talented scholars and investment professionals have worked through the steps needed to make better portfolio decisions. This history neatly divides into two parts, the

---

[11] Karam, P. Andrew. Undated. "John Napier Discovers Logarithms." *Encyclopedia.com*, https://www.encyclopedia.com/science/encyclopedias-almanacs-transcripts-and-maps/john-napier-discovers-logarithms

[12] Markowitz (2006) noted that the Italian statistician and actuary Bruno de Finetti did some work on mean-variance analysis with correlated risks in the 1940. However, even though de Finetti's statistical work was well known, including to Milton Friedman's collaborator Leonard "Jimmie" Savage, who was influenced by it, his mean-variance analysis was not known, other than to Italian actuaries, until Markowitz's 2006 article was published. (De Finetti did not apply mean-variance to investment portfolios; he was investigating questions related to insurance.)

first one (1952–1972) spanning the time period when the basics of modern finance – all unfolding from Markowitz's method of balancing risk against return – were established. The second (1973–2023) has been a period of application and refinement.

As we noted earlier, medieval history (as opposed to *Harry Potter*) teaches us that a Philosopher's Stone which turns base metals to gold doesn't actually exist. Likewise, there is no formula for making money in markets. However, there is a process and structure by which we can craft inputs that make sense in the context of one's investment beliefs, time horizon, and data availability. It involves Bayesian inference as well as modesty about what we can know about the future. That body of knowledge is as close as we will get to an investment Philosopher's Stone. It is fitting and proper to associate Harry Markowitz with the idea of the stone, because he always saw himself as a philosopher as well as a mathematician.

Markowitz optimization spawned two decades of frenzied research on the theory of capital markets, quite unlike any research in finance that had previously occurred.[13] Kenneth Arrow, James Tobin, and Paul Samuelson, all Nobel Prize winners, contributed greatly; but the best-known and most complete result, the Capital Asset Pricing Model (CAPM) of William Sharpe, was the first real general equilibrium model of the capital markets.[14]

Let's recall how Markowitz optimization, which is normative (it tells you how to do something), spawned the CAPM, which is positive (it seeks to explain how the world works). Transformations like this often occur in science, and it's instructive to examine how this one took place.

---

[13] A young Fischer Black, asked to consider finance as an area of study, derisively said, "I know how to balance a checkbook." This story (Mehrling 2005) indicates the low regard in which finance was held among serious scholars pre-Markowitz. In a wonderful irony, Black later became one of the greatest finance innovators of all time.

[14] John Lintner, Jan Mossin, and Jack Treynor all discovered versions of the CAPM at about the same time as Sharpe, but Sharpe was by far the best known and most vocal exponent of it.

Harry Markowitz, Bill Sharpe, and the CAPM

Markowitz's discovery didn't say what the world would look like if everyone followed his advice, but his protégé William Sharpe did. Sharpe conducted a brilliant thought experiment based on Markowitz optimization. He said that if:

(1) every investor sees the same "picture" (everyone has the same estimates of risk, return, and correlation for every asset or asset pair), and

(2) every investor behaves as Markowitz prescribed by optimizing their portfolios,

then *every investor holds the same portfolio*. Under such conditions, if every stock is to be held with no stocks left over, then that portfolio *must be* a cap-weighted index fund of all the stocks in the market. This is the central insight of the CAPM and is the best-known theoretical result in finance.[15]

Portfolio choice with riskless as well as risky assets

Sharpe, drawing on Tobin's (1958) two-fund separation theorem, then noted that, while everyone will hold the same portfolio of risky assets (let's call them stocks), some people will want less of that portfolio and others will want more of it because people differ in their risk tolerance. With that wrinkle added, all portfolios then consist of *combinations* of the cap-weighted market portfolio and "cash," where *cash* really means a long or short position in the riskless asset, usually said to be U.S. Treasury bills.

---

[15] We realize that calling this the central insight of the CAPM is unconventional. Many would say that the central CAPM insight is the relationship between beta risk and expected return, or the difference between diversifiable (unsystematic, security-specific, uncompensated, alpha) risk and undiversifiable (systematic, market-wide, compensated, beta) risk. However, both of these insights are only true to a first approximation – for example, there are lots of circumstances where diversifiable risk might be compensated. But it is incontrovertible that, given the usual assumptions, the efficient portfolio that Markowitz was so worked up about is an index fund! And it has to be a cap-weighted, and thus self-rebalancing, index fund.

We could have said "all *efficient* portfolios," where inefficient portfolios are constructed in some other way, but *if everyone optimizes there are no inefficient portfolios*. The CAPM world is stunningly simple, with investors only needing to make one decision: how much market risk to take – or, in Greek instead of English, what their beta should be.

Invoking the no-arbitrage or "no free lunch" condition, the expected return of *each individual stock* or other asset must therefore equal the expected return of the combination of the market portfolio and cash having the same beta as the stock. However, the portfolio will have less risk than the stock and is therefore to be preferred. This observation completes the CAPM. It can be summed up, again in Greek, by saying that beta is the only property of an asset that counts and that expected alpha is always and everywhere zero, for both individual assets and for portfolios. Realized alphas only differ from zero because the forecasts that went into setting the prices of the stocks in the market portfolio turned out to be incorrect.

The central place of the CAPM in the history of financial thought

If all of this were literally true, Markowitz really would have discovered the Philosopher's Stone because everyone would know exactly how to invest. The real world is, of course, more complicated than this and the CAPM is not a complete model of the way prices are set in the market. But without the starting point of the CAPM, which relies for its very existence on Markowitz optimization, we would have no macroconsistent or general-equilibrium model at all (because the pre-Markowitz discounted cash flow model says nothing about the aggregation of assets, only the value of a specific asset).

A great deal of elaboration and testing of the CAPM took place thereafter, along with more distantly related work summing to the body of knowledge we now call "modern finance" (a phrase that is morphing into "classical finance" as the seminal period recedes into the past). These efforts were complete by about 1972, with option pricing or, more generally, contingent claims analysis, being the last piece to fall into place. Readers wanting more details on this story should refer to Peter Bernstein's extraordinary books, *Capital Ideas* (1992) and *Capital Ideas*

Evolving (2007), as well as Ronald Kahn's short and luminous exposition, *The Future of Investment Management* (2018).[16]

Summing up this period in history, Bernstein wrote, "This little group of a dozen men have left us a heritage the value of which we cannot even begin to calibrate."

Challenging received wisdom, 1973-2023

As practitioners began to adopt MVO in their investment processes, the focus of research drifted toward problems in application. The contributions in this era fell into three broad groups: explaining and forecasting stock (or stock market) returns, incorporating liabilities or spending into the MVO framework, and optimization as a statistical estimation problem.

Explaining and forecasting stock returns, largely by identifying common factors but also by observing time-varying risk premia, became its own genre and industry and is one of the dominant threads in modern finance.[17] Although the CAPM says there is only one factor (the market), it turns out that is an oversimplification and much of modern active management is based on common factors in stock returns other than the broad cap-weighted market. This analysis is, of course, an aspect of crafting optimization inputs, Markowitz's Stage 1.

Recognizing an investor's liability or spending needs as an asset held short in an optimizer is another post-1972 innovation: Marty Leibowitz and his

---

[16] Bernstein (1992); Bernstein (2007); Kahn (2018).

[17] In 1960, Lawrence Fisher and James Lorie of the Graduate School of Business at the University of Chicago (now the Booth School of Business) and Louis Engel of Merrill Lynch embarked on a project to determine "how much gain or loss an investor might have realized if he had bought all the New York Stock Exchange common stocks" using machine readable data from the New York Stock Exchange and other sources (Fisher and Lorie 1964). By the time they were done, the Center for Research for Security Prices (CRSP) at the University of Chicago held a vast library of connected data on asset returns, company-specific accounting data, and general economic data. The avalanche of empirical work based on the CRSP data files, which includes a number of Nobel Prizes, continues today.

team at Salomon Brothers in the 1980s contributed much of this literature, mostly in the context of a defined-benefit pension fund with known liabilities.[18] The third thread is optimization as a statistical estimation problem, and we focus on that next.

Optimization as a statistical estimation problem

Markowitz himself, and others thereafter, recognized that optimization inputs are statistical estimates and thus subject to estimation error. First, the inputs required are forecasts of the future, and we know we cannot forecast the future, except with very wide error bands. If the inputs are taken from history, the implied assumption is that the future will be very much like the past; if the inputs involve modifying historical data, the assumption is that the person using the optimizer knows how the future will differ from the past. Either assumption is obviously dicey.

Richard Michaud (1989) was the first to conduct a fully organized review of this problem and set forth a widely used method for dealing with it. He showed how to calculate a "fuzzy efficient frontier" reflecting uncertainty about the inputs and, thus, the outputs.[19] Michaud pithily called the optimizer an "error maximizer" that turns bad inputs into even worse outputs – a compact and accurate assessment when MVO is naively applied to making portfolio decisions.

Survival bias

It's bad enough that we cannot know the future, but we don't even fully understand the past. For example, we cannot know the true historical mean return[20] of the stock market, because as Paul Samuelson (1994) said,

---

[18] See, as one of the earliest and best examples, Leibowitz and Henriksson (1988).

[19] Michaud's method, called statistical optimization, was the topic of an unprecedented four sessions at the Fall 1999 Q Group conference. (The Q Group is a semiannual, two-and-a-half-day discussion group for senior investment professionals with a quantitative focus, hence the "Q", and usually covers ten topics; that time, it dealt primarily with just this one problem.) Markowitz himself had described optimization inputs as a statistical estimation problem in his original 1952 paper, but he did not follow through to the logical conclusion of a "fuzzy" or indeterminate frontier. Michaud called his method "resampling" but "statistical optimization" is much clearer and was the title of the Q Group program.

[20] The population mean (of the distribution from which the one sample of the past was drawn) as opposed to the sample mean (the history that happened to occur this one time).

"we have only one sample of the past." In a different "run" of history, something very different would have happened. And our long-term data on stocks and bonds come from the most successful countries (primarily the U.S. and U.K.) in the most successful centuries (the 19th, 20th, and a little piece of the 21st) in the history of the world. Surely this history is upwardly biased! One cannot expect a literal repeat of these spectacularly favorable conditions in all or even most future scenarios.

William Goetzmann, a celebrated Yale historian and financial economist, has written extensively about this "survival bias" and is the foremost exponent of survivorship as a source of possible error in forecasting. His frequent collaborator, Philippe Jorion, suggested early on (Jorion 1986) that optimizer inputs should be adjusted for survival bias in the historical data; and Jorion and Goetzmann (1999) documented the extent of the bias. How exactly to make this adjustment is another paper.

Black-Litterman: A Bayesian approach to optimization

In 1990, drawing on ideas floated much earlier by James Tobin and Bill Sharpe, Fischer Black and Robert Litterman proposed a Bayesian way to estimate expected returns that blended prior knowledge (that of all the participants in the market combined) with a given investor's unique knowledge, preferences, or biases. Litterman (1990) wrote,[21]

> As is well known...standard [MVO] is not well behaved. Optimal portfolio weights are very sensitive to small changes in expected excess returns. Thus, the...Black-Litterman model began with a financial engineering question – "How can we make the standard portfolio optimizer better behaved?" – rather than...as a natural extension of the global CAPM equilibrium.

But Black-Litterman, as ingenious an adaptation of Markowitz and Sharpe as has ever been devised, became a natural extension of the global CAPM equilibrium.

Black-Litterman starts with the obvious (once it's been said) observation that the cap-weighted market portfolio of every risky asset in the world is the outcome of every investor in the world buying the securities they want

---

[21] Litterman (1990), page 78. A more accessible writeup is in Black and Litterman (1992).

and shunning the ones they don't want. If all investors optimize, which you'll recall is also the assumption behind the standard CAPM, then this world market portfolio is Markowitz efficient.[22] Through reverse optimization one can discern the underlying risk and return assumptions, which are definitionally market-consensus assumptions.

This set of assumptions becomes the starting point (the Bayesian "prior") for an investor's custom portfolio. Then, instead of requiring the optimizing investor to input estimates of risk and return, Black and Litterman ask the investor only to state how her risk and return assumptions *differ* from the market's assumptions and to state her degree of confidence in her own assumptions (versus those of the overall market). From this, the Black–Litterman method derives a unique Markowitz-efficient asset mix for that investor. We will return to this idea when we make our recommendation for optimizer inputs.

Theoretically inclined readers will note that, like the ordinary CAPM, this is a general equilibrium model. It takes into consideration how every investor in the world behaves (or should behave), not just one particular optimizing investor. It is macroconsistent in that if everybody used the model, all assets would be held with none left over.

There are other important innovations in optimization but we can't describe them all. Having recounted much of the history of innovation in optimization, it's time to complete "your job," Markowitz's exhortation to the user of his optimizer technology to come up with sensible inputs. Of Markowitz's two-stage process, we now turn to Stage 1, forming the inputs.

---

[22] *Roll* (1977) identified the world portfolio as being the theoretically relevant risky-asset portfolio for the CAPM analysis. Among others, Ibbotson and Siegel (1983) estimated the historical returns on such a portfolio. A more up-to-date estimate of world-portfolio returns is in Doeswijk, Lam, and Swinkels (2020).

The Philosopher's Triangle: Implementing Markowitz's Stage 1

Using Bayesian thinking, we now combine the prior from Black-Litterman – the return and risk assumptions embedded in the world wealth portfolio – with other information unique to a given investor. We illustrate with a triangle (Exhibit 1) a range of MVO risk-return estimates using three well-known and available sets of risk and return forecasts: (1) the expected returns from the world portfolio, (2) capital market assumptions developed by an expert or group of experts chosen by the investor, and (3) the expected returns implied by the weights in the investor's existing portfolio.

The triangle

At the upper left vertex of the triangle in Exhibit 1, point A, we find the world market wealth portfolio of risky liquid assets. The theoretically ideal portfolio at point A contains every return-generating asset in the world, including real estate, human capital, and illiquid portfolio investments, but we need an accurate time series of returns for each asset class so we are limited to liquid, tradeable assets.

Exhibit 1 — MVO Stage 1 inputs: Three sets of expected returns and volatility

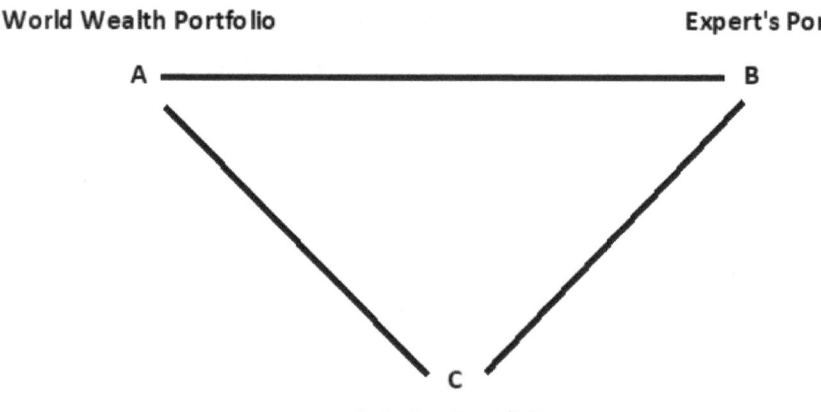

The logic behind using the world market wealth portfolio is that the weights have been produced by the collective decisions of every investor in the world, including Harry's practical men of good judgment. Thus, the weights in this world portfolio reflect the market *already having done the optimization for you*.[23] This approach is closely related to Black-Litterman and relies on the assumption that the world portfolio is efficient because it has been produced by the collective efforts of all market participants, who in aggregate can be presumed to clearly see the conditions they face and make rational choices, even though any one participant may not.

At point B, the upper right vertex, we find a hypothetical portfolio constructed using the risk and return forecasts provided by an expert or group of experts. Such forecasts can be obtained from your favorite academic or consulting firm, or produced by your staff if there are experts among them. It is not a consensus forecast; it is the set of forecasts that, based on your choice of experts, you would implement if you faced no transaction costs, legacy holdings, position limits, or other frictions keeping you from allocating assets as you think best.

The line joining points A and B is a continuum, from expertise contributed by everyone in the world (point A) to the expertise of an individual or small group whom you've selected (point B). As you move rightward along the line, you lose the influence of one knowledgeable investor after another, but you also lose the influence of people who know nothing (and don't know that they know nothing). So, you may either gain or lose forecast accuracy as you move along that line.

---

[23] This successful child has many fathers, notably Tobin (1958) and Sharpe (1964). In a corporate communication, Quantor Capital writes,

> At first, this portfolio was just an idea, a theoretical construct...Tobin [1958]...posited that there exists what he called a single "super-efficient portfolio" that was the perfect balance between risk and reward...Sharpe [1964] argued that Tobin's super-efficient portfolio was the global market portfolio, which would be composed of all risky assets proportionally weighted by their total market value...
>
> ...[T]here are some who contend that such a portfolio still exists in theory only...Roll [1977]...argu[ed] that a true market portfolio would include every risky asset: not only stocks and bonds, but also real estate, commodities, collectibles, and anything else of value that could be traded. In short, he argued that a global market portfolio is an interesting but unachievable ideal.

Later, Ibbotson and Siegel (1983) indicated that, for an all-asset portfolio to be efficient, it should also include non-tradeable assets such as human capital, making it even more unachievable.

The vertex at the bottom, point C, is your portfolio as it currently stands. It probably reflects a mix of influences: earlier optimizations, market movements that have not been neutered through rebalancing, legacy positions or other idiosyncratic holdings, position limits from your investment policy statement, and possibly restrictions (say, from an ESG policy) on what you're allowed to hold.

Obtaining the expected returns and risks for the world and existing portfolios

The expert's portfolio inputs are the expected return for each asset, the risk of the asset (represented by standard deviation in MVO), and the correlation of each asset pair. The standard deviation and correlations are typically estimated from historical data. To reverse-engineer the expected returns for the world and expert portfolios, one starts with the known portfolio weights and runs a "reverse" optimization, an established and accepted MVO-based procedure that identifies what the optimizer inputs would have to be for the given set of portfolio weights to be Markowitz efficient. We now have portfolio weights and risk and return expectations for each vertex of the triangle.

This is a good place to share a key insight from adding the reverse optimization to the decision process: by making the risk and return expectations in your portfolio explicit, you must confront how they differ from those of either the world portfolio or the expert portfolio. Waring and Ramkumar (2008) powerfully made the point that the risk and return forecasts implied by some investors' portfolio weights are "far out there." Therefore, unless you believe in the accuracy of such far-out estimates, say a 10% annual return premium of emerging market equities over developed markets, or a 2% risk estimate for a portfolio of nominally market-neutral hedge funds, you shouldn't hold the asset – at least not in the weight that it represents in the current portfolio.

This is also a good place to repeat Richard Michaud's important insight that we referenced earlier in this essay: MVO is an "error maximizer" that turns bad risk and return inputs into even worse outputs (portfolio allocations). Therefore, when examining and judging expert inputs, yours or an advisor's, the rule of thumb is that when odd combinations of risk and return are observed, they are probably wrong, and likely to contribute to Michaud-like error maximization.

Using the information in the three sets of portfolio weights

Now, how do we combine these three parcels of information?

In the spirit of Bayesian statistics, we suggest choosing a point on the line from A to B that corresponds to the *intensity of your belief* in the forecast accuracy of A versus B. In other words, whom do you trust, and how much do you trust them – everyone in the world, or the group of experts you've selected? This is a reasonable question and we are not suggesting that the whole-world answer is the correct one. There are many uninformed people in the world and many of them invest money without giving a moment's thought to any of the issues in this article.

Having chosen a point on the line connecting points A and B as the target, examine where C, the existing portfolio, sits in comparison. The investor needs to move from C toward the point on the line connecting A and B, but how far? To answer that question, the investor must weigh the cost of getting to the portfolio she wants against the opportunity cost of *not* getting to it.

Is the portfolio you have, the portfolio you want?

Now, imagine a line connecting point C with the chosen point on the line from A to B. This new line (not shown) represents the decision of how far to move from "the portfolio you have" to "the portfolio you want." While the decision of where to be on this line is based on an assessment of transaction costs, hard-to-trade positions, position limits, other portfolio restrictions, and in some cases taxes, those should be secondary considerations.

At this point, having completed Markowitz's Stage 1 (our version of it, obviously, is not the only possible one), it's time to move on to Stage 2, running the optimizer itself. Our readers know how to do this and we'll stop.[24]

---

[24] Running the optimizer is not simply a matter of turning on a machine and waiting for the results. There are many subtleties and implementation issues. Users of optimizers should be familiar with these issues and need to address them before accepting optimization outputs uncritically.

Conclusion: How Markowitz's philosophical and mathematical contribution changed the future

Until 1952, investment decision-making was about valuing and choosing individual securities. Analysts used discounted cash flow (DCF) calculations on a stock-by-stock, bond-by-bond, real-property-by-real-property basis. This tool set was solid and had existed for hundreds of years, having started with Fibonacci's rudimentary DCF model in the year 1202.[25] Progress over the next 750 years was incremental.

Then came Harry Markowitz and his two 1952 papers, "Portfolio Selection" in the *Journal of Finance* and "The Utility of Wealth" in the *Journal of Political Economy*,[26] that created an entirely new science of investment decision-making that we know today as modern portfolio theory (MPT), by introducing its first major tool, mean-variance optimization (MVO). This was a leap from one kind of finance to another that no one had thought of before. This jump merged expected utility theory from classical economics with the applied mathematics of non-linear optimization from the new field of operations research.[27]

---

[25] As documented in Goetzmann (2004). Leonardo of Pisa, called Fibonacci ("son of Bonacci"), was best known for his number sequence (1, 1, 2, 3, 5, 8, 13, etc.) but made contributions in many fields of inquiry, including his transformational book, *Liber Abaci* (Book of Calculation), that brought Hindu-Arabic numbers to the West from South Asia and North Africa and transformed commerce. (Before that, Roman numerals were used.) He was one of the first Renaissance men.

[26] Many of you may be asking, "Wait! What? Where did this second paper come from? Did somebody find it lost in the stacks at the Regenstein library?" The answer is that when you talked to Harry about MVO, especially about the inputs in Stage 1, he always talked about both the *Journal of Finance* (Markowitz 1952a) and *Journal of Political Economy* (Markowitz 1952b) papers. To him they were a matched pair. He really was what his degree was: a Doctor of Philosophy.

[27] Operations research – sometimes called management science – was originally developed during and for World War II, with famous algorithms like "maximum matching" that were used to match refugee pilots who spoke the same language to fly airplanes in the Battle of Britain. The post-war outpost for much of this work was the RAND Corporation (where "RAND" stands for "research and development"). It's no surprise that the first two giants of modern portfolio theory, Harry Markowitz and Bill Sharpe, both worked at the RAND Corporation in the 1950s.

After almost seventy-two years, this new science of investment decision-making has been tested, deepened, and expanded by the giants who followed Markowitz and Sharpe, the little group of a dozen men of whom Peter Bernstein spoke so fondly. Many of them, like Markowitz and Sharpe, were also recognized with Nobel Prizes in Economics, and over time there came to be many more than a dozen of them. MVO and MPT have proven to be the breakthrough that changed the angle of progress in the fields of finance and investment management as profoundly as Newton changed the angle of progress in physics and Darwin in biology, albeit on a different scale. Because investing provides the financing needed for productivity growth, GDP growth, and improvement in human welfare, Markowitz's innovations have also changed the angle of human progress.

But Harry did leave us one thing still to do: to determine how to combine history, economics, mathematics, and judgment to determine the estimates required in his Stage 1 – and to do so in a way that enables everyday investors, including pension fund boards, mutual fund managers, consultants, portfolio advisors, and individuals, to implement Harry's directive that "the first stage starts with observation and experience and ends with beliefs about the future performance of available securities."[28]

We hope that Harry Markowitz, in his role as a philosopher as well as an economist, would approve of our suggestions for "combining statistical techniques and the judgment of practical [individuals]" in the pursuit of better and less risky investment returns for all classes of investors.

REFERENCES

Bernstein, Peter L. 1992. *Capital Ideas: The Improbable Origins of Modern Wall Street*. Hoboken, NJ: John Wiley & Sons.

Bernstein, Peter L. 2004. *Capital Ideas Evolving*. Hoboken, NJ: John Wiley & Sons.

Black, Fischer, and Robert Litterman. 1992. "Global Portfolio Optimization." *Financial Analysts Journal* (September/October).

---

[28] Markowitz (1952), page 1, sentence 2.

Dimand, Robert W. 2009. "The Cowles Commission and Foundation on the Functioning of Financial Markets from Irving Fisher and Alfred Cowles to Harry Markowitz and James Tobin." *Revue d'Histoire des Sciences Humaines* 2009/1 (no. 20), pp. 79-100.

Doeswijk, Ronald Q., Trevin Lam, and Laurens Swinkels. 2020. "Historical Returns of the Market Portfolio." *Review of Asset Pricing Studies,* Volume 10, Issue 3 (October), pp. 521–567, https://doi.org/10.1093/rapstu/raz010.

Goetzmann, William. 2004. "Fibonacci and the Financial Revolution." NBER Working Paper 10352, https://www.nber.org/papers/w10352.

Ibbotson, Roger G., and Laurence B. Siegel. 1983. "The World Market Wealth Portfolio." *Journal of Portfolio Management,* Vol. 9, no. 2 (Spring), pp. 5-17.

Jorion, Philippe. 1986. "Bayes-Stein Estimation for Portfolio Analysis." *Journal of Financial and Quantitative Analysis,* Vol. 21, no. 3 (September), pp. 279-292.

Jorion, Philippe, and William N. Goetzmann. 1999. "Global Stock Markets in the Twentieth Century." *Journal of Finance,* Vol. 54, No. 3 (June), pp. 953-980.

Kahn, Ronald N. 2018. *The Future of Investment Management.* Charlottesville, VA: CFA Institute Research Foundation, https://www.cfainstitute.org/en/research/foundation/2018/future-of-investment-management

Karam, P. Andrew. Undated. "John Napier Discovers Logarithms." *Encyclopedia.com,* https://www.encyclopedia.com/science/encyclopedias-almanacs-transcripts-and-maps/john-napier-discovers-logarithms

Leibowitz, Martin L., and Roy D. Henriksson. 1988. "Portfolio Optimization Within a Surplus Framework." *Financial Analysts Journal,* Vol. 44, Issue 2 (March).

Litterman, Robert ("Bob"). 1990. "Beyond Equilibrium: The Black-Litterman Approach." In Litterman, Robert et al. 1990. *Modern Investment Management: An Equilibrium Approach.* Hoboken, NJ: John Wiley & Sons.

Markowitz, Harry M. 1952a. "Portfolio Selection." *Journal of Finance,* Vol. 7, No. 1 (March), pp. 77-91.

Markowitz, Harry M. 1952b. "The Utility of Wealth." *Journal of Political Economy,* Vol. 60, no. 2 (April), pp. 151-158.

Markowitz, Harry M. 1990. "Foundations of Portfolio Theory." Nobel Lecture (December 7), https://www.nobelprize.org/uploads/2018/06/markowitz-lecture.pdf.

Markowitz, Harry M. 2006. "De Finetti Scoops Markowitz." *Journal of Investment Management,* Vol. 4, No. 3 (October), https://papers.ssrn.com/sol3/papers.cfm?abstract_id=934412.

Mehrling, Perry. 2005. *Fischer Black and the Revolutionary Idea of Finance.* Hoboken, NJ: John Wiley & Sons.

Michaud, Richard O. 1989. "The Markowitz Optimization Enigma: Is 'Optimized' Optimal?" Financial Analysts Journal (January/February).

Roll, Richard. 1977. "A Critique of the Asset Pricing Theory's Tests, Part I: On past and potential testability of the theory." *Journal of Financial Economics*, Vol. 4, issue 2 (March), pp. 129-176.

Rowling, J. K. 1997. *Harry Potter and the Philosopher's Stone.* London: Bloomsbury.

Samuelson, Paul A. 1994. "The Long-Term Case for Equities (and How It Can Be Oversold). *Journal of Portfolio Management*, vol. 21, no. 1 (Fall), pp. 15-24.

Sharpe, William F. 1964. "Capital Asset Prices: A Theory of Market Equilibrium under Conditions of Risk." *Journal of Finance*, Vol. 19, Issue 3 (September), pp. 425-442

Tobin, James. 1958. "Liquidity Preference as Behavior Towards Risk." *Review of Economic Studies,* Vol. 25, No. 2 (February), pp. 65-86.

Waring, M. Barton, and Sunder R. Ramkumar. 2008. "Forecasting Fund Manager Alphas: The Impossible Just Takes Longer." *Financial Analysts Journal*, Vol. 64, issue 2 (March/April).

Copyright © 2023 CFA Institute. All rights reserved. Reproduced by permission.

Chapter 8. Would Charles Darwin Have Been a Good Investor?

Laurence B. Siegel
June 2023

I wanted to write Pulak Prasad's *What I Learned About Investing from Darwin*, or something very much like it, 40 years ago. My first published article, written in 1982, began: "The economy of man was Charles Darwin's inspiration for his theory of natural selection."[1] I then quoted Darwin:

> I happened to read...Malthus on *Population*, and being well prepared to appreciate the struggle for existence which everywhere goes on from long continued observation of...animals and plants, it at once struck me that under these circumstances favorable variations would tend to be preserved and unfavorable ones to be destroyed. The result of this would be the formation of new species.[2]

Pulak Prasad
Source: https://medium.com/authority-magazine/pulak-prasad-of-nalanda-capital-on-the-5-essentials-for-smart-investing-1d7c2a9035ff

My article then outlined the ways in which evolution and economics are similar, explaining change through time as the result of variation and natural selection. Clearly, there's a book in there somewhere. It is just as well that I did not write it, because Prasad, an Indian investment manager writing about Indian markets, has done so with market knowledge vastly superior to what I had at age 28 or, probably, now.

---

[1] Siegel, Laurence B. 1982. Foreword to Roger Ibbotson and Rex Sinquefield, *Stocks, Bonds, Bills, and Inflation: The Past and the Future*. Charlottesville, VA: CFA Institute Research Foundation.

[2] *The Origin of Species*, p. 7 (1859 [1909, Harvard Classics edition, in the introduction]).

I would not have emphasized "how to pick stocks" as Prasad does, because I don't know how — I barely know how to pick funds — and I don't think you can teach that in a book. Another downside of Prasad's book is that the connections between evolutionary theory and investment management sometimes feel forced. But Prasad writes about biology and evolution with the brio of a gifted science teacher, a most welcome change from the prosaic tone that characterizes so many investment books.

Prasad has a deep understanding of the ways in which ideas from evolution apply to businesses and the economy, and thus to investment management. He might have spent more effort on the ways in which they *don't* apply. Having stated my caveats, I recommend this book with considerable enthusiasm.

Three rules for winning

Prasad makes two Warren Buffett-like recommendations for managing an active equity portfolio successfully...

1. Don't lose money — which he translates into "don't take big risks," because it's impossible to entirely avoid losing money if you're buying equities.
2. Buy high-quality companies at a fair price.

...and one that I associate with Jack Bogle:

3. Don't be lazy — be *very* lazy

The book is organized around these three themes, in each case relying on links between Darwin's evolutionary theories and the economics behind active equity management. But I won't cover these topics in the order in which Prasad presents them. Instead, I devote this review to just two of the basic evolutionary concepts — convergence and signaling — that Prasad uses to inform his investment strategy. At the end I'll say a few words in favor of laziness.

What is evolution and what does it have to do with economics and investing?

As background for convergence, signaling, and the other evolutionary ideas in Prasad's book, let's look at the many parallels between biological evolution and the operation of the economy — acknowledging that there are areas where the metaphor doesn't apply.

I start with a precise definition of "evolution," because the word is often used loosely just to mean change or improvement. That's not its scientific meaning. In biology, evolution is a change in the genetic makeup of a population over time. More precisely, it's a change in the relative frequency of *alleles* (gene variants) in that population, due to the joint effects of (1) random variation and (2) natural selection — the latter sometimes called "survival of the fittest," a vivid but imprecise phrase I expand on below.[3] (An allele is "one of two or more alternative forms of a gene that arise by mutation and are found at the same place on a chromosome" — that is, it is not just any variation in a gene, but a specific kind.[4])

If two subsets of a population change enough in their genetic makeup that they can no longer reproduce with each other, they are regarded as new species, as Darwin said in the quote above. Further evolution can cause, over very long periods of time, divergence so profound that the species look like they come from different planets. Eagles and crocodiles, both descended from archosaurs, are an example.[5]

---

[3] A third mechanism, called genetic drift, has been discovered "recently" (in the last 75 years) but it is not particularly relevant to investing. A good explanation is at https://en.wikipedia.org/wiki/Genetic_drift as it was accessed on June 14, 2023.

[4] The quote is from *Oxford Languages*, https://languages.oup.com/google-dictionary-en/

[5] Over even longer periods, plants and animals have a common ancestor, as do all living things on earth (including single-celled organisms). We know this from analysis of the DNA in their cell nuclei. This is one of the most astonishing findings of evolutionary theory.

The operating instructions of evolution

To see how evolutionary concepts can be repurposed as business management ideas, let's review the basic "operating instructions" of evolution:

- Competition (Darwin's "struggle for existence" — not everyone survives long enough to reproduce)

- Mistakes (most variations are useless or harmful)

- Speciation (some new variants of organisms succeed and, over time, become new species)

- Convergence (very different species, faced with similar problems, come to resemble each other)

- Differential reproduction rates, consisting of (1) the probability of surviving to reproductive age, and (2) the number of offspring you produce if you do reach that age; and

- Natural selection, or "survival of the fittest."

I earlier described this last principle as imprecise. Sure, only the fittest survive — but fittest for what? If it only means the fittest *for survival*, the phrase is tautological and meaningless.

Herbert Spencer, and then Darwin who loved and adopted the phrase, meant survival of those variations that were "fittest" for (that is, best adapted to) the immediate, local environment.

But, at least initially, Spencer and Darwin did not quite finish the thought. All organisms are well enough adapted to their immediate environment that they thrive there, so "survival of the fittest" is better understood as fitness for surviving *possible future change*.[6] Do you see the business analogy?

---

[6] And it is not clear in advance what the change will be. So, a genetic variation in an organism can be well adapted to one possible future outcome (say, warming of the climate) but poorly adapted to another (say, an increase in the population of predators).

By recasting natural selection as survival of the fittest, Spencer should be credited, even more than Darwin, with pulling economics and evolution together. He described one aspect of evolution as "opportunistic expansion into empty ecological niches [along with]...extinction...[that] happened due to large shifts in the...environment."[7] This description fits the story of business expansion, competition, and demise perfectly.

To round out the list of operating instructions, note that all organisms — not just intelligent ones — try, as hard as they can, to influence their environment to their own advantage. The outcome of these many processes is *profound change over long periods of time*.

This is what happens in the economy and markets too. See the self-explanatory Exhibit 1.

Depending on what actually happens, the organism will either thrive or go extinct. Evolution is powerfully influenced by randomness.

[7] *Principles of Biology* (1864) — this is astonishingly modern talk for 1864! Spencer is blamed, fairly or not, for the dog-eat-dog philosophy called Social Darwinism, which basically says that you get what you deserve. Yet one of today's most popular scientific themes, evolutionary psychology as popularized by E. O. Wilson and Steven Pinker, owes much to Spencer, who has been partly rehabilitated. A worthwhile discussion is at
https://www.smithsonianmag.com/science-nature/herbert-spencer-survival-of-the-fittest-180974756/.

Exhibit 1 — Evolution of U.S. industries since about 1800, as shown by relative market cap of the industry

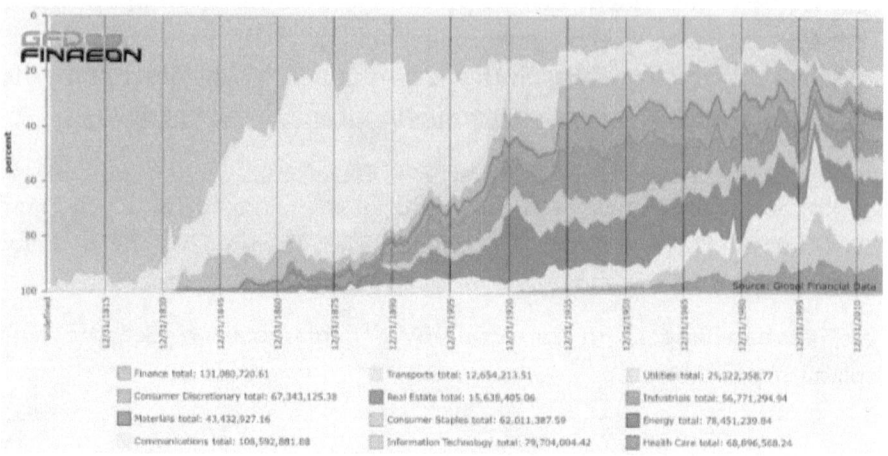

Source: https://finaeon.globalfinancialdata.com

Of the two concepts I cover, signaling applies more directly to business and investing, but convergence is a more profound and universal idea. So I begin with convergence.

Convergence: On fish, dolphins, and ichthyosaurs

Why do fish, dolphins, and ichthyosaurs (an aquatic dinosaur) look so similar, despite having radically different ancestry? Why do birds, bats, and pterosaurs (a flying dinosaur) all sprout wings where their forearms "belong"? The reason is called *convergence*, the tendency of disparate organisms facing the same problem to come up with similar solutions.[8] If you want to swim fast, the streamlined, finned design of fish and dolphins

---

[8] Some of my writing, like much evolutionary writing, makes it sound as though evolution has a mind of its own. It does not. Neither do species that "do" thus-and-such to adapt to their environment, or to become better adapted to possible future environments. It's just a figure of speech. So is "design," which makes it sound like there's a designer when there is not.

is just about the only design that will work. (That is why submarines also look like fish and dolphins.) Darwin understood this. He wrote,

> Animals, belonging to two most distinct lines of descent, may readily become adapted to similar conditions, and thus assume a close external resemblance.[9]

A particularly vivid illustration of convergent evolution is the similarity between Australian marsupials and non-Australian placental mammals. Each marsupial seems to have a placental counterpart that looks and functions similarly but comes from a different bloodline. Exhibit 2 shows an example.

Exhibit 2 — Gray wolf and Australian (Tasmanian) thylacine

Source: https://theaveragescientist.co.uk/2023/02/22/convergent-evolution-when-winning-designs-strike-back/

Australia and Asia separated, due to continental drift, about 100 million years ago when no mammal of modern design yet existed. That is long enough ago that, the thylacine, sadly now extinct, and the wolf have no common ancestor that looks anything like them — early mammals looked more like the reptiles from which they're descended. The wolf and

---

[9] Darwin, Charles. 1859. *The Origin of Species.* John Murray, London, UK, p. 427

thylacine came to look alike over millions of years because they faced similar challenges in adapting to their respective niches — the need to catch fast-moving prey, chew and digest it, stay warm in a cold climate, and so forth. In fact, the "dog design" and the "cat design" are the only surviving carnivore designs because they seem to be the only ones that work, all of nature's other experiments in carnivory having gone extinct.[10]

This apparent pairing of an Australian marsupial and a Eurasian/North American placental mammal, physically similar but genetically almost unrelated, is repeated many times across different creature designs. This shows that convergence is not just an oddity applying to wolves and thylacines, but a recurring theme in evolution. The reason is that there are typically *only a few ways* — sometimes only one way — *to solve a problem*, as we saw with fish, dolphins, and submarines.

Convergence investing

Now, what does all this evolutionary biology have to do with stock picking?

Although Prasad buys companies like any other stock picker, he thinks of himself as buying *industries* instead, because all the companies in an industry compete in the same ecosystem and face similar problems. As a result, their profits tend to cluster around the industry median. That's the business analogue of convergence in biology. (I'm oversimplifying for brevity's sake.) Some industries, often the most boring ones, offer large profit margins almost as a matter of course: "sanitaryware" (toilets) and job bulletin boards are his examples. Others, typically glamour industries, offer low ones: airlines, the quintessential glamour stocks of the last century, have earned a cumulative loss over their entire existence!

But Prasad identifies exceptions to the boring/value vs. glamour/growth rule, for example information-technology outsourcing companies, which

---

[10] Except for the thylacine! And, remarkably, the thylacine looks like a cross between a dog and a cat, despite having lines of ancestry quite distant from either. It is so dog-and-catlike that it is sometimes called the Tasmanian wolf and at other times the Tasmanian tiger. The evolutionary pressures faced by its ancestors pushed it toward both the (unrelated) dog design and the (unrelated) cat design, winding up somewhere in the middle. A richly detailed discussion of the evolution of carnivores is at https://en.wikipedia.org/wiki/Carnivora.

typically earn huge returns on investment. Competition among these semi-glamorous companies doesn't seem to drive down profits as one might expect. You have to look at industry data and macroeconomic conditions (the ecosystem beyond the industry), not just judge an industry based on its superficial appearance.

Prasad sums up his convergence philosophy by noting that, like animals or plants trying to solve a problem and converging on similar solutions, "there are only a few ways for a business to succeed." His advice is to "identify...a convergent pattern of success or failure" in businesses and, of course, buying the likely-to-be-successful ones.

This is easier said than done. And Prasad admits that the rule works except when it doesn't.

Assessing convergence-based investment strategies

If these homilies are what Prasad got out of Darwin's writings on convergence, they're not wrong, just a bit *anticlimactic*. It's true that the industry factor explains a large proportion of a given stock's return. But company strategies and decisions matter. Investors in Ford Motor Company and Packard Motor Company had profoundly different experiences. *A priori* it was not obvious that they would: they were in the same highly profitable industry and differed mostly in size and strategy. Ford's large size and diversification were advantages, but so is specialization — Packard made luxury touring cars, a strategy that has worked well for Daimler-Benz! Packard went out of business because it made a major strategic mistake. It tried to compete with Ford and GM by expanding into unfamiliar markets for which it had no talent.[11] Prasad's method might have missed this difference.

Prasad admits that his formula does not always work and cites Amazon, which he didn't buy, as an example. He avoided it because it started out in a

---

[11] https://www.hagerty.com/media/car-profiles/10-reasons-why-packard-died/.

glamor industry (internet retailing) — and he expects to miss the next Amazon too. But he says that the opportunity cost of missing an Amazon is offset by the consistent profits from buying "high-quality companies at a fair price" and being "very lazy." I'll return to laziness later (because I'm lazy).

More recently, the computer industry has provided huge returns to investors. Yet, while Apple and Microsoft have grown to be trillion-dollar corporations — there are only five in the world[12] — many computer companies have failed or deeply disappointed, including former greats such as Digital Equipment, Compaq, and the technologically superb Cray Research.[13] Although the business ecosystem has rewarded innovation in computers beyond imagining, it was possible to lose money by choosing stocks poorly. The evolutionary approach to investing, or more properly *this* evolutionary approach, has its limits.

But one can imagine many other investment disciplines grounded in biology and evolution, because the basic principle is sound and provides a pathway for thinking differently about investments, surely the key to beating the market or a benchmark.

Signaling

Even closer to the essence of business strategy than convergence is *signaling*, an element of game theory.[14] Game theory, in economics, asks how one should behave when the results depend on how others behave. This idea applies in business because companies maximize their profits in the face of

---

[12] The others, as of this writing, are Amazon, Alphabet (Google), and Nvidia.

[13] Larry Smarr, a distinguished computer scientist, called Seymour Cray "the Thomas Edison of the supercomputing industry."
https://www.washingtonpost.com/archive/politics/1996/09/24/computer-pioneer-injured/d173707b-7dc2-4fec-84c6-dfb13a86c7b7/.

[14] Game theory in economics was developed by John von Neumann and Oskar Morgenstern (*The Theory of Games and Economic Behavior*, 1944, https://www.amazon.com/Theory-Games-Economic-Behavior-Neumann/dp/8401848504/) and John Nash (the subject of Sylvia Nasar's 1998 biography *A Beautiful Mind*, https://www.amazon.com/Beautiful-Mind-Sylvia-Nasar/dp/1451628420/r made into an Academy Award-winning movie in 2001). Nash's concept of game-theoretic equilibrium is described at https://en.wikipedia.org/wiki/Nash_equilibrium (caution, this article is quite detailed and advanced).

competition from other companies that are trying just as hard and employ people who are just as smart. Most businesspeople know they are playing this game, so applying formal game theory to business is not a stretch.

Evolutionary game theory arose later and asks the same question about species.[15] The evolutionary version was developed by scientists who were familiar with economic game theory and intuited — correctly, it turned out — that it would apply even more directly to biology than to economics.

Central to evolutionary game theory, and to security analysis, is *signaling*. Prasad writes,

> Signals have evolved specifically to alter the behavior of the receiver in ways that benefit the signaler and are [intended to] influence the behavior of prey, predators, mates, competitors, friends, and family. While we call ourselves investors, an evolutionary biologist would not be remiss in branding us as "signal decoders." As outsiders to a company, the only thing we rely on is signals being emitted by companies — some direct and others indirect; some comprehensible and others bizarre; and most important, some honest and others dishonest.[16]

According to evolutionary theory, signals are likely to be honest only when they involve some sort of sacrifice or cost borne by the signaler. According to Prasad,

> In 1975, Amotz Zahavi, an Israeli evolutionary biologist, proposed his famous *handicap principle* which asserts that only those signals that are costly to produce (and hence are handicaps) can be considered reliable. For example, male elks with larger antlers attract more mates presumably because their message to female elks is: look how healthy and virile I am because I carry these massive unwieldy antlers.

It's possible that big antlers help their bearers fight, but the peacock's magnificent tail has no known function other than to show females that

---

[15] See https://plato.stanford.edu/entries/game-evolutionary/ for a description, again quite advanced. The seminal work in the field is Maynard Smith, John. 1982. Evolution and the Theory of Games. Cambridge, UK: Cambridge University Press.

[16] In CEO World, at https://ceoworld.biz/2023/04/07/what-i-learned-about-investing-from-darwin/.

the male has so much vigor he can afford to waste it on a very expensive (in metabolic terms) decoration.

The behavior of rich human males is similar. Rather than or in addition to advertising one's athletic ability — a more direct way of demonstrating fitness — they buy fast cars, big boats, and lavish homes, again demonstrating the ability to expend resources frivolously. The Lambo is the human "peacock's tail."

Exhibit 3 — *The handicap principle in bird and man*

Nature, I guess, has a sense of humor — it selects for individuals who conspicuously waste resources over those who merely demonstrate that they have plenty of them.

Signaling in business

Applying the handicap principle to stock picking, investor should avoid companies that waste resources on *dishonest* signaling, but buy those that send out *honest* signals. Analysts should therefore ignore signals that are costless (or nearly so) to the signaler. Prasad's examples of worthless signals include press releases, interviews, investor conferences, road shows, and earnings projections. There are no consequences for being wrong, no skin in the game.[17]

In contrast, worthwhile signals, which are costly to the company, include *past* financial performance and the company's achieved competitive

---

[17] Earnings projections are Prasad's bugaboo, not mine. Companies that miss their earnings estimates are often punished harshly in the market, indicating that they do have skin in the game. (Maybe this isn't true in India — I have no idea.)

position in the industry. These demonstrate a history of having produced a high return on capital. Not only *can* such a company do something right, it *has done* so, repeatedly so as to produce the observed results – and many have the people and culture needed to do it again.

Prasad thus invests in companies that display these characteristics. His investment management firm has done well, partly because it operates in the emerging Indian market where price is often quite distant from value. Signal-based investing is not, however, a fail-safe formula for success (nothing is). IBM Corporation did a great many things right, dominating its industry for decades, before it faltered in the 1990s.[18] The same can be said of many other once-great companies, so beware of taking Prasad's signaling advice too literally.

"Don't be lazy — be very lazy"

If there's one lesson in Prasad's book that is hard to argue with, it's that lazy investors tend to be winners. Buy—hold—forget is a good general strategy, as long as your memory comes back when it's time to rebalance (very important). Buying only index funds is even lazier and usually more financially rewarding.

But Prasad means something else by "lazy." He notes that a company's long-term fortunes vary less than its short-term ones. Earnings surprises are mostly noise. So are stock price fluctuations, he argues. "News" is noisier than either.

He cites as an example L'Oréal, which meets his "buy" criteria by doing one thing well for a long time and making large profits. He then lists 65 (count 'em!) news stories about L'Oréal that surfaced between 2009 and 2021, ranging in tone from slightly bad to very bad. He then pointedly asks, "Would you have stayed invested?" Most readers would say no.

L'Oreal's stock price, quoted in dollars, rose from $18.15 on January 2, 2009 to $95.42 on December 31, 2021. It also paid a total of $7.63 in dividends over

---

[18] A thoughtful analysis is at https://manavsplace.medium.com/marketing-why-ibm-faltered-2b328b2a66e2.

the period, plus some extra money from reinvesting the dividends in the rapidly appreciating stock.[19]

Be lazy — but not crazy. Buy-and-hold almost always beats frequent trading, and always beats noise trading (trading not based on information). But, as I noted earlier, some companies do everything right until they don't, or until a competitor wipes the floor with them.

Conclusion and advice to investors

I had fun reading *What I Learned About Investing from Darwin*. But I learned more about biology, a field in which I'm already somewhat well read, than about investing. Many investors who are avid readers will come to the same conclusion. The classics of investment literature — Burton Malkiel's *A Random Walk Down Wall Street*, Charles Kindleberger's *Manias, Panics, and Crashes*, Peter Bernstein's *Against the Gods*, and Nassim Taleb's *Fooled by Randomness*, to name my favorites — are the finance liberal-arts education every serious investor needs.[20] Prasad's *Darwin* book is an elective course, likely to enrich readers' understanding of the investment thought process but not revolutionize it.

Prasad valiantly tries to apply evolutionary theory to investing at a level granular enough to be useful. Mostly he succeeds — and the book is a pleasant, lively read. But investors should not overapply the lessons of evolution any more than they should ignore them. Read this book; then, think for yourself and apply many disciplines, not just that of evolutionary biology, to the selection of securities.

---

[19] These are actually quotes for the L'Oréal ADR (American Depositary Receipt), traded on the NASDAQ as LRLCY.

[20] I leave out Benjamin Graham and David Dodd's *Security Analysis* at my peril — it is the foundation of the modern practice of active management — but most advisors and their clients are not about to become security analysts.

Chapter 9. How Venture Capital Thrives by Betting on Weirdness

Laurence B. Siegel
June 21, 2022

Who would want to be tasked with investing their own and other people's money in companies run by weirdos and jerks? But that turns out to be one of the most important skill sets shared by successful venture capitalists.

"Reasonable people," begins Sebastian Mallaby in his excellent history of venture capital investing, "well-adjusted people…without hubris or naïveté, routinely fail in life's important missions by not even attempting them…Khosla himself was an unreasonable man, creatively maladjusted."

Vinod Khosla is the venture capitalist who backed the startup company, Impossible Foods, that makes the Impossible Burger. (It's a plant-based burger that has become wildly successful because, unlike earlier veggie burgers, it tastes good.) Although each venture-capital success story is different, Mallaby – the author of *The Man Who Knew*, a biography of Alan Greenspan that I reviewed in Advisor Perspectives in 2016[1] – finds a common thread: All of them involve unreasonable, maladjusted people who are a pain in the neck. Mallaby describes Khosla as "cocky and obnoxious…one part tyrant, two parts visionary."

Sebastian Mallaby
Source: http://4.bp.blogspot.com/-5Ee6vRWXzQk/Ufcu-9Lm3OI/AAAAAAAAowQ/Bao3nEM63Xk/s1600/SebastianMallaby-CFR-bio-pic.jpg

---

[1] https://www.advisorperspectives.com/articles/2016/12/05/how-should-history-judge-alan-greenspan

But Khosla is not the inventor of the Impossible Burger. That's Patrick Brown, who is even more unreasonable. A celebrated geneticist, Brown wanted to *put the meat industry out of business*. Most inventors would be satisfied with their product achieving a decent market share and making them rich. Brown wanted to destroy an industry he regarded as harmful and save the world thereby. Livestock farming takes up one-third of the world's agricultural capacity and produces a lot of carbon emissions; Brown wanted it to disappear.

His dream was that "nobody would eat ground cow flesh again." Impossible!

Mallaby's new book, *The Power Law*, elegantly shows how these impossible dreams get funded, and then either win big or (much more frequently) lose everything. That is where the power law comes in.

What is the Power Law?

The book's title, *The Power Law*, is meaningful to people who work with data but will be a mystery to everyone else. It's an important concept from statistics, so I'll start by describing it. Have you ever noticed that the sizes of cities, businesses, and many other phenomena in life follow a pattern like this?

Exhibit 1 — Power-law distribution

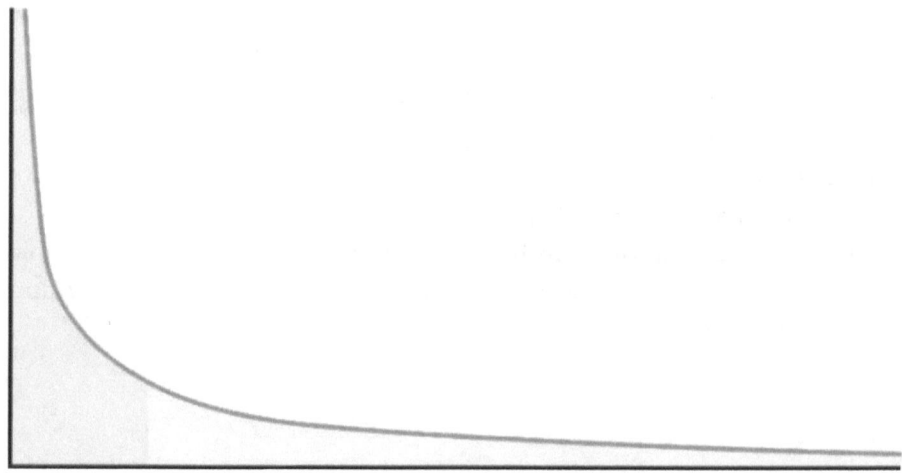

Source: https://en.wikipedia.org/wiki/Power_law#/media/File:Long_tail.svg

Cities are an example. You can picture New York, the largest U.S. metropolitan area, at the top of the curve in Exhibit 1. Los Angeles, about two-thirds as large, is farther down.

Chicago, about two-thirds as large as Los Angeles, is farther down still — and so on down to the multitude of small cities making up the "long tail" to the right. The city example describes an exponential series (example: 1, 1/2, 1/4, 1/8), not a power series (1, 1/4, 1/9, 1/16), but the two ideas are similar – a number that decreases quickly and approaches zero while never quite reaching it. Although the book's title refers to a power series, it is not clear whether Mallaby is using the term literally or figuratively. Either way, it fits the general pattern of private equity returns.

The Power Law vs the Normal Distribution

Mallaby compares the power-law distribution to the much more familiar normal distribution. In a normal distribution, outliers don't matter much. Men's heights are normally distributed, so if you removed Lebron James from a room of 100 otherwise randomly selected men, their average height would go down by only a fraction of an inch. But wealth follows a power law, so if you take Elon Musk out of a room of 100 randomly selected people, or even rich people, their average wealth plummets.

In a phenomenon that follows a power law, outliers matter tremendously.

The Power Law and Venture Capital

What does all this have to do with venture capital? It turns out that the returns on venture capital investments follow a power law. (I am talking about the returns on the companies that are in the VC firms' portfolios, not the VC funds themselves.) The power, in this case the ratio of the return on the #2 company to that of the #1 (and so on down), is much less than two-thirds. According to Mallaby,

Y Combinator, which backs fledging tech startups, calculated in 2012 that three-quarters of its gains came from just two of the 280 outfits it had bet on. "The biggest secret in venture capital is that the best investment in a successful fund equals or outperforms the entire rest of the fund," the venture capitalist Peter Thiel has written.

The source of this winner-take-almost-all effect is the fact that, in the venture world, or at least the technology part of it, success leads to more success in an explosive pattern.[2] It's not like the ordinary investment management business where styles such as growth and value run in cycles with the result that, as Charles Gave said, you are "one day a rooster, the next day a feather duster."[3] Mallaby argues that the explosion upward is due to a network effect that you find in the tech sector but only rarely in the rest of the economy:

> After the invention of the semiconductor, or after the invention of the Ethernet cables that hooked personal computers together, usage picked up gradually and then exploded upward in an exponential curve; this was the innovation power law that underlay the financial one observed in venture-capital portfolios.

A little later, the internet did something similar, but at an even faster rate, almost vertical.

The Mothership

An earlier story reflecting this same phenomenon, which Mallaby recounted with a historian's attention to detail, is that of Fairchild Semiconductor, the mothership of venture capital, in the late 1950s. It housed a Who's Who of future tech-company billionaires: Gordon Moore (of Moore's Law), Robert Noyce, Andy Grove, and Eugene Kleiner who

---

[2] The explosive effect may not be as powerful, or may not exist at all, in other types of venture-funded businesses such as manufacturers and retail stores.

[3] Personal communication. Charles Gave is a founder of Gavekal Group, an investment research firm. Before that, he ran the investment management firm Cursitor-Eaton.

would later establish the iconic VC firm Kleiner Perkins. Arthur Rock, a New York-based broker who would later become one of the world's great venture capitalists, backed it.

Fairchild Semiconductor's founders in 1957. Left to right: Gordon Moore, C. Sheldon Roberts, Eugene Kleiner, Robert Noyce, Victor Grinich, Julius Blank, Jean Hoerni, and Jay Last. https://www.chipsetc.com/fairchild-semiconductor.html

Unsurprisingly, they were all engineers (except Rock, who financed the venture from outside it). Our modern world was built not by statesmen, scientists, or financiers, but by engineers.[4]

What became of this little group? In 1968, Moore and Noyce founded Intel, for a long time the world's largest semiconductor manufacturer. "Intel Inside®." (Manufacturers of parts and ingredients struggle for name recognition even if they are blindingly rich.) Grove became president of Intel in 1979. Eugene Kleiner joined with Tom Perkins, Frank Caufield, and Brook Byers to form what would become the most recognizable name in venture capital investing; Kleiner Perkins dominated Silicon Valley for four decades before its influence started to fade about a decade ago. It funded or co-funded, among hundreds of other companies, Amazon, Genentech,

---

[4] William Shockley, the Nobel Prize-winning physicist for whom nearly all of these men worked before launching their venture, was a scientist as well as an engineer (professor of electrical engineering at Stanford). Note that he did not jump aboard the Fairchild Semiconductor train and was almost certainly not asked to; the group just described, known as the Traitorous Eight, seem to have gotten their nickname by joining together in rebellion against Shockley (yet another "tyrant" by Mallaby's reckoning).

Google, Netscape, Sun Microsystems, and Twitter.[5] The impact of the Fairchild "alumni association" on modern life is incalculable.

Flower Children vs the Mayflower

Most of the successful startups in the last 40 years have been in the western United States, mostly in northern California. Yet VC as a business concept originated in the Northeast with Laurance Rockefeller, Jock Whitney, Georges Doriot, and others profiled in the early chapters of Tom Nichols' book *VC: An American History*, which I reviewed in *Advisor Perspectives* in 2019.[6]

Why the move to the West? "We owe it all to the hippies," said the musician-businessman Bono (Paul Hewson). Under the influence of Stewart Brand, author of the *Whole Earth Catalog*, the freewheeling and nonconformist culture of Bay Area hippies collided with that of inquisitive computer scientists at Stanford and Berkeley in the late 1960s and early 1970s, and a new culture of hackers, tech dreamers, and startup founders emerged.[7] I had a job interview with the late Apple executive Jef Raskin in 1977 and the atmosphere of his lab in a remote part of northern California – not the Apple headquarters – resembled that of a hippie commune. (I was not selected.)

The east-west schism had taken shape earlier, as the Fairchild crew negotiated with their East Coast bankers. Mallaby recalls:

> [Robert] Noyce wanted instinctively to run Fairchild without any divisions between bosses and workers…[T]here would be a level playing field, a ferocious work ethic, and a belief that every last employee had a stake in the firm.

---

[5] Genentech, the first major biotech company, doesn't seem to fit in. But venture investing is about more than what we usually call "technology." Medicine is technology too, and Genentech (now part of Roche) is where synthetic human insulin comes from — perhaps more important, if you are a diabetic, than any of the other companies.

[6] https://www.advisorperspectives.com/articles/2019/07/08/the-history-and-future-of-venture-capital-investing. Note the old-money pedigree in the Northeast: Rockefeller and Whitney.

[7] A history of this period is in Markoff, Robert. 2022. *Whole Earth: The Many Lives of Stewart Brand*. New York: Penguin Random House.

In [Tom] Wolfe's telling of this story,[8] "...Fairchild Semiconductor's East Coast overlords...could never fathom this...ethic. [They] had a feudal approach:...there were kings and lords, and there were vassals and soldiers."

Sequoia Capital's Don Valentine described the Eastern money men as "people with hyphenated names or Roman numerals after their last name, direct descendants of immigrants who arrived on the Mayflower." Imagine a group of casually dressed, computer-toting hippies asking them for large sums of money.

It was not a foregone conclusion that the unstructured West would beat the button-down Northeast. But, by the late 1970s, with the founding of Apple in Silicon Valley and Microsoft in Seattle, it did, and Western dominance of venture capital in the United States has only grown stronger since then.

Peter Thiel, Founders Fund, and the Power Law

Peter Thiel
Source: https://www.usatoday.com/story/tech/2014/10/12/peter-thiel-on-apple-mbas-and-startup-creation/17059735/

Fast forward a couple of decades (Mallaby's book is *long*) — past the founding and funding of Microsoft, Apple, Google, and Amazon. It's 2004 and the venture capital industry is booming, thanks largely to big institutions — university endowment funds, pension funds, charitable foundations — perceiving that private capital, of which VC is a part, offered a better return than the stock or bond markets. Having started a half-century earlier as a rich man's hobby and then a niche activity in the Boston and San Francisco suburbs, VC has gone mainstream. It's an *industry*.

---

[8] Wolfe, Tom. 1983. "The Tinkerings of Robert Noyce." *Esquire* (December), https://web.stanford.edu/class/e145/2007_fall/materials/noyce.html

Peter Thiel is an odd duck even by the standards of the VC duck pond. A gay conservative libertarian Republican German American, Thiel annoyed much of the VC community with his kooky projects (life extension and seasteading), lawsuits, and constant political proselytizing.[9] He is also brilliant and mega-rich, having co-founded PayPal, set up a hedge fund called Clarium Capital, and founded the security company Palantir. He was the angel investor behind Facebook. He is closely associated with Elon Musk, with whom he is said to have (surprise!) a love-hate relationship.

Having nothing to do (!) and recently emerged from fights with other Silicon Valley bigwigs such as Sequoia Capital's Michael Moritz, Thiel set up his own venture capital firm, Founders Fund. Mallaby writes,

> The name signaled the ethos: founders who had created companies like PayPal were out to back the next entrepreneurial cohort, and they promised to treat this new generation with the respect that they themselves had wished for.

It sounded very groovy, very Californian. It would also become one of the most successful VC firms of the new century.

At the beginning of this article, I quoted Thiel saying that the best investment in a successful fund was often the only one that made any money. Thus, writes Mallaby,

> Thiel was the first VC to speak explicitly about the power law. Past venture investors, going back to Arthur Rock, had understood full well that a handful of winners would dominate their performance. But Thiel went further in recognizing this as part of a broader phenomenon.

Because Mallaby's expansion on this point is the central theme of the book, I quote him at length:

> Thiel went further in recognizing this as part of a broader phenomenon…the "Pareto principle" or 80-20 rule [says] that radically unequal outcomes [are] common in the natural and

---

[9] According to seasteading.org, "seasteading means building floating societies with significant political autonomy." The organization reports having seven active projects, one of which is underwater (intentionally). For Thiel's writings, see https://thememeticist.com/other/2020/07/28/thiel-online-writing-list.html.

social world.

Mallaby describes the economist Vilfredo Pareto's observation, around the turn of the last century, that 80% of the land in Italy was owned by 20% of the people, and that this inequality could be observed in many different contexts. "It was therefore not just a curiosity that a single venture-capital bet could dominate a whole portfolio. It was a sort of natural law," writes Mallaby. He continues:

> Thiel was methodical in thinking through the implications of this insight...He argued, iconoclastically, that venture capitalists should stop mentoring founders...The power law dictated that the companies that mattered would have to be exceptional outliers;...[t]he founders of these outstanding startups were necessarily so gifted that a bit of VC coaching would barely change their performance.

The most successful companies in the Founders Fund portfolio, a colleague of Thiel's observed, were often those with which VCs had the least involvement. In Mallaby's words,

> [T]he art of venture capital was to find rough diamonds, not to spend time polishing them...[If] the power law dictated that only a handful of truly original and contrarian startups were destined to succeed, it made no sense to suppress idiosyncrasies...the wackier the better. Entrepreneurs who weren't oddballs would create businesses that were simply too normal...[and] would have occurred to others.

And that is how the power law — not just the theory of it, but the practice — became the central principle of venture capital investing.

Y Combinator

Y Combinator has the coolest company name in the Valley. It sounds like they are breeding new companies in a biochemistry lab.

The brainchild of Paul Graham, Y Combinator provides the exact same deal to every venture: $500,000 to "accelerate" the growth of the business, regardless of its size and financial condition. (It is not the only accelerator firm.) Over 20,000 companies apply each year, and the acceptance rate is 1.5% to 2%. In a beautiful demonstration of the power law, the rewards to Y Combinator are few and big: "We now have more than 110 companies valued over $100M and more than 25 companies valued over $1B," according to the company web site. Most of the $500,000 investments are a total loss.

Paul Graham
Source: https://www.paulgraham.com/

You could be forgiven for thinking this sounds more like a MacArthur Foundation "genius grant" than an investment (Y Combinator also gives away money to nonprofits.) Graham would fit in at a foundation or university — he is something of a philosopher whose blog posts are legendary for their intellectual quality.[10] But Y Combinator is not a foundation. Graham and his partners care very much about money; they just earn it in an unconventional way, breaking all the rules of traditional VC investing. They pursue extreme diversification, invest small amounts, take an unusually small stake in the company (7% plus some optionality), and bring the entrepreneurs together in a bootcamp-like atmosphere.

Their try-everything approach gets results. Among Y Combinator's successful investments were Airbnb, Dropbox, Doordash, and Reddit.

Put enough smart and ambitious people (many of whom are visibly crazy) together in a few hundred square miles of north-central California real estate and you get some unexpected outcomes. Although I'm just guessing, Y Combinator is probably Stewart Brand's favorite VC.

---

[10] http://paulgraham.com/articles.html

Uber: Ideas having sex

Uber is one of my favorite companies to write about, because it did almost everything wrong and still succeeded at disrupting one of the most entrenched industries in existence — the taxicab cartel. The company was run by a jerk, broke laws intentionally, and changed the rules on drivers so often as to infuriate half of them. (The other half, who treated the situation as a game to be mastered, did very well.)

Maybe they're black hats, but without Uber breaking the cartel and creating a free market in rides, we would still be chugging around in taxis that, as George Will wrote in 2003, "were last inspected at Studebaker dealerships and are driven...by strangers driven by strange demons."[11] (I've saved that quote for 19 years, waiting to use it.)

Uber's great innovation wasn't dynamic pricing (which responds in real time to changes in supply and demand); the airlines had been doing it for decades. It wasn't the use of mapping and geolocation software to enable drivers and passengers to locate each other, although that was important. It wasn't the hiring practices, where drivers could work as many or as few hours as they wanted and have other jobs. The innovation was doing *all these at the same time.*

Matt Ridley, that brilliant and controversial chronicler of human progress, asserts that new ideas come from old ones having sex.[12] It's a vivid image. Computer + telephone = internet. Horse and carriage + engine = car (with an unemployed horse left over). Uber is a particularly salient example of ideas having sex, with at least three different threads of invention combining to produce the resulting leap in utility.

---

[11] Will, George F. 2003. *With A Happy Eye, But...* New York: Free Press, p. 163.

[12] In *The Rational Optimist* (2011), which I reviewed in 2012, https://larrysiegeldotorg.files.wordpress.com/2017/07/ap-ridley-pdf.pdf

Why are so many founders and CEOs "not nice"?

While Mallaby does not tell the full story of Uber, he draws a valuable lesson from what he describes as the company "going off the rails." "Founders Fund made an expensive error," he continues,

> by refusing to invest in...Uber; its bratty founder, Travis Kalanick, had alienated [the fund's managers]. "We should be more tolerant of founders who seem strange or extreme," [Peter] Thiel wrote, when Uber had emerged as a grand slam. "Maybe we need to give assholes a second and third chance," [Founders Fund principal Luke Nosek] conceded contritely.

It's a lesson I would have preferred not to learn. Founders and CEOs are often not nice. Kalanick fits the mold, which was perfected a long time ago by James H. Patterson, the S.O.B. founder of National Cash Register. Mallaby refers to many tech-company leaders as "tyrants"; in addition, Steve Jobs and Bill Gates, heroes to many, have been described similarly. All of us are rooting for businesses to be led by good human beings, but there is something about successful large-company entrepreneurship that is correlated with an aggressive and even bullying personality.

It is probably for the best that Kalanick was replaced by a more responsible and law-abiding CEO. But, without Kalanick's hardball tactics, Uber would not have gotten a foothold (nor would have Lyft, which hitched a ride on Uber's earlier aggressiveness). Our travel about town would still be guided by strange demons, and we would still be paying monopoly prices for a service that belongs in the competitive economy.

There's a broader lesson here: Venture capital and the companies it backs play a vital role in the economy and in the rapid rate of technological progress that we've become used to, even when they are not well behaved. Disruption is not pretty.

Conclusion and advice for investors

The Power Law is a story book, a *history* of the U.S. venture capital industry as told by its people, practices, and products. It is plausible bedtime reading. Despite the mathematical title, the book has no math beyond what I've presented and does not rely on data or academic studies. Only a natural storyteller like Mallaby can capture the essential weirdness of many entrepreneurs and venture capitalists. They make hedge fund managers, profiled in Mallaby's earlier book, *More Money than God*, look like boring conformists.

Nor does *The Power Law* give investment advice, but I will: These stunts are performed by trained professionals — don't try them at home.

Individual investors and their advisors should avoid venture capital investing entirely. (I might make an exception for those with true inside information about ventures started by people they know personally, as long as the information is legal. Even then, do it in small doses.) The "good" VC funds, the ones like Accel Partners and Founders Fund that see the most attractive startups, are closed to all but a few institutions and families who commit to investing in the funds in good times and bad. The not-so-good funds lose money; sadly, those are the ones that investors can gain access to. (Unlike in the public equity market where manager results are more random, there are "good" and "bad" VC funds because the most successful entrepreneurs keeping going back to the same firms for more funding, causing yet another explosive process.)

The power law surely contributes to plight of the average VC fund. Given the pervasiveness of failed startups, it is essential that VC funds get to invest with the few that produce outsized returns. But the structure of the VC industry dictates that those investments are divvied up among the elite firms at the top of the pyramid.

Even though they shouldn't invest in VC, individual investors will be holding many of these companies in their portfolios once they go public. They will consequently be buying the stocks that entrepreneurs and venture capitalists are selling. Companies founded by entrepreneurs and backed by venture capitalists are the seed corn of our economy. We only get to enjoy the meal once the seeds have been nurtured (or, more often, allowed to die) by the venture capital community, but investors need to understand where new companies come from, and why.

Chapter 10. Financial Folly, Religious Frenzy and the Delusions of Crowds

Laurence B. Siegel
May 8, 2021

What do financial folly and religious frenzy have in common? This question has not been carefully explored since Charles Mackay's spectacular 1852 study, *Extraordinary Popular Delusions and the Madness of Crowds*.[1]

But, in a recent book, William Bernstein, a well-known economic historian, neurologist, and investment manager, makes the connection even more strongly than Mackay did. The title of his book, *The Delusions of Crowds*, explicitly pays homage to Mackay's classic. Bernstein's delightfully written book is as worthy a read as Mackay's.

To make the comparison between religious frenzy and financial foolishness come alive, I'll hop around through the centuries and reflect on the Anabaptist mania in Germany in the 1500s, the commendable

William Bernstein
Source: http://www.bogleheads.org

rise and sad fall of the American entrepreneur Samuel Insull in the early 1900s, and other topics as diverse as Ronald Reagan and red calves. It may sound like I've been consuming some formerly controlled substances, but there is a method to my madness. To investigate the links between

---

[1] Mackay, Charles. 1852. *[Memoirs of] Extraordinary Popular Delusions and the Madness of Crowds.* http://www.gutenberg.org/files/24518/24518-h/24518-h.htm#image07

religious and financial weirdness in anything like a serious way – what Bernstein asks us to do – it's necessary to go into detail on some classic examples of each. So that's what I've done.

Why investors should care about irrational behavior

Investors should be keenly interested in irrationality — in all aspects of it. Classic finance theory assumes that people are hyperrational, selecting portfolios that are mathematically optimal in their balancing of risk, return, and correlation. From all possible optimal portfolios, they select the one that maximizes their utility, taking into account their aversion to risk.[2] No one believes this, but the mistakes of millions of investors should cancel out, so that by analyzing markets as if people were rational, you should get a good approximation of reality.

Except when you don't.

Financial markets burgeon with bubbles, crashes, high-priced stocks of companies with no earnings or revenues, and investors who act against their own interest. The recent headlines about GameStop, Bitcoin, Ark Invest, and the use of highly leveraged options by individual investors are reminiscent of the stories told by Mackay and Bernstein. To understand markets, it's vitally important to figure out what's going on when prices depart – in either direction – from fundamental value by large amounts.

And I'm not just talking about the stock market. Government bonds are priced in classic Mackay fashion — discounting the hereafter.[3] An Austrian

---

[2] In a radical and invaluable simplification of this method, the capital asset pricing model, or CAPM, says that investors should simply form portfolios out of two assets: (1) the market capitalization-weighted portfolio of all risky securities, that is, an index fund; and (2) cash or some other asset deemed to be riskless. This simplification, the brainchild of William Sharpe and several others, made optimization practical by greatly reducing the number and difficulty of needed estimates and calculations.

[3] In 1928, economist Max Winkler said the stock market was discounting not only the future but the hereafter. The quote has been repeated endlessly and has been attributed to just about every market sage and wag since that time.

government bond maturing in June 2120, almost 100 years from now, recently sold at a yield of 0.45%.

Traders aptly call it the Semper Augustus bond in reference to a beautiful tulip involved in the Dutch tulip mania of 400 years ago.[4] A Semper Augustus tulip bulb briefly cost as much as a house.

Semper Augustus tulip
Source: Wikimedia Commons

Religious frenzies and financial manias

It is timely to look not just at extreme behavior in financial markets but in other spheres of human activity. Bernstein's choice of religion as the comparable sphere is understandable, although I quarrel with some of the logic and tone. In particular, religion at its worst can be unbelievably destructive: The Thirty Years' War between Catholics and Protestants in 17th century Europe cost that *continent* about 20% of its population. Germany lost at least one-third of its citizens. In contrast, financial panics (the usual endgame of manias) almost always end in recovery and opportunity for investors. While I don't mean to trivialize losing one's money, there is a qualitative difference between that and losing one's life.

---

[4] Bhansali, Vineer. 2021. *The Incredible Upside-Down Fixed Income Market: Negative Interest Rates and Their Implications.* Charlottesville, VA: CFA Institute Research Foundation. Available as a free, ungated download at https://www.cfainstitute.org/-/media/documents/book/rf-publication/2021/rf-bhansali-negative-interest-rates.ashx.

Yet there is something out of balance about Bernstein's demonization of religion. Religion may be based on an illusion of supernatural control over human affairs, but it is still on net a good thing. It evolved because it binds societies together with a common understanding of the world and human nature, and because it sets norms of behavior that are otherwise very difficult to enforce. Moreover, the greatest human need other than mere physical survival is community. Religion creates communities that are intermediate in size between families or villages at one end, and the entire human race at the other. While I believe that religion is a human invention, it is an incredibly valuable one if not perverted in some of the ways that Bernstein describes.

Religious madness: The Anabaptist insanity of 1533-1535

I start with religion because that is where Bernstein starts and where he places the greatest emphasis, unlike his previous books which are mostly about investing and the historical development of the world economy.[5]

An Anabaptist believes in adult baptism, on the ground that an infant cannot commit consciously to the Christian life; the word comes from the Latin for "second baptism." This doctrine sounds harmless and much less strange than many religious practices that are widely accepted. Yet, between 1533 and 1535, the "Anabaptist madness" seized northern Germany and let to an orgy of killing, by and of Anabaptists, that Bernstein chronicles in almost too-graphic detail as an iconic example of religious insanity.

---

[5] Bernstein's books on the economy are his most valuable, in particular *The Birth of Plenty: How the Prosperity of the Modern World was Created* (New York: McGraw-Hill, 2004), which was one of the inspirations for my book, *Fewer, Richer, Greener: Prospects for Humanity in an Age of Abundance* (Hoboken, NJ: Wiley, 2019); and *A Splendid Exchange: How Trade Shaped the World* (London: Atlantic Books, 2008). Previously, he wrote *The Four Pillars of Investing: Lessons for Building a Winning Portfolio* (New York: McGraw-Hill Education, 2002), which should be read by all investors. The pillars are theory, history, psychology, and "business" — the last one meaning that brokers and investment managers exist to make a profit.

Financial Folly, Religious Frenzy and the Delusions of Crowds 161

A peaceful moment in the Anabaptist Rebellion c. 1535:, Jan van Leiden tauft ein Mädchen (John of Leyden Baptizes a Maiden), Painted by Johann Karl Ulrich Bähr, Oil on canvas, 1840. Source: https://tsup.truman.edu/files/2016/01/FalseProphets-LookInside.pdf

What happened? In thrall to an end-times narrative that pops up repeatedly in the history of religion, the Anabaptists expected the world to end. As a portent, citizens of the Westphalian city of Münster reported seeing three suns.[6] The Book of Revelation indicates that, in the end times, a select group will be saved and another, much larger group will be destroyed.

The Anabaptists believed, naturally, that they would be among the select. So did their opponents. In addition, each wanted to do their opponents a

---

[6] Anyone with a passing knowledge of atmospheric science knows that "sun dogs," a pair of bright sun-like lights in the sky appearing on each side of the actual Sun at a 22º distance, are an occasional local phenomenon due to refraction by ice crystals. I have seen them myself. So maybe the people of Münster saw three suns. Religious hustlers and other con men have always used rare astronomical or meteorological phenomena, such as eclipses and comets, to persuade others that something supernatural is taking place.

favor by converting them, thereby saving them from eternal damnation. Convert or die; that is how religious wars "work."

If, in our own culture, we have an impression of Anabaptists at all, it's usually a positive one; the peaceful and quaint Amish of my native Ohio, a subgroup of Anabaptists, are prosperous farmers who seem content to live and let live.[7] In contrast, the Anabaptists of the Münster rebellion were maniacs:

> Some lifted themselves up in crazy dances as if about to fly... Some collapsed face down on the ground... some lay in the soft mud, rolling themselves over and over... Some howled with gleaming eyes. Some frothed at the lips. Some made threats while shaking their heads and gnashing their teeth... Some cried, some laughed. We, on the other hand, did not so much laugh at their crazed madness but grieve.

wrote a young German, Hermann von Kerssenbock, quoted by Bernstein.

The Anabaptists also violently took over the city of Münster, prompting a year-long siege that resulted in starvation for the city's hapless citizens.

What was done *to* the Anabaptists after the city was taken by the besiegers at least matches what was done *by* the Anabaptists. The torture and execution of the Anabaptist leaders was unusually cruel, even for the late medieval/early modern culture that inspired *Game of Thrones*.

I tend to think of religious manias, and political ones such as the French Revolution, as being driven ultimately by earthly concerns. These typically include hunger, hatred of those in power, and fear of rapid change, as well as by hope for something better (usually rendered in the afterlife in the religious case, and in an earthly utopia in the political one). People are not necessarily crazy to react to their circumstances by holding extreme views. However, as we have seen, they can become crazy when reinforced through close proximity to a large number of other people sharing those views. The madness of crowds.

---

[7] Today, there are many other Anabaptist groups in the U.S. and Europe, including the Mennonites and the Church of the Brethren. They number about 4 million and are all peaceful.

With the benefit of distance, we can laugh at the tulip bubble, the internet bubble, and the ridiculous pumping-and-dumping of GameStop. We can only shudder at the tale of the first Anabaptists.

An "electric" example of financial engineering gone wrong

There is no example of financial irrationality that can match the worst instances of religious irrationality. Financial chaos occasionally leads to death: The suicides of Jesse Livermore, Madoff fraud victim Thierry Magon de La Villehuchet, and 20-year-old Robinhood customer Alexander Kearns were tragic.[8] But most episodes of financial folly are transient and do little lasting damage; the worst ones, such as the crash of 1929, are more enduring but still end in recovery.[9] More typically, the impact of a financial bubble or crash is exaggerated by the lurid stories told by those who were most deeply involved.

Let's look at one of Bernstein's examples. Everyone knows about 1929, the dot-com bubble, the crash of 2007-2009, and the recent melt-up in stock prices. Historically minded investors are also aware of tulips, John Law's Mississippi Company bubble, and the South Sea Bubble. (The South Sea Company had nothing to do with exploiting the riches of the South Pacific; it had the appalling objective of transporting African slaves across the South Atlantic.) Bernstein tantalizes us with just a few bumps in the history of capitalism, preferring to dwell on religious frenzies. But, to tie the narrative back to investing, I'll focus on a lesser-known financial episode that he chronicles: the decline and fall of Samuel Insull and his tangle of electric utility companies.

Insull's biographer Gary Hoover writes,[10]

---

[8] I'm leaving out examples where the decedent was, or appeared to be, guilty of a major crime.

[9] The Great Depression was an economic crisis, not strictly a financial crisis. Historians are still unsure whether a sharp turndown in the real economy caused the stock market crash of 1929-1932, or the reverse. So I differentiate between the Depression and the market crash.

[10] Hoover, Gary E. 2021. "From Hero to Hated: America's Most Tragic Entrepreneur," American

Few business leaders or entrepreneurs in American history have done more to enable progress and prosperity than Samuel Insull, a name little known today. Yet eighty years ago, he was one of the most famous people in America and Europe – and one of the most despised... He did more to bring electricity to America than any person outside its inventors. Sam Insull put together an energy empire worth billions, only to see it disappear from his grasp in the Great Depression. What happened then is one of the great tragedies of business history.

Associated with Thomas Edison from an early age, the English-born Insull cobbled together a portfolio of electric utilities that boggled the mind. Bernstein describes it: "He stacked hundreds of companies into layers, with the bottom layers sometimes owning pieces of those at the top of the structure." The layers included "'superrich cream' and 'super-superrich cream' that came from stacking multiple organizational levels."

Samuel Insull (right) in better days with Thomas Edison
Source: American Business History Center

Does this sound like a 2008-style mortgage pool? Or is it more like a fund of funds of hedge funds, a so-called f-cubed?

> From 1929 to 1932, electric utilities performed like the Dow Industrials: down almost 90%. A company would have to be entirely unleveraged, and also lucky and well managed, to survive this. But many companies did. Market researcher Michael Painchaud identified stocks that were not just survivors but winners (they rose in price) over the brutal 1929-1931 period.[11] There was one electric utility common stock (American Electric Power), three utility preferreds, and a host

---

Business History Center (website, January 14), https://americanbusinesshistory.org/from-hero-to-hated-americas- most-tragic-entrepreneur/

[11] https://www.cnbc.com/id/27404980

of familiar industrial names, many of which survive today. But Insull's conglomerate did not survive.

Bernstein recounts:

> In April 1932, just three months before the...market... bottomed, his bankers summoned him to a New York office and informed him that they would not support him further. "Does this mean receivership?" he asked. "Yes, Mr. Insull, I'm afraid it does." The damage to the investing public was immense...by 1946...amount[ing] to $638 million. By that year, the stock market had largely recovered.

Furious investors, opportunistic politicians, and the media ganged up on Insull, who was indicted on dubious charges of fraud and embezzlement. He and his wife quietly fled to Paris. "ALL EUROPE HUNTING INSULL," screamed the *Chicago Daily Tribune*. He was extradited to America and placed on trial. Ten days before his 75th birthday, Insull was acquitted. He stood trial two more times on other charges and, again, was acquitted. He died in Paris four years later.

Hoover concludes:

> Investors who held onto their Insull securities generally turned out okay.... [W]hen the Depression finally ended and stocks rebounded, the total losses on all Insull securities were about 24 percent of the amount invested. None of the companies went bankrupt. The strongest company, Commonwealth Edison, never missed a dividend. Today the company has morphed into Exelon, America's largest electric company...[with] revenues exceeding $30 billion per year.

Hoover's comments about Insull's sad end are well worth repeating:

> Sam's wealth had fallen from a peak of $150 million to a mere $10,000.
>
> On July 16, 1938, seventy-eight-year-old Samuel Insull died of a heart attack while awaiting a train in a Paris Metro (subway) station. Since he had no wallet and no money, the newspapers declared that he had died a pauper. Yet everyone who knew Sam knew he went nowhere without his wallet, usually with

perhaps $1,000 in cash in it. So Sam's body had been robbed. Biographer Forrest McDonald closes his story with the line, "And so, in his death, as in his life, Samuel Insull was robbed, and nobody got the story straight."

The Lord gave, and the Lord hath taken away. –Job 1:21

Insull left behind Chicago's beautiful Civic Opera Building, large donations to African American charities, parts of Chicago's elevated and electric interurban railways, and a company (Commonwealth Edison) that was one of the first to provide the package of employee benefits now standard. This in addition to the electric infrastructure that was his main business. The moral lesson: Even a company that improves society in profound ways, run by a brilliant businessman and generous philanthropist, can ruin some investors if its financial structure, the liability side, is no good. As with most financial disasters, the culprit was leverage. The same tale would be told, with different characters, countless times over the subsequent century.

The other moral lesson: Life isn't fair.

Some concerns about the message of the book

Bernstein provides entertainment, education, and erudition. Who else could name-drop Abraham, Jesus, the monk Joachim of Fiore (1135-1202), the mathematician Eric Temple Bell, Pythagoras, Francis Bacon, and science writer Michael Shermer in one page (page 38)?

But Bernstein should not equate all religious feeling with its worst examples. If one judges Jews by the most shocking parts of Deuteronomy (many too distasteful to mention here), or Muslims by the political/military rather than the spiritual definition of jihad, the results are not pretty. One should avoid judging any large group by the actions of a tiny number of fanatics, past or present. That is not how Jews and Muslims conduct themselves.

Bernstein versus the dispensationalists...and Ronald Reagan

Yet Bernstein holds a view of "dispensational" Protestant Christians that resembles what we might think of Jews and Muslims who take the weird exhortations in their ancient texts literally and act on them. (A dispensational Christian believes that history and the future are divided into about seven distinct periods, the last one being a 1,000-year reign of Christ on Earth — the Millennium — as promised in the Book of Revelation. This reign will end in "God's final judgment" and the end of earthly existence. According to this belief system, we are now in the period just before the Millennium, which is supposed to end with a "great tribulation," or time of trouble, before the reign of Christ begins.)

Obviously, we'd want to keep a close watch on political and religious leaders who believe this literally, because we have the technological power to end the world as we know it, and someone might want to hurry the process along.

In this vein, Bernstein tars Ronald Reagan with the dispensationalist brush. There is some evidence that Reagan held those views with varying degrees of seriousness over his lifetime, including when he was president. But the Reagan I remember was a tolerant man and responsible president, owing much more philosophically to William F. Buckley than to any religious figure. While the most extreme of Reagan's religious beliefs may have spooked secular observers, Reagan the president governed without a hint of them influencing his decisions. He was a very conventional secular conservative.

In a lengthy and detailed study of Reagan's religious convictions and their influence on his policies, James Green, a British history student and now a barrister, writes:[12]

---

[12] Green, James. 2009. "Reagan, Armageddon, and the 1984 Presidential Debate: On the Overlap of Political and Apocalyptic Discourses in America." University of Bristol, Department of Historical Studies, http://www.bristol.ac.uk/history/media/docs/ug-dissertations/2009green.pdf

> Reagan's rhetoric [has] been labelled "cold war fundamentalism," comprising an emotional patriotism and portrayal of the conflict in absolute terms. [This] yielded apocalyptic language, and parallels to dispensationalist discourse about foreign policy. However, the symbolic language he deployed did not...define his political behaviour; neither direct military conflict nor a nuclear apocalypse ever came...Indeed, his policies were...more nuanced...than his rousing speeches...; although Reagan did pursue a military build-up in his first term, he later...cultivate[d] more amiable relations with Russia than had existed for decades, including steps towards nuclear disarmament.

Reagan later sought nuclear disarmament of the whole world. I wish he had succeeded.

Bernstein's attack on Reagan weakens his brief against religion. Many people are religious. Most of them are utterly harmless and do good things. Reagan kept his beliefs a private matter, and cooperated effectively with people whose religious views were fundamentally different than his own.

The Red Calf

The Delusions of Crowds is worth the purchase price if only for the chapter title Apocalypse Cow. It refers to a holy cow (sorry, couldn't resist) that was born with an unusual red coloration in Israel in 2018. Some ancient Jews errantly worshiped a golden calf; a few modern ones, plus some Christians, briefly believed that a red one signaled the fulfillment of a Biblical prophecy of the end of days. As always, the end came and went without incident.

Still, the episode forced the question: Are we as gullible as we were 3,500 years ago? I don't think so; red cow disease appears to infect only a tiny minority of human beings, and is far less dangerous than the real mad cow disease.

Concluding thoughts on religion

The beliefs of evangelical Christians sound wildly fanciful and dangerous when rendered literally, but so do the beliefs of all religions, including my own (Judaism). The story of Abraham and Isaac, the cornerstone of three major world religions representing 55% of the world's population, is one of the most distasteful in all of literature. Polytheistic religions are no less fanciful, and more fun to read about — their gods are some bad actors. Behind all this wildness is the necessity of leaders, in trying to bind their people to a religion, to make extreme demands of their followers. That is the only way they can divert the people from going about their business, ignoring religious leaders' commands to do good or evil.[13]

And, as all religions start out extreme, they all become more moderate as they adjust to the realities of living in this world — Judaism in the sixth century A.D. and Christianity gradually in the centuries leading up to the Enlightenment. Islam began to modernize in the nineteenth century, then reversed in the last 50 years. When the Muslim reformation takes place, we'll say we saw it coming all along.

Contra Bernstein, then, religion is a two-sided coin, inducing good and harm that must be weighed against each other.

Advice for investors

Bernstein writes so skillfully and vividly that he can convince readers of almost anything. I believe that religious nuttiness and financial foolishness are separate phenomena, linked by the fact that human nature is inherently flawed but otherwise quite dissimilar. Neither problem is about to disappear even as we learn more about our psyches.

---

[13] www.bbc.com/future/article/20190418-how-and-why-did-religion-evolve.

But financial recklessness is easier for an investor or advisor to avoid than religious folly. If you don't understand or don't like the valuation, leverage, or underlying business of a security or fund, don't buy it.

Technology

The era of modern technology started in the eighteenth century with steam engines and other hallmarks of the Industrial Revolution, but took off with astounding breadth and speed in the last thirty years. We still can't fully appreciate how new ways of thinking, new sciences, and new inventions will change our world.

Wayne's Favorite: Mark Mills on the Cloud, the Robot Revolution, and Machines That Think. (Do not confuse this author, the tech guru Mark P. Mills, with Mark Mills, the prolific fiction writer.)

—W.H.W.

Chapter 11. Henry Kissinger on the Promise and Threats of AI

Laurence B. Siegel
November 2023

At this horrible moment in history, it's reassuring to find out that serious thinkers have long been reflecting about national and global security and the way that AI interacts, or might interact in the future, with military and strategic matters. Thus, *The Age of AI (And Our Human Future)*, by Henry Kissinger, Eric Schmidt, and Daniel Huttenlocher, is keenly relevant even though the book is two years old, an eternity in AI-space.

Henry Kissinger
Source: https://commons.wikimedia
.org/wiki/File:Henry_Kissinger_13877.jpg

However, the book is not a great read. It's wordy, repetitive, and jargon-filled. I struggle to recommend reading the whole thing. But, in light of our current onslaught of challenges, Chapter 5, "Security and World Order" (pages 135-176), is worthwhile. I begin my review with some comments on that chapter and then move on to the economics of AI and related topics.

About the Authors

It's a surprise to find that Henry Kissinger has written a book at all — he's 100 years old. It's even more surprising to find that the book is about artificial intelligence, a recent outgrowth of the computer industry, which in turn is younger than Kissinger himself. He was a grown man of 22 when

ENIAC, the first general-purpose, programmable electronic computer, creaked to life at the University of Pennsylvania.[1]

Eric Schmidt, the second author of *The Age of AI*, is the former CEO of Google. It was not a surprise to see his name on the cover, along with that of Daniel Huttenlocher, who is the first, and so far only, dean of the Schwarzman College of Computing at the Massachusetts Institute of Technology.

Much of *The Age of AI* reads like a primer on the topic, addressing questions that all of us have thought about recently. These top-level questions include:

- Is AI really *intelligence*? Or is it a simulacrum of intelligence, a very clever computer program designed, built, and controlled by humans?
- How will we benefit from AI?
- Is AI dangerous?
- What are the consequences of AI for national security?

The authors also try to answer more profound, but perhaps unanswerable, questions such as,

"When AI participates in assessing and shaping human action...what, then, will it mean to be human?" They offer some beautiful words on the topic:

> Human identity may continue to rest on the pinnacle of animate intelligence, but human reason will cease to describe the full sweep of the intelligence that works to comprehend reality...[O]ur emphasis may need to shift from the centrality of human reason to the centrality of human dignity and autonomy...

But that, to me, is a way of saying "we don't know."

---

[1] Kissinger immigrated to New York with a group of young people all about the same age, fleeing the Nazis with their parents, in 1938 when he was 15. They all attended the same New York public high school. Most of them became distinguished in one field or another. But I've heard secondhand that only Kissinger retained his thick Central European accent — the others spoke unaccented English later in life. The person who told me this thinks that Kissinger's accent is partly a put-on, designed to make him sound even smarter than the smart youths he immigrated with. (At that time, German was the language of science and academia.)

The Age of AI is silent on many of the issues that investors care about: What are the consequences of AI for the economy? Will it set off an economic boom, like those in the past that were fueled by the discovery of a new resource? Will it put a large number of people out of work? How should investors respond? Although *The Age of AI* does not have an economic slant, I'll address these issues from my own point of view.

Finally, a question that has popped up recently is: Will AI cause human extinction? No, it won't. I'll get back to that, in a suitably mocking tone, after discussing defense and the economy.

Eric Schmidt
Source: https://commons.wikimedia
.org/wiki/Category:Eric_E._Schmidt#/media/F
ile:Eric_E_Schmidt,_2005_(looking_left).jpg

Artificial intelligence, war, and the avoidance of war

What's the worst-case scenario? Probably not the silly, but widely circulated, fantasy of an AI that is instructed to make as many paper clips as possible and turns every atom in the universe, including us, into paper clips. No, the ability of AI to start a nuclear war — whether by following an evildoer's instructions or just by blundering — is probably AI's greatest danger. It is the one that Kissinger, Schmidt, and Huttenlocher (henceforth KSH) focus on, so I will too.

Blundering into a nuclear war?

Here's a catastrophic scenario that many of us have thought about: An AI-governed missile system is programmed to launch nuclear weapons at an enemy only in the face of overwhelming evidence that the enemy has already begun a nuclear attack. The AI "believes" it has that evidence. But the AI is wrong. There's no attack. The AI counterattacks anyway.

A global thermonuclear war results.

AI is often wrong, as you know from your infuriating experiences with Siri or Alexa. The stakes are low — you try to drive to an address that doesn't exist, or order chow mein when you meant to order chow fun. But an AI missile system is obviously high-stakes. If you're thinking "they would build that system with much more accuracy and many more safeguards," you're right — they would.

Daniel Huttenlocher
Source: https://computing.mit.edu/daniel-huttenlocher/

But our missile detection systems were always built with the intention of being fail-safe. That did not make them fail-safe. They have mistaken a Norwegian spacecraft launch, a harmless Soviet weapons test, and the moon rising over the horizon — *the moon!* — for nuclear attacks. Only human intervention stopped these mistakes from turning into catastrophes. The closest call was on September 26, 1983, when a mid-level Soviet military man, Stanislav Petrov, found that his missile detection system was reporting a U.S. nuclear attack in progress. *Sensing* that there was something wrong with the information, that the U.S. "attack" wasn't real, Petrov disobeyed orders to retaliate and is widely credited with having saved the world.

AI doesn't have feelings or hunches or doubts — and it doesn't have a conscience. It can act too quickly for human intervention, and is motivated to do so because any hesitation could result in an AI-directed counterattack that is also too fast for human intervention.

Also, Stanislav Petrov should have won the Nobel Peace Prize. What do KSH have to say about this?

> The range of activities an AI is capable of undertaking...may need to be adjusted so that a human retains the ability to monitor and turn off or redirect a system that has begun to stray...[and] such restraints must be reciprocal...Major powers should pursue their competition within a framework of verifiable limits.

This is fairly weak tea. International agreements, mutual inspections, and willingness to share some secrets make up the peacekeeping framework that Henry Kissinger had a role in building. It worked when only the U.S. and the Soviet Union had nuclear capabilities. *Doveryai no proveryai* — trust but verify.

Those were Cold War safeguards. Today, rogue states and non-state actors could conceivably build a nuclear weapon. If you consider North Korea to be a rogue state, one already has. Russia is on the edge of being a rogue state. And AI is much easier to develop than a nuclear weapon. Here's a grim thought: if an AI in a non-nuclear country, acting under someone's instructions, *fools* enough people into thinking the country has nuclear capabilities, we could wind up in a "hot" war.

Using AI to do good

These risks are real, and KSH describe them vividly. But the benign case for AI is even more powerful. We've had some sort of AI for generations; we call it "automation," and it has helped consumers and boosted the efficiency of the economy immensely. Your car's automatic transmission, which shifts gears at exactly the right moment, relies on hydraulic logic circuits, a form of AI that has been around for 90 years and doesn't even use electricity. Industrial robots have been working in factories since the 1960s. They used to be fairly stupid, requiring human instruction for every little task; now they "figure out" what needs to be done and how to do it. But they were using AI the whole time. AI is a tool, and any tool can be used for good or ill.

The authors' best example of using AI to do good is the discovery of a new antibiotic. The drug researchers "developed a 'training set'," KSH write, "of two thousand known molecules," teaching the AI about the chemical properties and ability to inhibit bacterial growth of each.

From this training set, the authors note, "the AI...identified attributes that had not...been encoded [and]...that had eluded human conceptualization..." They continue:

> When it was done training, the researchers instructed the AI to survey a library of 61,000 molecules...that (1) the AI predicted would be effective as antibiotics, (2) did not look like any existing antibiotics, and (3) the AI predicted would be

nontoxic. Of the 61,000, one molecule fit the criteria. The researchers named it halicin — a nod to the AI "HAL" in the film *2001: A Space Odyssey*.

Halicin works against three previously drug-resistant strains of bacteria. While humans could probably have teased out this result eventually, the opportunity cost of the effort involved would have impeded research on other needed drugs. AI performed the work cheaply and well.

Turn it off?

If AI behaves badly, turn it off! That's what KSH suggested when discussing military applications, and it makes intuitive sense. What's wrong with this idea?

Nothing, in principle. It's exactly what you should do. But turning off a decentralized and intentionally redundant computer system is not easy. You can't turn the internet off. That is why DARPA, the U.S. Defense Advanced Research Projects Agency, created the internet in the first place — to make sure that if one part of their global communications system failed, the rest of it would keep humming. So disabling an out-of-control AI that has the nuclear football might be harder than it sounds.

The Economic Promise Of AI

Enough of this doom and gloom talk. Let's look at the upside.

Almost every economist, financial analyst, and business strategist who has written about AI in the recent past believes AI will increase productivity and thus GDP. Discovery of a new resource or general-purpose technology (AI is both) has always made work easier, workers more productive, and goods and services cheaper in real terms.[2]

---

[2] "Real" conventionally means "adjusted for inflation," but it can also mean that a quantity is expressed in terms of the number of hours of work needed to produce it. The number of hours can be, but need not be, difficulty-adjusted. See Baily, Brynjolfsson, and Korinek (2023) https://www.brookings.edu/articles/machines-of-mind-the-case-for-an-ai-powered-productivity-boom/

How much more productive? An April 5, 2023 Goldman Sachs report[3] says that generative AI could increase global GDP by 7%, or about $7 trillion. If that's a one-time pop, which their report seems to imply, that is only two or three years' global growth: the global GDP we'd expect in 2100 without AI will arrive in 2097. That would be a disappointment for such a large and potentially risky change in technology.

An increase in the slope or rate of global GDP growth, at least for some years, would be a much better outcome and seems more likely given the history of other general-purpose technologies such as electricity, air travel, and the internet.[4] The productivity gains from these innovations didn't happen for a while, and the commercialization of AI will follow the same trajectory.

McKinsey & Company corroborates Goldman's estimate of a $7 trillion addition to global GDP but says that their number is for the impact of *generative* AI alone,[5] while *at the same time* forecasting a change in the slope of growth:

> Generative AI could enable [additional] labor productivity growth of 0.1 to 0.6 percent annually through 2040... Combining generative AI with all other [automation-related] technologies, work automation could add 0.2 to 3.3 percentage points annually to productivity growth.[6]

To sum up, McKinsey adds the impact of generative and non-generative AI to arrive at an overall "total AI economic potential" of $17.1 trillion to $25.6 trillion, one-sixth to one-fourth of global GDP.[7] This is equivalent to adding *another United States* to the world economy.

---

[3] https://www.goldmansachs.com/intelligence/pages/generative-ai-could-raise-global-gdp-by-7-percent.html

[4] In the same publication, Goldman also projects a 1.5% per year boost to productivity over the next decade, a forecast inconsistent with the forecast of a 7% increase in global GDP. A 1.5% annual increase compounds to 16%, not 7%.

[5] They give a range, $6.1 trillion to $7.9 trillion.

[6] https://www.mckinsey.com/capabilities/mckinsey-digital/our-insights/the-economic-potential-of-generative-ai-the-next-productivity-frontier

[7] The "total potential" is expressed in dollars of productivity as an annual rate and is incremental to (added to) the productivity that would occur without the AI.

AI and unemployment

This increased productivity means that fewer workers are needed to produce the same output. But we do not use the greater efficiency to produce the *same* output! We produce more, or better, or just different goods and services. If you told a 1950s machine operator, who would eventually be replaced by a computer, that his grandchildren would find employment as computer-aided design engineers, social media marketers, and artificial intelligence researchers, he would have thought you were crazy. But that is what happened. Each technological advance of the last 250 years caused some sort of panic about unemployment at the time, yet the number of people working has grown each time.

If, over the very long term, increased automation really took away jobs on net, the unemployment rate would be sky-high and increasing. It isn't. Exhibit 1 shows that while the U.S. population grew from 63 million in 1890 (the first year for which reliable unemployment data exist) to 334 million today, the unemployment rate fell to roughly 4% in every business boom during that long period. Every single time. I call this number the Magic 4%. Obviously, a massive number of jobs were created as we experienced one "job-destroying" technological revolution after another.

Exhibit 1

Source: Siegel, Laurence B. 2019. *Fewer, Richer, Greener*. Chart based on data sourced and organized by Wikipedia user Peace01234. 1930–2009 data are from Bureau of Labor Statistics, employment status of the civilian noninstitutional population, 1940 to date. 1890–1920 data are from Romer (1986). 1920–1930 data are from Coen (1973).

Labor force participation

But hasn't the labor force participation rate fallen, making the Magic 4% more of a statistical artifact than a fundamental economic truth?

You bet it has. Your forebears, if you go back far enough and are not descended from royalty, worked from sunup to sundown at backbreaking work that barely yielded enough food for those doing it. Children worked about as hard as adults. The labor participation rate was, in round numbers, 100%.

From that inauspicious start, the only possible direction for the labor participation rate to go was down. This represented tremendous progress and is part of what has made modern life bearable or enjoyable. There is more to life than work, work, work — and one of the main reasons for developing any technology, including AI, is to make work easier and leisure more available.

But this does not mean that AI lacks an economic downside. It will put some people out of work who cannot realistically be retrained. The amount of labor market churn due to AI could be very large. According to Ethan Ilzetzki and Suryaansh Jain, writing for VoxEU,[8]

> The World Economic Forum concluded in October 2020 that while AI would likely take away 85 million jobs globally by 2025, it would also generate 97 million new jobs in fields ranging from big data and machine learning to information security and digital marketing.[9]

This outcome may cause social unrest. It will almost certainly fail to improve the lives of the hard-core unemployed. And it may stimulate political demands for more social benefits or a basic income guarantee, further burdening taxpayers including those not yet born.

Implications for investors

Investors are mostly concerned with corporate profits, not economic productivity *per se*. But, while workers and consumers will and should get part of this new bounty, shareholders are in a position to benefit handsomely. In this sense, the emergence of AI as a new resource or general-purpose technology is strongly bullish. Global equities offer the best medium for taking advantage of this opportunity.

The improvement in efficiency will not arrive all at once, and there will be losses to some companies while others gain. I would not buy "AI stocks" as currently understood. They've already soared. And the stocks that will benefit the most in the long run may be very different from the current holdings of AI-oriented funds. Recall the great internet bubble that peaked in 2000. Amazon and Google were "buys" even at those elevated prices if you could manage to hold them through the subsequent bumpy ride, but many of the other bubble stocks are now worthless or nearly so. Meanwhile, quite a few companies formed after the bubble have thrived. At any rate, the benefits of AI may accrue more to companies that use AI effectively — which could be in any industry — than to those that produce the AI technology.

---

[8] https://cepr.org/voxeu/columns/impact-artificial-intelligence-growth-and-employment

[9] Note that, while these sound like big numbers, each represents just over 1% of the world's population.

While the upsides of AI may be primarily economic, its potential downsides are not. They are social, cultural, military, psychological, and some would say existential.

Will AI cause human extinction?

Thankfully *The Age of AI* does not touch on the current craze for saying that AI will cause the human species to go extinct. It won't. There are 8 billion of us and world population hits a new high every day. A species which does that is not a good candidate for extinction anytime soon. We are also good at defending ourselves from existential threats, as we can see just by looking at those population numbers. Human extinction caused by AI is about as likely as human extinction caused by climate change — the likelihood rounds to zero. Both AI and climate change are real risks. But killing everyone in the world — that's what "extinction" means — is incredibly hard to do. About 70,000 years ago the world's human population contracted to the point where we can see the residue of the "bottleneck" in the genes of people living today. We don't know what caused the mass dying — an asteroid impact (geologists say there wasn't one), climate change (climatologists assure us that the ice ages were survivable through migration), or maybe a disease. But we're here, so we know that humans survived some sort of terrible catastrophe.

Today, we have an array of tools that our 70,000-year-ago ancestors didn't have: weather satellites, ships, airplanes, instant global communication, antibiotics, and lots and lots of money. We can even nudge a small asteroid out of its path so it doesn't strike Earth. (A large one would be a problem.)

Other than nuclear war, the biggest risk is probably some sort of AI-engineered bioweapon. But nature engineers those all the time and, despite tragic losses of life, we find ways to fight back and survive. Moreover, we have already developed horrifically destructive bioweapons; luckily they have not been used. AI-generated ones are unlikely to be worse.

So extinction is the least of my worries.

Beware of hyperbole!

Almost everyone who writes about AI falls into the trap of overstatement. I thought that the serious-minded KSH team might not, and much of the book is not overstated, but they offer this proposition:

> Only rarely...has technology transformed the fundamental political and social structure of our societies...The car replaced the horse without forcing a fundamental shift in our social structure. The rifle replaced the musket, but the general paradigm of conventional military activity remained largely unaltered...But AI promises to *transform all realms of human experience*.[10]

In a tweet, Yann LeCun, an NYU professor and chief AI scientist at Facebook, fired back:[11]

> More than stone tools? Fire? Agriculture? Metal technology? Writing? Mathematics? Gunpowder? Printing press? Steam engines? Aviation? Computers?
>
> Not mentioning religion? Feudalism? Theocracy? Rationalism? Capitalism? Communism? Fascism? Liberal democracy?

LeCun has injected a dose of sobriety into this fanciful discussion. Thank you, Professor.

Conclusion

AI is a tool, invented by humans to make various tasks easier. While it will have formidable power, we should not cower before it in the illusion that it is something greater than us that we cannot restrain. The great line in the 1931 movie *Frankenstein*, "You have created a monster and it will

---

[10] Italics added.

[11] 9:32 a.m., May 13, 2023 on X (the website formerly known as Twitter). LeCun posts as @ylecun.

destroy you," remains a fixture in our minds 92 years later and 205 years after Mary Shelley wrote the novel on which it was based.[12]

Why? Because the idea that we've created something beyond our control is a recurring fear throughout history. The fear has usually — not always — turned out to be unfounded. We can reassure ourselves that, as Mark Mills said to me, AI is just "really good automation." But, like nuclear technology, AI can be used by bad people to do bad things — or by careless people who do bad things without intending to. We had best be prudent.

---

[12] Spoken by "Dr. Waldman," played by Edward Van Sloan affecting a heavy Central European accent. Contrary to what some people remember, Frankenstein is not the monster, but the doctor who created him.

Chapter 12. Cloudy with a Chance of Technological Breakthrough

Laurence B. Siegel
April 4, 2022
Updated December 2023

"I thought you said the cloud was secure."

Will the cloud drive massive increases in productivity and wealth — as the internet did before it? That is the central question asked by Mark Mills in his stunning new book, *The Cloud Revolution.*

Little changes sometimes morph into very big ones by stealth: you don't see the big change coming until it has enveloped you. This is how ARPANET, an obscure Defense Department project started in 1966, came to infiltrate every aspect of civilized life as it expanded into the global wireless internet.

More often, little changes fizzle out or have a gradual, evolutionary influence. Which path will the emergence of the cloud, the latest "new new thing" in information technology, take?

Mark P. Mills
Source: http://theamericanenergynews.com/shale-oil-big-data-analytics-26feb16/

In *The Cloud Revolution*, the physicist and venture capitalist Mark Mills says that the cloud is "as different from the Internet as the [Internet] was different from telephony." He argues that it has already started to spark an economic boom that will transform life more profoundly than the internet did. If he's right, the implications for investors are remarkable: a continuation of the long bull market and spectacular returns for the most directly affected companies. If his forecasts are exaggerated, investors need to be more careful.

What's the Cloud?

Before exploring the merits and demerits of the cloud, it behooves us to ask: What is it?

The internet, parent of the cloud, was famously described as "everybody's computers, connected";[1] actually, it's that plus the infrastructure that

---

[1] http://www.uky.edu/~sdbaker/tel101/w5net.ppt

allows them to be connected. There's a physical Internet "backbone," but the distinctive part of the infrastructure is a set of standards or protocols, such as TCP/IP, that make it possible for these computers to "understand" each other's "languages." The Internet fell together almost by accident, and it's a remarkable piece of collective engineering.[2]

Unlike the internet, which is the combination of all these physical and ethereal parts, Mills writes, "The cloud is not an ethereal thing; it's a physical infrastructure. By all measures — dollars, physical equipment, square feet of buildings – it's the biggest infrastructure humanity has ever built."[3] A piece of this infrastructure, located in Las Vegas, is shown in Exhibit 1.

Exhibit 1 — Switch Inc. data center in Las Vegas

Source: https://www.switch.com/photos

---

[2] This is not to say that the Internet evolved without intelligent design. Tim Berners-Lee *invented* the Web browser, Alan Emtage the search engine. These are individual accomplishments. ARPA at the Department of Defense developed elements of the Internet, including TCP/IP and packet switching, without which the whole thing would have failed. But there was no central authority saying, "We need to connect everybody's computers — let's figure out the needed steps and assign each of them to somebody" as one would if building a car. In that sense, the Internet fell together — it is an accident of history.

[3] Not from the book, but from a blog post by James Pethokoukis and Mark Mills on the American Enterprise Institute web site at https://www.aei.org/economics/5-questions-for-mark-mills-on-the-cloud-revolution/.

Mills continues,

> One square meter of a typical cloud data center has about a thousand times more comput[ing] horsepower than the whole world had in the early '80s, and we're building out data centers at ... the rate of about 10 million square feet a year. And data centers, interestingly, cost about the same to build [in dollars per square foot] as a skyscraper like the Empire State Building or the World Trade Center.[4]

In other words, the cloud is very un-cloudlike in the ordinary sense of the world; it's a *thing*. It is not the internet. It interfaces with and acts as part of the internet. It consists of data centers like the one shown above, in every part of the world, along with wired and wireless means of transmitting data from users to these centers and back again. The cloud is an energy and materials hog on a mammoth scale. Mills predicts that it will be the largest infrastructure project ever.

Obviously, an infrastructure investment on this scale has profound implications for investors. On the construction side, trillions of dollars will flow to the energy and materials sectors. (Cumulative costs have already passed $1 trillion.[5]) On the usage side, the cloud's proponents argue that radically more abundant, faster, and cheaper information will have beneficial effects on almost everything. I'm not entirely sure, but it's possible.

Recentralization

In the last generation, we've been sold hard on the virtues of decentralization. The internet is decentralized and has benefited us beyond measure. DeFi, decentralized finance, an emerging blockchain-based set of technologies for storing, verifying, and transacting financial and real assets, has promise – and problems.

---

[4] Also from the Pethokoukis and Mills blog post.

[5] https://a16z.com/2021/05/27/cost-of-cloud-paradox-market-cap-cloud-lifecycle-scale-growth-repatriation-optimization/

Partly Cloudy with a Chance of Technological Breakthrough

As with any new technology, some of the claims regarding "decentralized everything" are exaggerated. Some things are done better when decentralized (love and marriage); some are done better when centralized (clearing of financial transactions). Bitcoin is the ultimate decentralized "currency"; *TIME* Magazine warns us that "because there is no centralized authority that manages Bitcoin, transactions cannot be reversed and mistakes cannot be rectified."[6] When my bank screws up, I talk to the manager, someone with the authority to fix the problem. Central authority in some settings is very valuable.

The cloud swims against the tide of history – it's *centralized*. Unlike the traditional Internet, the cloud needs only one copy of every piece of software. It needs only one copy of every piece of data. In fact, the cloud started out as a way to provide "software as a service" (meaning: software for which you have to pay a recurring subscription fee, because you don't own it). To that, the cloud adds remote data storage as a service, so you don't have to buy, maintain, and keep track of storage devices.[7]

These centralized attributes cause *everybody's computer to be exactly the same*. OK, "exactly" is an exaggeration because keyboard layouts and screen specifications differ, as well as some other details. But, as long as you can identify yourself to the cloud, you can use your data, as well as the software to which you're entitled, on any computer. You don't need to own a device at all! The one at the public library is fine. We may be headed toward "hardware as a service."

So much for decentralization being the only trend we need to follow.

---

[6] Prasad, Eswar. 2021. "The Future of Crypto Is Bright, But Governments Must Help Manage the Risks." TIME.com, Posted October 22, 2021 at https://time.com/6108232/bitcoin-cryptocurrency-future-blockchain-regulation/.

[7] Initially I was furious that I had to pay a recurring fee for something that I could have owned for cheap. But, as with most price increases, I am getting used to it. And cloud storage has saved my hide when I've lost files or destroyed a hard drive.

Rematerialization

Mills is in part a materials scientist, and he devotes three chapters to materials, a much-neglected component of technological change. He writes,

> ... [A] popular notion has it that society is "dematerializing" ... The proposition is that, as economies become increasingly service-dominated, accelerated by the Amazonification and Uberization of everything, "the need for resource-intensive manufacturing is not inevitable." Materials and materials-centric industries are, in this worldview, passé.

The quote-within-a-quote is from Andrew McAfee's *More from Less*, the gospel of dematerialization, which I reviewed in favorable terms in Chapter 3 of this book. My 2019 book, *Fewer, Richer, Greener,* also has a chapter on dematerialization, drawing on McAfee's and others' work. I pointed out (in the book review, not the book) that a $1,000 smartphone has capabilities that, as best you could replicate them, would have required equipment costing $32,136,910 as recently as 1985. "Drop the $32 million Cray-2 supercomputer (which has the same processing power, 1.9 gigaflops, as a good smartphone) and it's $136,910," I wrote.

In the time since I started writing *Fewer, Richer, Greener*, the Apple A17 Bionic chip, which powers the iPhone 15 Pro, has been released and can do 3,425 gigaflops. That's an 1800-fold improvement in about seven years.

Dematerialization is thus the main trend, and it is not going away. But let's give Mills' rematerialization hypothesis a fair hearing. It has merit and, while his narrative below digresses from the cloud a bit, it's fun to read about the progress in a field, materials science, that few of us know anything about:

> A century ago, cars were manufactured only using a handful of materials: wood, rubber, glass, iron, copper, vanadium, and zinc ... Today a car ... is built from more than three dozen different nonfuel minerals, including increasingly a mélange of the 17 so-called "rare earth" elements. Similarly, while a cellphone circa 1980 contained a couple of dozen elements from the periodic table, today's smartphones exploit the properties of over 70 different types of atoms ...

Mills then lists (and describes, but I'll leave out the descriptions) some new kinds of materials:

> Electronic textiles...biocompatible materials...transient electronics...adaptive materials...self-healing materials...programmable materials...self-assembling materials.

Then there are biomimetic (life-imitating) materials, such as artificial skin. With materials science leaping ahead in these ways, we should not expect just dematerialization, which dominates the popular-economics headlines, but also some rematerialization. Nor are most of these advances going to save on energy: finding, mining, processing, and using these exotic materials are all energy-intensive activities.

Finally, Mills reminds us, the cloud itself is *extremely* energy-intensive: "The pattern-learning phase for a single artificial intelligence application can consume more compute energy than 10,000 cars do in a day."[8] Wow. Maybe we ought to weigh the costs and the benefits of cloud-based AI applications more carefully.

And, according to Mills, the cloud is so productivity-enhancing that it is subject to a Jevons problem. William Stanley Jevons, a nineteenth-century British economist, found that the cheaper coal became, the more total spending on coal (P x Q, the price times the quantity of coal purchased) grew instead of shrinking as one might guess from the lowering of price. The reason was that the low prices spurred new uses for coal, and caused coal to displace competing energy sources, so that Q grew faster than P shrank. Mills believes that the cloud's energy use will increase substantially, despite energy becoming cheaper as renewable and nuclear power sources come onstream. If he's right, we should invest in energy producers. But investing in advanced materials producers is more fun and might even be more profitable.

---

[8] https://www.manhattan-institute.org/our-love-of-the-cloud-is-making-a-green-energy-future-impossible. In a 2020 article, a New York Times reporter, Steve Lohr, argues, contra Mills, that the cloud is making previously very energy-intensive applications less costly in terms of energy: https://www.nytimes.com/2020/02/27/technology/cloud-computing-energy-usage.html.

How big is it?

Like the friends of the legendary fisherman who let the *really* big one get away, we want to know, "How...big...is...it?" How big is the cloud now? How big is it likely to get?

The most salient way in which the cloud differs from previous computing environments is data storage capacity, so let's answer the question in those terms. A decade ago, reporter Tuan Nguyen impressed even himself by noting that the total data storage capacity of the world was 295 exabytes, which is 295 billion billion bytes.[9] By 2025, with cloud build-out expected to be nowhere near complete, total cloud capacity (about half of the world's overall data storage capacity) is expected to be 100 zettabytes.[10] A zettabyte is a thousand exabytes.

A word has already been coined for 1,000 zettabytes — "yottabyte" — and, given the growth rate I just documented, it will be needed before the end of this decade. Linguists and wags are busy inventing words for new powers of 1,000: a hellabyte (a hell of a lot of bytes) or brontobyte stands for 1,000 yottabytes. (I'm not joking, although maybe the inventor of these words was. But you can bet they'll be used.) And 1,000 brontobytes, that is, 10^{30} bytes, is a geopbyte; I can't even pronounce it.[11]

What is the cloud for?

What good is all this data storage?

---

[9] https://www.zdnet.com/article/what-is-the-worlds-data-storage-capacity/

[10] https://www.cloudwards.net/cloud-computing-statistics/

[11] Wait, there's more. Mills writes, "Arrays of communications hardware propel bytes along 'highways' constituting not only roughly three billion miles of glass cables, much of it buried, but also the equivalent of another 100 billion miles (that's 1,000 times the distance to the sun) of invisible connections forged by 4 million cell towers." Billions and billions. I'd argue that all that stuff is the Internet and the mobile phone network, not the cloud, but the cloud would be pretty useless without it.

It was said about the Internet that no one initially knew what it was for; you just had to connect everyone's computers together and see what happens. We can say the same thing about the cloud.

Here are some examples of very large data storage requirements: photography, medicine, geolocation. We'll go through these very quickly.

Photography

There are more than five billion smartphone users, all wanting to save their photos and videos. Five billion phones, times 10 photos a day, times 365 days per year, times two megabytes per picture is 36 quintillion bytes (36 exabytes) of data recorded each year, plus all the forwards and downloads. Multiply by some modest number for videography instead of photography. Whether this usage is frivolous or purposeful, somebody is paying for it, and will pay more in the future (see my comment earlier about the Jevons problem); that's what investors should be focused on.

Medicine

But the benefit goes well beyond me being able to see billions of sumptuous meals, kittens, and vacationers posing in front of tourist sites. A doctor can look at a patient's MRI from her computer on another continent. It is conceivable that microrobots traveling through patients' blood vessels, in search of cancer cells to destroy or brain cells to repair, could take many more pictures or movies than 36 quintillion bytes' worth per year. Remote surgery requires not just a large but also a very fast data feed from the surgical site to the surgeon — and back. When something, in this case both storage and data transmission, becomes very cheap, it's hard to forecast the uses to which it will be put.

Geolocation

With cheap cloud data storage and fast transmission, my Uber driver can find my destination without having any idea where it is. GPS, which is mostly a cloud application, does the thinking for him. Eventually autonomous driving, admittedly a long way off for safety and liability reasons, will make the Uber driver look unimpressive. The data feed from the self-driving car to the cloud and back is so large, and the need for speedy communication so intense, that the *speed of light* is a constraining factor, causing the system to need subsidiary servers that are physically closer to the car than a central cloud data bank could ever be.

This all sounds like science fiction written by a high school student, but it's real or will be, and it adds up, significantly boosting productivity growth. If the 1.7% to 1.8% per year long-term growth rate of productivity, and thus global per-capita income, is going to continue far enough into the future to make us all "rich" by current standards, which is to say that everyone can become middle class, we will need innovations on this scale. That is the main takeaway from Mills' book, and I hope that in his enthusiasm he is not exaggerating too much.

Other cloud applications

I've already alluded to AI/ML, artificial intelligence and machine learning, as a use of the cloud. The amount of hype behind AI/ML is staggering. The internet of things (IoT), which uses billions of little "sensors" that collect data and communicate with each other while leaving us out of the loop until we need to be in it, is a cloud application too. And then there is the internet of bio-nano-things (IoBNT).[12] (Seriously.) That's a new name for what I described earlier, sensors or microrobots swimming around in my bloodstream looking for, and stopping, trouble.

Life is becoming a science fiction story.

The Roaring Twenties?

So far, this has been the decade from hell: a war lost in Afghanistan, another one raging in Ukraine as I write, a vicious attack on Israel, a deadly pandemic within recent memory. Fortunately, U.S. markets have held up well. But they are high-priced, and thus offer less future upside than they would at more typical valuations.

---

[12] Akyildiz, I. F., M. Pierobon, S. Balasubramaniam, and Y. Koucheryavy. 2015. "The Internet of Bio-Nanothings." IEEE Communications Magazine – Communications Standards Supplement (March), https://mbite.unl.edu/files/papers/2015/j1.pdf

Technology, however, has a way of progressing under the surface even when world events are chaotic. Technological advances during the Great Depression decade of the 1930s, including safe passenger aviation and efficient long-distance telephony, were some of the most rapid and profound in history. The 2020s will roar in this sense; in 2030 we'll look back on current technology as primitive, and the cloud will have played a role in that transformation.

But the book's subtitle — "How the Convergence of New Technologies Will Unleash the Next Economic Boom and A Roaring 2020s" — promises more economic insight than it delivers.

Mills is not an economist, although because he is a venture capitalist, you'd think he could phrase his forecasts in more explicitly economic terms. The book is, thus, almost entirely about technology. To give an economic flavor to his narrative, he uses the Kondratieff wave, the long-term (roughly 60-year) cycle that, according to its discoverer, reflects the amount of time it takes for a truly revolutionary technology to be born, grow to meaningful size, and reach maturity – after which the cycle starts anew with a different revolutionary technology.

This cycle, in Kondratieff's view, causes the economy to grow and stabilize in a roughly 60-year rhythm. While many economists believe that a longer cycle, corresponding to "industrial revolutions," better fits the data, the basic idea of economic cycles is sound. (Stalin didn't think so, and banished Kondratieff to Siberia for showing that progress isn't linear.)

But, if even half of the technological change that Mills forecasts comes to pass, the 2020s will be as disruptive, and potentially profitable, a decade as has ever occurred.

Reflections on *The Cloud Revolution* and productivity

Mills' wrote *The Cloud Revolution* to set forth the technological innovations that we can expect, in practically every field of endeavor, from cloud computing and its offshoots. My purpose in this review is to note that technological innovation leads to productivity growth, which is the only way to achieve increased per capita wealth and income. It is productivity growth that leads to profit growth, which in turn creates sustained investment returns.

But we are left with some unanswered questions:

- Will cloud computing decrease costs in the economy overall, and/or extend the reach of what the economy can accomplish, enough to advance macro productivity?
- Will it increase the network effect (the rise in the value of a technology caused by more people adopting it)?
- What are the known things that we cannot do today that we could do if the cloud's capabilities materialize as Mills forecasts — for example, 3D printing that is accurate and affordable enough to change the concept and practice of manufacturing? Effective and commonplace remote surgery?

The answers are implied in the book's many detailed stories, but Mills could have provided a concise summary, focusing on what are awkwardly called "takeaways." One could argue that the whole book is a takeaway, but such a response ducks the obligation to readers to provide something quotable to report to their friends, colleagues, and fellow readers.

We are also interested in the downside. "Digitalizing what we see and do," Mills's phrase, does not overcome the objection that there is not much truly new information, just a very large increase in the number of bits produced by digitizing it. All this data collection and storage has a cost in energy, materials, and human effort — are we sure that the cost does not exceed the benefit? "Where is the knowledge that we have lost in information?" asked T.S. Eliot more than a century ago.

Business does not always get things right. The new cable-technology companies at the turn of the century pursued the 99.999% (five 9s) reliability of the Bell System. But customers wanted mobility, streaming audio and video, and multiple functionality (the smartphone) and would have been happy with five-8s, 88.888% reliable, phone service — static and dropped calls. Replacing today's highly successful internet ecosystem with a cheaper cloud ecosystem might well bring little gain or an actual loss — the cloud-based Office 365 application suite is notoriously awkward and unreliable.

While Mills' book is weak on these tradeoffs and should treat them more explicitly, his erudite histories of work, machines, and energy are terrific, and they alone make the book an important read, especially in the context of the long-term improvement in productivity and progress that the cloud can generate.

Implications for investors

Whether or not Mills is right about the cloud being a vast leap beyond the internet, it's coming, and the energy, materials, and real estate needed to build it will be purchased. Buy the companies that are selling blue jeans to the gold miners: mining companies, advanced materials producers, and producers of the energy that the cloud will consume.[13] Maybe even the real estate on which cloud facilities will sit. Buying cloud service providers is too easy; everybody's doing it, and the prices are already high. (Switch, whose data center is shown on page 2, had a P/E of 133 in early 2022. The company has since been acquired by Digital Bridge.)

However, if the cloud is the energy and materials hog that it appears to be, and energy does not become radically cheaper (if you wait long enough it will, but few people have that long an investment horizon), then energy and materials costs will constrain the otherwise remarkable potential of this new industrial sector.

The global economy will get whatever efficiency benefits or cost savings that flow from use of the cloud, as with any other technological improvement. The latter — the extent to which the cloud revolution extends to the economy more generally — is the tricky part, hard to assess.

---

[13] I do not recommend specific companies in any of my work. Also, I am not a registered investment advisor or broker/dealer, nothing in this publication should be construed as investment advice, etc.

Conclusion

Mills is a man of many talents and accomplishments. His eclectic knowledge makes the book a satisfying read. It could have been 400 pages on circuits and switches, but Mills is far too intellectually curious to do that to us. He surrounds his paean to the cloud with very strong auxiliary material, including meditations on why technology matters, how technological revolutions unfold, and what could go wrong. Mills's ability to do this shows why the best books on a technical topic are written by a specialist who can double as a generalist.

This is a futuristic book. There is always a hint of P. T. Barnum in books that predict a technology-driven economic boom and productivity party. Mills keeps the Barnum-isms to a minimum and, much to his credit, comes close to saying that there's no such thing as a futurist: "We're all forecasters." All of us embed forecasts, explicit or implied, in everything we do.

The Cloud Revolution is a worthy and challenging read, and I highly recommend it.

The author wishes to thank Stephen Sexauer, CIO of the San Diego County Employees Retirement Association, for introducing me to the book and to Mark Mills, and for contributions to this article that are right at the cusp of co-authorship (which he graciously declined). The section on Reflections is his thinking, restated in my words. –W.H.W.

Chapter 13. Mark Mills on the Cloud, the Robot Revolution, and Machines That Think

Edited by Laurence B. Siegel[1]
April 2023

On February 25, 2023, I heard Mark Mills, a physicist, venture capitalist, and author of *The Cloud Revolution*, which I reviewed in this space on April 6, 2022, speak at a meeting of the Global Interdependence Center in La Jolla, California. This is a heavily edited transcript of his speech, not an original article by me. Without further ado...

Of Tabulators and Tractors

Mark Mills: Thank you, and thanks to the Global Interdependence Center.

The putative title of my talk is "The Technology of Money" because most of this conference so far has been about crypto, but I don't want to talk about the machines that facilitate finance — that facilitate transactions — that can trade wealth. Those machines are *tabulators*. I contrast these with *tractors*, which I'll get to in a moment.

---

[1] All exhibits are copyright © 2023 by Mark P. Mills, except for Exhibit 5 which was graphed by Laurence B. Siegel using FRED data, and Exhibit 6 which was constructed by Siegel and Stephen C. Sexauer. This article is not copyrighted. It is a heavily edited transcript of a speech by Mills and is protected under CC BY-NC-ND 4.0, which enables readers to redistribute it freely, with attribution, for noncommercial use. Incorporation in derivative works, beyond commonly understood "fair use," and including re-publication in other media, requires written permission of the authors.

In 1952, for the first time in human history, a machine tabulated an election result. Walter Cronkite hesitated to release the results because the machine predicted that Eisenhower would win. He thought all the experts were right that Adlai Stevenson would win. He was wrong, the machine was right.

The very first commercial computer was bought by Bank of America to process checks. Although it was ridiculously expensive, it could process 40,000 checks an hour while humans were doing it at 200 checks per hour. So, it's beyond obvious why they used a computer to facilitate the recording of transactions moving through their system.

Mark P. Mills
Source: City Journal

Cryptocurrencies are like that. They use a set of rules to process a transaction. Exhibit 1 is a graph of the total equity market cap, or value, of all cryptocurrencies combined from 2016 to date. The graph is about two weeks old and shows that total crypto market cap is around $1 trillion. A trillion dollars is a lot of money, but the world's a big place, and crypto represents only 0.05% of the stored value of all forms of financial assets in the world.

Exhibit 1 — "Tabulators" and "tractors" compared[2]

Machines that facilitate finance vs create wealth

Tabulators

Crypto capitalization ($ trillion)

Tractors

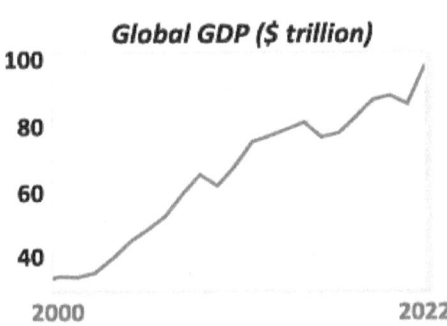
Global GDP ($ trillion)

What I want to talk to you about, what I'm far more interested in, is the class of machines that includes tractors. Those that *create* wealth. Tractors are a classic example of a tool for wealth creation compared to what they replaced.

So, the really interesting issue for me, which I wrote about in my book, *The Cloud Revolution*, is: what are the underlying technology trends that facilitate not just exchange but also wealth creation? The world produces $100 trillion worth of goods and services every year — that is, global GDP is $100 trillion, and it's been growing. Its growth does not look anything like the cryptocurrency bubble. It's slow and steady and confers over time huge gains in standards of living for so many.

So let me focus on machines that increase productivity, in effect the "tractors" of the future. Most people know, if they studied economics, that

---

[2] Capitalization is a stock and GDP is a flow, so they cannot be compared directly.

productivity growth is what drives So let me focus on machines that increase productivity, in effect the "tractors" of the future. Most people know, if they studied economics, that productivity growth is what drives economic growth. Robert Solow received the Nobel Prize for documenting that fact. By "technology" he didn't mean Bitcoin, or ultrafast computers, or spacecraft. He meant technology in the broad, correct sense of the word: inventions and innovations that help you do more with less. Technology is the primary driver of the wealth and the productivity of the world.

There are patterns to technology's progress. My book is really about these patterns, but because I have limited time, I will illustrate them with just four examples.

The benefits of technological change come slowly

The patterns of technological innovations are non-linear, and take longer than most imagine. After radical innovations or discoveries emerge they then, always, take a while to be perfected. Of course, when they're perfected, there's a tipping point, a take-off point where they start to get used a lot. This is obvious, but what's interesting is that the timing of the patterns is pretty consistent over the ages. Introduction in 1908 of the Ford Model T marked the beginning of the auto age in earnest, but that was over 20 years after the first car was invented.[3]

Aviation grew from a concept to a big business in steps as well. The first scheduled airline passenger service in the U.S., operated by Western Air Express, took off in 1926 — again, about 25 years after the Wright Brothers. It took another 25 years, plus a few, to enter the jet age, which made flying

---

[3] Karl Benz, in 1886, is usually credited as the foundational inventor, although France's Nicholas Joseph Cugnot built a steam-powered tractor in 1769. See "Who Invented the Automobile?" (undated), Library of Congress, https://www.loc.gov/everyday-mysteries/motor-vehicles-aeronautics-astronautics/item/who-invented-the- automobile/. It is widely believed that a century earlier, in the 1670s, Ferdinand Verbiest built a small prototype (too small for a driver and unable to be steered) of a self-propelled steam vehicle.

fast and convenient — the Boeing 707 was introduced in 1957, and the sky was the limit after that. Computers — it's the same thing. Commercial computer mainframes came on the market roughly 20 years after the first electronic computer, and it was another 25 years before what we think of as the computer age took off.

The era we're in now, the age of the cloud, is just now getting moving, 25 or 30 years after the first cloud data center, Santa Clara Exodus, was built in 1995. This rhythm seems to apply to robotics too, and most other foundational technologies.

So, there's a predictable and understandable lag between the development of a new technology and its widespread adoption and influence on the economy. Solow famously said in 1987, "You can see the computer age everywhere but in the productivity statistics." Twenty years later you *could* see it in the productivity statistics.

Higgledy piggledy growth[4]

So let me tell you where we are today with computing power in economic terms. Any economist wants to know the progress in how much of a good or service you can buy for a dollar. In the case of computing power, what you're buying is computations per second. This is true whether you're buying the machine, leasing it, or using it remotely in the cloud.

The history of modern computation is one of growth at increasing rates, as Exhibit 2 shows. It's an exponential curve. During the first age of electromechanical computing, the economic value of these machines increased sevenfold per decade. You got seven times more value, measured as the number of computations per second, each decade. Later, the first electronic age increased value by 16-fold per decade, a much faster growth rate.

---

[4] This phrase refers to the title of a 1962 article by I.M.D. Little, well known to historians of finance and business, which basically showed that a company's earnings cannot grow to the sky. It is at https://onlinelibrary.wiley.com/doi/pdf/10.1111/j.1468-0084.1962.mp24004001.x

Exhibit 2 — Quantity of computational services that can be purchased per dollar, 1900–2020 (log scale, base 10)

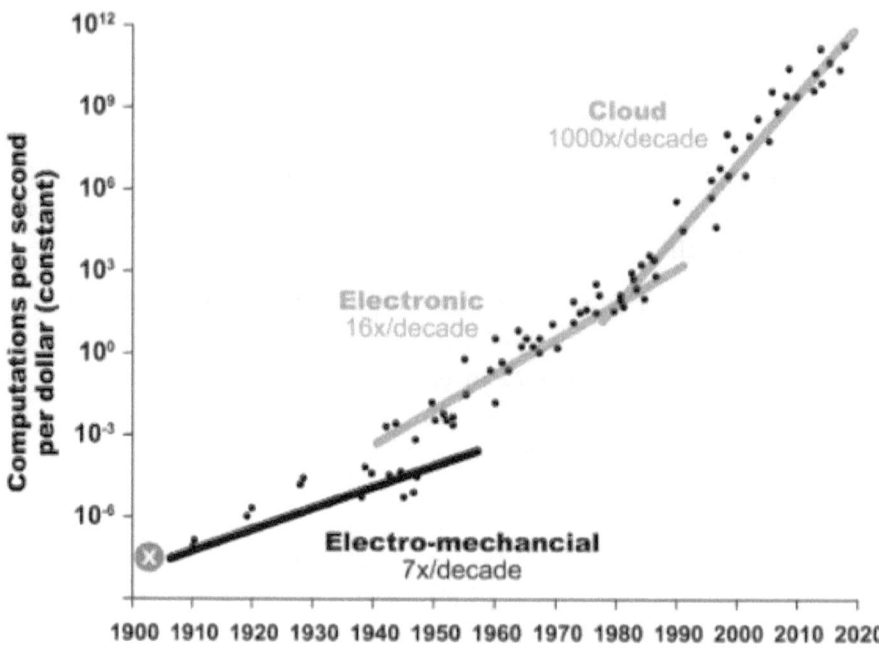

But, in the age of the cloud, value has been going up 1000-fold per decade.

You can compare this to the improvement in the economic cost or value of transportation services — how much it costs to move goods or to go somewhere. It's also an exponential curve. Exhibit 3 shows that the economic efficiency of transportation services also grew by a thousandfold, but that happened over the entire 20th century — it took 100 years. We're now doing that every 10 years in computation services. This is consequential in ways that are hard to sort out.

Exhibit 3 — Amount of transportation that can be purchased per dollar, 1700–2100 (projected), log scale (base 10)

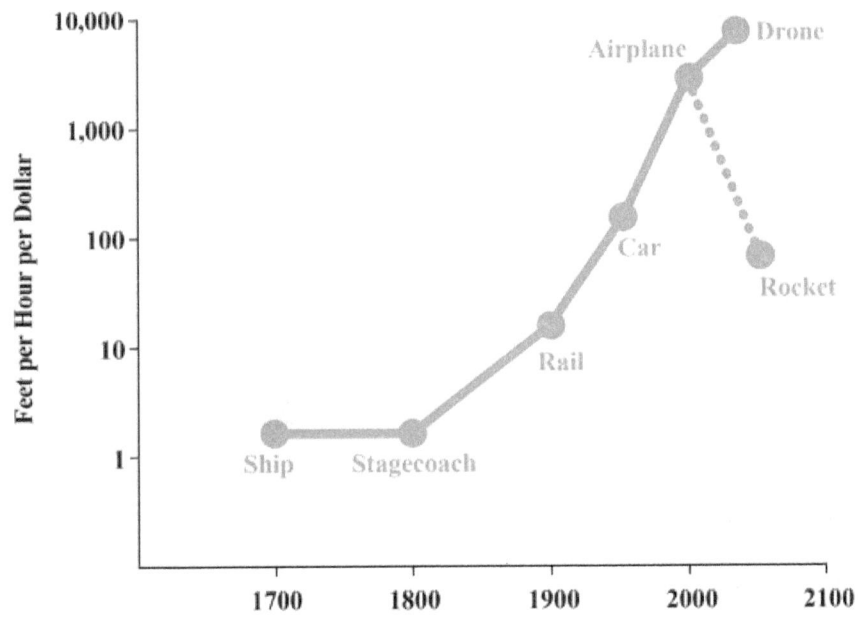

An inference chip the size of a dinner plate

Coming back to the machine realm, let's consider a little-known company called Cerebras. It's a commercially viable post-startup company. It manufactures a new class of inference chip — not a computer chip *per se*. In the world of artificial intelligence, you're doing inference, not computation. I know roughly where I want to drive. The answer isn't computational in the sense of 1 + 1; it's continuous adaptation to changing circumstances. To do that, all the early machines used computation chips to perform inference but used brute force, which is very inefficient, like using a helicopter to fly across the Atlantic.

Or you can build an inference chip. Graphics processing units (GPUs), what NVIDIA began to produce 25 years ago, are inference chips or engines, which was the class of processing unit that enabled the efficient use of artificial intelligence software. We get things like Siri and Alexa because they do pattern recognition on your smartphones, which requires inference.

The inference chip in Exhibit 4, made by Cerebras, is the size of a dinner plate. It came into commercial being 25 years after the first AI chip, echoing the pattern I discussed earlier. This chip processes images, and does inference 10,000 times faster than the fastest NVIDIA GPU. It's now a commercial product, not an idea.

Exhibit 4 — Cerebras WSE-2 computer chip, shown in spatial context

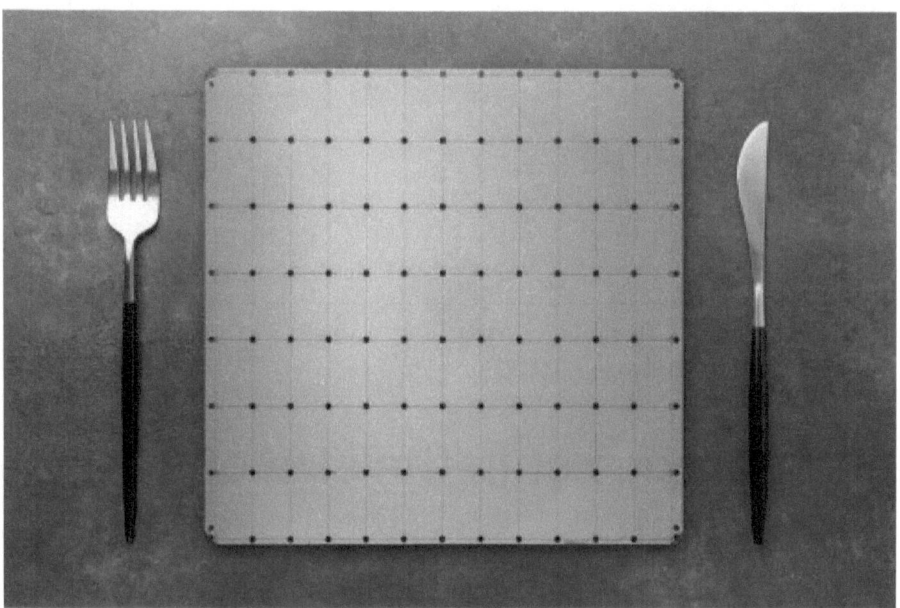

For those of you who, like me, also work in the energy domain, you'd be interested to know that this one chip uses 15 kilowatts of electricity. This is the capacity of three typical houses, or one very large house in La Jolla, running 24/7.

This chip has 3 trillion transistors on it. It's an astonishing engineering feat. It allows you to do inference faster, easier, and cheaper even though it's very expensive, each costing about $1 million.[5] A group of these chips

---

[5] This is one three-millionth of a dollar, or one thirty-thousandth of a penny, per transistor.

was assembled in December 2022 — 16 of them — to make what's called an exaflop supercomputer. (An exaflop is one quintillion, or 10^{18}, floating-point operations, or flops, per second.) The previous exaflop supercomputer was a $600 million, 47,000-processor machine at the Oak Ridge National Labs that requires 25 megawatts to run. The Cerebras exaflop supercomputer using 16 of these dinner-plate chips requires just 2 megawatts and costs $30 million to build. They built it in one week.

Where is this supercomputer going to reside? In the cloud. It's not going to sit in your smartphone. It will sit in the cloud and it will do inference. It will make ChatGPT smart. ChatGPT is already smarter than Siri and Alexa by a lot. All of us had the experience of trying to convince Alexa or Siri to understand English. ChatGPT is better. ChatGPT is still C–, maybe D+.[6] This additional leap in AI processing power will make chatbots, which are central to making a lot of financial transactions easier, actually useful, and a lot else besides. I think this is consequential, if not revolutionary.

The cloud as an engine of economic growth

The essential contention of my book is that we are at a dislocation, a pivot in history in the functionality, reach, scale of the cloud that is humanity's newest infrastructure. The cloud is not the internet — the cloud uses the internet. The cloud isn't about doing computation (though it can) but providing inference and advice; it isn't about just storing data or cat videos, though it does that too. Of course the cloud stores the unbelievably massive amount of data produced every day, about so many aspects of commerce. The cloud is a utility for providing advice and support to the economy at large. Of course it is the engine that makes crypto work, but that's just one use of it, and not a very large one.

---

[6] At the time Mills said this, ChatGPT-4 had not yet been released, and when it was, it answered questions at about an 11th grade level. However, in August 2024, Tyler Cowen reported that the latest version of ChatGPT-4 had answered an economics question (about the Alchian-Allen Theorem) at a level I'd describe as that of a first-year economics PhD student or a very well-prepared college senior. This is a huge improvement in a very short time.

Exhibit 5 shows spending, in constant (2012) dollars, by U.S. businesses on IT services and hardware starting in 1947. There's no sign that this is peaking soon or even leveling off.[7] Businesses don't buy non-useful things. Businesses are spending a trillion a year now, in the United States alone, to buy information processing and the means of acquiring information. That's meaningful.

Exhibit 5 — Private fixed investment in information processing equipment and software, 1947–3Q2022

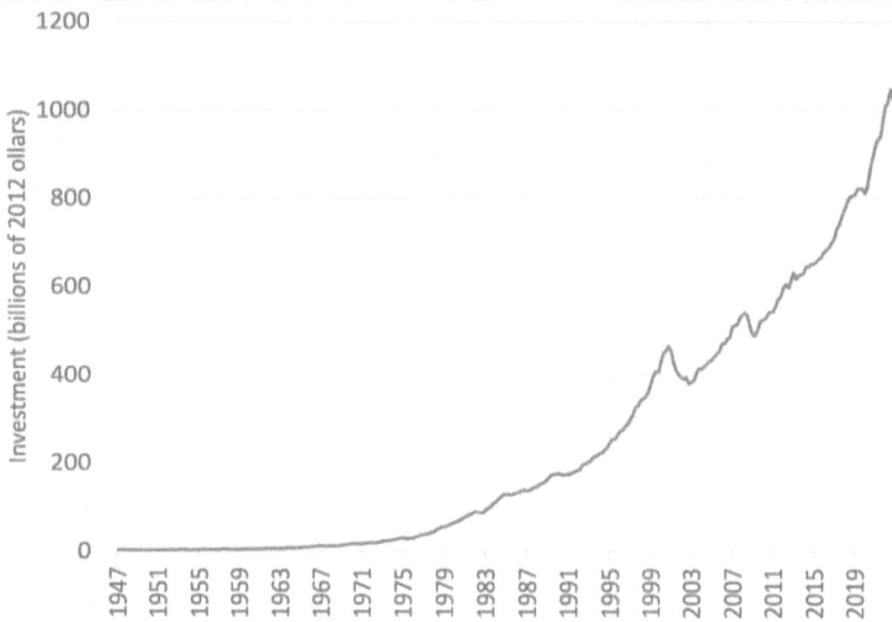

Capital spending on global cloud infrastructure now exceeds global capital spending by all electric utilities combined, even though we're electrifying everything. And the growth rate of spending on the cloud is far greater than the growth rate of spending on electric utilities. If you think in real estate terms, the cloud is a network of buildings and communication systems and end-devices, and the buildings at the core of the cloud, the datacenters, are the size of skyscrapers in square footage — a million

---

[7] However, the growth rate has decreased, as you'd see if the y-axis used a log scale. (I used an arithmetic scale to emphasize the sheer volume of investment.) But growth rates invariably slow as the denominator becomes enormous, 'hiding' the continuing rapid rate in absolute growth.

square feet under one roof. They cost about the same per square foot to build as a skyscraper. They rent for five times as much per square foot as a skyscraper, and they consume 100 times as much power per square foot as a skyscraper. The world has built about 1,500 skyscrapers over the past century, and over 5,000 enterprise, skyscraper-class, datacenters in the past couple of decades; the latter is expanding far faster than the former. It gives you some sense of where the world's cloud infrastructure is going, and the scale of its energy appetite.

Much more important is the economic impact of the marginal dollar spent on the cloud versus spending on other things. The marginal dollar spent on steel, a new car, any new physical asset typically gives you a new asset that is better, but only a little bit better. But each marginal dollar spent on the next unit of IT hardware or service is not just a little bit better. It's getting better at the rate I showed you earlier — a thousandfold per decade. It's an astonishing economic accelerator.

That will, inevitably, show up in the macroeconomic data. The cloud is blowing away the traditional production function.

Not enough people? Build robots...lots and lots of them

Let's turn to a couple of ideas on labor and employment that relate to our previous speaker, Patrick Harker [president of the Philadelphia Fed]. He said we don't have enough people, and I agree with that. In fact, Elon Musk has said the same. The world is looking at a very bad demographic path, for lots of reasons, as couples are choosing to have fewer and fewer children, in many cases none at all.

One of the functions of the cloud — one of the functions of AI — is to address the longstanding challenges in labor markets. AI deployed in robots is already starting to migrate into these markets, especially those that involve manual labor. The absence of robots in businesses is startling. Some 90% of the manufacturing businesses in the United States don't have a single industrial robot. You can invert that: 90% of the industrial robots are in 10% of the businesses. This may be because robots, until now, have only been good at doing highly repetitive tasks that very large businesses undertake.

Until now, there haven't been robots that are useful, mobile, and adaptive, and can work alongside people in multi-function tasks that characterize the majority of industrial businesses. The class of mobile robots is now at a take-off point, again coming about 25 years after the first viable ones were built. Nearly one million such units shipped last year.

The robot of the last era was the robot that you bolted down and set to doing some kind of highly repetitive task. The very first robot to do that was in 1961. It was called Unimate. In fact, that year it showed up on Johnny Carson's TV show and was also installed for the first time in a General Motors factory, making that factory the most productive one in the world. Every automaker on the planet chased that. The vast majority of industrial robots installed thus far have all been focused on and effective at doing the highly repetitive mass-production tasks with the automotive industry the utterly dominant (stationary) robot buyer.

In a coincidence, one of the first commercially available useful mobile robots showed up 61 years later *on the same stage* that Unimate appeared on, with Johnny Carson's stage now being used for the Jimmy Fallon show. You can see "Spot," a walking dog-like robot, appear with Fallon here.[8] Other examples of current robotic advances are here,[9] showing an industrial use case for Spot — safety inspections — and here,[10] an example of a pre-commercial anthropomorphic warehouse machine from Agility Robotics.

But if you really want to be impressed, check out the motor skills of Boston Dynamics' Atlas robot. You can see Atlas do some funky fifties-style dancing with some "friends"[11], navigating a parkour course,[12] and being helpful around a workshop.[13] "His" feats in the last video seem to involve reasoning as well as athleticism. Atlas, and its competitors, are not

---

[8] https://www.facebook.com/FallonTonight/videos/tonight-showbotics-boston-dynamics-robot-dances-to-bts-ioniq-im-on-it/345579204239794/
[9] https://www.youtube.com/watch?v=iiiPOKoI2gE
[10] https://www.youtube.com/watch?v=hD4NiXg861c
[11] https://www.youtube.com/watch?v=fn3KWM1kuAw
[12] https://www.youtube.com/watch?v=tF4DML7FIWk
[13] https://youtu.be/-e1_QhJ1EhQ

imaginary concepts but machines on the cusp of commercial viability with profound implications for productivity in markets where there is an endemic and worsening labor shortage.

How do we get all these jobs done?

Spot and Atlas, plus ChatGPT, and all the dozens of similar machines in pre-commercial development, are in fact revolutionary. Five years from now, the economists at the Federal Reserve will look back on this time period as a pivot in which we solved an interesting problem. How do we get the jobs done that are underserved, undesirable?

Exhibit 6 uses Federal Reserve data to categorize all of U.S. labor into a two-by-two matrix: routine versus non-routine, and cognitive work versus manual work.

Exhibit 6 — Evolution of job quality in the United States, January 1983–August 2022

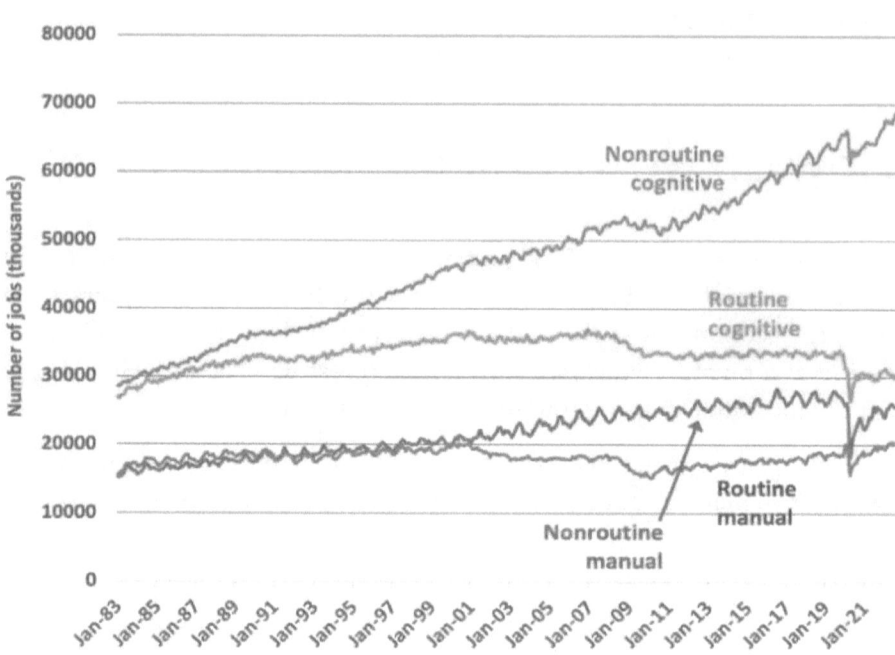

Source: Siegel and Sexauer (2023), using data from FRED, Federal Reserve Bank of Saint Louis.[14]

You can see that, over the last 40 years, there was essentially zero change in the absolute number of people engaged in routine tasks in both the manual and cognitive labor categories, despite a big increase in population. All the growth in labor has been in non-routine work, both cognitive and manual. If we don't have enough people to do the non-routine jobs where demand is growing, we can find them by moving them out of routine task. This latter transition is made possible by amplifying routine labor efficacy, i.e., reducing the number of people doing routine work (both manual and cognitive) and adding more robots, both physical machines and virtual AI robots like ChatGPT. Routine tasks are precisely where those technologies are best suited.

---

[14] Siegel, Laurence B., and Stephen C. Sexauer. 2023. "Longer, Healthier, Happier: Why Working Longer Improves Almost Everything." Journal of Retirement (May 24)

Doing that frees up capital, frees up people from doing the worst jobs, enhances productivity, and allows wage growth without wage inflation. So I think the Fed's challenge in tamping down inflation will be solved — I'll be slightly provocative–much more effectively by facilitating the deployment of new machines than by manipulating interest rates and raising business taxes.

Macro observations and conclusion

Two quick macro observations: The job openings ratio — the ratio of U.S. jobs available to the number of people that are available to be employed — just flipped. We now have more jobs than people available. You all know that. And, second, the demographic shape of the global labor pool has flipped: the working-age population is shrinking as a percentage of the total population. This is happening in just about all countries, but is most visible in the United States, Europe, and China.

We're going to need ChatGPT-class machines on steroids, and we're going to need many more robots. We will get them; dozens of innovators are building them and even the most famous modern machine innovator, Elon Musk, has joined the pursuit recently announcing Tesla's plan to build an autonomous, mobile, humanoid robot. The announcement is worth seeing.[15]

All this means that the average productivity growth rate will tilt back up. Exhibit 7 shows the five-year trailing productivity growth rate in the United States. The underlying technology trends tell us that it will rise to the historical average and beyond. The data are beginning to show that already.

---

[15] https://www.youtube.com/watch?v=UXHoWNfjJYM

Exhibit 7 — U.S. productivity growth rate, trailing five-year average, 1955–2020

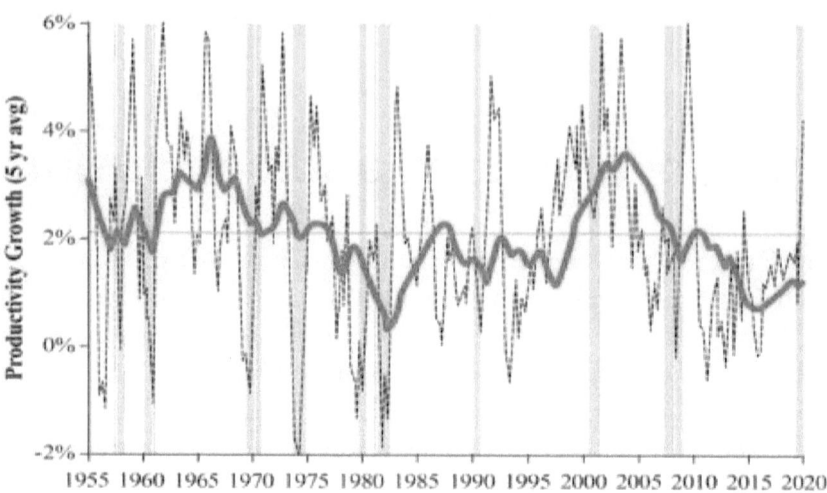

Source: Mark Mills

So, I expect these technologies will bring profound dislocations, and wealth creation. There's more pent-up growth than most people realize. Economists, not to be unkind because most of you are economists, have historically been profoundly bad in predicting economic dislocations caused by technology. But they've been very good at hindcasting the impacts of technology dislocations once they happen and framing the resulting economic rules of the road. Let's not insult them, because those rules do matter. Thanks.

Mark P. Mills (speaker) *is a physicist, a Manhattan Institute senior fellow, a faculty fellow at Northwestern University, and partner in Montrose Lane, an energy-tech venture fund. He is author of* The Cloud Revolution *(2021),* Digital Cathedrals *(2020), and* Work in the Age of Robots *(2018), and co-author of* The Bottomless Well *(2006). He served as chairman and CTO of ICx Technologies, and co-authored a tech investment newsletter, the Huber-Mills Digital Power Report. Prior to that, he served in the Reagan White House Science Office and worked in the*

commercial nuclear industry. He began his career as an experimental physicist and development engineer in microprocessors and fiber optics, earning several patents while working at Bell Northern Research and RCA. He holds a BSc, Honours, in physics from Queen's University, Canada. His website is https://www.tech-pundit.com.

Laurence B. Siegel (editor) may be reached at lbsiegel@uchicago.edu. His website is http://www.larrysiegel.org. –W.H.W.

Chapter 14. Why Are Elephants So Smart and Buildings So Short?

Laurence B. Siegel
September 2023

We can and do build very tall skyscrapers. But they are impractical money losers because so much floor space is taken up by elevators. A new book explains the interplay between size and scale, and what it means for our economy and investments.

Vaclav Smil, the 80-year-old Czech-Canadian scientist whom Bill Gates cites as his favorite author, rarely disappoints. Smil's 2022 book, *How the World Really Works*, is a superb paean to the physical world and its primacy in our lives — warning us that idealistic techies are wrong when they claim that teraflops and petabytes are what matters. As the economist and book reviewer Michael Edesess noted in *Advisor Perspectives* last year,

Vaclav Smil
Source: Yale University

> If you're a modern techy, you might say [that]...the four pillars of modern civilization...[are] something like the microchip, the cloud, the internet, and wi-fi. Nope, says Smil. The four pillars of modern civilization are cement, steel, plastics, and ammonia.[1]

"He's right," concludes Edesess, as do I. The material world matters. Many of us, dazzled by information technology, underestimate the importance of natural resources, materials science, and good old-

---

[1] https://www.advisorperspectives.com/articles/2022/06/13/were-living-in-a-material-world

fashioned heavy industry. (Without synthetic ammonia, used to make fertilizer, half of us would starve. Good to know.)

How the World Really Works also puts a dent in the hopes of energy-transition enthusiasts.

It will take a lot of time, money, and materials. Previous energy transitions took 40 to 60 years, Smil argues, and this one probably will too.

Building on his long-running effort to describe the physical world in intuitive language, Smil has come out with a new book, *Size: How It Explains the World*. But I'm reluctant to recommend *Size*, not because it is a bad book, but because so many books on related topics, including most of Smil's, are better. The two-and-a-half chapters on scale are quite good — they are the second half of chapter 4 and all of chapters 5 and 6. The connections Smil makes between Galileo, Jonathan Swift, animals, plants, and buildings regarding the effects of scale are Smil at his best.

But buying this book and reading the whole thing — just because Smil wrote it — seems like a poor time allocation decision when both Geoffrey West's superb Scale, which I reviewed very favorably,[2] and Sebastian Mallaby's *The Power Law* (the latter being about scaling in venture capital, for the investment-minded) are easier and more fun to read.[3]

The chapters in *Size* that are not about scale are filler, mushing together some vaguely size-related concepts such as the golden ratio in art and architecture, the science of ergonomics, and the basics of normal and Pareto (power-law) probability distributions.

In this review, I focus on Smil's scale chapters. I then discuss size and scale in business, a topic that Smil does not cover.

---

[2] https://larrysiegel.org/the-rules-of-growth-organisms-cities-and-companies/

[3] I reviewed *The Power Law* at https://larrysiegel.org/how-venture-capital-thrives-by-betting-on-weirdness/.

Why are elephants so smart and buildings so short?

Scale sounds like just as abstract a concept as size, so let's make it more concrete. As Smil (and West) use the word, it's the way the size of one thing varies with a change in the size of some other related thing. For example, one might guess that the brain-to-body-mass ratio of an animal would predict its intelligence, but the prediction is wrong until you correct for scale. An elephant's brain is small relative to its body but its intellect is impressive; the tiny tree shrew has the largest brain of any animal relative to its body but that does not make it smart. The elephant is smart partly because of its brain-to-body ratio, but – this is important – partly because its brain is so big in absolute (not relative) size.

The overarching principle is that the brain-to-body-mass ratio that maximizes intelligence is smaller in big animals and bigger in small animals. The relation among these variables is *nonproportional*. (To explain why would take a whole book, so I won't try.)

Nonproportional scaling factors are observed all over the place. Brian Potter, an engineer who writes about the economics of buildings, explains:

> As a building gets taller, more and more elevators are needed to service the upper floors, which intrude on the floors below. The result is that a taller building must devote proportionally more and more of its space to elevators.[4]

Exhibit 1 - Empire State Building and surrounding area in 1931

Most buildings are short — one of them is a spectacular anomaly

Source: https://gothamtogo.com/wp-content/uploads/2021/06/unnamed-1.png

---

[4] https://worksinprogress.co/issue/why-skyscrapers-are-so-short/

For a one-story building, and most two- and three- story buildings, the ratio of elevator space to building space is zero. For the tallest buildings, it can be 40%. That is why, in Potter's words, "skyscrapers are so short."

Skyscrapers aren't short compared to other buildings, but they're short relative to what they could be if there were no scaling effects. Moreover, the structures near them are often surprisingly short, suggesting that very tall buildings might be a peacock's tail, showing the world how wasteful the builder can afford to be. Exhibit 1 is a famous example from 1931, combining the comical and the majestic. (The dirigible adds a nostalgic note — did people really ride in those? Across the Atlantic?)

Later, as land values rose, the city filled in and the Empire State Building doesn't look as out of place today as it did then. However, the world's tallest building has moved offshore — it's currently the Burj Khalifa in Dubai — and *that* one looks as out of place as the Empire State Building did in 1931. Extreme tallness in buildings is mostly a money-losing monument to the ego of the builder.

Brobdingnag and Lilliput

Smil introduces us to these scaling concepts by way of Jonathan Swift's *Gulliver's Travels*. As most schoolchildren know, normal-sized Lemuel Gulliver visits a race of tiny people one-twelfth his height (so about six inches tall) and a race of giants twelve times Gulliver's height (so about 72 feet tall). In describing these characters, Swift commits a bonehead error — he "built his masterpiece," Smil writes, "on the mistaken assumption that such a thing...is perfectly possible" with no change in the way the creatures look and behave.

Smil notes that Swift would not have made that mistake if he had read Galileo's *Dialogue Concerning Two New Sciences*, written in 1638, some 84 years before *Gulliver*. We tend to think of Galileo as an astronomer because of his mammoth contribution to that field, but he was also a general scientist of remarkable ability. His description of the way that scale affects the proportions of animals, summarized by the Brazilian physicist Francisco Rodrigues in an article in *Medium*,[5] is still our best understanding 400 years later.

Exhibit 2 – Little and big
Gulliver among the Lilliputians; the King of Brobdingnag examines Gulliver

Source: https://gulliverstravels.fandom.com/
wiki/Lilliputians?file=Lill-01.jpg

Source: https://www.metmuseum.org/art/
collection/search/391822

Smil dissects the Gulliver problem in several additional pages of detail, explaining that a Brobdingnagian, if he had the relative proportions of a normal human but were 72 feet tall, would weigh 116 tons, more than the largest known dinosaur. His legs would crumble from his weight unless they were several times thicker than an elephant's, and he would have many other traits that we'd consider deformities. In other words, he would not look human at all, and could not run, jump, or do many other physical things that a human easily does.

The six-inch-tall Lilliputians would also have scale-related problems, albeit different ones — though, as shown in Exhibit 2, they'd be able to ensnare big Gulliver if, like ants, they banded together.

---

[5] https://francisco-rodrigues.medium.com/power-law-universality-in-nature-c933f271bda8

The tale of a whale, a bird, and a tree

But wait...there *is* an animal that weighs more than 116 tons! You've probably already guessed that it's a blue whale, the largest animal ever known to have existed. It can survive and thrive because it lives in the water. Weighing almost nothing after accounting for water displacement, the blue whale functions beautifully in its own environment. It is, however, a complete disaster in any other environment. It can't even stand up or walk. The scale of the whale requires that it be aquatic for its entire life.

At the other extreme, a small bird called the bar-tailed godwit has flown 8435 miles, from Alaska to the Australian island of Tasmania, without stopping. (See Exhibit 3.) It comes pretty close to living in thin air, needing to touch down only to rest and find food. Note that this avian ultramarathoner must carry the many calories needed for this trip in its body; there are no bird restaurants in the sky. A larger creature could not possibly do this — consider how many times a human being trekking that many miles would have to stop and eat.

Thus, Smil concludes, the possible variations in the physique and behavior of a living creature are tightly constrained by their size. In case you're thinking that this law doesn't apply to plants, you'd be wrong – it just applies differently. Not needing to move about, a plant can grow larger than any animal.

Exhibit 3 – Bar-Tailed Godwits

Source: https://www.npr.org/2022/10/28/1132171095/a-non-stop-flight-from-alaska-to-tasmania-may-be-for-the-birds-and-a-possible-re

The world's heaviest tree, the General Sherman sequoia in California, is 276 feet tall and weighs 566 tons, as much as five blue whales; the world's *tallest* tree, a skinny California coast redwood called Hyperion, stands 380 feet high – taller but not as heavy. No tree is likely ever to grow much taller or heavier than these behemoths because it would collapse of its own weight.

The laws of scale that apply to animals and plants, but with different parameters, also apply to buildings, cities, microchips, and everything else...

All businesses great and small

...*including businesses*. Here's the bridge between Smil's intellectual horseplay and the world of investing: the scale of a business is fundamentally important to its organization and behavior. Like our tall building that needs a lot of elevators, a multinational corporation requires many more layers of management than a taco stand. From that perspective, a large business can look very inefficient. But large size also conveys many advantages (economies of *scale*) to a business, the most obvious of which is bulk purchasing. In a Darwinian fashion, the market weighs the advantages and disadvantages of large size and a balance is reached for each kind of business, just as it is reached for each species of plant or animal.

So, aircraft manufacturers are large and handicraft shops are small. We already know this, but it's helpful to understand why. The reasons emerge from the laws of scale.

Size, scale, and stock selection

Investors are, of course, intimately familiar with one dimension of size – the market "cap" of stocks. From 1926, when reliable data begin, through about 1980, small-capitalization stocks outperformed large ones by a fat margin – enough, on average, to spawn a whole new category of mutual funds and other investment vehicles. Starting about when the small-cap effect was discovered around 1980, however, the effect disappeared and the two size categories fought to a tie. (See Exhibit 4.)

Exhibit 4 — U.S. small-cap versus large-cap stocks, nominal total returns, 1927-2018

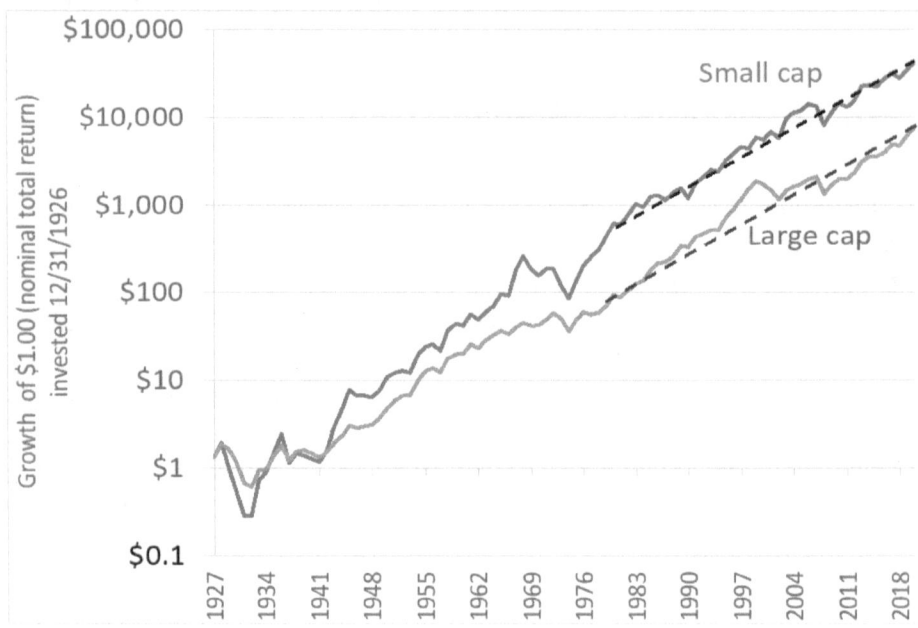

Source: Rajnish Mehra, "Presentation by Rajnish Mehra." In Siegel, Laurence B., and Paul McCaffrey. 2023. Revisiting the Equity Risk Premium. Charlottesville, VA; CFA Institute Research Foundation, https://rpc.cfainstitute.org/research/foundation/2023/revisiting-equity-risk-premium-2021, p. 53, redrawn using log scale

This is not to say that small caps started to have the same return as large caps year after year — they often diverged widely — but there has been no *net* size effect from 1980 to 2023, with small caps winning in some periods and large caps in others. Thus, while it looked for a while as though small size conveyed big advantages to publicly traded companies, that turned out to be a mirage.

But equity analysts look at other aspects of size: a company's revenues, profits, number of employees, geographic extent of its market, land area of the physical plant, and so forth. One reason to make such a careful study of size is to determine if the company is well positioned to create a quasi-monopoly or earned monopoly in some aspect of its business. If it is, that makes the company worth more. It's hard for small companies to earn monopoly profits unless the monopoly is very localized or the company makes a niche product; to play that game you want to be as big as possible.

Another reason to be concerned with company size is to forecast how much regulatory attention will be focused on the company; here, large size is a disadvantage. Still another reason is to assess the likelihood of labor unionization — big companies are more susceptible to it.

Moreover, companies are subject to scaling effects, meaning that the impact of size on success can be nonlinear (in either direction). Small companies have the advantage of being nimbler and more experimental — look at the private-equity energy sector today — but some things can only be done efficiently by large ones. Interconnecting the country for electric, telecommunications, water, and natural gas utilities is an example; we have more than a century of evidence that natural monopolies exist in those businesses. The large-cap companies that did this work were good stocks to own while the quasi-monopolies lasted.

Note that radio, which provides a similar service but doesn't need wires or pipelines (so there is much less capital outlay), has never been a natural monopoly, and small stations often became industry pioneers and big profit-makers.[6]

Only a Google-sized company could have digitized a large fraction of the world's books. Sadly, Google must wait for the laws to change so the public can read the books; only a few selected parts, for example the British Library's vast antiquarian (pre-1877) collection,[7] have been allowed to circulate. But this currently stranded asset will someday have tremendous commercial value. Some stocks should be expensive, and the stock of Google's parent company, Alphabet, certainly is.

In business as well as in biology, architecture, and just about everything else, scale matters.

---

[6] Professional economic historians and other sticklers will note that the first radio networks (CBS and so forth) were in fact linked by wires. That phase, however, did not last long and does not appear to have been a critical aspect of that industry's history.

[7] https://www.bl.uk. As of press time, the collection is unavailable due to a cyber-attack on the British Library. Efforts are being made to restore the website.

A broader view of Vaclav Smil's work

I close with an overview of Vaclav Smil's *oeuvre* and how *Size* fits into it. As an energy expert, Smil often finds himself at the center of a whirlwind of passionate opinion on the topic. He is called a pessimist by optimists and an optimist by pessimists. To this, he replies: "I am neither a pessimist nor an optimist. I am a scientist."[8] He tries to calm the passions by taking moderate positions, emphasizing solutions rather than imminent disaster. But, like any human being, he does not get everything right.

Must growth come to an end?

In a widely quoted sound bite in his 2019 book, *Growth*, Smil wrote that "[G]rowth must come to an end. Our economist friends don't seem to realise that." This quote has been used by the degrowth movement to support their cause and by techno-optimists to illustrate how wrong a great scientist can be. In fact, the quote is both exactly correct and profoundly wrong.

No physical quantity can grow at a positive rate forever. That is about as incontrovertible a fact as exists in the universe.

What our economist friends know that Smil does not, however, is that what people try to maximize is *not a physical quantity*. People try to maximize *utility* — the amount of satisfaction or usefulness they get out of whatever they're consuming. Theoretically, utility *can* grow at a positive rate indefinitely. Whatever satisfaction or usefulness you got out of a given pile of goods and services this year, you might be able to get a little more next year. Maybe it's just a matter of becoming more psychologically well-adjusted, or maybe the quality (not the quantity) of the goods and services will have improved.

While projecting this betterment out *forever* is a stretch, this principle focuses the mind on utility not being constrained by physical limits. Utility exists only in people's minds, so there are no limits to it.

---

[8] In *How the World Really Works*.

Dematerialization

There's more good news. We are not only getting more utility out of the pile of goods we produce — we are using fewer resources to make them. This is called dematerialization and is another path to sustainable growth. Not only do our economist friends know that — so does Smil, who wrote a book about it, called *Making the Modern World: Materials and Dematerialization* (2013). It is not entirely optimistic and he does not think dematerialization will solve all of our resource problems, but he is keenly aware of the phenomenon.

Smil recognizes that some further increase in resource use is necessary and good. Some people — several billion of them — need more stuff. "Too many people still live in conditions of degrading and unacceptable material poverty," he writes, and "all of those people...need to consume more materials *per capita* in order to enjoy a decent life."

Smil's book on dematerialization is worthy, but if you want a much shorter and easier read on the topic, check out chapter 23 of my book, *Fewer, Richer, Greener* (2019). The chapter is titled "Dematerialization: Where Did My Record Collection Go?" and is available as a free download.[9] If you access it, please do not redistribute or repost it. Smil's work features prominently in my book chapter.

Side trips

Smil has written more than 40 books. *Size* fits into this body of work awkwardly. Many writers, some successfully and others not, veer off into topics that are not their core expertise but that they find interesting: Edgar Allan Poe wrote a textbook on mollusks, and Robert Louis Stevenson wrote a nonfiction book celebrating laziness. *Size* has the same feel, that of an author exploring a side path. So do Smil's *Why America Is Not a New Rome* and *Should We Eat Meat?* (Hmm.)

Smil has it in him to write an engrossing and informative book on size, scale, proportion, and related concepts. He did not do so. Although it contains some fine chapters, *Size* does not hang together as a book.

---

[9] The chapter is at http://larrysiegel.org/books/frgchapters/chapter23/. Unlike this article, the book chapter is copyrighted material and should be treated as such.

Exhibit 5 — Dematerialization in one lesson
Use of nine basic commodities in the US, 1900-2010

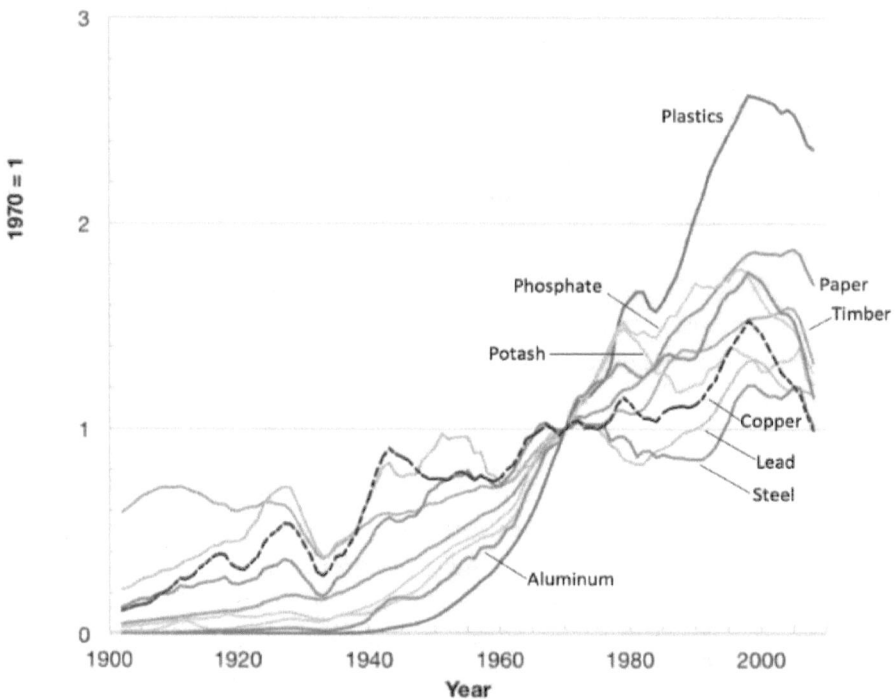

Source: https://issuu.com/alcorlife/docs/cryonics-magazine-2022-04/s/17507406.
Note: The data are normalized so that 1970 = 1.00, so that all the lines intersect in that year. This is just a graphing technique and does not imply that there was anything special about the year 1970 in the commodity market.

Advice to readers and investors

Investors should treat *Size* as deep background. Most investors would be well advised to read other books on related topics, such as Geoffrey West's *Scale* and Pulak Prasad's *What I Learned About Investing from Darwin*, which I also reviewed in *Advisor Perspectives*[10] — if they want to study

---

[10] https://larrysiegel.org/can-evolutionary-biology-inform-investing/

these ideas. An economy is much like an ecology, and investors should be aware of the recent literature that clarifies and builds on this connection.

Smil's writing style is heavy, packed with information. Many readers prefer a breezier approach, but Smil is such a knowledgeable writer, thinker, and researcher that one would be remiss to skip him entirely. So, if you want to learn about size and scaling, read *Scale* — and if you want to know how the world really works, read Smil's *How the World Really Works*.

The author thanks Stephen C. Sexauer, CIO of San Diego County Employees Retirement Association, for helpful comments and revisions. –W.H.W.

Political Economy

I had a big argument with Larry over this title: shall we call it Political Economy or Public Life? I thought, "Political Economy was too academic, too snobby." He convinced me with the following message:

> *Encyclopedia Britannica* (which still exists!) defines Political Economy as "the branch of social science that studies the relationships between individuals and society and between markets and the state."

I can't summarize it better than that.

Wayne's favorite: Johan Norberg's Plan to Save the World Through Capitalism

—W.H.W.

Chapter 15. Johan Norberg's Plan to Save the World Through Capitalism

Laurence B. Siegel
April 2024

Do we need a "capitalist manifesto"?

At least six authors have thought so, enough to write books having that title. First, Louis Kelso and Mortimer Adler, as a team, in 1958; then Andrew Bernstein, Gary Wolfram, and Robert Kiyosaki earlier in the current century; and now Johan Norberg, the celebrated author of *Progress*, which I reviewed favorably.[1]

All of these works are counterweights to Karl Marx's *Communist Manifesto*, which has been aptly described as the "most destructive book ever written."[2]

These authors are onto something. Anti-capitalist sentiment has reached a fever pitch, even in the United States where capitalism has had its greatest success. The three most popular magazines in the U.S., by monthly website visits, have had this to say about capitalism (I'm cherry picking, of course):

> "In order to understand the brutality of American capitalism,

---

[1] https://www.kelsoinstitute.org/pdf/cm-entire.pdf
https://niagarapencentre.com/shop/product/the-capitalist-manifesto-by-andrew-bernstein-paperback-indigo-chapters-coles-04f924
https://www.goodreads.com/book/show/18922722-a-capitalist-manifesto
https://www.richdad.com/capitalist-manifesto
https://www.cato.org/books/capitalist-manifesto
Plus Jesse Kelly's 2023 book, *The Anti-Communist Manifesto*, if you want to count that.

[2] *Mein Kampf* is a close competitor, but its impact was not as widespread as that of *The Communist Manifesto*, adherence to which tyrannized one-third of the world's population for much of the twentieth century, and which still strongly influences the government of China (pop. 1.4 billion, 18% of world population).

you have to start on the plantation." – Matthew Desmond, *New York Times Magazine*, August 14, 2019

"A way of life that is dying [is] the culture of competitive individualism, which in its decadence has carried the logic of individualism to the extreme of a war of all against all." – Christopher Lasch, *People* Magazine interview by Barbara Rowes, July 1979

"Unless it changes, capitalism will starve humanity by 2050." – Drew Hansen, *Forbes*, February 9, 2016

Concerning that last quote, the *Forbes* magazine slogan, printed on the cover of every issue, is "Capitalist Tool." Published by Steve Forbes, the magazine is as full-throated a cheerleader for capitalism as Norberg, if not more so.

Yet Hansen's article claims that that "capitalism has...devastated the planet and has failed to improve human well-being at scale."[3]

Failed to improve human well-being at scale? Is Hansen kidding? We've experienced a two-and-a-half century economic superboom that started with almost universal extreme deprivation and that has, thus far, made half the world's population middle class.[4]

(Norberg correctly credits free markets and free trade — the building blocks of capitalism — for this astonishing change.)

---

[3] https://www.forbes.com/sites/drewhansen/2016/02/09/unless-it-changes-capitalism-will-starve-humanity-by-2050/?sh=34ec9bc17ccc

[4] https://www.brookings.edu/articles/a-global-tipping-point-half-the-world-is-now-middle-class-or-wealthier. As described by Brookings, the World Bank defines the global middle class as consisting of people who can consume $11 to $110 per day, per person, measured in 2017 U.S. dollars. That's a very wide range, with no natural intuition as to how well a person lives on that amount of money, so the World Bank describes it thus:

> Those in the middle class...can...buy consumer durables like motorcycles, refrigerators, or washing machines. They can afford to go to movies or indulge in other forms of entertainment. They may take vacations. And they are reasonably confident that they and their family can weather an economic shock...without falling back into extreme poverty.

Johan Norberg's Plan to Save the World Through Capitalism

Capitalism has had an even better run recently, with the globalization of prosperity. By 1980, the United States, western Europe, and Japan were already rich, but 40% of the world's population still lived in extreme poverty ($2.74 per person per day in today's money).[5] The turning point was the adoption of the essential elements of capitalism (not the whole package) in China around that time,[6] and in India a decade later. Since that time, and not just in those two giant countries, the world's poor have gotten dramatically richer, even as the wealth of the rich has soared too.

Johan Norberg
Source: Cato Institute

Thus, given the ill repute into which capitalism has fallen in some circles, we need a capitalist manifesto! And Norberg, who rarely disappoints, has provided a good one — not quite a great one — in *The Capitalist Manifesto: Why the Global Free Market Will Save the World*. I recommend this book even though it isn't an amazing read like Norberg's 2016 bestseller, *Progress*, and despite most readers already being familiar with the arguments in it.

---

[5] The World Bank's 2017 definition of extreme poverty, inflated to 2024 prices.

[6] It's been said that while the Chinese government describes its system as socialism with Chinese characteristics, it's really "capitalism with capitalist characteristics." (Example: https://marxistleninist.wordpress.com/2011/05/19/a-question-of-state-revolution-china-market-socialism/, in the comments.) More seriously, Weijian Shan, a Hong Kong private equity manager, has made the case that this perception is correct at https://hbr.org/2021/05/americans-dont-know-how-capitalist-china-is. Under the leadership of Xi Jinping, China has been backsliding, but from a much richer starting point than the country has experienced at any time in its history.

The usual arguments for free markets

There's nothing in the philosophy behind *The Capitalist Manifesto* that isn't in Milton Friedman's *Capitalism and Freedom*, written more than 60 years ago. This isn't a complaint; the tried principles are still true. The specifics of Norberg's book are, of course, much more in tune with today's realities, but the underlying ideas are the same.

For that matter, they're the same as those in Adam Smith's eighteenth-century masterpieces, *The Wealth of Nations* and *The Theory of Moral Sentiments*. Readers seeking to deepen their knowledge of the thinking behind a free society should read the latter — Smith was anything but amoral, and he did not only care about money.

Norberg makes the usual arguments for a global free market, borrowed from Smith, Friedman, and many others. Because you know them already or can look them up, I'll add my own (also borrowed):

- Market economies are the best way to allocate resources efficiently because, as Friedrich Hayek said, they push decision-making out from the center to the endpoints where the information is.

- The supply-demand-price mechanism gathers and communicates information about what needs to be produced in a way that no central authority can mimic.

- Capitalism is morally better than other systems because it requires only voluntary effort and exchange. Any other system relies on coercion.

Norberg uses the example of coffee to describe the communication aspect of the price system. Channeling Leonard Read, who wrote "I, Pencil" in 1958 to show how the price system induces people from all over the world to cooperate (mostly unknowingly) to make a writing implement that no single individual in the world knows how to make,[7] Norberg does the same thing for coffee:

> I can't make a cup of coffee; neither can you. In fact, no one can make a cup of coffee. Those invigorating drops are the result of lots of people's knowledge, skill and hard work that no single person can undertake...

...a helpful (if unoriginal) story that Norberg then fills in with several pages of detail. But, at least for those familiar with Read's pencil, Norberg hits a truer note with a thought from Frédéric Bastiat:

> One day in the middle of the 19th century, a young Frenchman from the countryside [Bastiat] visited Paris. It fascinated him that millions of people there slept peacefully even though they would die within a few days if transports from all over the country did not continue to flow to the big city....How could it be that this huge marketplace was filled every morning with almost exactly the number of goods that the inhabitants needed...? What....is the secret and ingenious power that governs this complicated system...?...That power is nothing but prices and the profit motive.

Yes, we depend on prices and the profit motive for our literal survival. Without them, the commissar would occasionally get it right, but eventually we'd be eating like North Koreans.

Is economic freedom on the wane?

The twenty-first century has been a rough ride for freedom, both economic and political. Authoritarian governments have gained at the expense of full democracies, and even in politically free countries the intrusion of governments into the economy grows and grows.

Why the backsliding? Because freedom is hard. You have to figure out what actions are in your best interest, and then do them. These decisions

---

[7] https://oll.libertyfund.org/titles/read-i-pencil-my-family-tree-as-told-to-leonard-e-read-dec-1958

may not work out. In free markets there are winners and losers; nobody wants to be a loser, so some people prefer a system where you don't have to play the game.

In contrast, being told what to do is easy. The Old Testament had something to say about that. David Mamet explains:[8]

> The Jews were led through the Sea of Reeds and, in the desert, complained, and wished to return to Egypt and slavery. Life in Egypt was by no means perfect; its only attraction was the absence of the necessity of choice. But it made all people equal. No slave need choose between good and evil, morality and immorality...

...nor, it must be said, did they need to find a way to eat. Slaves are fed.

Thus the current revival of interest in authoritarianism. But freedom is not only a necessity for the soul — it enriches the wallet. The pie is so much bigger in a free-market world that even the losers live much better than the typical "non-loser" citizen in a centrally planned economy.

Despite some recent setbacks, the struggle for freedom is gradually, and haltingly, being won. According to the Fraser Institute, a Canadian free-market think tank, economic freedom reached its *all-time* high in 2016, with only a modest fall-off afterward, as shown in Exhibit 1; the big boost came between 1985 and 2000.

---

[8] Mamet, David. 2011. *The Secret Knowledge*, New York: Sentinel (Penguin), p. 51.

Exhibit 1

Source: 1970-2021 data from https://www.fraserinstitute.org/economic-freedom/graph.
1950-1965 data from Lawson and Murphy. (2019).
https://www.cato.org/sites/cato.org/files/pubs/efw/efw2019/efw-2019-chapter-3.pdf
Note: Y-axis is magnified. (This is apparently an unforgivable sin in data graphics.)

But the recent decline is alarming. That's not because of its size, which is small – it only takes us back to 2011 levels – but because of the dramatic collapse of freedom in a few strategically important places: Venezuela, Hong Kong (ouch) and, briefly but destructively, Sri Lanka. The citizens of these countries deserve better.

Is China a paper tiger?

Fortunately for us investors, Norberg does more than just cheer for capitalism. In filling in his thesis, he provides a few (not enough) insights that, if correct, can help long-term investors think more clearly about the future.

Most notably, he calls China a "paper tiger," hinting that maybe we've overinvested in it, and also that we're too afraid of it. As evidence of China's weakness, he cites

> [s]ome researchers [who] disassembled an iPhone 7 that sold for $649. They observed that the manufacturing cost of just over $237 (which looks like $237 of...imports [from China to the U.S.]) in the data tables mostly consists of components that have previously been imported to China, such as American, Japanese, Korean and Taiwanese microprocessors, memory chips, and displays. But some are, of course, Chinese labour and parts. How much? Just under $8.50 – not much more than an hourly US minimum wage. The "biggest winner" receives only 1.3% of what you pay for an iPhone.

Most of the rest goes to developed-country workers in various trades and professions. "Reshoring" iPhone manufacturing would not help the U.S. because the increase in the cost of iPhones would swamp any extra income the reshoring would generate for American workers, and because the U.S. is already getting much of the purchase price.

This analysis is correct and clever. But, on the larger question of China's role, I disagree with Norberg. If the Chinese contribution to the world economy were as puny as its contribution to the dollar value of an iPhone, the standard of living in China would be a fraction of what it is. China's PPP GDP per capita — a measure used by economists to compare living standards across countries and across time — is almost one-third that of the United States and half that of moderately prosperous Portugal. You can't get there by sewing T-shirts and making toys. China's manufacturing ability, and now its services and information industries, are formidable.

I don't think China is a paper tiger. Under less-than-ideal conditions – a veneer of Communist ideology, a horrible history, and very limited freedoms even today – the Chinese people have created for themselves an economy that is the envy of developing countries everywhere. China's newfound prosperity is real, as anyone who has visited the country in the 1980s and then again recently will tell you. (Although their movements will be monitored, foreign visitors can go almost anywhere they want in China — they are not seeing Potemkin villages.)

If Norberg is correct and China's influence really is declining, however, we should be very concerned about its aggressive behavior in the military sphere. Authoritarian governments often make up for their shortcomings by picking fights. And China is a major nuclear power with the world's largest army.

The environment and climate change

But hasn't capitalism been the driving force behind increasing CO_2 concentration in the atmosphere, leading to global warming?

Yes and no. The driving force is people wanting to use energy and the things you can produce with it — food, manufactured goods, transportation — to better their lives, and capitalism has provided them a way to do that. In the poorest countries, an adequate supply of energy is the difference between a miserable life and a dignified one. Norberg recalls:

> A few years ago, I visited a small, poor village in the Atlas mountains in Morocco. I got to spend time with a friendly family who lived…close to nature. From the outside, it looked like a simple but good life…But when I asked the father about their lives, he gave a long list of everything they…desperately longed for: a water pump [with which to] water the crops, a refrigerator to store food, and lighting so kids could read in the evening. He wanted to be able to charge a telephone to keep in touch with the outside world…All these needs could be summed up in a single wish: that the power lines would finally reach all the way to their little village.

That is not the worst of it. "Without electricity and gas," Norberg continues, "the family cooked and warmed itself in the same way as 3 billion other people do: by burning solid fuel indoors…" Burning wood and dung (yes, dung) indoors results in the death of about two million people annually from respiratory diseases.

Do we really want to take energy *away* from these people? No — advocates of "degrowth," that is, producing and consuming less to limit fossil fuel usage, have not thought this through. The hoped-for energy transition will take money — boatloads of it — and only a rich society can muster the needed resources.

Again, capitalism is what produces rich societies. In Norberg's words, degrowth "would be the worst thing we could do for the world – and for the planet…Poverty is one of the most expensive ways to save the planet, even apart from its effect on the poor themselves."

As my friend and frequent co-author Stephen Sexauer has written, "To get green, get rich."

Was 1950s America a worker's paradise?

We hear, with increasing frequency, that the United States was better off when we didn't trade much with the rest of the world. Americans had more choices when they enjoyed the full range of job opportunities, from coal mining (oops) to automobile manufacturing, that have since flowed to the developing world now that trade is freer. The 1950s and 1960s are said to be the peak of our remembered prosperity.

How much of this story is true? Many economists and writers, not just Norberg, have noted that factory work in the U.S. in the 1950s was often irregular, ill-paid, and brutal. Norberg writes, "As a steelworker in Pennsylvania warned his children, 'come in this place, you don't know if you're coming out. And if you do, you might be missing an arm, or eye, or leg.'" (Of course, this was capitalism too — it's not all desk work and committee meetings.) A lucky few, mostly working for big corporations, had steady work at union wages but that was the exception, not the rule, and even these workers, when asked, said they were doing it so their kids wouldn't have to.

What's more, union wages in Detroit factories in 1953 averaged $1.30 an hour. That's $15.21 in today's money. Some golden age.

Norberg powerfully proves the point that, as has often been said, "Nothing is more responsible for the good old days than a bad memory."[9] Yet Norberg's summary of his section on labor markets contains a weird misstatement: "The whole narrative of the lost golden age of factories is based on a single American city [Detroit] in a single year [1953] during the very peculiar time after World War II, when Europe's industry lay in ruins."

Oops, not really. Good factory jobs really did exist in most cities and lasted more than a year. I can vouch for it; I grew up in Cleveland near the General Electric and Parker Hannifin plants, and many of the workers there, who were my neighbors, had jobs that lasted for years and owned their own modest homes.

Whatever the actual conditions were — and, obviously, they differed for each person — these folk memories always contain a grain of truth. Factory jobs were a big step up from the workers' — or their fathers' — farm jobs. Moreover, we probably enjoyed more social peace when everyone in town, from the factory owner to the janitor, sent their kids to the same comprehensive high school where they all had to learn to get along. (Black Americans would be justified in disputing this claim.)

But I agree with Norberg that this memory of "shared prosperity" — ironically, now a Communist Chinese slogan — grows rosier with the passage of time, as memories tend to do, and that the reality was closer to what Norberg describes. We don't want it back.

Who lost the right-wingers?

Traditionally, in the U.S., Europe, and Western offshoots, the political right has been pro-capitalist. But no more — at least, not consistently. Norberg is dismayed that many of his onetime right-leaning allies have taken up protectionism and isolationism, which are patently anti-capitalist. And he takes abuse from the left too:

> Twenty years ago free trade was considered bad because *we* exploited *them*; now it is considered bad because *they* exploit

---

[9] Usually attributed to the curmudgeonly columnist Franklin P. Adams (1881-1960).

us. Twenty years ago, capitalism was wrong because supposedly it made the world's poor poorer. Now it is wrong because it makes the poor richer.[10]

Reviewing *The Capitalist Manifesto* for the American Institute for Economic Research, Joakim Book (a good name for a book reviewer) concludes: "These days, Norberg is as likely to be called a woke, globalist leftie as he was a crazy, right-wing, capitalist lunatic in the 2000s. Frustrated, Norberg remarks that *he's* not the one who changed."[11]

The meaning of life?

Bravely or foolishly, Norberg titles his last chapter (other than a brief epilogue) "The Meaning of Life." In it, he defends capitalism from what he calls "the last line of defence against free markets": the charge that it overlooks, or cheapens, or destroys the things that matter most.

In this meandering chapter, Norberg discusses the connection between money and happiness, the naïveté of communitarian anti-capitalism, and the fatuousness of "post-liberal" writer Patrick Deneen's reactionary social vision. Norberg's defense is quirky and I find it a little unsatisfying, so let me offer mine, which arrives at the same place as Norberg's but by a different path.

Capitalism is an economic system, not a comprehensive philosophy of life, although it's consistent with the Enlightenment ideal of individual self-sovereignty. The *purpose* of an economic system is to allocate scarce resources to unlimited wants and needs, but the *fruit* of such a system is money, ideally in the hands of the people who produce those resources. Thus, we can think of capitalism as providing a way for people to make money.

---

[10] Apparently because making the poor richer causes them to contribute more to global warming. (I am guessing at what Norberg means; he didn't spell it out.)

[11] https://www.aier.org/article/johan-norbergs-the-capitalist-manifesto-a-review/

And, in a zinger that should have been printed on the book cover, Norberg writes that "the best thing about having money is that you can think about things other than money."

This comment recalls John Adams a quarter of a millennium earlier:

> My sons ought to study mathematics and philosophy, geography, natural history, naval architecture, navigation, commerce and agriculture in order to give their children a right to study painting, poetry, music, architecture, statuary, tapestry, and porcelain.

That's a pretty good statement of the meaning of life. And that's why Norberg had the gall to say, in the book's subtitle, that global free markets will save the world. You can't actually save the world, which is a collection of flawed human beings pursuing goals that are often beyond our reach. However, as Tyler Cowen says in the subhead of his mega-popular economics blog, Marginal Revolution, we can take "small steps toward a much better world."[12]

And a world organized around the classically liberal principles set forth in Norberg's manifesto would, indeed, be a much better world.

---

[12] https://marginalrevolution.com

Chapter 16. Paul Samuelson and Milton Friedman, The Frenemies Who Defined 20th Century Economics

Laurence B. Siegel
September 2021
Revised December 2023

The British journalist Nicholas Wapshott's *Samuelson Friedman*, a sequel to his earlier *Keynes Hayek*, promises an exciting Shootout at the OK Corral but doesn't deliver. (The silly book titles don't help either.) Nobel laureates Paul Samuelson, left of center, and Milton Friedman, firmly on the libertarian right,[1] had much in common – both made the study of the supply-demand-price system their life's work. They admired each other's superb technical skill and were on friendly terms personally. While the two men differed profoundly in their policy views, as revealed in their alternating columns in *Newsweek* from 1966 until 1984, Wapshott focuses on the men, not the policies. He thus misses a great opportunity to educate readers on the central economic debate of our time – the question of how large a role government should have in society.

The two economists differed not only on specific policies but also on the theories that gave rise to the policies. Did Keynesian or neoclassical economics paint a more accurate picture of the forces that shape the economy? Samuelson favored the Keynesian view; Friedman, the neoclassical. In an interview, Wapshott said that *Samuelson Friedman* was conceived as a sequel to his earlier book, *Keynes Hayek*, which portrayed two men with similarly contrasting views.

---

[1] Economically but not socially; Friedman was a libertarian, probably the best-known one of all time.

Both men had weaknesses. Samuelson had an oddly soft spot for central planning and infamously forecast that the Soviet Union would overtake the U.S. economically by the 1980s. (He later updated his forecast to the 1990s and eventually abandoned it.) Yet Samuelson's most renowned work in government was as an advisor to President Kennedy, a cold warrior and no leftist. Friedman's greatest weakness, a rigid absolutism about monetary policy that set him on a collision course with President Nixon, was also his greatest strength: he did not bend with the political winds and stood firm in his convictions.[2]

A word on Nicholas Wapshott

Wapshott's approach to describing a political battle is refreshing: until the end of the book, he takes no obvious side in the Samuelson-Friedman debate. He thus avoids the acrimonious tone that poisons many books on political economy. Having been a biographer of many apolitical people – actors Rex Harrison and Peter O'Toole, and director Sir Carol Reed, among them[3] – Wapshott seems comfortable being, or at least appearing

---

[2] But Friedman was not that inflexible: In https://www.thedailybeast.com/nicholas-wapshott-a-lovefest-between-milton-friedman-and-jm-keynes (gated but free to first-time viewers), Wapshott writes,

> [In] his buried essay on Keynes, Friedman ...[a]bruptly dismiss[ed] Hayek's notion that big government tends to curb the rights of individuals... report[ing] that, in Britain, where government was administered with integrity and honesty, governments have grown large without endangering the public good.
>
> From his time in England, Friedman learned that "Britain retains an aristocratic structure, one in which noblesse oblige was more than a meaningless catchword. Britain's nineteenth-century laissez-faire policy produced a largely incorruptible civil service, with limited scope for action, but with great powers of decision within those limits. It also produced a law-obedient citizenry that was responsive to the actions of the elected officials operating in turn under the influence of the civil service.
>
> While big government in Britain did not tend to be tyrannical, it was "very different in the United States," which "has no tradition of an incorruptible or able civil service." Quite the contrary...

The "buried" essay is https://www.richmondfed.org/~/media/richmondfedorg/publications/research/economic_quarterly/1997/spring/pdf/friedman.pdf.

[3] Also, oddly, the pop star George Michael (in a book co-authored with Wapshott's brother Tim).

to be, neutral. Interestingly, he has kept both his right- and left-leaning credentials burnished: he worked for Tory icon William Rees-Mogg at the *Times* of London and joined the neoconservative New York *Sun* as national and foreign editor in 2006, where he spoke admiringly of Ronald Reagan's legacy. But he also writes for the socialist *New Statesman* and teamed up with celebrity editor Tina Brown to establish the mostly progressive *Daily Beast*.

That said, the book builds toward a strong preference for Samuelson's policies that Wapshott keeps fairly well hidden until he sums up the legacies of the two men in terms of their relevance to the cure for the Global Financial Crisis of 2007-2009. In Wapshott's view, Keynesian remedies ended a crisis that was caused by letting markets "run wild," a policy he says that Friedman would have favored.[4]

Wapshott's prose is not bad but it doesn't sparkle. You have to be interested in Samuelson and Friedman specifically, not just in the economic debate framed by the two men, for *Samuelson Friedman* to hold your attention. In addition, as the popular economist and author Noah Smith said about the *Keynes Hayek* prequel, "you won't learn much economics from this book, which is mostly an account of the lives and labors of its two protagonists."[5] That's disappointing compared to what an author more interested in the history of economic thought could have delivered.

Because of this, I focus in this review more on the economics of Samuelson and Friedman and less on the personalities.

---

[4] Wapshott also, absurdly, blames the Trump presidency and the attempted "coup" of January 6, 2021 on the pernicious influence of Friedman's small-government thinking. Friedman would have thought the anti-intellectual Trump repulsive. I suspect that none of the thugs and clowns who broke into the Capitol in 2021 had heard of Friedman or could explain why "that government is best which governs least" (Thoreau's, not Jefferson's, aphorism).

[5] http://noahpinionblog.blogspot.com/2012/11/keynes-hayek-by-nicholas-wapshott.html

About Paul Samuelson

The public face of Paul Samuelson (1915-2009) is his mega-successful *Economics* textbook,[6] plus his *Newsweek* column. Among economists, however, he is regarded as possibly the greatest mathematical economist of all time. For this revolution in economic analysis, and for his lucid explanation of Keynesian theory, he won the 1970 Nobel Prize in economics, the first such prize won by an American.

Paul Samuelson in the 1990s
Source: https://economics.mit.edu/faculty/samuelson/photos

Samuelson is also blamed by some for turning economics almost single-handedly from a storytelling discipline, akin to history, into a mathematical nightmare. The last time a top economics journal could be easily read by a nonspecialist was in the 1950s, just before Samuelson's influence peaked.[7]

At any rate, because of Samuelson's ubiquitous textbook, a generation of undergraduates from the 1948 first edition to sometime in the 1960s learned (inaccurately) that Keynesian macroeconomics was the only macroeconomics that mattered. Then, while personally remaining a Keynes acolyte, Samuelson began to revise his book to reflect a more ecumenical approach, absorbing influences from Friedman and many others. His "neoclassical synthesis" integrated ideas from the older economics of the nineteenth century into the Keynesian framework. He also gradually began to include in his book alternative approaches to

---

[6] Still in publication and still mega-successful, with later editions co-authored with 2018 economics Nobel Prize winner William Nordhaus.

[7] In 1987 the American Economic Association founded a nontechnical or "storytelling" journal, the excellent *Journal of Economic Perspectives*, specifically to address that problem. A few specialties in economics, especially economic and business history and the history of economic thought, are still (somewhat) nonmathematical.

macroeconomics such as Austrian free-market economics, Marxian economics, and institutionalism.

Paul Samuelson on investing

Most mainstream economists haven't contributed much to finance; Samuelson did so lavishly. He developed several of the seminal ideas defining modern portfolio theory and the understanding of investment risk. His 1965 paper, "Proof That Properly Anticipated Prices Fluctuate Randomly,"[8] uses theory to demonstrate what Eugene Fama, at roughly the same time, demonstrated using data: it's hard to beat the market. While Fama's advocacy of efficient markets is better known, Samuelson's is just as important in that (with James Tobin, Kenneth Arrow, and others) he established the microeconomic foundations of modern finance. Without these foundations, finance stands alone, separate from the rest of economic theory; with them, it is fully integrated into the larger world of economic thinking.

In a 1994 paper in the *Journal of Portfolio Management* entitled "The Long-Term Case for Equities (and How It Can Be Oversold),"[9] Samuelson addressed time diversification. Many boosters of the long-term case for equities, notably Jeremy Siegel, have proposed that long-term investors face less risk than short-term investors because, in the long run, stocks have time to make up for short-term losses. Historically that has certainly proved to be true – at least in successful countries like the U.S. and U.K.[10]

---

[8] Samuelson, Paul A. 1965. "Proof That Properly Anticipated Prices Fluctuate Randomly." *Industrial Management Review*, Vol. 6 (Spring), pp. 41-49. Note that this groundbreaking finance paper was published in a fairly obscure journal even though Samuelson was probably the world's best-known economist at the time. I'm guessing that is because mainstream economics journal editors didn't think finance was in their bailiwick.

[9] Samuelson, Paul A. 1994. "The Long-Term Case for Equities." *Journal of Portfolio Management*, Vol. 21, issue 1 (Fall), pp. 15-24.

[10] An extensive literature on "survival bias" asks whether the experience of long-term successful countries like the U.S. and U.K. is representative, or more likely, upward biased in that it overstates the returns that can be expected when you don't know in advance whether a country's stock market will succeed. See various chapters in Goetzmann, William N., and Roger G. Ibbotson, 2004, *The Equity Risk Premium: Essays and Explorations*, Oxford, UK

But, Samuelson countered, "Time spent waiting to recover from crashes is also time spent waiting for more crashes." Thus, while stocks should be expected to beat bonds in the long run, there is no assurance that this will happen. The risk of being invested in the stock market does not tend to disappear over time. Rather, in nominal terms, the stock market is riskier than fixed-income assets over all time horizons. In real terms, the stock market is still riskier than fixed income unless there is a hyperinflation or the serious threat of hyperinflation.[11]

Samuelson is correct. To have even the *possibility* of a high rate of return, an investor must take the risk associated with having a large weight in stocks. However, we must make this choice without relying on any belief that a long holding period eliminates or substantially reduces this risk.

This thinking places Samuelson, mostly celebrated for his macroeconomic insights, in the first rank of academic *investment* pioneers.

About Milton Friedman

While Milton Friedman (1912-2006) was about as well respected as Paul Samuelson as an economic theorist and empiricist, it's in promoting the public understanding of economics that Friedman was really at his best. He is pictured here in his natural habitat, which is in front of a TV camera. His explanations – of how capitalism and freedom are related, how choice empowers

Milton Friedman in his natural habitat – PBS
Source: https://www-tc.pbs.org/fmc/interviews/images/ihr2friedman.ing

---

Oxford University Press.

[11] The discussion in this and the next paragraph is paraphrased from Siegel (1997), which I wrote after I heard Paul Samuelson speak on the topic. Siegel, Laurence B. 1997. "Are Stocks Risky? Two Lessons." *Journal of Portfolio Management*, vol. 23, no. 3 (Spring), pp. 29-34.

the consumer, and how monetary policy was to blame for the Great Depression and the great inflation of the 1970s – are timeless. He influenced a generation of young people, including the incredible 52% of University of Chicago undergraduates who, at the peak of his influence late in the twentieth century, chose economics as their major.[12]

Friedman the monetarist

Friedman is best known for turning the equation of exchange, an old concept expressed by the accounting identity $MV = PQ$, into a *theory* of how prices and inflation are determined. (This equation means that the quantity of money, M, times the velocity of money, V, equals the sum of the dollar volume all transactions in the economy, $P \times Q$, in any given period.) Friedman's theory, called the Quantity Theory of Money,[13] says that, all other things equal, an increase in the quantity of money will cause prices to rise by the same proportion. If Friedman's theory is correct, and it certainly was at the time (it now requires modification because of changes in the institutional structure of the economy), we have a way to explain inflation and, if we can anticipate what the monetary authorities are going to do, a way to forecast it.

His classic 1963 work with Anna Schwartz, *A Monetary History of the United States, 1867-1960*, showed that the theory held up well over that period in the United States. It has been vindicated in other countries, including (to a first order) those that experienced hyperinflations such as Weimar Germany. Some recent research shows that the theory is incomplete in that it ignores the effects of fiscal policy that do not show up in the measured quantity of money, but that is a topic for another day.[14]

---

[12] Personal communication from the Dean of the College, John Boyer. (He thought the percentage should be lower, and it now is.) Full disclosure or true confession: I applied to the University of Chicago from high school in hope of studying with Friedman, but when I found out how tough a grader he was, I only audited the course. I nevertheless became acquainted with him through other channels. He had such a casual manner that when I met him for the first time, I thought maybe I was meeting a *different* short Jewish man in his sixties; I expected a dominating personality but he was modest and kindly. He signed my dorm's Monopoly™ board, adding the flourish "Down with monopoly!"

[13] Friedman was not the first to call this the Quantity Theory of Money, but he is the person most closely associated with it.

[14] See Cochrane, John H. *The Fiscal Theory of the Price Level*. Book draft,

Friedman's influence soared in the 1970s, after the predictions in his 1967 presidential address to the American Economic Association came true. In a PBS television appearance, he said,

> [I]n the presidential talk I...argued that, if you tried to follow the policy of using inflation to try to cut down unemployment. you would end up with both more inflation and more unemployment.... [Y]ou can't keep fooling the people all the time, and people will recognize what's happening, and as they recognize what's happening you'll have to have more and more inflation to achieve that objective. And even that won't work because people will catch on to it. And what happened in the 1970s [stagflation] was about as clear a demonstration of something that had already been predicted in advance as you could have.[15]

I'll return to the 1970s inflation episode later, in the section on Samuelson's and Friedman's time in public service.

Friedman and investment management

Friedman was not a finance scholar, but his insights into money have influenced every investment manager. By "money" I mean what Friedman meant at the time: currency in circulation plus checkable deposits in banks. These were (during Friedman's lifetime) non-interest-bearing instruments that could be used to trigger a transfer of real resources. All other assets, real and financial, are "not money" and need to be paid for with money – and you would expect to be paid with money when you sell them.[16]

This bright line between money and other assets has since been blurred by the Fed's payment of interest on reserves, and by the emergence of new sources of liquidity such as cryptocurrency and lines of credit backed by

---

https://www.johnhcochrane.com/research-all/the-fiscal-theory-of-the-price-level-1. The Cochrane book is very long and technical. With two colleagues, Thomas Coleman and Bryan Oliver, both of the University of Chicago, I am writing a short, nontechnical book about the Fiscal Theory, a part of which has been published as a CFA Institute Research Foundation brief, https://rpc.cfainstitute.org/en/research/foundation/2021/puzzles-of-inflation-money-debt.

[15] https://www.pbs.org/fmc/interviews/friedman.htm (undated).

[16] In the classic textbook explanation, this is the "medium of exchange" function of money. The other functions are as a unit of account and a store of value.

stock and bond portfolios and by real estate. Thus Friedman's Quantity Theory is not as directly applicable as it used to be. Even while Friedman was still alive and active, money market funds and other new financial instruments required an expansion in the definition of money for the purpose of estimating what inflation might be; we therefore have a whole family of monetary aggregates: M0, M1, and so forth through M6. But the basic principle, that the amount of money in circulation helps to determine the price level, remains sound.

Investment management requires estimates of future inflation for several reasons. One is that investors' liabilities or spending plans are sensitive to inflation. Another is that inflation is incorporated into asset returns in different ways for different assets: unexpected inflation hurts nominal bonds, leaves the value of TIPS bonds unchanged (if all other things are equal, but they're never equal), and typically hurts equities in the short run but not in the very long run.[17] An industry of "Fed watchers" has grown up around the perceived ability to predict inflation, as well as real output, based on the actual or expected behavior of the monetary authority. While Fed watchers do more than just look at monetary aggregates to forecast inflation, it is an important part of their job.

In addition, labor and materials costs and consumer spending are affected by inflation, so it is important for investors to keep their pulse on

---

[17] The effectiveness of TIPS in hedging against unexpected inflation was called into question in the 2022 inflation surge. Early in that period, the longest (30-year) TIPS bond had a pitiable real yield (yield not including future inflation adjustments) of -0.59% on December 3, 2021. After the inflation and the Fed's response to it, which involved one of the fastest interest rate increases in history, the 30-year TIPS yield mushroomed to +2.56% on October 25, 2023. This meant a capital loss to holders of 30-year TIPS of an astonishing 64.2%. Some hedge! But (1) nobody invests all their money in the longest TIPS bond – at least I hope they don't – and (2) the money then grows at the new, much higher interest rate instead of the original negative one.

At any rate, the huge price drop was caused not by the unexpected inflation itself – which would not, by itself, change the TIPS price – but by the Fed's unprecedented "quantitative tightening" response to it. That is what I mean by "all other things are never equal."

TIPS fans (I am one) may counter that a bondholder who doesn't look at interim price fluctuations but holds the bond to maturity will have been neither helped nor hurt by the unexpected inflation (except for a small amount of risk from having to reinvest coupon income at unpredictable rates). The higher nominal payouts from the bond caused by the inflation will be canceled out by the decline in the purchasing power of the dollars received. But not looking at the price is cheating. TIPS are not riskless.

monetary policy. Not all investment managers are monetarists in the Friedman sense, but almost all are aware of the importance of monetary policy and of resulting changes in the price level.[18]

Samuelson and Friedman in public service

I've drifted pretty far from my original goal, which was to evaluate Wapshott's account of the tension between the two great economists of the last half of the twentieth century. Let's now return to the book, and look at the area in which Samuelson and Friedman came into conflict the most, and where Wapshott focuses his attention: public service.

Samuelson and Friedman got their start in public affairs by advising John F. Kennedy and his presumptive 1964 opponent Barry Goldwater respectively. While the two candidates differed on practically every economic issue, it was an amicable time: the candidates liked each other so much that they hoped to conduct the campaign *together* as a barnstorming tour – in Goldwater's private plane. And both were engaging, charismatic fellows with a gift for oratory. It would have been the campaign of the century.

Alas, it was not to be. Kennedy was assassinated and his successor Lyndon Johnson had little interest in Samuelson's theories, although he kept Samuelson on his team.

Meanwhile, Richard Nixon, another candidate with a limited interest in economics, rose to the top of the Republican Party and was elected president in 1968. Friedman would have been a natural advisor to the Republican who had defended free markets in his 1960 debates with Kennedy, but Nixon clashed with Friedman at every turn. Tevi Troy in *The Wall Street Journal* writes:

---

[18] I am mostly referring to active managers, including those who allocate actively between asset classes, but I really think all managers should be aware of monetary policy and its consequences because every pool of assets is gathered to pay for some sort of spending, which is affected by inflation.

In September 1971, Milton Friedman attended a meeting at the White House with President Richard Nixon and George Shultz, who was then director of the Office of Management and Budget but had previously taught at Friedman's University of Chicago. Nixon somewhat graciously tried to defend Shultz from Friedman's free-market wrath, telling the professor that Shultz hadn't been responsible for what Nixon called a "monstrosity" of a policy. Friedman's response was blunt: "I don't blame George. I blame you, Mr. President."

Friedman never again visited the Nixon White House or spoke to Nixon, but he was right. The freeze would have disastrous effects. Fortunately, Friedman's time advising presidents wasn't over... After [Ronald] Reagan was elected president in 1980, a very important someone in Washington was once again listening [to Friedman].[19]

Friedman, Reagan, and Thatcher

According to Wapshott, the tightly coordinated Reagan-Thatcher administration in the U.S. and U.K. adopted Friedman's purist free-market message wholly. This description is a little unfair – they didn't and couldn't make all markets "free" or unregulated. Regarding monetary matters, however, Reagan and Thatcher did what Friedman suggested: they adopted a cold-turkey cure for the inflation that was then raging out of control (13.3% in the U.S. and 18.0% in the U.K. in 1980).

As Exhibit 1 shows, the cure involved sending both economies into a deep recession by hiking interest rates to unprecedented levels: 22% in the U.S. and 17% in the U.K.[20]

---

[19] https://www.wsj.com/articles/milton-friedman-nixon-reagan-free-market-price-controls-11629327291

[20] These are short-term, central bank interest rates. Long-term bond yields peaked at 15.8% in the U.S. and 16.3% in the U.K.

Exhibit 1 — It was bad, very bad... Interest rates and inflation in the U.S., May 1954-August 2024. The U.K. experience was similar. Unemployment also reached very high levels in both countries

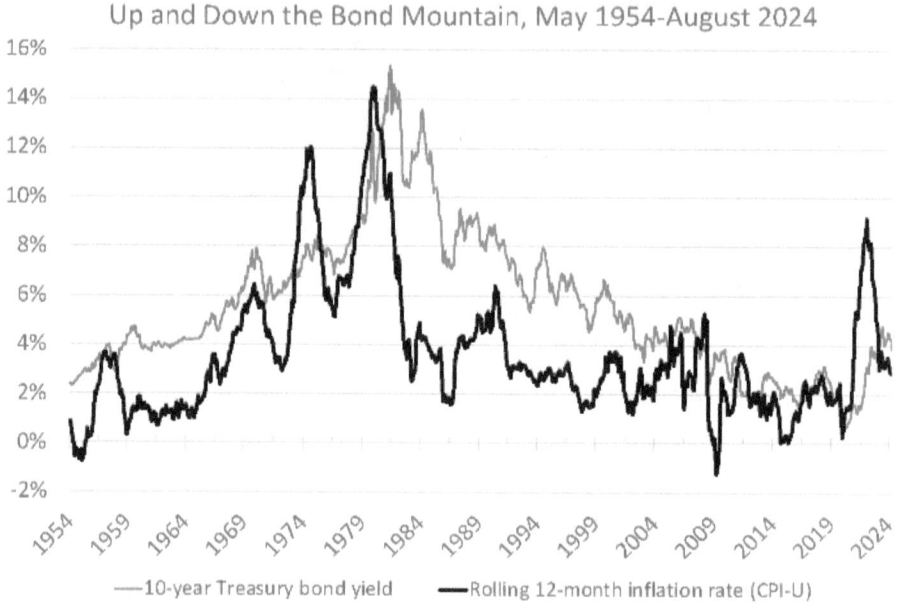

Source: Drawn by the author using data from FRED, Federal Reserve Bank of Saint Louis.

Younger investors who didn't live through this period should study the exhibit closely. Many now think of the 1970s and early 1980s as a historical oddity – or they don't think of them at all. I thought likewise of the crash of 1929 when I was a young analyst forty or more years ago. I should not have done so, and younger investors should not do so now. It's unlikely, but it could happen again.

The experiences of the U.S. and U.K. in this period were parallel but not identical. In the U.K., it took the 1978-1979 "winter of our discontent," which was really awful (see Exhibit 2), for the people to elect – out of desperation, a large Conservative majority whereby its leader Margaret Thatcher got Friedman's policy prescriptions enacted.

U.S. President Jimmy Carter's "malaise" speech, in which he didn't use the word *malaise* but should have, reflected, as in the U.K., not only a decade of capital destruction and a wrenching dislocation in the labor market but a general sense that the country was declining, perhaps beyond the hope of recovery.

Exhibit 2 — Stoke Newington, UK, in "the winter of our discontent" (1978-1979)

Source: https://flashbak.com/alan-denneys-photographs-of-stoke-newington-during-the-winter-of-discontent-in-1979-35474/

The call for "somebody to do something" grew from a whisper to a roar – until somebody, the voters, *did* do something. And, in both countries, it was a monetarist and free-market prescription which stopped inflation in its tracks and kicked off a generational bull market, but which also displaced old-economy workers, many of them forever. We are still feeling the reverberations of this disruption.

The economic ice bath worked wonderfully to bring down inflation. By 1983 the U.S. inflation rate had fallen to 3.1%, and the U.K. rate to 4.6% – but the sky-high interest rates required to bring down inflation froze the economy and generated equally sky-high unemployment. There was a nagging fear that the Friedman-Reagan-Thatcher team had overdone it.

Was there a less painful way to stop the destructive inflation of the 1970s and early 1980s? Probably not. Inflation happens because someone benefits from it: governments (which are typically net debtors), corporate and individual debtors, some trade unionists. To stop inflation, you have to stop providing those "rob Peter to pay Paul" benefits, meaning that Paul will be unhappy. Following Frédéric

Bastiat's nearly 200-year-old maxim,[21] those who are unhappy (with any given policy) scream bloody murder all day and night, and those who are happy sit quietly so as not to rock the boat. Thus, the inertia behind the status quo, in this case high inflation rates, is powerful.

When the ice bath began to have its effect, with inflation rates falling rapidly, there was concern among economists and politicians that the expected post-recession prosperity would kindle the inflationary fires once again, and that the wrenching economic adjustments that had brought down inflation would be for naught. That did not happen, and with the benefit of hindsight it is now evident that pursuing anti-inflationary policies with great vigor, as Reagan and Thatcher did, was the right decision.

But Wapshott does not agree:

> But Friedman's simple dogma, which seemed to make sense to a number of financial journalists, market analysts, and a clique in the Conservative leadership in the mid-seventies, ended its British life as an apologia postscript to a decade of unnecessary mass unemployment and painful lost opportunities.

Conclusion

The mismatch between the promise and delivery of the book begins with the subtitle, "The Battle Over the Free Market." While the two men disagreed very strongly about free versus regulated markets, the main tension described in the book is between monetarist and Keynesian macroeconomic theory and policy, a narrower question. Wapshott could have enlivened the book by noting that Samuelson sharpened his criticism of Friedman after the latter's death:

> At the bottom of this worst financial mess in a century [in 2008] is this: Milton Friedman–Friedrich Hayek libertarian laissez-faire capitalism, permitted to run wild without

---

[21] Bastiat said (I paraphrase) that any policy that benefits a small group of people will be sought by those people with great passion and effort, while it will only be opposed very mildly by those paying for it because that particular policy will only cost them a few *sous* (pennies). So government naturally grows and grows.

regulation. This is the root source of today's travails. Both of these men are dead, but their poisoned legacies live on."[22]

Ouch. Samuelson seems to have been a socialist who kept his edgier views quiet so that he could be more effective as an advisor to presidents and public intellectual in the capitalist United States. It's disappointing to find that out about a man who contributed so much to economics as it is practiced today.

To sum up, readers interested in the historic battles over how to fight the Great Inflation that peaked in the 1970s in the U.S. and the U.K. will find much of value in *Samuelson Friedman*. These battles have become relevant once again, forty-some years later. But those interested in the larger questions, including many raised by both Milton Friedman and Paul Samuelson in their long and multifaceted careers as economists, should look elsewhere.

---

[22] Samuelson, quoted in Henderson, David R. 2022. "Great stories and weak economics." *Regulation*, CATO Institute, Winter 2021-2022, https://www.cato.org/regulation/winter-2021/2022/great-stories-weak-economics

Chapter 17. Friedman's Bulldog? Edward Yardeni Presents a Brief for Capitalism

Laurence B. Siegel[1]
January 2022

A Personal Reflection

At some level you carry what you learned in school with you for the rest of your life. I went to the University of Chicago out of high school, hoping to study with Milton Friedman, who had published *Capitalism and Freedom* a decade earlier. I didn't wind up studying directly with Friedman but I got to know him through other channels and took courses from many of his friends and students including George Stigler, Yale Brozen, and Deirdre McCloskey.

Friedman's values, Chicago School economics, and classical liberalism have shaped my intellectual life — as has the unrelenting dedication to free inquiry of University of Chicago presidents Hanna Holborn Gray and Robert Zimmer. It was a great way to start my adulthood.

---

[1] The author thanks Stephen C. Sexauer for his extensive help, including significant passages (updated and modified) from a previous work by the two of us (https://larrysiegel.org/the-age-of-experts-a-review-of-marc- levinsons-an-extraordinary-time-2/).

Ed Yardeni's Three Cheers for Capitalism

I was therefore delighted to see that Edward Yardeni, a highly regarded investment analyst and consultant, has written *In Praise of Profits!*[2], a full-throated defense of capitalism, competitive corporations, and profits. In a time when free enterprise is under artillery fire and capitalism and capitalists (other than some tech company founders) are widely vilified, even "Two Cheers for Capitalism" are welcome. (That is the title of a 1978 book by Irving Kristol.) Yardeni offers three unapologetic cheers:

> Market-driven profit is the source of prosperity, not its nemesis… [M]ost entrepreneurs who succeeded…struck it rich by offering consumers goods and services that improved their collective well-being, often spotting consumer needs that no one else saw… Entrepreneurs, driven by the profit motive, are the ultimate source of prosperity that benefits everyone. Kill their profit motive, their entrepreneurial spirit and their work ethic, and you'll kill the golden goose.

No mincing words there.

A Balanced View of Progressivism

But wait — unlike many "conservatives" (Ed Yardeni says he is one, but a better word is liberals as in "classical liberals"), Yardeni has kind words for progressives:

> Progressives no doubt mean well… [They] have made a great deal of progress in expanding the social safety net provided by the government to help people in need. Among their major achievements are Social Security, Medicare, Medicaid… [a long list follows].

---

[2] I leave out the typographically awkward exclamation point after this. *In Praise of Profits* is volume 6 of a longer series by Yardeni titled Predicting the Markets. It can be obtained at https://www.amazon.com/ Praise-Profits-Predicting-Markets-Topical/dp/1948025124.

In fact, one of his subchapter titles is "In Praise of Progressives." Much of *In Praise of Profits*, then, is a less a direct presentation of the virtues of capitalism than an attempt to educate progressives on why the problems they seek to solve will be helped by more capitalism, not less.

The popularity of radical leftism among today's young people and some of their foolish elders strikes me as bizarre — like Elvis Costello, they want to bite the hand that feeds them. Because of shoddy education, young progressives don't see where their own future prosperity will come from; being young and not having yet accumulated capital like their parents, they think they never will. It was ever thus — I thought the same thing 50 years ago when I was a young dummy, as did my father at the same age, and probably his father who was born in the 1880s. From my grandfather to today, U.S. real GDP per person is up over 10 times. Capitalism and the pursuit of profits created this progress.

Yardeni, then, does the much-needed work of explaining to progressives where progress comes from. I would have been hard pressed to write such a sympathetic book addressed to progressives. I thank Yardeni for doing so.

On the one hand, on the other hand

Moreover, Yardeni is, to his credit, a two-handed economist. He sees both sides to most questions. Not only does he praise his progressive opponents (who, the somewhat progressive author Steven Pinker says, "hate progress"), he joins them in hating crony capitalists. He documents the contribution to the economy of small corporations, partnerships, and sole proprietorships, often neglected by those who focus on the S&P 500 as the metric of business success. He is concerned about executive compensation that is hundreds of times that of the firm's median employee.

What is economics for?

Yardeni calls for economics to play an activist role:

> The latest (19th) edition of *Economics* (2010) by Paul Samuelson and William Nordhaus teaches students that economics "is the

> study of how societies use scarce resources to produce valuable goods and services and distribute them among different individuals." ...[But] I've learned that economics isn't a zero-sum game as that definition implies. Economics is about using technology to increase everyone's standard of living... Free markets provide the profit incentive to motivate innovators to solve this problem... From my perspective, economics is about creating and spreading abundance, not about distributing scarcity.

This provocative paragraph accurately reflects a fundamental division in economics. First and foremost, the goal of economics has been, and probably should be, what Milton Friedman called "positive," simply trying to understand how the economy works — how people behave in their roles as consumers and producers. ("Descriptive" is a better word with less baggage.) Let's learn some physics before we design rockets.

But Yardeni's view reflects the hope, shared by most economists, that their skills and observations can be used to improve everyone's lives. That's "normative" or prescriptive economics, used by policymakers. In view of the great mistakes that have been made by applying economic thinking to social engineering, Yardeni does us a favor by narrowing the discussion. He argues that his goals — creating and spreading abundance — can be fostered *by making profits*. Only profitable companies can generate well-paying jobs, fund large research and development projects, and provide the atmosphere and infrastructure needed to attract and retain high achievers.

But first, a word from your accountant

All this political economy is great fun and a worthy topic for a discussion at the University Club or a classroom, but there's some practical learning to be had from *In Praise of Profits*. It's about accounting — in particular, the way that profits fit into our system of National Income and Product

Accounts (NIPA) designed by the Nobel Prize-winning economist Simon Kuznets and others almost a century ago.[3]

During the Great Depression, economists realized they did not have the tools to understand what was going on. They had primitive measures such as railroad car loadings, but much more was needed. Simon Kuznets, a Byelorussian[4] Jewish immigrant who taught at the University of Pennsylvania, responded to this need by developing a method of "national income accounting." Kuznets added up the dollar value of all the transactions in the economy over the span of a year, netting out intermediate transactions to avoid double counting, and called it Gross National Product (GNP), from which GDP was later derived.

Kuznets's method assesses the long-term growth rate of the economy quite nicely, although many economists quibble about its biases and shortcomings. Kuznets was well aware of these, stating that "the welfare of a nation can scarcely be inferred from a measure of national income." Still, having nothing else to work with, economists found GNP to be a vast improvement over the primitive measures they had been using to cope with the mystery of the economic collapse of the 1930s.

After World War II, which ended the Great Depression, Congress passed the Full Employment Act of 1946, which conveyed to the U.S government responsibility for full employment, stable prices, and growth in output.[5] To assess how well they were doing, Congress mandated that unemployment, a consumer price index, and GDP measures be used. These measures are generally well constructed but are nevertheless imprecise indicators of economic well-being. Nevertheless, our leaders govern based on these NIPA data.

---

[3] National product as a concept is much older and dates back to the Frenchman, Pierre le Pesant de Boisguillebert, in the 1690s, but Kuznets was the first to design a practical implementation of it and come up with accurate estimates.

[4] Byelorussia is the name for Belarus that was in use at the time.

[5] For a fuller description of this period, see my article with Stephen C. Sexauer at https://larrysiegel.org/the-age-of-experts-a-review-of-marc-levinsons-an-extraordinary-time-2/.

Millions and millions of profitable businesses

Yardeni shows how the profits of public and private corporations, partnerships, and sole proprietorships fit into this picture. There are more than 6.8 million corporations in the U.S., *plus* partnerships, sole proprietorships, and individuals reporting income from a business or profession.[6] Profits of non-S&P 500 companies are nearly as large (40% vs. 60%) as the profits of the S&P 500, and the *dividends* of non-S&P companies are much larger (64% vs. 36%) than those of the S&P because of S corporations passing their profits through to their owners in the form of dividends.

In 2018, Yardeni notes, there were 27.1 million proprietorships, and 4.0 million partnerships with 27.4 million partners. So, the number of pass-through business owners and partners totaled 54.5 million; adding in the 6 million corporations, there was one business for every 5-1/2 Americans (men, women and children)!

Profits, then, are vital to our economy and way of life and do not all go to "fat cats." They mostly go to us, the people, in the form of business income as well as dividends and capital gains on the stocks in our retirement plans and other investments.

A book that serves two masters

Yardeni's slim volume, accompanied by oodles of graphs and charts (actually printed in the book, not on a web site!), has two flaws:

1. *Yardeni should have written two separate books.* He tries to serve two masters. He starts with a serious discussion of profit in a

---

[6] "Admittedly," writes Yardeni, "these numbers are inflated by partnerships that are limited liability companies (LLCs)," dominated by real estate partnerships that often are small holdings indeed. To manage liability, it has become customary for landlords to establish an LLC for each building they own.

national income accounting sense: what "profit" means, how to calculate it, how it fits in with other macro concepts such as unemployment and economic growth. This would be book one and provides valuable education, but it pulls the reader's attention away from what Yardeni told me was his main purpose, which was to write a Capitalist Manifesto — book two.[7] A lively video interview of Yardeni conducted by Josh Brown and Ben Carlson is a better manifesto. Two tight books would be a better one-two punch.[8]

2. *Yardeni's discussion of profits completely leaves out the cost of capital.* If you have deployed capital in an enterprise and only earned what you could have earned by putting the same amount of capital into the public markets, your entrepreneurial effort hasn't made you any money! An economist would say that your profit is zero. Any discussion of the role of profit in the economy should give the concept of the cost of capital (properly, the opportunity cost of capital) a central place.

Ignoring the opportunity cost of capital is a major omission. The concept is centuries old: in a survey taken *in the 1830s*, a group of businessmen said, "no profits should be considered earned until the fair rate of return on capital [that is, the opportunity cost of capital] is taken into account."[9] This is as well-established an economic concept as has ever existed.

No one can efficiently deploy resources without considering what the best use, next best use (and so forth) of that resource might be. Capital is one of the most important of those resources and is the one being discussed. A brief treatment of capital costs as they affect the measurement of profits would have greatly improved the book.

---

[7] As of January 2024, the interview was at https://www.youtube.com/watch?v=tQqFCGcWvCU. Since this article was first published, Johan Norberg has written a wonderful book called *The Capitalist Manifesto* (https://www.amazon.com/Capitalist-Manifesto-Johan-Norberg/dp/1838957898/). Several older books bear the same title, including a 1958 book by Louis Kelso and Mortimer Adler.

[8] Because *In Praise of Profits* is part of a series of books, this suggestion is not all that unrealistic.

[9] As reported by Gary Hoover in a personal communication. Hoover, a retired serial entrepreneur and university lecturer, is founder of the American Business History Center, http://www.americanbusinesshistory.org.

Which way is forward? Closing thoughts on progressivism and progress

One of the odd features of today's progressivism is that it looks for inspiration not to the future, but to an imagined past of shared prosperity and social harmony. The postwar period of American hegemony, say 1947-1973, in the wake of a catastrophic war in Europe and Asia, is regarded by some as a model for the future. During that period, many, but not all, Americans saw themselves as belonging to a very large and growing middle class. Rich, poor, and those in between went to the same schools, spoke the same language, and shared the recent memory of a brutal war. Although more and more people were moving to cities and suburbs, small-town living — where people from all walks of life rub shoulders and are forced to get along — was the predominant memory, and for many the present reality.

But because both Yardeni and I are economists like many potential readers of this review, I want to look at the economic data — not just reflect casually on our past — to judge progress. In 1947, U.S. GDP per capita was $14,018 (in the "2012 dollars" used by the St. Louis Fed to make comparisons across time); by 1973 it had grown to $26,758. In 2020, it was $58,759. And we have much cleaner air and water, incomparably better medical care, cheaper and safer travel, and almost free instant communication. This is priceless progress.

Setting aside emotion and invoking rationality, would you rather live in a 1973 $26,735 GDP per capita country or today's United States with per capita income of $58,759?

These observations call forth the question: Why are the good old days so often perceived as better than the present, even if they're not? Steven Pinker writes,

> [T]he negative coloring of...misfortunes fades over time. As the columnist Franklin P. Adams pointed out, "Nothing is more responsible for the good old days than a bad memory."[10]

---

[10] In his book *Enlightenment Now! The Case for Reason, Science, Humanism, and Progress.*

We also confuse our own situation with that of the commons. Beyond a certain age, life becomes a race against diminishing capability. As Pinker says, "we mistake a decline in our faculties for a decline in the times." Each of us is getting closer to death each year. But society isn't getting closer; because of increasing longevity, it is actually getting farther away from death.

Last word

The University of Chicago professor Peter Leeson, who has carefully studied the relationship between economic systems and developmental success in different countries, would heartily approve of Yardeni's book and his crusade to reform progressivism so that it supports progress once again:

> Unless one is ashamed of unprecedented increases in income, rising life expectancy, greater education, and more political freedom, there's no reason to be a milquetoast defender of capitalism. That is what sprawling free markets have meant for countries that became more capitalist over the last quarter century... I also find that the two cheers for capitalism variant that desires markets, but "within reason," is wrong... Development is monotonically increasing in capitalism. Maximal capitalism begets maximal development.[11]

I'm pretty sure he's right.

Self-plagiarism warning: This paragraph (of mine and Pinker's), starting with "Then why are the good old days" and ending (ironically) with "death," is repeated from my 2018 review of *Enlightenment Now!* at https://larrysiegeldotorg.files.wordpress.com/2018/05/ajo-siegel-pinker.pdf

[11] Leeson, Peter T. 2010. "Two Cheers for Capitalism?" in *Symposium: Peter Berger's Achievement in Social Science,* Soc (2010) 47: 227–233, published online at https://www.peterleeson.com/Two_Cheers_for_Capitalism.pdf

Chapter 18. Why Joel Kotkin's Fear of American Neo-Feudalism Is Unfounded

Laurence B. Siegel
December 11, 2022

Joel Kotkin, an urban geographer, demographer, and prolific futurist, argues in a new book that the United States is headed toward "neo-feudalism." The original feudalism of the Middle Ages bound most individuals into a fixed position in the social hierarchy. Kotkin sees something similar emerging in our future.

But his evidence is unconvincing.

Rather than feudalism, we are headed toward hyper-capitalism, where each person is an entrepreneur constantly selling his or her services to the highest bidder. Thus, although it's beautifully written, pleasantly brief, and full of interesting information, Kotkin's book, *The Coming of Neo-Feudalism*, fails to persuade.

Joel Kotkin
Source: http://www.joelkotkin.com/

The dark vision of a sunny man

Want to be afraid…really afraid?

Kotkin writes,

> A poll conducted by the [Victims of] Communism Memorial Foundation in 2016 found that 44% of American millennials favored socialism while 14% chose fascism or communism. By 2024 millennials will be the country's biggest voting bloc by far.

Coming from a man whose disposition has been sunny for his entire career, and whose books and articles promote "an America where solutions trump ideology," this nugget is not good. We have always had socialists and communists in our midst, but fascism? Really?

I don't necessarily believe the poll. Other surveys of the young, admittedly from before the pandemic and current economic uncertainty, showed that they favor "economic moderation" while holding liberal social views.[1] The poll results are surprising as well as alarming.

Here's a more typical Kotkin prognostication, from 2010:

> ...[I]f we look beyond the short-term hardship [of the Great Recession], there are many reasons to believe that America will remain ascendant well into the middle decades of this century...[O]ne important reason is people. From 2000 to 2050, the U.S. will add another 100 million to its population...putting the country on a growth track far faster than most other major nations in the world. And with that growth...will come a host of relative economic and social benefits.[2]

This 2010 quote exemplifies the sunny Kotkin I know and love, and whom I invited to speak at a conference I helped organize a few years back.[3] His talk was received with great enthusiasm — although a few audience members, recalling the zero-population-growth *zeitgeist* of their youth, were surprised to hear Kotkin tell them they should have more children.

A feudal future...or maybe not

Yet Kotkin has soured on America's future. If we are careening toward neo-feudalism, I don't want to go along for the ride. The original feudalism, in the Middle Ages, was a system of personal relationships, enforced by custom, between members of various rigidly defined and hereditary social

---

[1] Russell Dalton of UC Irvine, writing at
https://www.press.umich.edu/9526877/politics_of_millennials.

[2] AOLNews.com, March 15, 2010.

[3] Institute for Quantitative Research in Finance (The Q Group), meeting in Dana Point, CA, Fall 2012.

classes. The livelihood of each person was both guaranteed and limited by their place in the feudal system. It was terrible.[4]

Kotkin sees similar power imbalances, reminiscent of feudalism, growing out of the exaggerated inequality into which our society has evolved. Our class system, such as it is, includes the super-rich captains of technology, finance, and entertainment; rank-and-file workers; and an underclass consisting of those made unemployable by that very technology.[5] These three classes are familiar leftovers from the factory system.

However, we've also sprouted more exotic groups such as the "precariat" — gig workers who are getting by but always at risk of destitution — and a new bourgeoisie of graduate school-educated professionals who are called funny names by pundits. If you are reading this, you probably belong to this last group, called the clerisy by Samuel Taylor Coleridge in 1830, and more recently the creative class by Richard Florida, bobos by David Brooks, and (I love this) the X people by Paul Fussell.[6] Reflecting the polymathic economist and historian Deirdre McCloskey's influence on my thinking, I'll just call them the bourgeois. I will return to this theme later.

---

[4] Although feudalism has its sentimental admirers, the great French historian Fernand Braudel (1902-1985), who has studied medieval and early modern European history probably more intensively than anyone else, gets the last word. Kotkin writes, "Braudel paints the grim reality of life for European peasants [in that era as] a life of 'almost total deprivation.' Peasants had practically no furniture, often not even a table, and they sold their better food products — like wheat, eggs, poultry, and lambs — to their social superiors, contenting themselves with millet and maize supplemented by salt pork once a week."

[5] "Such as it is": The U.S. has never really had a class system in the British sense. What Americans call "classes" are really income categories and are very fluid. They are less fluid than they used to be, but social structure is always more fluid when a country is going from poor to rich; the starting point matters. Meanwhile, immigrants, many of whom are doing spectacularly, find the U.S. much more fluid than where they came from. The length of the line of people waiting to get into a country is a surefire indicator of that country's relative desirability.

We still find that many wealthy people come from modest circumstances, and a current trend is for the children of the bourgeois to be *downwardly* mobile for voluntary reasons. There is no landed aristocracy to speak of. That said, the cognitive élite, discussed later in this article, has become increasingly concentrated in their own communities and isolated from the other groups, as described vividly in Charles Murray's *Coming Apart* (2013).

[6] All three terms are used by David Brooks in this bit of undeserved self-flagellation: https://www.afr.com/world/north-america/how-the-bourgeois-bohemians-broke-america-20210824-p58lch.

Are we headed toward feudalism, or something else?

What is feudalism? According to the *Encyclopedia Britannica*,

> [It] was characterized by the absence of public authority and the exercise [instead] by local lords of administrative and judicial functions...and the prevalence of bonds between lords and free dependents (vassals). [The bonds]...were forged by the lords' bestowal of property, called "fiefs," and by their reception of homage [i.e., a formal pledge of loyalty] from the vassals. These bonds entailed the rendering of services by vassals to their lords (military obligations, counsel, financial support) and the lords' obligation to protect and respect their vassals.

Does that sound like the United States you see in 2022 or at any time you imagine? If not, you understand what I find unsatisfying about this book. It assumes we will stay on the narrow path that Kotkin thinks we're on, which is unlikely even if he is correct about us currently being on that path. The book therefore makes a forecast which will turn out to be wrong.

If not headed toward neo-feudalism, where are we headed? Feudalism is based on fixed economic roles for the various components of society and thus fixed wealth shares. The U.S. economy is anything but fixed. The giants of the "old" telecom industry, itself dating only from the breakup of AT&T in 1984, are already gone or are shells of their former selves. The new tech titans are founders of social media and internet retailing companies — industries that weren't in anyone's wildest imagination 30 years ago.

We will have a few enduring winners, producing new Warren Buffetts, but most of today's darlings will crash back to earth and their founders will climb down the wealth rankings as quickly as Engine Charlie of General Motors did a couple of generations ago. The 1970 list of largest-cap companies, or richest men, looks completely unfamiliar now.

This wildly competitive mêleé has no chance of turning into an ossified "neo-feudal" structure. It is hyper-capitalism, not feudalism paleo or neo.

Not a Gilded Age, but a Golden Age for the cognitive élite and a tarnished Silver Age for the rest

There is a vague resemblance between the present and future I'm describing and the capitalist milieu of the Gilded Age, but with profound differences. A few entrepreneurs in technology and finance, sometimes called "robber barons" in reference to the Gilded Age kingpins, have produced much of the wealth of the country and have been rewarded with a much smaller, but still immense, share of the wealth of the country.[7] Their employees toil in infinitely better conditions — mostly comfortable offices, hospitals, and schools instead of dangerous mines, factories, and farms — and earn a rate of pay (adjusted for inflation) more than five times that of the Gilded Age midpoint year of 1885.[8] Yet there is still a vast gulf between the two groups' standards of living, far larger than what prevailed in the egalitarian middle of the twentieth century.

To round out the contrast between feudalism and either the original Gilded Age or what I anticipate in the future, there's no "absence of public authority"! There wasn't in 1885, there isn't now and, importantly,

---

[7] The historian Burton Folsom, writing for the Foundation for Economic Education at https://fee.org/articles/how-the-myth-of-the-robber-barons-began-and-why-it-persists/, makes the case that the "robber barons" were not robbers but more like today's tech entrepreneurs — mostly deserving of their fortunes despite their flaws. I agree with Folsom but I won't quarrel with "barons," because tech entrepreneurs live better than any baron of old could have imagined.

[8] The Gilded Age, so named by Mark Twain and Charles Dudley Warner, is usually defined as 1870-1900. I started my calculation with the average wage in 1885 of a New York carpenter, an upper middle-skilled trade at the time, which was $2.99 per day [obtained from https://fraser.stlouisfed.org/files/docs/publications/bls/bls_0499_1929.pdf, p. 162]. (The investment analyst Meryl Baer, who compiled similar data, notes that "most workers did not earn that much money" [https://bizfluent.com/info-7769323-history-american-income.html].)

I annualized this amount, assuming a five-day week and 50-week year, to $747 per year, and assumed that was the entire income of a family of four. A $747 annual income inflates to $22,963 in 2022 dollars. I compare this to the 2022 median family-of-four income in New York State of $117,706, a 5.13x "raise" in real terms. This analysis is admittedly very superficial, but it is a reasonable first cut at the question of how much the U.S. standard of living has increased over the last 137 years.

technology is enabling public authority to grow even more powerful in the future. If the bourgeoisie existed in feudal times, it was tiny, consisting of a nascent merchant class plus the intellectuals of the church and the king's court. Today it approaches 20% of the entire population, one of the great achievements of our society. It will grow larger still.

Whatever you want to call our unequal but prosperous world, today or in the foreseeable future, it's not feudalism.

Bountiful times for the cognitive élite

What I expect — with which Kotkin concurs in his other works but not here — is the continued growth of the cognitive élite, the winners of what David Freedman, writing in *The Atlantic* in 2016, called the "war on stupid people."[9] That's not quite fair, because the cognitive élite bears no malice (that I know of) toward the less intellectually able, but the smart are getting all the money while there just isn't that much for "stupid" people to do. This trend will continue and accelerate. Despite the valid complaints of young college graduates struggling to get a foothold in the economy, more and more of the future workforce will be educated and specialized and will enjoy even higher standards of living than they do today.

Consider the slice of recent history in Exhibit 1:

---

[9] www.theatlantic.com/magazine/archive/2016/07/the-war-on-stupid-people/485618/

Exhibit 1 — *Evolution of job quality in the United States January 1983–August 2022*

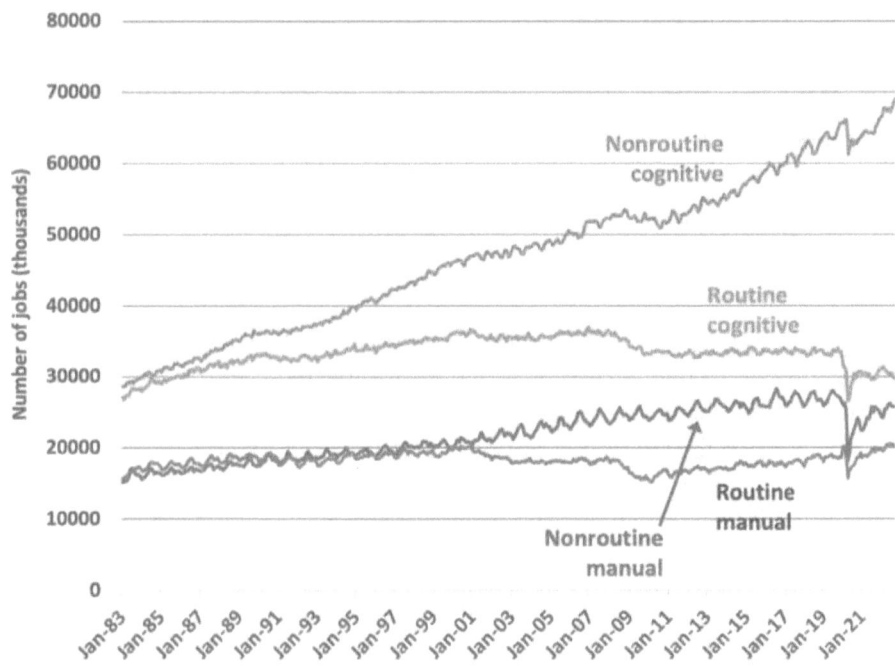

Source: Siegel and Sexauer (2022), using data from FRED, Federal Reserve Bank of Saint Louis.[10]

The data speak for themselves. The trend toward non-routine cognitive jobs is dramatic and enduring. As machines, including AI, do more of our grunt work, the cognitive élite will grow and grow. Put your thinking caps on.[11]

Why do I call the future for the other three job categories a "silver age"? Because most people, at all skill levels except the highest, lived very poorly until sometime in the last century. (Read Dickens, or Upton Sinclair's *The Jungle*. The latter was written in your great-grandfather's day, not that long ago.) It's better now. There is no comparison between lower-status workers' living standards, even in the fairly recent past, with their living

---

[10] Siegel, Laurence B., and Stephen C. Sexauer. 2023. "Longer, Healthier, Happier: Why Working Longer Improves Almost Everything." *Journal of Retirement* (May 24).

[11] When *The Economist* ran a much earlier (2014) version of this chart, they gave it a one-word title: "Think."

standards today. The silver is a little tarnished, but it's a silver age for the common man.[12]

However, positional goods (being better off than your neighbor) are important too. This is deeply embedded in our DNA. No one wants to be consigned permanently to a proletarian class because of their immutable characteristics, even if they are eating well and living in air-conditioned quarters, surrounded by modern appliances and online stimulation. They want to be valued. They want respect and appreciation as well as better pay. They also crave upward mobility and job security.

Some of this inequality is the result of technological change and we're just going to have to live with it. But overall standards of living will continue to rise, and the tide has fortunately turned in favor of higher wages and greater respect for labor. We are not creating a serf class.

The marriage of capitalism with liberal democracy, placing the sovereignty of the individual at its core, will win the competition among systems of social organization because it is the only system we know of that makes people rich. As I write this, people in Russia, China, and Iran are agitating for the economic and humanistic freedoms that we have but that many of us take for granted.

Sooner or later, they will get them. We had better not let ours disappear. I now touch on a couple of specific issues raised by Kotkin.

No bourgeois, no democracy?

Kotkin's thinking draws on that of the social historian Barrington Moore, Jr., who is known for the aphorism, "No bourgeois – no democracy."[13] *The*

---

[12] Unfortunately I am not writing in German, where *mensch* means human being, as in the rights of man or Darwin's descent of man. A male human being is *Mann*. I apologize for any offense taken by female human beings — but you should blame the Anglo-Saxons of old, not me. In German and some other languages there is no such confusion.

[13] Moore, Barrington, Jr. 1966 [1993]. *The Social Origins of Dictatorship and Democracy: Lord and Peasant in the Making of the Modern World*. Boston: Beacon Press, 1993. Moore, a Harvard professor, lived from 1913 to 2005.

Coming of Neo-Feudalism features this quote conspicuously. What are Moore and Kotkin talking about?

Moore, a controversial figure often described as a Marxist, argued that all successful democracies have been created and stewarded by the middle and upper-middle classes, not the proletariat from whom Marx claimed to draw support. He was exactly right. To avoid becoming mob rule, democracy requires informed voters and even better-informed elected officials, drawn from a population that is accomplished enough to have earned at least modest prosperity and respectability. The alternative is Venezuela or Argentina, the world's first formerly developed countries.[14]

Deirdre McCloskey, about whom I have written previously,[15] agrees and lays out her case in exquisite detail. Her Bourgeois Trilogy, a three-volume masterwork detailing the role of the middle class in building the good society, argues that if everyone adopted bourgeois values, most of our social problems — not just those caused by poverty, but those due to deteriorating personal and community values — would disappear. That is not about to happen, but it is an ideal to work toward.

As noted earlier, the bourgeois in the United States are a larger share of the population than in any other society in human history. This is a good thing. Although human variation assures that we won't make everyone bourgeois, we should at least provide a stepladder to the bourgeoisie that anyone can use or not use according to their preference and ability. Our sprawling state university and community college system is testimony to the fact that we're already trying.

---

[14] In 1950, Venezuela was the fourth richest country in the world (https://www.weforum.org/agenda/2017/09/ venezuela-was-once-twelve-times-richer-than-china-what-happened). Recently many Venezuelans have faced starvation. Argentina is better off, but its status in the world economy has plunged almost continuously for a century.

[15] In Chapter 1 of this book, "Deirdre McCloskey and Art Carden Explain How the Modern World Came to Be," and in my 2019 book, Fewer, Richer, Greener.

The "gated" city

Kotkin's area of greatest expertise is urban geography, so it's here that we'd expect his best insights.[15] He observes that our great cities have become what he calls "gated" — more economically segregated — even as relations among racial groups have improved. In addition, always a contrarian, Kotkin builds on his long-standing skepticism about gentrification. He argues, instead, that expansion of the urban footprint — what many call sprawl — is beneficial because it lowers prices and gives people of ordinary means a decent place to live. These are reasonable thoughts, even if they push hard against the current wisdom, which favors Europe's compact cities (surrounded by green space) as well as the small number of "European" cities in the United States.

But, using Chicago as a case study, Kotkin does not get the human geography of that city quite right. He relies on the widely repeated observation by Pete Saunders, an urban planner who is black and lives in Chicago, that his city (where I also live) is one-third San Francisco and two-thirds Detroit.[16] That's shorthand for one-third playground for the affluent and two-thirds impoverished ghetto.[17]

Saunders's comment is outdated at best. Chicago is one-third San Francisco, one-third Detroit, and one-third East Los Angeles, where Hispanic newcomers have transformed once-sleepy factory neighborhoods (essentially all white) into lively, if in places a little tatty, *barrios*. The Hispanic population of Chicago now surpasses that of blacks and is upwardly mobile, albeit from a low level, supporting Kotkin's view that immigration conveys large benefits.

All of our cities have vibrant immigrant neighborhoods built and run around family capital and hard work. These ambitious families are taking advantage of opportunities for economic improvement that the U.S.

---

[16] The relevant Saunders article is at https://urbanreforminstitute.org/wp-content/uploads/2019/01/Toward-More-Equitable-Urban-Growth.pdf.

[17] While San Francisco is *priced* as an affluent playground, the quality of life in many parts of the city has decayed beyond belief due to homelessness, drug addiction, and open-air drug trafficking. Chicago has less of this because of the forbidding weather.

uniquely provides. The "gated" city is way too broad a generalization and doesn't match up to the dynamic nature of everyday life in the U.S.

One last thought about Kotkin's urban analysis: while the middle class is in trouble within the city limits of Chicago and other "global cities," it is mostly thriving in the suburbs and particularly in smaller, cheaper cities. This isn't exactly a secret. Kotkin would have found less of a trend toward feudalism if he had looked at Salt Lake City, Columbus, and Nashville instead of New York, Los Angeles, and Chicago.

Is Kotkin's perspective liberal or conservative?

Yes, it is.

Readers can be forgiven for finding Kotkin's political stances puzzling. He's an eclectic centrist who left the Democratic Party after decades of loyal support, alleging that his former party has abandoned working people and instead taken up the causes of identity politics and anti-growth.[18] Over the last decade or so, Kotkin has taken positions on the center-right that infuriate so-called progressives. Most notably, he is "pro-choice on urban development,"[19] disdaining the bicycle-and-latte crowd that would have us all live like residents of Amsterdam (for our own good) and favoring urban sprawl when and where that is what people want.

Kotkin has been courted by the pro-business, growth-oriented right, and he now writes for several publications associated with that tendency. But he is also shunned by those on the right who loathe his pro-immigration stance and other liberal positions.

Jonathan Swift said that you can tell a genius by "the dunces...all [being] in confederacy against him."[20] Modernizing Swift's wisecrack, when the

---

[18] www.dailynews.com/2016/07/29/what-happened-to-my-party-joel-kotkin/

[19] The "pro-choice" quote is actually from Kotkin's long-time collaborator, Wendell Cox.

[20] Swift, Jonathan. 1706. "Thoughts on Various Subjects, Moral and Diverting," Famously quoted in, and used to craft the title of, John Kennedy Toole's *A Confederacy of Dunces* (ca. 1962 [posthumous, 1980]), which is included in many lists of the greatest novels of all time.

wing nuts on both sides of the political spectrum are arrayed against you, you must be doing something right. Kotkin is.

Conclusion

There is much to admire about Kotkin. He writes about compelling topics. He follows nobody's party line. His deep knowledge of urban history and geography, and his small-L libertarianism, give him a generous view of population growth and urban development that is a refreshing change from the hectoring tone of much of today's opinion writing.[21]

Yet there is something deeply unsatisfying about Kotkin reaching back to the 12th century to find a metaphor for the kind of society that he fears we are turning into. We will not become a feudal or neo-feudal society. Thus, *The Coming of Neo-Feudalism* is his weakest effort so far. I do not recommend the book. It is a better use of your time to read his other works, many of which are superb. I am particularly fond of Kotkin's much earlier *The City: A Global History* and *Tribes*, modern classics that nudged pop sociology in the direction of real science and serious analysis.

But if I'm wrong and feudalism is coming back, don't buy stocks — buy indulgences.

The author thanks Stephen Sexauer, CIO of the San Diego County Employees Retirement Association, for his review and comments. –W.H.W.

---

[21] Not that unlimited population growth is desirable or even physically possible. Kotkin draws a bright line between developed economies, for which he believes population growth is mostly beneficial, and poor countries that need to curtail their population growth (and in many cases are finally doing so).

Provocative

This is our catch-all title for topics that lie on the fringe of Larry's home base. If you want a quick dose of some fascinating topics, read these selections first.

Wayne's favorite: The Many-Faceted Mind of Will Goetzmann.

I have chatted with Will, who is a walking encyclopedia on topics ranging from the discovery of prehistoric coins to his enjoyment of ice dancing. His writing dazzles the reader with the breadth of his understanding.

— W.H.W.

Chapter 19. How to Think: Steven Pinker's Instruction Manual for Your Brain

Laurence B. Siegel
December 6, 2021

An urban legend has Amos Tversky, the late co-founder (along with Daniel Kahneman) of behavioral economics, asking a computer scientist what he was working on. The computer man responded, "I study artificial intelligence." Tversky, a notorious smart aleck, responded, "I study natural stupidity."

Steven Pinker has studied natural stupidity more carefully than any other living writer. Trained as a cognitive psychologist and linguist, Pinker's books on human behavior include *How the Mind Works*, *The Blank Slate*, and *The Stuff of Thought*. Pinker became one of the world's foremost public intellectuals with his book on the decline of violence over time, *The Better Angels of Our Nature*, and its sequel, *Enlightenment Now*, which I reviewed in Advisor Perspectives on December 7, 2021.[1]

Steven Pinker
Source: https://stevenpinker.com/photographs-steven-pinker

---

[1] https://www.advisorperspectives.com/articles/2021/12/07/steven-pinkers-instruction-manual-for-your-brain

Why we need to learn how to think

Pinker goes back to basics with *Rationality*, a beautifully written book on *how to think*. Why do we need to be taught how to think? Our brains evolved under conditions very different from those we face now, so that our instincts that promoted survival under those conditions may harm us today. We mix up logic with emotion, data with information, and information with wisdom.

Rationality is a step-by-step guide to unmixing these and using hard-headed logic to arrive at useful conclusions.

Readers with a business or economic education will find the material in *Rationality* familiar and a bit elementary. However, Pinker has an unusual gift for clarity of expression and effectively draws in readers who think they know this stuff already. He takes the reader through the building blocks of rational thought: logic and the perils of logical fallacies, probability, Bayesian inference, risk and utility, signal detection and statistical decision theory, game theory, correlation and causation, and behavioral and cognitive biases. That's the outline of the book, which I enthusiastically recommend.

It's not possible to go over all this material — basically, a college-level course in how to think rationally — in a book review, so I'll focus on three chapters of particular interest to investors: (1) Bayesian inference; (2) risk and utility (briefly); and (3) signal detection and statistical decision theory (that's how investors pick asset managers). The other topics are very important, but most of them, especially correlation/causation and behavioral biases, have been covered in other literature familiar to most educated readers.

Bayes' wonderful theorem

Scott Alexander, pseudonymous author of the popular and kooky intellectual blog Astral Codex Ten, posted the following recently:[2]

$$P(A|B) = \frac{P(A) \cdot P(B|A)}{P(B)}.$$ All the rest is commentary.

Huh?

Those familiar with Jewish texts will recognize the second expression immediately: Rabbi Hillel of Babylon, asked by an onlooker to explain the Torah while standing on one foot, said "What is hateful to thee, do not do unto thy neighbor... The rest is commentary."

The first, more challenging expression is Bayes' theorem, which provides a formula for blending one's prior knowledge (sometimes called prior belief) about the likelihood of a phenomenon, $P(A)$, with experimental evidence, B. The "posterior", $P(A|B)$, "probability of A conditional on knowing B," blends that experimental evidence with the prior to arrive at the best estimate of the likelihood of that phenomenon given both sets of information (the prior and the experiment).

Alexander is implying that the theorem is the most important lesson you will ever need. I'm not sure about that, but it's one of the most important.

Developed by the Reverend Thomas Bayes (1702-1761), Bayesian inference is one of the most useful concepts in statistics and in human thought. It is also one of the most confusing. Yet, without Bayesian inference, our thinking about the likelihood of events will be muddled and wrong. Steven Pinker gives Bayesian inference a central place in his instruction manual for your brain.

The most confusing part of Bayesian inference is why one's prior beliefs should have any weight at all. Suppose I believe the moon is made of green

---

[2] Formerly Slate Star Codex. http://astralcodexten.substack.com. Alexander is part of the "rationality community"; Pinker is on the fringes of it.

cheese. Or that flying as a passenger in a commercial airplane is more dangerous than piloting a hang glider. Or that bitcoin is going to $1 million.

That's not what prior belief (or "Bayesian prior") means – not even close – although students of statistics can be forgiven for making that mistake, because part of the mystery surrounding Bayes' work is his fault. He never wrote up his research, and what remains of it is found in a nightmarish mathematical paper *about* Bayes, written by one Richard Price in 1763.[3]

A Bayesian "prior," then, has nothing to do with the silly beliefs listed above. Forget that you ever heard the word "belief" in the context of Bayes. A Bayesian prior is *prior knowledge*, specifically the probability you would assign to an event before that event occurs. That probability, $P(B)$ in the above expression, is the "base rate" or likelihood that events of that general kind will occur.

This is best taught by example. (A full explanation of the Bayes theorem is too lengthy to include here; read Pinker's book or check out the "Bayes theorem" and "Bayesian inference" Wikipedia entries.[4]) Here is the University of Chicago professor Thomas Coleman's example, similar to Pinker's but simpler:[5]

> Consider breast cancer, which is relatively rare in the general [female] population (say, 5 in 1,000). Thus, the prior probability that a woman has breast cancer, given no symptoms and no family history, is only about 0.5%. Now consider the woman undergoing a mammogram, which is roughly 95% accurate (in the sense that the test falsely reports a positive result about 5 percent of the time).
>
> What is the chance that, if a patient has a positive mammogram result, she actually has breast cancer? The temptation is to say 95% because the test is 95% accurate, but

---

[3] Price, Richard. 1763. "An Essay towards solving a Problem in the Doctrine of Chance. By the late Rev. Mr. Bayes, communicated by Mr. Price, in a letter to John Canton, A. M. F. R. S." *Philosophical Transactions of the Royal Society of London.* 53: 370–418. It has never been clear what text is Bayes' and what is Price's.

[4] https://en.wikipedia.org/wiki/Bayes_theorem and https://en.wikipedia.org/wiki/Bayesian_inference

[5] Coleman, Thomas S. 2011. *A Practical Guide to Risk Management.* Charlottesville, VA: CFA Institute Research Foundation, p. 43.

that [is wrong]...Out of a pool of 1,000 test-takers, roughly 5 (5 in 1,000) will actually have cancer and roughly 50 will receive false positives (5% false-positive rate, 5 in 100, or 50 in 1,000).

That is, there will be roughly 55 positive test results, but only 5 will be true positives. This means the probability of truly having cancer given a positive test result is roughly 5 in 55, or 9% — not 95 in 100 or 95%.

Pinker comments,

The most popular answer from a sample of doctors given these numbers ranged from 80% to 90%. Bayes' rule allows you to calculate the correct answer: 9%. That's right, the professionals with whom we entrust our lives flub the basic task of interpreting a medical test, and not by a little bit.

Bayes' theorem, then, is a good place to start learning about how to think rationally. It could be a matter of life or death. And "what is the base rate?" is a good question to ask in any situation requiring forecasts and estimation of probability.

Risk and utility

Pinker explains risk and reward, not in relation to investing, but in terms of gambling and other choices. This is a good decision given that his primary audience consists of general readers with no special investment knowledge; investing is packed with other confounding variables, making the risk-reward relationship in that field counterintuitive. ("I want investments with low risk and high reward!")

Moreover, investment advisors and other financial professionals who need a tutorial on the basics of risk and reward should find another occupation.

But there is a gem in Pinker's otherwise humdrum risk-return chapter. For investors and (especially) economists, the most fun part of the chapter is Pinker's treatment of the silly charge that economists believe people are robotic utility maximizers who engage in coldhearted calculations before making decisions:

> Some theories are unlovable. No one has much affection for the laws of thermodynamics... [because they rule out] a perpetual-motion machine. Ever since Darwin proposed the theory of natural selection, creationists have choked on the implication that humans descended from apes...
>
> One of the most hated theories of our time is rational choice...[or] *Homo economicus*... What exactly is this mean-spirited theory? It says that when faced with a risky decision, rational actors ought to choose the option that maximizes their "expected utility"...People interpret it as claiming that humans are, or should be, selfish psychopaths.

Fortunately, Pinker doesn't believe for a moment that expected-utility theory is mean-spirited, or that people are or should be selfish monsters. He's raising a straw-man argument to show how silly the charge really is.

I do not find these theories unlovable at all. Theories like these are what allows us to make sense of the universe. I never expected to create energy out of nothing and was not disappointed to find out we couldn't. I am proud of my simian cousins. Evolution is one of the most beautiful theories ever imagined.[6]

Pinker's demolition of the straw man teaches one of the most important lessons in how to think. The lesson is in understanding the role of a theory. Economists (with a few exceptions) do not believe, any more than Pinker does, that people should make cold-hearted calculations before making any decision. Instead, they believe that economic choices can be analyzed *as if* people were utility-maximization machines. There is a big difference.

"As if" is the key here and is part of every economist's vocabulary. In the social sciences, a theory, such as utility theory, is *supposed* to be a stylized or simplified model of reality — not a full description of it. A full description of the conditions under which people make economic decisions would involve understanding the neural architecture of our

---

[6] Even though it is a theory of differential death rates, which sounds a little ghoulish. If a species has arranged its affairs so that all its offspring survive, as humans have mostly done, it doesn't evolve. See the Yale finance professor Roger Ibbotson's fascinating discussion at https://www.youtube.com/watch?v=ElEGOsN5qA4.

brains, the influence of evolution and experience on our animal natures and, even more fundamentally, the actions of the chemicals in our bodies.

Economics does not try to do all that. What economics does is to *momentarily pretend* that the world is simpler than it is, to make analysis possible. That is one reason the analysis is not always correct, but without the "as if" assumption there would be no analysis at all.

Statistical decision theory: Distinguishing signal from noise in manager selection

Statistical decision theory sounds very complex and geeky, something only an engineer would love. But it's just Pinker's moniker for statistical significance and how it captures "real" (in this case, economic) significance. Pinker adds the phrase "signal detection" to his chapter title because statistical decision theory is what enables us to distinguish signal from noise.

This issue is at the heart of asset manager selection, the principal activity of many investment advisors.

Signal detection helps us answer this question: "How confident can we be that manager A, having beaten manager B by x% over such-and-such a period, is really the better manager rather than just lucky over that past time span?" (Manager B can be the benchmark, or an index fund.) The excess return that we can attribute to skill and not luck is the signal and is the part of the return that we can reasonably expect to persist in the future (although even that will fade over time). The rest of the return variation is noise.

As this example suggests, statistical significance is harder to interpret than most people think: Distinguishing signal from noise is challenging. For example, if an investment manager has an alpha (measured over some past period) with a T-statistic greater than 2, an investor may feel "confident," based on the use of the term *confidence interval* to describe the error bars around an estimate, that the manager is adding value.

Note the tense of the expression, "adding," implying continuation of the past into the future. With this T-stat, an investor is likely to conclude that the manager is a good choice for beating his or her benchmark in the future. After all, the evidence is that, in the one "run" of the past that we have available to study, the manager did beat the benchmark with 100% certainty.

But that one run of the past will not occur again. In the future, which is what we're concerned about, what is the probability that the manager with a T-stat of 2 will beat the benchmark again?

Naively, if the run in the future were drawn from the exact same distribution as the past period that we examined, the answer would be about 95%, based on our understanding of statistical significance and T-stats. But we don't know what distribution the future run will be drawn from. There is an infinity of possible distributions that could have produced the one run that happened, and only one of those – and we cannot know which one – did. And we are just as clueless about which one will produce the next run, in the future when our money will be at work.

Past performance is not as good an indicator of future performance as the naïve interpretation of statistical significance might suggest. No wonder so many people buy index funds!

How common is "statistically significant" alpha?

In a long-ago study I did with my friends Ken Kroner and Scott Clifford at Barclays Global Investors,[7] we found that, over 1980-2000, only 10 out of 494 managers (in all asset classes) had alpha T-stats greater than 2. Only 224, fewer than half, had positive alphas at all! So, although the very best active managers produced results far in excess of what could be explained by random variation, "statistically significant" active management alpha is

---

[7] Siegel, Laurence B., Kenneth F. Kroner, and Scott W. Clifford. 2001. "The greatest return stories ever told." *Journal of Investing* (Summer). The article is gated, but an ungated article based on the same data and conclusions is at https://larrysiegeldotorg.wordpress.com/wp-content/uploads/2014/07/barclays-greatest-ii.pdf.

rare in the long run. You needed to have special knowledge of the manager's people, philosophy, and process — plus some plain old luck — to have a good chance of picking winning managers over that period, and presumably also today.

Why progress is possible but not inevitable

In Pinker's other books, he has been enthusiastic about the possibility of progress — especially moral progress, something that most other progress advocates avoid discussing. *The Better Angels of Our Nature* shows, mostly convincingly, that both state-sponsored violence (war) and interpersonal violence (as revealed by murder statistics) have declined dramatically over the centuries when measured on a *per capita* basis. By this measure, even the 20th century "hemoclysm" (his coinage), consisting of World Wars I and II and the Chinese and Indian civil wars, is not much of an outlier; long-forgotten catastrophes such as the Chinese War of the Three Kingdoms (A.D. 184-280) were much worse when measured by the percentage of the population that died.

In a later book, *Enlightenment Now*, Pinker attributed this decline in violence, as well as other elements of the improvement in living conditions over the centuries, to the European Enlightenment of the 1600s and 1700s. He asks us to embrace Enlightenment values, fearful that if we do not do so, we will be governed by the strong rather than the wise, and without the consent of the governed. Some current political trends around the world make this fear realistic. The liberal triumphalism of the late 20th century now seems like a dispatch from a lost world.

As a result, while Pinker believes that progress — economic, environmental, and moral — is possible (after all, we got here), it is not guaranteed. When people abandon the rationality so carefully cultivated by civilized people from the ancient Greeks to the Renaissance Italian humanists to the Enlightenment philosophers of whom Pinker is so fond, progress goes into reverse. And when things go wrong, they can go very wrong very quickly. Thus Pinker's passion for teaching the elements of rationality in this book, something one might think is no longer needed — but it is.

Why rationality matters

Let's pursue this line of thinking, key to Pinker's philosophy, in a little more detail. The most important chapter in his book is the closing one, "Why Rationality Matters." Becoming rational can be viewed simply as an accumulation of skills, something that can be taught to any willing learner. Most of the readers of this review will have had some of this training.

But why is it so important to learn to be rational? We're apes who are only a few hundred thousand years removed from the savanna where our instincts evolved. Many of our instincts serve us very poorly under modern conditions. We make all kinds of cognitive errors and bad decisions because our ape brains (which contain lizard brains beneath) are doing the "thinking" for us. So being rational doesn't come to us naturally at all.

Starting with Aristotle and continuing through the present day, philosophers and students of the history and methodology of science have tried to coax us toward rationality. But most philosophy is written in unreadable jargon, tainting the whole field and making it hard for the most important messages – what I call "How to Think" – to get through.

Pinker argues that rationality is a pushback against the chaos of an indifferent universe; we use our intellect to try to make order out of that chaos. And we do that partly to satisfy our curiosity about how the universe works, but more importantly to better our lives: to make progress. Pinker writes,

> Having documented [human progress in two of my previous books], I'm often asked whether I "believe in progress." The answer is no. Like the humorist Fran Lebowitz, *I don't believe in anything you have to believe in.*[8] [Progress has occurred] not because of some force or...evolutionary law that lifts us ever upward. On the contrary, nature has no regard for our well-being, and often, as with pandemics and natural disasters, looks as if it's trying to grind us down. "Progress" is shorthand for a set of pushbacks and victories wrung out of an

---

[8] My italics and a nice phrase for repeating at parties.

unforgiving universe, and...needs to be explained.

"The explanation," Pinker continues, "is rationality." His take on how the process works is one of the most powerful closing statements in any book of this genre:

> When humans set themselves the goals of improving the welfare of their fellows...*and they apply their ingenuity in institutions that pool it with others'*, they *occasionally* succeed. *When they retain the successes and take note of the failures*, the benefits can accumulate, and we call the [result] "progress."[9]

There's the recipe:

- Establish and maintain institutions that pool the knowledge of groups of people and nurture *applied* ingenuity.
- Keep a record, not just of the successes but of the failures.
- Allow the benefits to accumulate — don't cut them off with bad policies.

Now, start cooking.

Last word

In *Rationality*, Steven Pinker presents a short but powerful total-immersion course in the elements of logical thinking. While some of the material is old hat to serious readers, *Rationality* is an exceptionally well-written refresher. Gary Geipel in *National Review* wrote that Pinker's chapters "might in different hands be impassable. Pinker makes them page-turners."[10] Read this book!

---

[9] My italics.
[10] www.nationalreview.com/magazine/2021/11/15/rationality-if-you-can-keep-it/

Chapter 20. Twenty Rules for Life: Morgan Housel's Antidote to Chaos

By Laurence B. Siegel
December 2020

In a fascinating little book, *The Psychology of Money*, the investment manager Morgan Housel provides more useful self-help advice than most authors who explicitly set out to do so.

My title and subtitle are a takeoff on Jordan Peterson's wildly successful book, *12 Rules for Life: An Antidote to Chaos*, a mostly abstract work of philosophy that nevertheless counsels such actions as cleaning your room. Housel's book, likewise, is an antidote to chaos and is shorter, simpler, and more accessible than Peterson's. Each of the 20 chapters of *The Psychology of Money* sets forth a rule for life that goes well beyond finance and that readers would generally – but not always – do well to follow.

Morgan Housel
Source: https://www.bajajcapital.com
/fintastic-talks/speakers/morgan-housel

I confess to a little disappointment when I first skimmed the book. It is brief, easy, and completely non-technical. I wanted to be challenged intellectually. But, when I read the book carefully, I found myself more challenged and rewarded *psychologically* – is Housel's take on human nature accurate? Are the common mistakes he documents that universal? Can we explain them through biology, psychology, and personal history, as Housel does? These are bigger questions than how much to save so you can retire at 65, how much to put in emerging markets, or how big the equity risk premium is. Housel addresses those questions fearlessly.

But sometimes wrongly.

All "rules for life" are too general, and it is fun to note the exceptions. Where I do so, I use the label "pushback" to alert the reader that I'm disagreeing with Housel or finding one of his rules incomplete.

Let's look at some of Housel's most striking rules.

"No one's crazy"

In Housel's first chapter, he asserts that our financial behavior, no matter how strange or self-defeating, isn't "crazy," but a product of our unique experiences. These can be personal, generational, ethnic, or anything else. For example, John F. Kennedy – that rarest of birds, a politician who spoke about himself truthfully – said, "I had no first-hand knowledge of the Depression. My family had one of the great fortunes of the world…I really did not learn about the Depression until I read about it at Harvard."

This was despite Kennedy having been 12 years old in 1929, when the Great Depression began, and 23 in 1940 when it was over. Is it possible to be that insulated from one's nearby surroundings?

My father, two years older than Kennedy, was thrown out of his house by both parents (separately) and was a street urchin at 13. Is it any wonder his only investments were cash and bank deposits, and that Kennedy was a daredevil? Neither was crazy; each was following his inner directive, shaped by personal experience.

But here's some pushback: People who follow the inner voice shaped only by their own experience don't seem very smart or inquisitive. A parade of gifted entertainers from Isaac Hayes to Johnny Depp have wasted their entire fortunes, close to a billion dollars in Depp's case. Is he crazy? I would say, "yes"; his inner voice is failing him on one of the most important issues in life, how to handle money.

Bill Gates was more than just lucky

In a chapter emphasizing the role of luck as compared to skill, ambition, and other traits of successful people, Housel notes that Bill Gates was startlingly lucky to be exposed to computers at a young age because, of the "roughly 303 million high school-age people in the world," Gates was one of the 300 who attended Lakeside School. Lakeside is a top-notch prep school in Seattle, and – almost uniquely among the schools of the world, in Housel's estimation – had a timesharing computer terminal.

Housel is right that we habitually underestimate the role of luck in life. An example close to the heart of investors is the topic of winning active managers. If all active managers did was to make random bets, about half of them would have above-average track records, obviously due to luck and nothing else. Active managers don't really do this – many have real skill – but it's hard to tell skill from luck just by looking at the numbers, and we're inclined to attribute most or all of the alpha from a favorite manager to skill. And, when they falter, as they inevitably do, we tend to write off the run of poor performance as just bad luck – without any hard evidence that either conclusion is justified.

Pushback: Lakeside was not "one of the only" high schools that had a computer; it was one of a small but not infinitesimal number. Mine, Hawken in Ohio, had one too, and I used it. I attended high school two years *before* Gates. Why am I not Bill Gates? Setting aside differences in innate ability, I'm not as motivated; I didn't care *that* much about computers; and I don't have the temperament of an entrepreneur. Two of my classmates became fairly famous computer scientists, but so did a lot of people of our generation.

Warren Buffett made 96.5% of his fortune after his 65th birthday

Yes, this little Housel tidbit is true. But it's not entirely fair. The first billion is always the hardest. In addition, Buffett is 90 years old. The increase in wealth between Buffett's 65th and 90th birthdays is an impressive but not miraculous 14.3%. He probably earned a higher return than that, because he spent some and gave a lot more away. But he had to have earned quite a bit more than 14.3% per year *before* he was 65 to accumulate $3 billion by that date. Most people never accumulate $3 million, much less $3 billion.

The lesson Housel draws from this story is that very long stretches of time in the market are the sources of some great fortunes. Get rich slowly. That's good advice: Start early and never stop. But, no matter how hard you try, you're not Warren Buffett (unless you *are* Warren Buffett and you're reading this).

Getting versus staying wealthy

"You should only have to get rich once," intoned Lyn Hutton, the respected chief investment officer of Commonfund Capital in a client meeting long ago. A later author, Russell Holcombe, used this aphorism as the title of his book. The saying could not be more right.

The tragic tale of Jesse Livermore is Housel's way of emphasizing this theme.[1] Livermore was one of the world's great speculators, traders, and short sellers ("the Great Bear of Wall Street") in the years leading up to the Great Depression. During the 1929 crash, he was short the market and increased his fortune while others were losing theirs – an event that may have been his downfall. He probably thought that he had special knowledge of how to time the market.

When the market crashed again in 1930, 1931, and 1932, Livermore turned bullish. He made large, leveraged purchases and lost everything. Deeply in debt, Livermore took his own life in 1940, about when the market would have made him rich again if he had been able to hold on. That is something that unleveraged investors can do if, unlike Livermore, they do not let their spending run wild.[2]

Keep some money for yourself.

---

[1] The real Jesse Lauriston Livermore (1877-1940), not the pseudonymous modern commentator who runs the excellent http://www.philosophicaleconomics.com blog, which I highly recommend.

[2] A fuller description of Livermore's life is in Chapter 10 of this book.

The art collector...or index fund manager?

Typical of Housel's little morality tales is the story of Hans Berggruen, the German art collector who, decades after he fled the Nazis in 1936, "sold part of his massive collection of Picassos, Braques, Klees, and Matisses to the German government for more than 100 million euros."[3] His secret, says Housel, was not skill at selecting great art investments, nor was it luck. The investment firm Horizon Research, quoted by Housel, argues that it was patience and diversification:

Hans Berggruen and one of his priceless Picassos
Source: https://www.nytimes.com/2007/02/27/arts/design/27berggruen.html

> The great [art] investors bought vast quantities of art. A subset of the collections turned out to be great investments, and they were held for sufficiently long periods of time to allow the portfolio return to converge upon the return of the best elements in the portfolio. That's all that happens.

Housel then explains,

> The great dealers operated like index funds. They bought [everything they could]. Then they sat and waited for a few winners to emerge...Berggruen could be wrong most of the time and still wind up stupendously right.

This is indeed how equity index funds work: as Hendrik Bessembinder, a professor at Arizona State, showed, only 4% of all stocks outperformed

---

[3] The Berggruen Museum in Berlin is named after him, its chief benefactor. Berggruen lived from 1914 to 2007.

low-returning Treasury bills over the period from 1926 to 2019.[4] But some of those that did were huge winners. Thus, the good performance of equity indexes over long periods of time is mostly caused by a select few issues. Which ones, you can't know in advance.

Pushback: While any given index fund works this way, a *portfolio* of index funds, diversified across asset classes, only does so if you never rebalance. Otherwise, the gains on the way to huge success are harvested early and reinvested in the less successful asset classes. This is the right thing for most investors to do. The purpose of rebalancing is to control risk. While the return on a never-rebalanced portfolio is indeed dominated by the return of its best investments, that portfolio could fall 22% in one day or 57% in a year and a half, as the S&P 500 did on October 19, 1987 and in 2007-2009 respectively. More recently, in early 2020, that same index fell 34% in 23 trading days. Ouch!

Another way of looking at this is that Berggruen did not care about risk. That is easier to do (or pretend to do) when you own assets, such as paintings, that are not marked to market. There is no way to measure or fully experience the risk of a sudden decline in the value of paintings, unless you are in the process of selling them. But investors in public securities markets *should* care about risk, and should not follow the Berggruen strategy, other than to the limited extent of buying and holding index funds (or other funds) and allowing them to appreciate up to the point where the size of the holding pierces investor's risk threshold.

Wealth is what you don't see

This is a quickie. My wife recently walked by a big fancy house and remarked, "So-and-so must be really rich. They just paid $2 million for that house." I replied, "Yeah, they used to have $2 million and now they don't."[5]

---

[4] Bessembinder, Hendrik. "Do stocks outperform Treasury bills?" *Journal of Financial Economics*, volume 129, number 3 (September), pp. 440-457.

[5] I was stretching a point; when you exchange cash for real estate, the money's not gone – you've just moved it from a liquid to an illiquid bucket. But a lot of people feel "house poor," suggesting that having a lot of money in an illiquid bucket is not all it's cracked up to be.

Housel makes this point vividly: Wealth is the part of your cumulative income that is *not consumed*. You can't see it. It is in the bank, or the stock market, or some other market. What you *can* see – consumption – is the part of the person's wealth that they used to have and don't anymore. If someone appears to be rich, you have no idea whether they are or not. Just ask Jesse Livermore.

History doesn't repeat itself

...but it rhymes, Mark Twain is supposed to have said. Look at the well-known Ibbotson chart, extended back to 1871 by Morningstar to get as long a time period as possible. It's hard to tell one half-century from another. The market booms, it crashes, it stabilizes, it booms, it crashes again. On the log scale used in the chart, the real (inflation-adjusted) level of the U.S. stock market total-return index fluctuates around a *straight line* representing compound annual growth of 6.8%. The straight line implies a stable or predictable rate of return. So, can't we foretell the future of investment returns by extrapolating the past? That worked well enough most of the time.

In addition, we can't tell by looking at the house whether it was bought with spare cash or with a mortgage at the outer edge of the buyer's ability to pay.

Exhibit 1

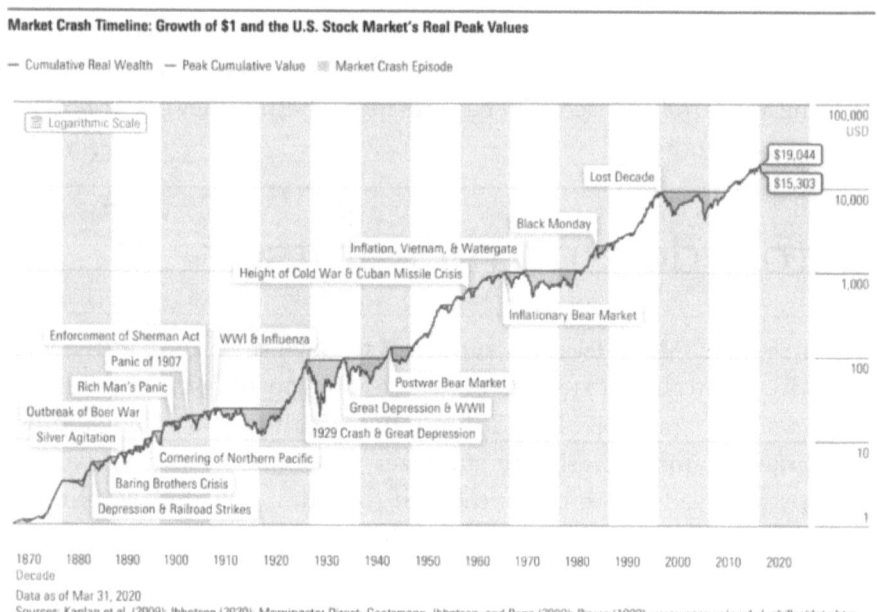

Source of the image: https://www.evidenceinvestor.com/what-previous-market-crashes-teach-us-about-this-one/ Reprinted by permission of Morningstar Inc., the underlying data source.

No, says Housel, echoing cautions expressed by Roger Ibbotson and many others since long-term historical market data first became available. Ibbotson and his colleagues would lower their forecasts of the future because interest rates are lower today than ever before,[6] and *possibly* because stock prices are high relative to historical norms. But Housel has a different set of concerns, related to changes in market structure and institutions:

> • Private equity as a means of financing business activity has become huge. We have less data on its historical performance than we do for public equities.

---

[6] They were when this article was written. No longer (as of 2024).

- The composition of the market keeps changing. Looking back over history, railroads, industrials, oils, and financials have each had their turn as the biggest components of indexes. Now it's technology. According to Housel, this has never happened before, but I would *push back* by saying that many companies that we now call industrials were the technological leaders of their time: Edison Electric (founded in 1880, about the time the extended Ibbotson chart starts), Westinghouse, AT&T, General Motors, IBM, Boeing, and many others.

- The mass popularity of individual investing for retirement only began with the invention of the 401(k) account, a little over 40 years ago. Meanwhile, traditional pension plans have all but disappeared outside the public sector.

Despite these profound changes, I agree more with John Templeton's aphorism, "the four most dangerous words in investing are 'It's different this time'," than with Housel's comic riff on it, quoting Ritholtz Wealth Management's Michael Batnick: "The 12 most dangerous words in investing are 'the four most dangerous words in investing are "It's different this time"'."

Meaningful changes are taking place all the time, but study the past carefully.[7]

The child is father to the man?

The child is father to the man, wrote Wordsworth,[8] but don't count on that working out exactly. Everyone changes, some more than most. Housel relies on this principle to argue that one's life plan must be flexible enough to allow for substantial change in oneself and one's goals and desires.

---

[7] To his credit, Housel softens his cautions about relying on history by saying, "The further back in history you look, the more general your takeaways should be. General things like people's relationship to greed and fear, how they behave under stress, and how they respond to incentives tend to be stable over time."

[8] "My Heart Leaps Up" (1802).

To drive home this point, Housel recounts the story of a young man, "the hardest-working guy I knew," who for many years wanted nothing other than to become a doctor. Despite only moderate ability, and 10 years older than his classmates, he powered through and got the coveted M.D. diploma.

How did that turn out for him? "Awful career, man." The stress and long hours had worn him out. He is not alone. Doctors are getting MBAs so they can work for or run biotech firms; some are simply selling their practices and are willing to do anything but doctoring. (I don't mean to discourage any would-be doctors among my readers.) One reason is that the industry has changed – in fact, it used to be called a profession and now it's better described as a regulated industry – but another reason, just as valid, is that the person you were at 18, pursuing a pre-med degree, no longer exists at 40 or 50.

Investors should be prepared for career changes and other surprises. *Mann tracht, und Gott lacht,* goes a Yiddish proverb (channeling a Biblical verse).[9] Man plans, and God laughs.

Optimism and pessimism: Mithridates, he died old

Are you an optimist or pessimist? I am a cautious optimist, and I have written a book reflecting that posture, *Fewer, Richer, Greener*. The title summarizes my vision of the future of humanity. I also acknowledge problems and suggest ways of fixing them.

Housel says that he, too, is an optimist by temperament. Yet, in a CFA Institute *Enterprising Investor* interview, he advocated balance, just as he does in the book:[10] "You need this barbell personality of optimism about

---

[9] Sometimes said to be Proverbs 19:21. I've used the German spelling because transliteration of Yiddish is a very inexact science.

[10] October 22, 2020, https://blogs.cfainstitute.org/investor/2020/10/22/morgan-housel-on-greed-and-fear-frugality-and-paranoia/

the long run of the market's ability to solve problems and create productivity and produce profits that accrue to shareholders."

"But that's just one side of the equation," the interviewer, Lauren Foster, remarked. Housel continued, "You also need pessimism about the short run...to survive long enough to benefit from the long run. I've often said, 'Save like a pessimist and invest like an optimist.' You need both and they seem contradictory: Long-term optimism and short-term pessimism, if not paranoia."

Yet Housel calls himself a "permanent optimist." Let's explore this idea a bit.

It's an odd optimist who is attracted to the bittersweet poetry of A. E. Housman, who in his famous poem beloved by cynical schoolboys, "Terence, This Is Stupid Stuff,"[11] argues that people who prepare for the worst are the happiest because all surprises are then pleasant surprises. I am that odd optimist, a fan of Housman's since late childhood. Housman's poem includes the tale of Mithridates, an ancient king who expected to be poisoned (a common fate for kings in those days) and steeled himself with small doses of various poisons so he would be immune. The poem concludes, "I tell the tale that I heard told/ Mithridates, he died old." The strategy works.

Housel seems to hold a similar view. Like me, Morgan Housel, while professing optimism, sees both sides: "Expecting things to be bad is the best way to be surprised when they're not. Which, ironically, is something to be optimistic about." This balance is what allows him to see the rich opportunities that await investors who commit capital to long periods of time in the market.

I told you this was no ordinary investment book. Or self-help book. It is new and different.

Conclusion

I close with two of Housel's reading recommendations from an interview with Chris Reining, a popular minimalist blogger and "supersaver":

---

[11] https://www.bartleby.com/123/62.html

Reining: You're a voracious reader. What book had the biggest influence on the way you think about money and life?

Housel: I'll give you two. *The Quest of the Simple Life* by William Dawson. It completely changed how I think about financial goals. *The Better Angels of Our Nature* by Steven Pinker. It made me a permanent optimist.[12]

I am not all that much into simplicity – I prefer a life rich in both experiences and material goods – but Housel is. Whatever your financial and personal goals, you will almost certainly get closer to them if you follow Morgan Housel's simple principles.

---

[12] Source: https://chrisreining.com/morgan-housel/

Chapter 21. Home, Home on the *Range:* The Advantage of Generalists over Specialists

Laurence B. Siegel
August 2019

A well-schooled generalist will outshine a specialist at a cocktail party, with an ability to thoughtfully contribute to conversations on any topic. But does that skill translate to better problem solving in all disciplines? That was the question David Epstein set out to answer in *Range: Why Generalists Triumph in a Specialized World*. And, as investors, we should be particularly interested in the aspects of the answer that pertain to investment management.

Everybody likes to be told they're wonderful. I read Epstein's *Range* with more than my usual enthusiasm. I'm a generalist, also called a polymath by those who love them and a dilettante by those who don't. I wanted to find out how my mile-wide, inch-deep knowledge of so many subjects is useful in life and admirable as a character trait.

What I got was a web of fascinating anecdotes, woven together by the theme I just stated, without a unifying theory or new way of looking at the world — which is what readers of quality popular-science books seek. Range is an easy, fun read. But, having placed itself in the big-think genre with a provocative one-word title alongside Geoffrey West's *Scale*, Jared Diamond's *Collapse*, and James Gleick's *Chaos*, Epstein's book does not measure up.

On genes, fat cells, and muscular abnormalities

Some of the anecdotes are truly impressive. Jill Viles, a teenage girl in Iowa afflicted with muscular dystrophy, found a genetic link between herself and an Olympic athlete in Canada, Priscilla Lopes-Schleip, with the opposite symptoms (muscular hypertrophy — big muscles — instead of dystrophy or wasting). What they had in common was a shortage of fat cells on their limbs, caused by a genetic defect. They had opposite symptoms because the defect was located at a slightly different place in the two women's lamin-A gene. The discovery was a startling display of intuition by Viles, an untrained "generalist."

But is Viles really a generalist, or a self-educated hyperspecialist on her own disorder, understandably obsessed since childhood with finding an explanation and possibly a treatment for her condition — and better informed on the topic than all but the most specialized neurologists? I'd go with this latter explanation. It often pays to be a generalist, but not in this case highlighted by Epstein.

By the way, there's a happy ending. Viles is now 44, happily married, and has a son who does not carry the defective gene.

The wicked and the kind

In Epstein's formulation, a *kind* learning environment is one in which intense study, repeated practice, and diligence are rewarded because the environment does not change much over time. "Golf, chess, classical-music performance, firefighting, and anesthesiology" are said to be kind learning environments.[1] The only one with which I have any familiarity is music, but he's right: when you practice a piece of classical music, you get better and better at it. The music doesn't mutate while you're mastering it, and audiences expect technical proficiency, not creativity; the composer provided the creativity.

I don't agree with him on firefighting, where conditions change in an instant and every building or forest is different; and anesthesiologists also need to adapt quickly to unexpected troubles. But the basic idea is sound: some environments can be mastered through diligence, the "ten thousand

---

[1] The quote is from Holt, Jim. 2019. "Remember the '10,000 Hours' Rule for Success? Forget About It" (review of Range by David Epstein). New York Times (May 28), https://www.nytimes.com/2019/05/28/ books/review/david-epstein-range.html (gated)

hours" of practice that Malcolm Gladwell, in *Outliers* (another one-word, big-think title), said was needed for extraordinary achievement.

Most learning environments, however, are *wicked*, says Epstein. These favor adaptable generalists. In a wicked environment, what you learn in one place or time period does not apply in the next one and may actually hurt you. Business management, investing, the sciences, and the humanities are such environments. A writer who only studies the craft of writing and does not live an interesting life will have little to say. A jazz (not classical) musician who plays a song the same way every time will be unexciting.

Closer to home, investment trends have swerved from value to growth to international to hedge funds to indexing and private equity in a couple of decades. A business can mutate a half dozen times in its lifetime: IBM started out as an analogue calculator company, then a typewriter company, then a mainframe computer company, then a microcomputer company, now a technical services company. Only a generalist or, in this case because it took more than a century, a series of generalists could manage such wrenching transitions.

Fox and Hedgehog
Illustration by Karel Franta

Isaiah Berlin, channeling the ancient Greek philosopher Archilocus, captured this distinction more poetically, categorizing people as foxes or hedgehogs: Foxes know many things, but hedgehogs know one big thing.

Ilana Redstone, an author affiliated with Heterodox Academy, captured this distinction beautifully (while admitting that it oversimplifies):

> ...Philip Tetlock, a professor at UC Berkeley, used this framework to examine the ability of "experts" to predict outcomes. Among other things (including an inverse relationship between fame and accuracy), he found that although hedgehogs were often quite persuasive in their

language — perhaps in part due to the strength of their convictions — foxes tended to be much better forecasters.

There were several reasons for this: foxes...possess[ed] intellectual humility. More importantly, they were willing to update their beliefs when presented with new evidence...This contrasts with the hedgehogs, who would sometimes stretch their overarching narrative beyond any range for which it was originally intended, and...more doggedly stick by their initial understanding of the world.[2]

Of course, most — maybe all — significant accomplishment is achieved by those who are a cross between fox and hedgehog. As Epstein acknowledges, it takes both general knowledge and developed specific skills to do anything hard. Fox to hedgehog is a continuum.

The battle hymn of Tiger's father

You knew immediately whom I was talking about, didn't you? Tiger Woods is one of the most famous people in the world, and he has never really done anything other than hit a ball into a tin cup a quarter mile away. There are other great golfers. But, for a long period, he was so much better than any of the others that a noted champion said Tiger was playing "a different game" from the one the speaker had mastered.

Can you imagine if a baseball player emerged who was so much better than other top players that, say, Alex Rodriguez would describe the new player as not playing baseball but a different game? Of course you can't. That's because the rewards for excellence in professional sports are so large, and the competition so tough, that the highest achievers cluster together, having similar records.[3]

---

[2] https://heterodoxacademy.org/prepare-students-foxes/

[3] Babe Ruth hit 60 homers in a season, the all-time record for decades. The much less well-known Jimmie Foxx and Hank Greenberg, playing in roughly the same era against similar pitching, both hit 58.

But Tiger stood out from a hypercompetitive crowd in exactly the way you wouldn't expect.

Epstein, a sports writer by background, observes that the young Tiger didn't want to do anything but play golf. At the age of *three*, "the boy shot 48, eleven over par, at a nine-hole course in California."[4] Tiger's father, Earl Woods, did not so much push the

> boy as allow the boy to pull him relentlessly. The elder Woods was responding to an intensely felt and completely unanticipated need and did the best he could.

The laid-back European upbringing of another champion

The Woods story, however, is an intentional misdirection. Epstein wants to *dispel* the notion that grit, single-minded focus, and 10,000 (or many more) hours are the sure path to reward. He immediately segues into a contrasting tale that suggests the grit theory is probably wrong, and cites the great tennis player Roger Federer as an example.

It was obvious to Federer's Swiss parents at an early age that he was athletic, but he didn't focus on any one sport. "As a boy, he played squash…[and] dabbled in skiing, swimming, wrestling, and skateboarding," Epstein writes. "He played basketball, handball, tennis, table tennis, badminton over his neighbor's fence, and soccer at school… Rather than pushy, a *Sports Illustrated* writer would observe that his parents were, if anything, 'pully'," urging him to "stop taking tennis so seriously" as he got older.

When the two men met for the first time in 2006, both at the peak of their respective games, Federer was a bit baffled by Woods. "I've never spoken with anybody who was so familiar with the feeling of being invincible," Federer recalls. "Even as a kid his goal was to break the record for winning

---

[4] A par 37 nine-hole course is a difficult course, not one designed for children or beginners.

the most majors. I was just dreaming of just once meeting Boris Becker or being able to play at Wimbledon."

Unlike Woods, Federer experienced what Epstein calls a "sampling period" wherein a young person (or, I guess, an older one) can try on various roles in life and figure out what they're good at, what is financially or spiritually rewarding, and so forth. Federer also sounds like a much better-adjusted human being than Woods.

Epstein sums up the tale of Roger versus Tiger by noting that many generalists have done well in the world, often outside their initial fields of interest:

> [S]ome of the people whose work I deeply admired from afar — from Duke Ellington (who shunned music lessons to focus on drawing and baseball) to Maryam Mirzakhani (who dreamed of becoming a novelist and instead became the first woman to win math's most famous prize, the Fields Medal) — seemed to have more Roger than Tiger in their development stories.

And, as Epstein notes, Charles Darwin started out on a path to become a medical doctor and then a preacher. Vincent van Gogh pursued a haphazard assortment of careers before settling on painting, "inspir[ing]," writes Epstein, "a widespread devotion that no artist, perhaps no person, has equaled."[5]

The tragic case of the failed O-rings

Epstein uses the Challenger disaster of 1986, in which the space shuttle exploded after the rubber O-rings used to join sections of the booster rocket failed, to illustrate the severity of the errors caused by overspecialization. The explosion killed all seven crew members, including two civilians.

The weather in Florida, where the launch was to take place, was unusually cold — about 40 degrees Fahrenheit — and NASA and Morton Thiokol engineers were concerned that the O-rings might fail. (Morton Thiokol was

---

[5] I'd quarrel with that: Shakespeare and Beethoven have adherents who are just as passionate; I am one. But van Gogh's art speaks to almost everyone, and is just as fresh now as it was in 1890, when he died.

The Advantage of Generalists over Specialists 323

the manufacturer of the booster rocket.) After much debate, both teams gave the fatal go-ahead to launch the rocket, basing their recommendation on an analysis of previous O-ring problems, illustrated in Exhibit 1:

Exhibit 1- Previous O-ring distress incidents graphed against ambient (outdoor) temperature: Problematic launches only[6]

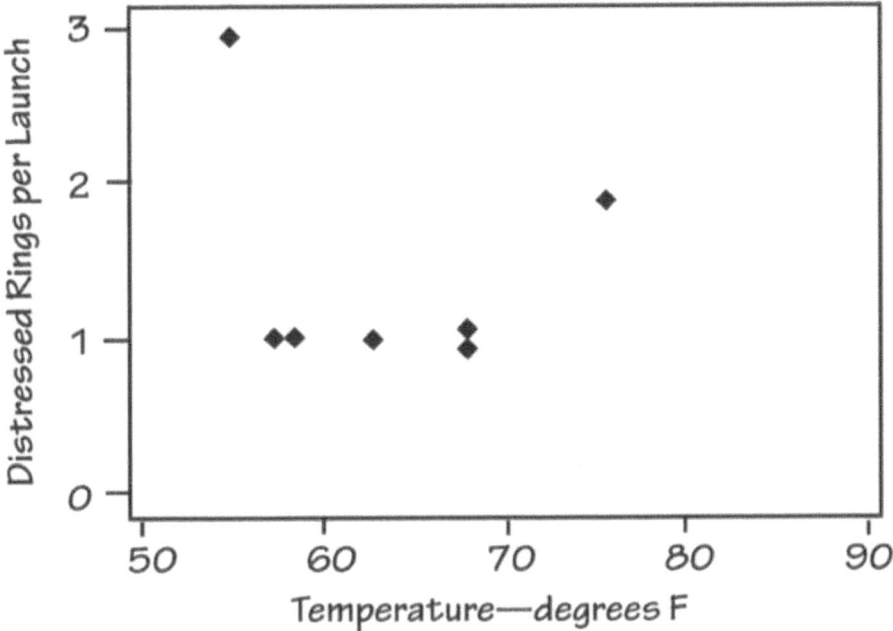

In the exhibit, there is almost no correlation between temperature and O-ring distress, although you could visually fit a slight negative relation (cold being worse than normal or hot temperatures) if you wanted to hang your hat on so few data points. The engineers who gave the go-ahead relied on this sparse data set.

---

[6] Source: Ranney, Gipsie. Undated. "Blind Spots in Learning and Inference." *The Systems Thinker* (online), https://thesystemsthinker.com/%EF%BB%BFblind-spots-in-learning-and-inference/. In Epstein's book, the space shuttle data are deliberately misrepresented as engine failures in race cars, for the purpose of teaching students about risk management, but he later reveals that they are data on O-ring distress (both erosion, which has never been fatal, and gas "blow-by," which destroyed the Challenger) on the space shuttle. Here, for clarity, I use the properly labeled data from Ranney.

What information was missing? Clearly, with hindsight, it was the launches that did *not* have an O-ring problem, as shown in Exhibit 2, which includes all launches, problematic and trouble-free:

Exhibit 2 — *Previous O-ring distress incidents graphed against ambient (outdoor) temperature: All launches*[7]

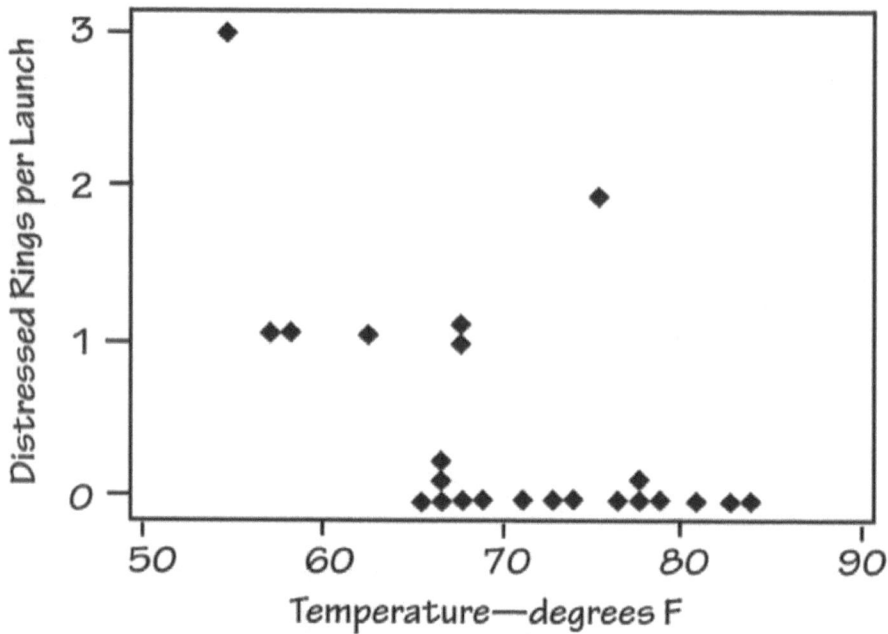

Exhibit 2 makes it painfully and tragically obvious that there is a correlation between temperature and O-ring distress: all of the launches at temperatures over 76, and all but one at temperatures over 69, were problem-free. *All* of the launches at temperatures below 64 were problematic. Launching at 40 degrees should have been out of the question.

While Epstein does not specifically blame the problem on overspecialization, the context in which he presents the case study makes it seem that way. In my view, though, the conflict was not between specialists and generalists at all — quite a few specialist engineers called

---

[7] Source: Ranney, Gipsie. Undated. "Blind Spots in Learning and Inference." *The Systems Thinker* (online), https://thesystemsthinker.com/%EF%BB%BFblind-spots-in-learning-and-inference/.

for caution and were outvoted — but between sober analysis and the do-or-die culture of the organization.

Yale professor Edward Tufte, a statistician, graphic artist, and sculptor, presented *the exact same analysis* in his magnificent *Visual Explanations*, a 22-year-old book that is known to everyone who deals with data.[8] It is not an obscure work — it is an acknowledged classic that, along with its three companion volumes, did present a new way of looking the world, the thesis being that the beauty and efficiency with which data are portrayed graphically are critical to affecting outcomes, including life-and-death ones. While the data are public information and anyone can write about them, Epstein should have acknowledged Tufte's role, especially given that Tufte testified in Congressional investigations of the Challenger disaster.

The most important equation in the world

If you're deciphering the architecture of the universe, or building a nuclear power plant, then $E=MC^2$ is pretty darned important. But if you're trying to make decisions with limited information, then the most important equation in the world is Bayes' theorem, set forth by Reverend Thomas Bayes in 1763:[9]

$$P(A \mid B) = \frac{P(B \mid A) \cdot P(A)}{P(B)}$$

where A and B are events and P( ) means probability.

---

[8] Tufte, Edward R. 1997. *Visual Explanations: Images and Quantities, Evidence and Narrative.* Cheshire, CT: Graphics Press.

[9] The work, *An Essay towards solving a Problem in the Doctrine of Chances*, was posthumous. Bayes died in 1761

In English, the probability of event A occurring, conditional on event B occurring, equals the probability of event B occurring conditional on A, multiplied by the ratio of the probabilities of the two events.

Still mystified? So are most people. Epstein gives a helpful example. Consider a physician making a diagnosis. The disease for which the doctor is testing is present in 1 of 1,000 patients, and the test has a 5% false positive rate. Assuming you know nothing about the patient's symptoms, what is the likelihood that a patient who tests positive for the disease does, in fact, have the disease?

"The correct answer is that there is about a 2 percent chance," Epstein writes. He continues,

> Only a quarter of the physicians and physicians-in-training got it right. The most common answer was 95%...[I]n a sample of 10,000 people, 10 have the disease and get a true positive result; 5%, or 500, will get a false positive; [so] out of 510 people who test positive, only 10, or 1.96%, are actually sick.

This is a straightforward application of Bayes' theorem. I'll skip the step where we fit the problem to the equation; Epstein's numerical explanation is good enough. The interesting part is that the missing information for the doctors who got it wrong — the base rate of 1 in 1,000 — was right in front of their face. It was just missing from their mind, from their field of view. And it was the key to getting an answer that is even close to being right.

Repeat after me, "What is the base rate?" If you train yourself to ask this question when trying to figure out the probability of something happening, you'll be way ahead of the game. "The base rate," of course, means "the probability of that event happening in the absence of any other information."

Most people learn Bayes' theorem at some point in their business education, or in math or statistics class or maybe in the social sciences. But very few fully appreciate what it means. That may be because the professor teaches the principle in terms of "priors" (which sound like silly preconceived notions) and "Bayesian adjustments" to the priors, based on "updated" information. But the prior, the base rate, is the most important piece of information. That's what the professors leave out.

If *Range* does nothing else, it is valuable in that it hammers this point into the reader's head.[10] How often do O-rings fail, out of all trials at all temperatures, not just in cold weather? What is the likelihood that the patient is sick, both before and after getting the knowledge that the diagnostic test is positive?

This is how generalists think, suggests Epstein. But properly trained specialists think this way too, if they are any good. The O-ring disaster and the misdiagnosed patient represent failures of both general and specialized education, and cannot be attributed to too much narrow knowledge.

Recommendations for readers

When I finished *Range*, I felt that I had read a psychology book. (The chapter title, "Flirting with Your Possible Selves," is a tipoff.) *Range* is a suite of compelling narratives, linked by a common thread — generalists outperform in unkind learning environments, which are the conditions most of us face — but it does not present a new theory or way of looking at the world.

That is not so much a criticism — if Epstein doesn't have a new theory, it's just as well he didn't make up a pretend one — as an unfair comparison with the greatest popular science books, which do open the reader's eyes to a new view of nature and mankind. This one does not measure up by that lofty standard. But it's still good summer reading, and serves as a welcome encouragement to generalists who have lost status and opportunity in an age that reveres technical expertise. History majors, take heart!

And Epstein is right that the most successful people will be those whose knowledge is what he calls "T-shaped" — both broad and deep — or, even better, M-shaped (broad in many areas and deep in a few adjacent ones). These shapes support the idea that general and specialized knowledge are

---

[10] Although, mystifyingly, Epstein never refers to Bayes by name or uses the words "Bayes' Theorem."

both important. You don't need to go back to the age of Leonardo da Vinci to excel as a jack-of-all-trades and master of at least one.

Advice for investors

Robert Hagstrom, author of the top-selling book, *The Warren Buffett Way*, wrote that investing is "the last liberal art," the last refuge of the generalist.[11] In his book with that title, Hagstrom recalled a talk by Charlie Munger, Mr. Buffett's sideman:

> Rather than discussing the stock market, he intended to talk about "stock picking as a subdivision of the art of worldly wisdom."...[H]e challenged the students to broaden their vision of the market, of finance, and of economics in general; to see them...as part of a larger body of knowledge...that...also incorporates psychology, engineering, mathematics, physics, and the humanities...[E]ach discipline entwines with, and in the process strengthens, every other.

By integrating all these disciplines, Hagstrom concluded, the student of markets can create "a latticework of mental models" that helps him or her better negotiate an often hostile terrain.

In the same spirit, Gary Hoover, the polymathic businessman and business historian who founded Bookstop,[12] wrote a book called *The Art of Enterprise*, which described entrepreneurship as "applied social science."[13] Business management and investing had better be undertaken by people with at least a little of the generalist in them, because they operate in an environment as wicked as one is likely to encounter.

---

[11] Hagstrom, Robert G. 2013 (second edition). *Investing: The Last Liberal Art*. New York: Columbia University Press.

[12] The first book superstore (founded 1982), which was acquired by B. Dalton and later sold to Barnes & Noble, thus forming the basis for Barnes & Noble Superstores.

[13] Hoover, Gary E. 2010. *The Art of Enterprise*. Out of print. PDF sold by the author at https://garyhoover.dpdcart.com/ product/136602.

The Advantage of Generalists over Specialists

In the investment field, we are often told to pay attention to alphas, betas, standard deviations, and correlations — the language of specialized expertise. I've argued elsewhere that such knowledge is important.[14] But investors also face the challenges of bull runs and bear raids, snake oil salesmen, black swans, and red herrings (a quasi-sarcastic term for private equity documents that promise boundless riches that rarely materialize). Are investors operating in a zoo?

Yes — the human zoo, with all the frailties that human beings have displayed since the beginning of time. To navigate this often unkind environment, one must be a zoologist, or, as we call students of the human zoo, generalists or humanists. First and foremost, we must understand the past and its endless variations on a few themes, notably greed, fear, and ignorance.

But we must also understand the upside, or we could not in good conscience be investors. We must observe that living conditions have been improving for at least two centuries and are likely to keep doing so for many more. Business men and women, scientists, engineers, artists and writers, and many others have contributed immensely to this Great Enrichment.[15] By investing wisely, one can participate in its continuance.

The author thanks Barton Waring for helpful comments. –W.H.W.

---

[14] Siegel, Laurence B. 2014. "Read Your Sharpe and Markowitz!" *CFA Institute Magazine* (September/October), https://larrysiegeldotorg.files.wordpress.com/2014/08/pages-from-cfa_s-0-14_8-18- 14-5-adobe-acrobat-pro.pdf

[15] Deirdre McCloskey's term (from *The Bourgeois Virtues*, University of Chicago Press, 2006), echoed in my 2019 book (*Fewer, Richer, Greener*, Wiley, http://www.fewerrichergreener.com).

McCloskey is one of the greatest generalists in economics, having held at the same time appointments in six departments at the University of Illinois at Chicago: economics, history, English, communication, philosophy, and classics. (In the last two, she was an adjunct.)

Chapter 22. "Money Changes Everything": The Many-Faceted Mind of Will Goetzmann

Laurence B. Siegel
April 2019

Will Goetzmann is no ordinary finance professor. His capstone book, *Money Changes Everything: How Finance Made Civilization Possible*, is a history of the world, centered around the idea that finance was necessary for civilization to flourish. Goetzmann is also a filmmaker and an expert on the art of the Wild West in the United States and of the Viking period in Scandinavia, the ancient history of stock markets, the original tulip bubble in the Netherlands, and neglected corners of the investment markets such as art and real estate.

William N. Goetzmann
Source: Yale School of Management

All that and he also wrote, with Roger Ibbotson, a volume of collected works called *The Equity Risk Premium: Essays and Explorations*, to which I contributed.

Will Goetzmann is the Renaissance man of the financial world.

After reviewing *Money Changes Everything*, I'll discuss some of Goetzmann's other works, including one that has nothing to do with finance.

The oldest stock in the world?

How old is the stock market? More generally, for how long has it been possible for individuals or groups of individuals to form joint-stock companies and seek equity financing, with the capital providers able to sell their shares *somewhere* ("on the open market" — it does not have to be a formal exchange) so they are not locked into the deal forever?

Until my work with Roger Ibbotson and Gary Brinson in the 1980s it was generally thought that the Dutch East India Company, founded in the 1600s, was the first joint-stock company. But we found a company, a water mill at Bazacle, near Toulouse, France, that had been continuously traded since 1372![1]

Of course, Goetzmann could not leave well enough alone. He traveled to Bazacle, visited the mill (it is still there), and inspected the medieval incorporation documents and shareholder records, some of which are shown in Exhibit 1. He and two co-authors found a treasure trove of information about the evolution of the corporation:

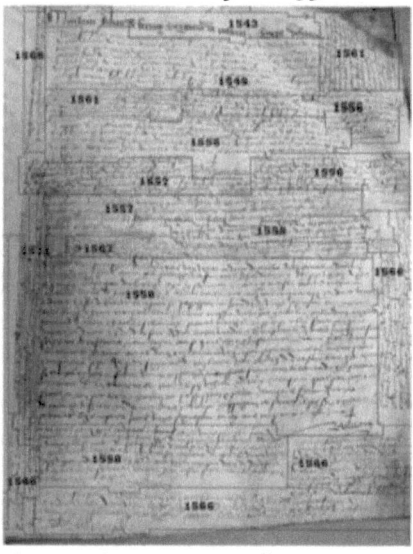

Exhibit 1 — *A register of pariers (shareholders) of the Société des Moulins de Bazacle from 1530*

Source: Goetzmann, William N. 2016. *Money Changes Everything.* Princeton University Press

> Shareholding companies that began in the 11th century formally incorporated themselves into two large-scale, widely held firms by 1373. In the years that followed they experienced the economic challenges and conflicts we now recognize as

---

[1] Ibbotson and Brinson, drawing on my unpublished research, dated the first trading of Bazacle water mill shares to the 1100s but later work showed that ownership of the Société des Moulins de Bazacle was formally divided into shares between 1369 and 1372. The company was nationalized in 1946 and is now part of Électricité de France. See Ibbotson, Roger G., and Gary P. Brinson. 1993. *Global Investing.* New York: McGraw-Hill.

> inherent in the separation of ownership and control. [T]he Toulouse firms developed institutional solutions including tradable shares, limited liability, governing boards, cash payout policies, external audits, shareholder meetings, and mechanisms for re-capitalization.[2]

"The Toulouse firms," Goetzmann and his co-authors write, "shed light on the necessary and sufficient conditions for the development of the corporate form."

Goetzmann and his co-authors also used the price and dividend history of almost 600 years of Bazacle mill shares to test modern asset pricing models! They write,

> We find a real average dividend yield of 5% per annum and no long-term price growth. Stationary dividends and stock prices enable us to directly study how prices relate to expected cash flows, without relying on rates of return....[V]ariations in expected future dividends explain between one-sixth and one-third of variations in prices.[3]

Money Changes Everything contains the short version of these stories, along with the fact that *ice floes* almost destroyed the mill in 1709. Toulouse is in the far south of France, close to the Spanish border and the Mediterranean. There really was a Little Ice Age!

I went into this level of detail on Bazacle because of my own interest in that particular company. Such detail, however, is typical of Goetzmann's treatment of every place and period in financial history that he investigated.

---

[2] Le Bris, David, William N. Goetzmann, and Sebastien Pouget. 2015. "The Development of Corporate Governance in Toulouse: 1372-1946." NBER Working Paper No. w21335 (July). Available at SSRN: https://ssrn.com/abstract=2629940. Quote from the abstract.

[3] Le Bris, David, William N. Goetzmann, and Sebastien Pouget. 2014. "Testing Asset Pricing Theory on Six Hundred Years of Stock Returns: Prices and Dividends for the Bazacle Company from 1372 to 1946." NBER Working Paper No. w20199 (posted June 11). Available at SSRN: https://papers.ssrn.com/sol3/papers.cfm?abstract_id=2448904. Quote is from the abstract.

The Roman Stock Exchange

As Goetzmann shows, the story of corporations, divisible ownership, and share trading goes back farther than medieval France. *Much* farther.

Goetzmann finds, in plain sight, evidence of financial technologies – loans, bonds, equities, options – going back about as far as recorded history goes: "By 3000 BCE, the ancient cities of the Near East had developed the fundamental tools of finance...[including] intertemporal contracts." The court records of classical Athens include disputes resolved using discount bond math. Perhaps the most compelling discovery regarding equities is that of the Roman stock exchange, depicted below:

Exhibit 2 — Temple of Castor and Pollux, Roman Forum

Photograph by the author

A stock exchange in the Roman Forum? Really? The picture shows what's left of the Temple of Castor and Pollux, an homage to gods, a religious institution. But Goetzmann writes, "At the steps of the temple, contracts were auctioned for Roman companies called *societas publicanorum*. Shares in these firms were also traded here, making this the earliest stock market...[O]ddly enough, [the temple columns look] not unlike the façade of the New York Stock Exchange..." And, in 59 BCE, Cicero accused a protégé of Julius Caesar of "manipulat[ing] share prices for profit — a tantalizing reference to early securities market fraud."

The oldest bond in the world

The ideas of compound interest and the time value of money are even older. The breeding habits of cattle provided the impetus for charging or receiving compound interest, the most basic concept in finance. Goetzmann writes, "If you lend someone a herd of thirty cattle for one year, you expect to be repaid with more than thirty cattle. The herd multiplies — the herder's wealth has a natural rate of increase equal to the rate of reproduction of the livestock."

Thus compound interest could be expected to appear on a wide variety of transactions, because competition will force other loans unrelated to cattle to bear fruit (another agricultural metaphor) at roughly the same rate. It is one more mental step to discount math and present value. Compound interest was used by the Sumerians, beginning something like 5000 years ago. Some of the words we use for money also refer back to cattle, such as "pecuniary," from Latin *pecus* (flock).

No one knows how old the oldest actual bond in the world is. But we do know that money lent at interest is about as old as civilization itself. According to Goetzmann, "[T]he financial architecture of the ancient Near East [included] loan tablets, mortgage tablets, leases, letters of credit, and [a] whole range of financial documents that sprung forth during Old Babylonian times," almost 4000 years ago in the age of Hammurabi, the lawgiver. These instruments certainly sound like bonds.

Let's now skip ahead to the dawn of the modern age, in northwestern Europe just before the Industrial Revolution.

The great mirror of folly

Money Changes Everything is the kind of history book in which basically all of the action takes place before modern times. By page 363 (out of 584) we are only up to the South Sea Bubble of 1720, which produced, among other things, the Dutch book that lampooned the bubble and its participants, *Het Groote Tafereel Der Dwaasheid*.[4]

Exhibit 3 — Detail from Het Groote Tafereel der Dwaasheid: A practitioner of WINDHANDEL (TRADE IN THIN AIR)

Source: https://www.donaldheald.com/pages/books/20771/john-law/the-great-mirror-of-folly-het-%20groote-tafereel-der-dwaashied-vertoonende-de-opkomst-voortgang-enSur

(Dutch is a wonderfully mysterious language, looking like a mashup of German, English, and Martian.)

The title means "The Great Mirror of Folly," and was the subject of another of Goetzmann's books. Co-authored with several other scholars, his book is also called *The Great Mirror of Folly* with the added subtitle, "Finance, Culture, and the Crash of 1720."[5] The crash of 1720 involved not only the South Sea Company, which was organized to trade in slaves, but also many other ventures. (The South Sea referred to in the company's name is the South Atlantic where much of the slave trade occurred, not the South Pacific.) The 1720 crash was probably the first highly correlated market decline.

If this *luftmensch* reminds you of the Wolf of Wall Street, Bernie Madoff, and Charles Ponzi all wrapped into one, you're not alone. Big money attracts big trouble, and scams and harebrained schemes are hardly new. With three centuries' distance, they can be pretty funny.

---

[4] The more famous tulip bubble was earlier, around 1637.

[5] Goetzmann, William N., Catherine Labio, K. Geert Rouwenhorst, and Timothy G. Young, editors. 2013. *The Great Mirror of Folly: Finance, Culture, and the Crash of 1720*. New Haven, CT: Yale University Press.

Financing civilization

I've given you a taste of the erudition and fun that permeates *Money Changes Everything*. But the book is too long and complex for me to do justice to it, even in a long-form review such as this one. It suffices to say that finance did indeed make civilization possible, in the sense that much of what we call "civilization" consists of large numbers of people cooperating to achieve things that one individual or small group could never possibly achieve. Such accomplishments — building a ship, organizing a large farming operation with complex division of labor, transporting goods safely over thousands of miles — take massive coordination, often over long periods of time and sometimes by people who will never meet and who may not speak the same language.

Those are the conditions in which finance, the branch of economics that deals with time and uncertainty, *must* be called into play. Money — and, in particular, the ability to combine different people's assets to form large pools of risk capital and the technology for making and enforcing commitments over long time spans — does indeed change everything.

Survivorship bias and long-run rates of return

One of Will Goetzmann's major contributions to investment finance is his careful study (with co-authors) of the role of survivorship bias in interpreting the long-run rates of return of capital markets. The basic idea is best understood at the country level. Unless we try very hard to correct the error, we only observe returns in countries whose markets have survived continuously to the present. This overstates the return that investors actually experienced.

Consider an investor in 1900, contemplating investing in the major markets of the world. The U.S., U.K., Canada, Switzerland, and a handful of other markets had no interruptions and the investments would have survived to the present, providing large profits. However, investments in Russia were worthless after the 1917 revolution, Chinese securities were worthless after the 1949 takeover by the Communists, and Japanese and German markets were interrupted by, respectively, one and two world wars. While China and Russia now have thriving markets, one would have had to inject new capital (from the labor market) in recent years to participate in these markets' current, if sometimes wobbly, success.

Global stock markets in the twentieth century

The theme of survival bias appears in many of Goetzmann's articles, most notably his paper with Philippe Jorion, "Global Stock Markets in the Twentieth Century."[6] The authors write,

> Long-term estimates of expected return on equities are typically derived from U.S. data only...[T]hese estimates are subject to survivorship, as the United States is arguably the most successful capitalist system in the world. We collect a database of capital appreciation index for 39 markets going back into the 1920s. Over 1921 to 1996, U.S. equities had the highest real return of all countries, at 4.3%, versus a median of 0.8% for other countries. The high equity premium obtained for U.S. equities there appears to be the exception rather than the rule.

If that is the case, then we'd better lower our expectations for future equity returns, because we don't know whether the countries we're invested in (presumably something close to a global cap-weighted portfolio) are going to be as successful in the future as *the United States* was in the past. Not as successful as global markets were in the past — as successful as the United States! That's a high bar, one we should not expect to be able to hurdle.[7]

Once you appreciate the explanatory power of survival bias, you tend to see it in everything. Wikipedia's survival-bias article applies the principle to "business, finance, economics, history, manufacturing and goods

---

[6] Jorion, Philippe, and William N. Goetzmann. 1999. "Global Stock Markets in the Twentieth Century." *Journal of Finance*, Vol. 54, No. 3 (June), pp. 953-980. The quote is from their Abstract.

[7] See also Dimson, Elroy, Paul Marsh, and Mike Staunton. 2002. Triumph of the Optimists: *101 Years of Global Investment Returns*. Princeton, NJ: Princeton University Press.

production, architecture and construction, highly competitive careers, the military, cats, tropical trees, [and] studies of evolution."[8]

If that seems a little farfetched, I'd add cosmology and the existence of life elsewhere in the universe.[9] More on that some other time; let's bring this discussion down to earth a little. Survival bias in architecture leads us to believe that all of the architecture of the past was glorious, because most old buildings (more than 80 or 100 years old) are beautiful. That's because the ugly, useless, or poorly constructed ones have been torn down! Are you beginning to see how widely this concept can be applied?

At this point the story gets personal...

...because, while I'm almost entirely sure I got the idea of survival bias in country stock markets from Will Goetzmann, he says he got it from me.

This kind of reverse rivalry gives me great pleasure. I hope he gets a kick out of it too. At any rate, in the late 1980s or early 1990s in connection with my background work for Ibbotson and Brinson's book *Global Investing* (mentioned earlier), I began including the mysterious-looking Exhibit 4 in my speeches and writing. It appears in *Global Investing* and then in my 1997 *Journal of Portfolio Management* article, "Are Stocks Risky? Two Lessons."[10]

---

[8] https://en.wikipedia.org/wiki/Survivorship_bias, as accessed on April 27, 2019. Repunctuated by me.

[9] In these contexts it's call the anthropic principle; see Penrose, Roger. 1989. *The Emperor's New Mind*. Oxford, UK: Oxford University Press. Wikipedia also has a good article on the principle at https://en.wikipedia.org/wiki/Anthropic_principle

[10] Siegel, Laurence B. 1997. "Are Stocks Risky? Two Lessons." *Journal of Portfolio Management*, vol. 23, no. 3 (Spring), pp. 29-34.

Exhibit 4 — Outcomes of a Diversified Global Portfolio of Investments in 1900

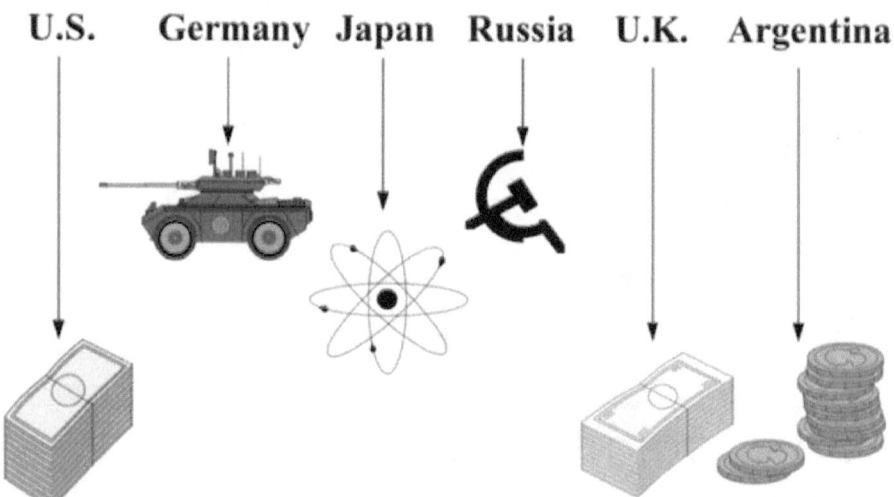

I shouldn't have to explain the similarity with the ideas in the Jorion and Goetzmann article cited earlier. Note that Germany only gets one tank, not two, because investors' claims that were extinguished in World War I didn't survive to be quashed again in World War II. And Argentina, with a pile of pennies, is there just to remind investors that not all surviving countries prosper. Investors in that once-wealthy country have done terribly.

By the way, I believe Goetzmann wins the originality claim because, while I probably wrote up this idea first, he was working with Ibbotson Associates, my employer at the time, as an outside consultant and I was strongly influenced by his ideas and research. If I didn't hear the idea from him at least in a casual conversation, then I'm a monkey's uncle.

I'd note, finally, that Jeremy Siegel (not my brother, although I don't always correct people on that question) has provided evidence that stocks, *but not bonds,* retained some residual value in Japan and Germany even as those countries' economies were destroyed by war.[11] When a government falls, its bonds become worthless with no hope of recovery, but

---

[11] Siegel, Jeremy J. 2008. *Stocks for the Long Run: The Definitive Guide to Financial Market Returns and Long-Term Investment Strategies.* Fourth edition, New York: McGraw-Hill.

corporations often survive the war and go on to prosper under the new government.

A brief visit to the *West of the Imagination*, with Will Goetzmann and his father

Will Goetzmann's varied interests beyond finance and financial history (or financial archaeology?) are illustrated by a book that is orthogonal to those topics, *The West of the Imagination*, co-authored with his father, the historian William H. Goetzmann. The threads that connect the two topics are a historian's eye for detail and love of the past.

Like many children of the 1950s, I wanted to visit — and maybe live in — the American West. Influenced by television, movies, books, and National Geographic's photography, I had a mental picture that was probably shared by tens of millions of children and young men and women of the time: gorgeous scenery, horses, adventure. (I didn't want to be an actual cowboy. The work was *hard*.)

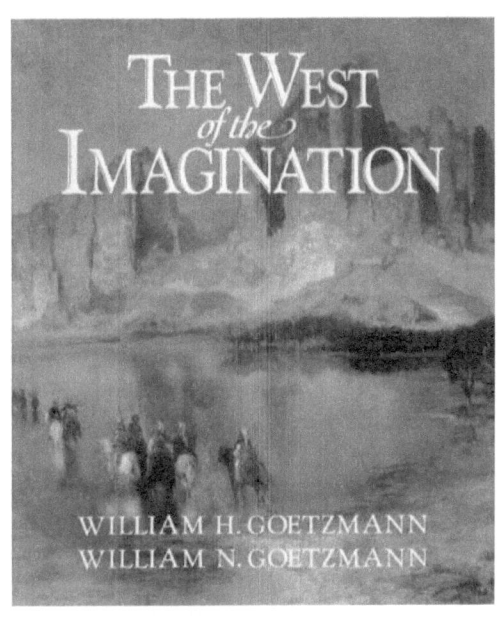

Source: http://viking.som.yale.edu/

The West of the Imagination chronicles the ways that the artists and photographers of the American West shaped both our accurate knowledge and our fantasies about that place and time. Their book was made into a PBS television series that aired in 1986.

The art discussed and displayed in the book ranges from the dramatic sculptures of Frederic Remington (himself a blue-blooded Easterner) to the modernist paintings of Georgia O'Keeffe and a great many lesser-known painters, photographers, and artisans.

Highly specialized thinkers and doers have made many of the most important discoveries in science, economics, and other fields vital to our well-being. It is hard to see how Maxwell's equations or the structure of DNA could have been discovered without their discoverers spending a lifetime of intense involvement in the details of their disciplines. But, if we assess a person's achievements according to how much beauty, enjoyment, and enrichment they generate, generalists are the most valuable innovators.

Will Goetzmann is one of them. May he inspire others to take such meandering paths through knowledge.

Chapter 23. Michael Lewis on the Unlikely Trio That Defeated the Pandemic

by Laurence B. Siegel
May 31, 2021[1]

The saga of local public health officials tasked with fighting epidemic disease, and their clashes with national health authorities who didn't care, was a perfect recipe for putting readers to sleep. But Michael Lewis made it into high drama.

I couldn't put it down. That's about the worst opening for a book review that I can think of, but I did read Lewis's *The Premonition: A Pandemic Story* in one sitting – despite my having gobbled up reams of literature about COVID-19 in the last year and a third.

This is the second of Michael Lewis's books about the micro-functioning of government. It is a sequel to his 2018 book, *The Fifth Risk*, which was about the Departments of Energy, Agriculture, and Commerce during the Trump administration. In that volume, Lewis coaxed us into appreciating the diligent work done by experts several layers down from the top, working in agencies that we know little about. (The first four risks are not specific threats but categories: severe and mild consequences, plotted against low and high

Michael Lewis
Source: https://commons.wikimedia.org/wiki/File:Michael_Lewis_2009.jpg

---

[1] The author thanks David Adler for his contributions.

likelihood. The fifth one is *project management*, as unlikely a topic for a page-turner as has ever been chosen.[2])

While *The Fifth Risk* chronicled the work of federal government employees, *The Premonition* focuses on the local ones who interact daily with the people they're sworn to protect. Of course, in a pandemic, local issues quickly become national and global ones, but it's at the level of homes, schools, and hospitals where the peculiar characteristics of a disease and the habits of the people who contract it are first noted. Only then does information filter through to the familiar national authorities.

The heroine and the heroes

The heroine of the book is Dr. Charity Dean, who started out in Santa Barbara, California's public health department, became assistant public health director for the state, and is now an entrepreneur and professor at the University of Southern California. In a *60 Minutes* interview, Lewis recalled, "Charity...thinks she's all alone, all alone in the world, aware in January that this pandemic [will] sweep through the United States and nobody's doing anything about it, including her state government."[3]

Charity Dean
Source: https://www.imdb.com/name/nm12579156/mediaviewer/rm4172400129/?ref_=nm_ov_ph

Soon, she is introduced to a renegade group of doctors called the Wolverines, named after a team of high-school guerrilla warriors in the 1984 movie *Red Dawn* (you can't make this up). As the team takes shape, her concerns begin to filter upward, but only after encountering roadblocks at the highest levels of government.

---

[2] Elsewhere in *The Fifth Risk*, the risks are enumerated as: (1) missing nuclear weapons and materials, (2) North Korea, (3) Iran's nuclear program, (4) a cyberattack on the electrical grid, and (5) project management.

[3] https://www.cbsnews.com/news/michael-lewis-premonition-60-minutes-2021-05-02/

The book, like many of Lewis', is built around an individual toiling in relative obscurity to achieve something good: think of Leigh Anne Touhy, who raises a very unusual son in *The Blind Side*, and Brad Katsuyama, who builds a system for defeating greedy high-frequency stock traders in *Flash Boys*. Accounts of ordinary people who turn out to be extraordinary are appealing – and Lewis is a master of the genre. Charity Dean is the key figure, but two Wolverines also play central roles in *The Premonition*.

The accomplices

Unlike Dean, Dr. Carter Mecher resided within the belly of the beast. A senior medical adviser at the U.S. Department of Veterans Affairs, Mecher wrote on January 28, 2020 that "WHO and CDC [were] behind the curve." On February 20 he warned that the outbreak of COVID on cruise ships was "a preview of what will happen when this virus makes its way to the U.S. healthcare system [and especially]…nursing homes. I'm not sure that folks understand what is just over the horizon."[4]

Both Dean and Mecher had already studied virus contagion in detail. Dean observed that schoolchildren socialize in much closer quarters than adults do. She believed that closing schools would be the most valuable action to take in a flu pandemic. (Unlike COVID, flu is serious in children and is easily transmitted by them.) Mecher was part of a federal group that performed battle-plan pandemic simulations using the Bush administration's template. The group, he said, "concluded they would soon need to move toward aggressive social distancing, even at the risk of severe disruption to the nation's economy and the daily lives of millions of Americans."[5]

If this policy had been adopted when Mecher and his colleagues recommended it, the virus might have been stopped early in 2020; that is,

---

[4] As reported by Adler, David, 2021, "Inside Operation Warp Speed: A New Model for Industrial Policy," *American Affairs*, Volume V, Number 2 (Summer). Plagiarism of a few words in this article is intended to be a compliment to Mr. Adler and is the result of me trying to write clearly, without quotes inside quotes.

[5] As reported by Lipton, Eric, et al., 2020, "He Could Have Seen What Was Coming: Behind Trump's Failure on the Virus," *New York Times* (April 11).

Ro, the transmission rate, might have fallen below 1. The endless lockdowns and ensuing economic catastrophe might have been avoided.[6]

Joe DeRisi is the third musketeer. (You knew there would be a tech genius in this story somewhere.) He is the biochemist and biophysicist at the University of California San Francisco who invented "the Virochip – a... chip with DNA sequences from every virus ever discovered," writes Steve Vasallo at Forbes.[7] "With this technology, Joe's UCSF lab can test blood or spinal fluid against every known infection, offering new hope for cases previously dismissed as undiagnosable." Not just every virus that affects humans, but viruses across the animal kingdom that have the potential to make the jump to people.

Put together Mecher, the government doctor; DeRisi, the virus hunter and inventor; and Dean, the battlefield commander – and you just might beat the virus, despite opposition from higher-ups, including the then-president, who didn't seem focused or aware of the danger. But this battle in the eternal war between humans and viruses would not be won right away. Hundreds of thousands of deaths and a devastating economic lockdown would intervene.

---

[6] This was, in fact, the original plan: "Two weeks to flatten the curve." Of course, they were the wrong two weeks; in late January 2020 the plan might have worked. However, there was never any guarantee that it would. We are now seeing that countries that seemed to have beaten COVID through early behavioral intervention, such as Taiwan, are now experiencing surges. It is possible that almost everyone in the world will eventually be exposed, with those protected early in the pandemic becoming vulnerable later, so that near-universal vaccination is the only answer. Fortunately, that is now possible.

My use of the word "catastrophe" is justified. At present, we are so far into the V-shaped recovery that it is hard to remember the severity of the COVID economic collapse. U.S. GDP contracted by 9.5% (not annualized) in one quarter, much faster than in any quarter of the Great Depression or any other historical depression. While GDP was not calculated in these old depressions, proxy measures show that the worst one-quarter decline in those periods was much less than that experienced in the second quarter of 2020.

[7] Vasallo, Steve. 2021. "Missionary Misfits: Meet Joe DeRisi, A Real-Life Virus Hunter." *Forbes* (March 8). Vasallo called it a computer chip but it is a glass microscope slide.

Pandemics that were and weren't

One lesson that these experienced pandemic fighters had learned from their past battles was that pandemics are not all equal. The devastating 1918 Spanish Flu, which killed 600,000 Americans and perhaps 50 million people worldwide, spread at a wild pace among the young. As already noted, Dean observed that closing the schools resulted in rapid control of the contagion.

Mecher compared the COVID virus to the more recent (2003) SARS epidemic, which was contained almost immediately:

Dr. Carter Mecher
Source: https://www.imdb.com/name/nm12579157/mediaviewer/rm3266430465/?ref_=nm_ov_ph

> The original SARS had infected only eight thousand people, killing eight hundred, before it was contained.[8] This new SARS [that is, SARS-CoV-2, the virus that causes COVID] had similar official stats, but he saw signs that the stats were misleading. The new SARS was spreading much more quickly from country to country...[and] was also eliciting very different [much more aggressive] behavior from the Chinese government.

Redneck epidemiology

Piecing together evidence like a movie detective and practicing what some derided as "redneck epidemiology," Mecher looked at details like Wuhan death notices – there were too many to be consistent with the official story – and the sudden appearance in Wuhan of a 1,000-bed quarantine hospital built in five days by the Chinese military. He also noted that about half of COVID cases were transmitted by people who had the virus but weren't sick. This fact made COVID incomparably worse than diseases where only

---

[8] That is a very high fatality rate, but a tiny infected population. The containment was successful.

the sick were contagious, because it was not possible to just remove sick people from the population and protect everyone else.

The disease was living among us and spreading fast.

SARS and MERS are under control. Ebola (not a coronavirus) ravaged three West African countries but did not spread beyond them. The difference between those threatened pandemics and the 1918 Spanish flu, it turns out, was in the social, not the medical, response. We don't have antiviral drugs (cures) for any of these diseases. Until the appearance of the COVID vaccine, all we had was behavioral protocols. The hated social distancing protocol was supported by a study, not just of the 1918 flu, but of the pandemics that weren't, where transmission was stopped by decisive early action.

The Wolverines' and Charity Dean's horrifying conclusion was that COVID-19 was not a repeat of the 1957 or 1968 flu pandemics or the SARS or MERS coronaviruses. COVID was 1918.[9]

Young men and fire

Part of Lewis' genius, as with any great writer, is in making unexpected connections. In the case of the deadly Mann Gulch fire in Montana in 1949, Mecher made the connection for him. Mecher "had fire on the brain," Lewis writes. "Fire was his favorite metaphor to convey how hard it was for people to wake up to a threat that grew exponentially." The Mann Gulch fire, initially thought to be "small and simple," turned into a nightmare that suddenly climbed a 76% slope and moved at 30 to 40 miles per hour. Only three of the 15 elite Forest Service smokejumpers there to fight it survived.

In a move that made the other firemen think he was crazy, the lead smokejumper (who survived) *intentionally lit* an "escape fire" that burned the grass in front of him. He safely trudged through the small fire and "felt

---

[9] Fortunately, the parallel is inexact. The 1918 Spanish flu pandemic attacked the young, while COVID principally affected the old and infirm. And, despite the matching numbers – approximately 600,000 Americans having died in each episode – our population today is three times what it was 102 years ago, so the per capita death rate is much lower.

the main fire passing by on either side of him, leaving him unscathed." This is now standard procedure.

The writer and University of Chicago professor Norman Maclean, best known for his short book, *A River Runs Through It*, also chronicled the Mann Gulch fire.[10] His book about it, *Young Men and Fire*, is also a classic... but not just because of its lessons for firefighters. Mecher heard a talk about the book and thought, "The Mann Gulch fire isn't about fire... It's also about pandemics," writes Lewis. Mecher jotted down lessons for fighting a raging pandemic including, "Figure out the equivalent of an escape fire."

Dean's escape fire

The escape fire materialized not in the brain of Mecher, but in an unrelated story Dean was telling herself about her own traumatic past experiences. (This plot twist was a little hard to follow, the only flaw I found in Lewis's narrative.) A trauma survivor – Dean's traumas appear to be sexual although we are never quite told –

> she [saw] the fire, growing exponentially, coming straight for her. In response she created an escape fire. Her escape fire was a story. In this new story she told herself about herself, she was never simply a victim. For whatever had happened she bore some responsibility.
>
> [The story] had turned her into an action hero...[s]he was put on earth to fight battles, and wars, against disease.

The newly minted action hero quit her county job and moved to the state health department in Sacramento. She then proceeded on a rapid upward path that ended in the White House, advising and conferring with Dr. Duane Caneva, the chief medical officer of the Department of Homeland Security. Caneva was, "a sometime antagonist [of Dean's] from her first days...as the number two public-health officer for California." She

---

[10] Maclean's *A River Runs Through It* (1976) was made into one of the finest movies of all time (directed by Robert Redford, 1992).

perceived Caneva as an agent of the Trump administration, caging child migrants from Mexico, and didn't at first realize that, in Lewis' words:

> there was this other Duane, who...belonged to this small, informal, almost secret group of...doctors who had once worked in the White House under Bush or Obama and were...now working, *without the White House's permission,* to coordinate some kind of national pandemic response... Duane Caneva wasn't a storm trooper for Donald Trump. He was part of the resistance.

She had been introduced to the Wolverines. She called it a "break glass group." In case of fire, break glass.

The surfer dude with a genius grant

Because Lewis pieces together a story that results in the eventual collision of three minds working at different times and in different places, some jumping around in time is required. Let's look at how the coronavirus that causes COVID was discovered.

In 2003, at the age of 33 with the look and manner of a surfer, the microbiologist Joe DeRisi was the first to identify SARS. Regarded as a genius, with that rubric confirmed by a MacArthur Foundation "genius grant," Lewis writes that,

> ... he'd been handpicked by UCSF's faculty to skip the usual postdoc stage of formal scientific training and been given his own lab – because they didn't want to waste a moment of his mind. "It's a mind without boundaries," said Don Ganem, a USCF microbiologist...who had pushed for DeRisi's hire. "It's a mind that is interested in everything and afraid of nothing. It's a bandwidth that is hard for most people to fathom."

The magic chip

DeRisi's invention, the ViroChip, made it possible to label the mystery illness arriving from China in late 2019 as a novel coronavirus. The chip, actually a glass microscope slide, holds genetic sequences from all 22,000 known viruses. When one passes unidentified genetic material from a virus over the slide, some of the material sticks. Whatever sticks is a match to the known viral material on the slide.

If it sounds like magic, it's pretty close.

Some of the genetic material from the mystery virus stuck to existing cow, bird, and human coronaviruses but was not an exact match to any of them. DeRisi concluded that it was a novel coronavirus, named SARS-CoV-2 by whoever gives official names to the nonliving (yet frantically evolving) bits of DNA or RNA, smaller than the shortest wavelength of visible light, that we call viruses.

Joseph "Joe" DeRisi
Source: https://www.ucsf.edu/news/2016/06/403141/joseph-derisi-elected-national-academy-sciences

The pop-up microbiology lab

By 2020, DeRisi ran not only his UCSF lab but also an outfit called the Chan Zuckerberg Biohub, created with a $600 million gift from the well-known tech couple. It was founded with the absurd goal of eradicating all diseases by 2100. (Diseases are not that stupid, and we are not that smart. We won't win. But maybe it's a way to get attention and attract the best people.) Chan Zuckerberg specialized in testing.

Once it got past the hurdle of not being trusted because it did not charge for its services and was funded by a disliked billionaire, the Chan Zuckerberg Biohub blew away the hospital/lab/regulatory agency combine.

Lewis writes, "On March 18, just eight days after the idea was born, the...Biohub's new COVID lab opened for business. It had taken Joe's new team two days less to build an entire lab than it was taking Quest Diagnostics and Labcorp to *process a single test*."[11] Efficient COVID testing had begun.

---

[11] My italics.

Into the Mann Gulch fire

On March 6, 2020, California governor Gavin Newsom convened a large group of experts. Dean was one, and she noted that when you have a virus that is spreading exponentially, there are no tests, and people with no symptoms can spread it:

> The only clear signal you get from the virus is death... [When] you realize that only half of 1 percent of the people who get [it] die, you can surmise that for every death, there are 199 people already walking around with it. That first death – which California had already experienced – was telling you that you had 200 cases a month earlier.

Assuming a reproduction rate of 3, Dean did the math and projected that seven weeks from today you'd have 11,809,900 cases. As much as 10 percent or so of those people, more than a million Californians, would need a hospital bed. Half of 1 percent, or a bit more than 59,000 people, would die.

This forecast assumed no mitigation – that nobody would do anything to stop the virus. There is always mitigation, if not imposed from above then by people making their own decisions about what risks to take. The forecast was, unfortunately, uncannily accurate despite the extensive mitigation (masks, lockdowns, and so forth) that took place. As of May 27, 2021, 63,214 Californians had died of COVID, consistent with Dean's estimate. More than 600,000 have died so far in the United States, and roughly 3.5 million in the world.[12]

---

[12] California data from the *New York Times*, https://www.nytimes.com/interactive/2021/us/california-covid-cases.html; U.S. and world data from http://www.worldometers.info. I ignore the controversy about having died of COVID (that is, as a direct result); dying *with* COVID (along with other direct causes of death); and dying *because of* COVID (including unrelated medical conditions that were overlooked or not treated, and so forth).

Government versus government

A lesser writer could have more starkly framed the story as underdogs versus the establishment, and that has a whiff of truth to it. A fairer interpretation, however, is that there are two establishments, one that is careerist and obstructionist, and the other consisting of diligent public servants, mostly at lower levels in various governments (local, state, and federal) and in universities and private industry, who not only know and care about their fields of expertise but also are able to occasionally persuade the top brass that they are right.

Lewis is not fond of the way that the top levels of government function. The CDC comes across particularly poorly in *The Premonition*. In a CFA Institute-sponsored interview, he said,

> We have an enterprise called the Centers for Disease Control, that actually isn't set up to control disease. This is putting it a little harshly, but if you had asked the [CDC] to *maximize* illness in America because of COVID, they might not have behaved all that differently from what they did.[13]

Other agencies are just as bad. Yet Lewis does not blame the individuals working at CDC. It's the *institutional structure* of government – the perverse incentives, the short tenure of political appointees, the many-layered bureaucracy, the redundant and competing agencies, the ever-present risk of being fired – that keeps government agencies from doing their job. We have much to learn from Lewis's micro-analysis of these structures.

---

[13] My italics. Lewis's interview, entitled "Looking Back to Look Forward: A Conversation with Michael Lewis," was conducted at the CFA Institute Alpha Summit, virtual conference, May 18, 2021.

"When someone convinces me that I am wrong, I change my mind. What do you do?"

During the pandemic, I thought that the delegation of disease-fighting authority to the states was a risky but promising experiment in data gathering. Different approaches to disease containment would yield differing results, and we'd quickly be able to figure out what was working and what was not. Also, state and local public health workers could make decisions based on what they were observing on the ground, right in front of them, rather than in a faraway place where they were getting information second- or thirdhand.

While we did get some worthwhile data out of the experiment, *The Premonition* convinced me that I was wrong. (That's why I titled this section with Keynes' famous wisecrack.) The U.S. is such an open society, with state boundaries so porous by design, that a national pandemic strategy would have been preferable – if real experts, not the careerist stick-in-the-muds who block their every move (and who appear as villains in Lewis's story) were in charge and had real power. Based on the parallels between COVID and 1918, social distancing and lockdowns should have been started much earlier. They would have also ended much earlier, with many fewer deaths and probably an open economy by summer 2020.

COVID's gifts

Everything, including a disease that has killed one American in 500, has an upside we can learn from. Lewis writes that a year into the pandemic Charity Dean thought of COVID as

> Mother Nature's gift to the country. The hardest part, to a public-health officer trying to control a communicable disease, was that you were always looking in the rearview mirror. COVID had given the country a glimpse of what Charity had always thought might be coming – a pathogen that might

move through the population with the aid of asymptomatic spreaders, and which had a talent for floating on air. Now that we knew how badly we responded to such a threat, we could begin to prepare for it. "Mother Nature," [she said], "has...tipped the odds in our favor."

This is too sanguine a conclusion because it has cost between 600,000 and 900,000 lives, in the United States alone, just to get this view out the front windshield. (It is like saying that we learn from losing a war. We do but we still lost.) We had some idea what was coming as far back as the Bush and Obama administrations, and should have been much better prepared. Unfortunately, several "pandemics that weren't" made us complacent. But now we're not. Dean is right that we will be much better prepared for the next pandemic.

But the gift that Dean didn't mention, one even more valuable than logistical preparation, is mRNA technology. It existed before COVID but we didn't know much about applying it. Now that we've had to sequence a rapidly mutating virus and develop an effective vaccine for it in a hurry, we know a lot.

Disease prevention using mRNA is, in fact, a general-purpose technology, adaptable to many viruses including those we don't know about yet – perhaps *all* viruses. David Adler wrote, "the Warp Speed people told me that the end of pandemics, or even infectious diseases, is now in sight, as are new cancer treatments. But then they dialed down their comments a bit."[14]

Even a fraction of that kind of success would be, in Neil Armstrong's unforgettable phrase, a giant leap for mankind.

---

[14] Personal communication, May 20, 2021.

Chapter 24. Malcolm Gladwell's "Talking to Strangers": On Preventing Financial Fraud and Worse

Laurence B. Siegel
November 12, 2019

> "There's always an easy solution to every human problem — neat, plausible and wrong."
>
> — H. L. Mencken, in "The Divine Afflatus," *New York Evening Mail* (November 16, 1917)

Talking to Strangers is not about talking to strangers. It is a manual on how to avoid being victimized or bamboozled by evil, slippery, or amoral people. Well-written (Gladwell is always entertaining) and opinionated, it is an annotated compendium of case studies on how some of the world's worst people got others — strangers — to believe their lies and get sucked into situations that range from merely unfortunate to profoundly tragic.

If you don't talk to strangers because you're afraid you'll become a victim, you'll never learn anything. Everyone except your mother was a stranger at some point in your life, and you only can learn by listening. The University of Chicago behavioral psychologist Nicholas Epley and Berkeley's Juliana Schroeder have a relevant take on talking to strangers, discussed in *Mom was Wrong: You Should Talk To Strangers*[1]. According to these authors, talking to strangers will make you happier (that is also my experience). Now, back to Gladwell, who does provide a helpful

---

[1] https://www.chicagobooth.edu/media-relations-and-communications/press-releases/mom-was-wrong-you-should-talk-to-strangers

service, although not as helpful as one might want and certainly not the one advertised in the title.

The book has considerable flaws. Like much of Gladwell's work, it oversimplifies complex problems and overcomplicates simple ones.

Investors will be most interested in Gladwell's recounting of how Bernie Madoff fleeced rich people and philanthropic institutions out of an astonishing $50 billion, providing a billion-dollar windfall for lawyers and misery for everyone else involved. But I'll start with Adolf Hitler, because he continues to fascinate and horrify, and Gladwell has much to say about him.

Gladwell introduces a couple of psychosocial concepts that he finds useful in explaining the behavior revealed in his stories. One is "default to truth," the idea that we assume, at least until we encounter contrary evidence, that what someone is telling us is true.

The other is "mismatch," a conflict between a person's inner intentions and the way they present themselves. Hitler was a spectacular example of mismatch, in that, unless you were looking closely, his public persona seemed to belie his genocidal intent.

The consummate attractor

So, how did Adolf Hitler, a deranged man with murderous intent, come to rule one of the world's most literate and cultured countries? Didn't his history provide some clues?

Of course it did. A quick glance at his manifesto, *Mein Kampf* (1925), reveals that it prefigured almost everything he said and did as *führer*.[2] Yet even the sophisticated Jewish newspapers of 1920s Germany pretty much ignored the book. The *Times of Israel* recently reported:

> [W]hen *Mein Kampf* came out for the first time, 91 years ago, German Jews hardly noticed it... [T]he Jews' reaction to Hitler's

---

[2] http://www.greatwar.nl/books/meinkampf/meinkampf.pdf. Just looking for a copy of *Mein Kampf* was a little unnerving. It appears in a bibliography as Hitler, A. (1925) – just like a normal person. Hitler has reached such a pinnacle in the mythology of evil that when we see his name in context of other people, in this case other authors, it seems significantly out of place.

screed, or rather the lack thereof, ...said Othmar Plöckinger, who recently published a 700-page book with many historical sources dealing with *Mein Kampf,* was a kind of not wanting to waste time with such nonsense."[3]

And, although *Mein Kampf* did not specifically discuss genocide, Lorraine Boissoneault writes in *The Smithsonian* that "as early as 1922, [Hitler told] journalist Josef Hell, 'Once I really am in power, my first and foremost task will be the annihilation of the Jews.'"[4]

Hitler bowing to Hindenburg, March 21, 1933
Source: https://encyclopedia.ushmm.org/content/en/photo/adolf-hitler-greets-paul-von-hindenburg

Gladwell suggests the probable reason that Hitler succeeded in coming to power despite flashing all the warning signs of a madman was that he epitomized the mismatch between intent and presentation that characterizes bad guys. He was "a consummate attractor," said Sir Martin Gilbert, the official biographer of Churchill. Neville Chamberlain, the British prime minister who infamously sought to appease Hitler, was not the only one fooled. Gilbert recalled that other world leaders who met Hitler, having prepared themselves for a monster, thought he was "not such a bad chap."[5]

Commenting on the photo of Hitler bowing to Hindenberg, an internet history blogger writes,

---

[3] https://www.timesofisrael.com/why-jews-couldnt-care-less-about-mein-kampf-when-it-first-came-out/

[4] https://www.smithsonianmag.com/history/first-moments-hitlers-final-solution-180961387

[5] Personal communication, 1996. Gilbert made these remarks in an investor meeting of Cursitor-Eaton Asset Management Company at which I was present.

"Hitler was an actor with several characters in his repertoire: there was the messianic [ranter]; there was the courteous Bavarian gentleman; there was the outraged victim; there was the Nietzschean supervillain; the dinner party bore... The real fascination here is that Hitler is playing a very rare role captured perfectly by the camera: the deferential servant of the German state. Hindenburg is the embodiment not only of the German army, but of the German Empire...,and Hitler in bowing the knee to the German President is showing his understanding of his debt to the chthonic spirits of German history."[6]

The news photo from March 21, 1933 that appears above was circulated worldwide, and shows Hitler deferring (exaggeratedly, I'd say) to Paul von Hindenburg, the taller, older, and handsomer man who would hand Hitler the reins of power, very much against his better judgment. Hitler isn't dictating to anybody, and the pose suggests humility and supplication, not command. I've included the excellent caption provided by "Dr. Beachcombing," the pseudonymous history buff who posted the photo.

The lesson, says Gladwell, is that when there is a severe case of mismatch, we are easily fooled. It is part of human nature to assume that what someone is telling us is true, or at least that they believe it to be true. While assuring Chamberlain and others that he meant no harm, Hitler intended the opposite. The price the world paid was enormous and its repercussions still haunt Europe and beyond.

Foxy Knoxy

Some of Gladwell's efforts to fit history to his theories, however, come up short. (That is the problem with "one explanation for everything" books.) He cites the travails of Amanda Knox, the young American who struggled — eventually successfully — for eight years to clear her name after a highly

---

[6] http://www.strangehistory.net/2016/03/25/image-hitler-bows-to-hindenburg/. Commentary by "Dr. Beachcombing."

problematic murder charge in Italy, as a case of mismatch. She acted guilty, Gladwell argues, even though she was not, hence the miscarriage of justice.

I've only followed the case in the news media, not researched it more thoroughly as Gladwell apparently did, but he got the gist of it wrong. A good shave with Occam's Razor — the principle that the simplest explanation for something is usually the best one — sheds some light. Knox behaved oddly, not because she was guilty or because of what Gladwell calls her inherent "youthful American goofiness," but because she was in shock from her roommate's murder and terrified of being punished for a crime she did not commit. Her ability to act normally was switched off by the circumstances. And, for bored and ambitious Italian police and prosecutors, she was a prize catch: a very attractive young foreign woman — an American, yet! Most murderers are threatening-looking men; she was different.

Knox did behave a little weirdly, but that is different from "acting guilty." People react to tragedy and the extreme stress of being a murder suspect in unpredictable ways — I know I would. She was also alleged, by police and the media, to have acted "brazen and sexual" when, Gladwell argues, she had actually been a shy misfit in high school.

Amanda Knox
Source: https://ew.com/article/2013/05/01/amanda-knox-interview-diane-sawyer/

But Americans, garrulous and assertive by global standards, strike many people as brazen, and most 20-year-old women are interested in sex. These are not the "tells" of a murderer.

Finally, given her last name and her appearance, it would be surprising if she had *not* picked up the nickname Foxy Knoxy as a middle-school soccer player. It is utterly bizarre that the nickname she acquired as a youth was taken as a sign of guilt in a murder case.

There is nothing about this case to suggest that Knox was anything but an innocent victim of incompetent and possibly malicious police work. The "mismatch" between a guilty demeanor and factual innocence simply isn't there.

What are Ross and Rachel feeling today?

Gladwell focuses in some detail on the *transparency problem*, the question of whether people reveal their true feelings through their body language and facial expressions. He notes that the actors in the TV series *Friends* are so transparent that you can usually follow the complex and silly plot twists even if you have the sound off. They are actors, not people in real life, and they are trained to translate the thoughts and feelings in the script into obvious behavioral cues. They can act out a fake smile or a real one, an affectionate hug or a romantic one, an angry or a disappointed frown, depending on what is called for.

Sendhil Mullainathan, behavioral economist at the University of Chicago's Booth School of Business

As a result, you think you're perceiving their true feelings. Of course, what the actors are feeling is that they'd like to go home, and are glad to be making so much money for easy work. You are mixing up the actor and his or her character, which is exactly what's intended.

But *Friends* is not real life. In real life, people sometimes don't reveal their true feelings through facial and body language. That's why, according to a group led by the University of Chicago economist Sendhil Mullainathan, *a computer makes better bail decisions than a judge*.[7]

The computer, Gladwell explains, went through a list of 554,689 defendants in New York City, of which judges had released just over 400,000 on bail. The computer had access to the same formal information (rap sheets, demographics, and so forth) as the judges, and made

---

[7] At the time he did this work, Mullainathan was at Harvard.

its own list of 400,000 people to release. It was a bake-off: man versus machine. Who made the best decisions? Whose list committed the fewest crimes while out on bail and was most likely to show up for their trial date? The results weren't even close. The people on the computer's list were 25 percent less likely to commit a crime while awaiting trial...

That's really scary. We place our freedom, maybe even our lives, in the hands of people who are much worse at reading the landscape of human emotion and intent than a machine that can't see, hear, empathize with, fear, or hate us and can only process highly stylized information. No wonder Amanda Knox was wrongly accused of murder.

The $50 billion con man

We now arrive at "default to truth." The following statements are true: Bernie Madoff founded the firm that developed the technology enabling the over-the-counter "pink sheet" stock market to morph into NASDAQ. He was non-executive chairman of NASDAQ. His firm was the largest market maker on the NASDAQ and, in one particular year, was the sixth-largest market maker in the overall securities business.

Would you have believed him if he said he was also an asset management whiz whose fund delivered truly exceptional returns with very little risk? A lot of wealthy and accomplished people did, to the tune of $50 billion. The problem was that, as we all now know, it was all a scam, a Ponzi scheme. There was no fund. He paid early investors off with the money received from newer ones.

Madoff's shenanigans were exposed when Harry Markopolos, an obscure security analyst, "couldn't figure out what Madoff's strategy was," according to Gladwell. If anyone was qualified to figure it out, it was Markopolos, who had his own hedge fund and had been asked by investors to copy Madoff's strategy so he, too, could make spectacular returns for them. Markopolos went to the SEC and to the then-prestigious prosecutor Eliot Spitzer (who later became governor of New York and resigned due to a prostitution scandal), and the mammoth scam was eventually uncovered, but not before the disbelieving SEC officials and the future governor gave Markopolos a lot of resistance.

"It may be fun to be fooled"

I wish there were some new insight in Gladwell's retelling of the Madoff tale, but there isn't. It's unsatisfying to be told that the existence of a man whose intent and demeanor didn't match, and who could get people to believe his lies, reveals something profound about human nature that we didn't already know. Being fooled by con men and swindlers is a recurring theme in every culture.

In fact, the momentary pleasure of being conned makes up an entire literary genre. Almost a century ago, the great *New Yorker* journalist Joseph Mitchell discovered a local bum with literary pretensions and a blue-blooded background, Joe Gould, who told such fabulous lies and exaggerations that he became the subject of Mitchell's best-loved articles.[8] Gould said he was writing "an oral history of the world" (he later added "in our time"), which he claimed was the longest book ever written. The work was not entirely imaginary: he quoted sections of it at length. Little of it, however, had been written down; it was, in fact, an *oral* history, resident in Gould's head.

The poet e. e. cummings, a contemporary and neighbor of Mitchell's and Gould's in Greenwich Village, got wind of this and wrote a couplet that sums up Madoff's scam better in two lines than Gladwell did in many pages:[9]

> it may be fun to be fooled
> but it's more fun...to be little joe gould

And it was fun to be Bernie Madoff while the party lasted.

---

[8] Mitchell, Joseph. "Professor Sea Gull" (1942) and "Joe Gould's Secret" (1964), in The New Yorker. Compiled in Mitchell's [1993] *Up In the Old Hotel*, New York: Penguin Random House.

[9] This is part of a longer poem: http://3bpoetrythoughts.blogspot.com/2013/04/ee-cummings-little-joe-gould-has-lost.html. It was, in fact, not much fun to be Little Joe Gould when he was not wowing the literati: he spent much time in mental institutions, and medical examinations found that he had experienced intermittent starvation.

Bernard Madoff, https://www.biography.com/crime-figure/bernard-madoff, (left), Joe Gould, drawn by Al Hirschfeld, https://www.newyorker.com/, (right)

We all want to believe there is more than meets the eye. People become careless when they become believers. Madoff took advantage of that universal weakness. That's all there is to the story, except that $50 billion is a lot more money than is usually lost when the confidence man comes to town.

The mystery of suicide

Too much of Gladwell's book is about suicide and sexual abuse, problems that are not amenable to simple solutions. While Gladwell's writing on these topics is competent and sensible, he imposes his communication theories on them. Doing so is more confusing than helpful.

The book is, in fact, framed by two takes — at the book's beginning and end — on the death of Sandra Bland, a young African American motorist who killed herself a few days after being jailed for an unwarranted and illegal traffic stop. Gladwell describes the misfortune as "what happens when a society does not know how to talk to strangers." I'd say it's what *sometimes* happens when an abusive cop encounters a deeply troubled citizen; if enough such encounters take place, eventually someone will die.

Some people are resilient, while others are easily pushed over the edge. Bland was the latter.

Gladwell overanalyzes the situation, finding that the policeman did "exactly what he was trained to do." Of course, he did not intend to kill anyone (and he did not do so). But, in an escalating confrontation between a policeman and a motorist, it's the policeman's duty to try very hard to de-escalate. The evidence that he did so is thin.

Sylvia Plath

Gladwell also devotes close attention to the suicide, in 1963, of the 30-year-old poet Sylvia Plath, about whom much has been written already. He attributes her suicide to the "coupling" of two risk factors: lifelong suicidal tendencies, made evident by her writing and mental health history; and the easy availability of "town gas," a carbon monoxide-heavy byproduct of coal production that was in wide use in British households of her time. (Town gas was later replaced with much safer natural gas.)

Gladwell's argument appears to be that if it had been harder for Plath to commit suicide — if there were no town gas in her oven — she might not have done it; most suicide attempts fail. Gladwell cites as supporting evidence the fact that the overall suicide rate in Britain fell quite a bit when town gas was eliminated. The problem is that Plath was about as determined a suicide as could be imagined. She was not crying out for help; she wanted to die. And so she did.

Do poets die young?

In a related thought, Gladwell informs us that "poets die young," and that does feel right. We think immediately of Keats and Byron, who died very young of natural causes, as well as Plath, and "Chatterton, the marvellous Boy, / The sleepless Soul that perished in his pride."[10] (The couplet is Wordsworth's; Thomas Chatterton killed himself at 17.)

---

[10] https://www.poetryfoundation.org/poets/thomas-chatterton

But do we have data on the average lifespans of poets, or are we engaging in availability bias because a few have died young and suicide is so shocking? It is also easy to think of poets who lived a long time: Henry Wadsworth Longfellow, Walt Whitman, and Robert Frost, the greatest American poets, come to mind. They lived to 75, 72, and 88 respectively.[11] Bob Dylan is still kicking at 78.

In a review of Gladwell's book, critic Andrew Ferguson notes that there is no occupational category in the U.S. for poets so we have no demographic data to study. Ferguson also traces Gladwell's claim that poets commit suicide at rates "as much as five times higher than the general population" to a study of 36 British and Irish poets *in the eighteenth century*, of whom two killed themselves. (Chatterton was one of the two.)

Anyone who works with data even casually will see the problem: The sample is way too small, as well as being out of date. Reviewing Gladwell's body of work, he often makes confident claims based on a thin reed of evidence.

How sexual abuse happens

Gladwell also analyzes the case of Brock Turner, the Stanford rapist. Again, I'd apply probabilistic thinking rather than miscommunication and misrepresentation. Some tiny percentage of men are rapists by temperament, and will take advantage of anyone in a vulnerable position. Most men, of course, are not, but it's hard to tell rapists from non-rapists just by looking. If there are enough encounters between, on the one hand, a large population of men, and on the other hand a large population of women who are "so out of it [due to drinking] that she doesn't understand what she is doing," some women will be raped. That does not excuse the rapist at all — it is just a fact.

More interesting is the awful case of Jerry Sandusky, the Penn State coach who molested innumerable boys and young men while being lionized by a community that regarded him as a hero. Sandusky is an example of

---

[11] A lifespan of 75 or 72 was well above average in the 1800s, when Longfellow and Whitman lived. It seems youngish now. Times and medical technologies have changed.

mismatch. His good deeds, which were many, were apparently a cover for his one goal, which was to have access to underage boys. His friends and associates had no way of knowing, and the instinct of his adoring public was to defend him. Many of the boys thought it was their duty to keep quiet or to pretend they liked the contact — at any rate, they were not believed, until they were.

The Sandusky story is the Hitler story in miniature: consummate attractor, reportedly kind to dogs and children, widespread adulation, not such a bad chap. A recipe for disaster, if the person in question is of bad intent.

Roasted by Andrew Ferguson

Book reviewers read other reviewers at their peril. It is too easy to be influenced by a persuasive rant or rave. But the estimable Andrew Ferguson of *The Atlantic*, whom I mentioned above, touched a nerve when he found *Talking to Strangers* vacuous.[12] I had the same feeling — that I had sat through the last of one too many sequels to an originally interesting movie. Ferguson writes,

> Gladwell's many critics often accuse him of oversimplification. Just as often, though, he acts as a great mystifier, imposing complexity on the everyday stuff of life, elevating minor wrinkles into profound conundrums. [The] pop...social science [promoted by Gladwell] specializes in taking axioms known to every 19th-century schoolteacher and duding them up as *heuristics* or *effects* or *biases*... Gladwell is both a sucker for and a master of this kind of obfuscation.

This critique, besides being sublimely funny, rings true. Gladwell has promoted catchphrase-style explanations for phenomena before: we all know the "10,000-hour rule." However, we don't know if it's true; if it is, there are major exceptions such as Mozart, who wrote exquisite music before he was old enough to have done anything for 10,000 hours. The

---

[12] https://www.theatlantic.com/ideas/archive/2019/09/when-malcolm-gladwell-says-nothing-at-all/597697/

"tipping point," obviously not a Gladwell original but sold hard by him, has been burned into our vocabulary to the point that it sounds like ancient wisdom — which it probably is.

In *Talking to Strangers*, the less-than-catchy catchphrase is "default to truth." *Of course* the default position when hearing something is to believe that it is true. We wouldn't be able to function otherwise: "What time is it?" "Three-fifteen." "Says who?"

But don't we also know not to believe everything we hear? Aren't we conditioned by common sense and experience to take people's words with a grain of salt, and to check out other evidence? If it's obviously mid-morning, we'd be justified in challenging the person telling us it's three-fifteen.

And we should be more guarded when a person is trying to sell us something or influence our behavior in an important way, especially when it comes to money. That is what most people do, whether they've been enlightened by Malcolm Gladwell's advice or are simply responding to the instincts that human beings have evolved over tens of thousands of years.

Recommendations for readers

Beware of one-variable explanations. Popular science and popular psychology writers love them because they provide a convenient way of organizing a book and distinguish their work from other, similar efforts. Gladwell is prone to this tendency.

Gladwell is an entertaining and appealing fellow. At age 56 he still looks like a teenager from a distance. He knows how to give a speech. But he has a packaged style, in Ferguson's words "introduc[ing] us to historical oddities, revisionist interpretations of the past, the frontiers of social science, the backstories behind recent headlines, all strung together along a single provocative thesis." The fact that the style can be effective does not mean that the single thesis is right — or, if it's right, that it is new and helpful.

An inability to see another person's bad intentions behind their façade of honesty and benevolence is *not* the root of all evil. Evil is the most complex puzzle man faces: Every religion, and every irreligious philosopher, deals with it in one unsatisfactory way or another. It is the ultimate multivariate problem. After thousands of years of intense study, we do not know much about it. We should study the matter with multiple points of view, rather than accepting simple explanations.

Advice for investors

To avoid becoming a pigeon of the next Madoff, do your own investigating. It still may not work — some bad outcomes are not preventable. But if Madoff had really been making bets of the size he claims, traders taking the other side of those bets would have surfaced. They didn't, and that should be enough to cast suspicion. When, many years ago, a Goldman trader told me that they traded with Enron frequently and always "won," I knew that something was rotten in the state of Enron. I did not know what, and I was not in a position to do anything about it. But I did not buy the stock.

Don't rely on the due diligence of others. Many investors tell me that they believe a particular alternative investment is "kosher" because Harvard, Yale, or some wealthy foundation or family is participating in it. They can afford to lose a sizable chunk of their money. You can't. If an investment doesn't make sense *to you*, if there are red flags, don't buy it.

Last word

Gladwell's book can be summed up — maybe a little unfairly — in the one-liner spoken by the prison warden played by Strother Martin in the film *Cool Hand Luke*: "What we've got here is...[pause]...failure to communicate." Such a failure can lead to untold damage and destruction. But it is not a satisfactory single explanation for all human misery. Malcolm Gladwell comes close to saying that it is. He should try harder.

Index

A

Abraham (Biblical), 166, 169
abundance, 19, 42, 70, 85, 95, 160, 268, 371
accelerator (in venture capital), 152, 211
Accel Partners, 155
active management, 43, 116, 142, 258, 298, 305
Adams, Franklin P., 9, 245, 272
Adler, David, 19, 341, 343, 353
affluence, 34, 37, 46, 70, 284
Afghanistan, 7, 87, 196
Africa and Africans, 6, 65, 71, 73–74, 80–81
    geniuses in, 74–75, 77
    nations, 81
    ordinary, 81
    slaves, 163
    unbanked, 81
Agility Robotics, 212
agriculture, 9, 35, 48–49, 184, 247, 341
airplanes, 46–47, 87, 183, 294
Alaska, 224
Alchian-Allen theorem, 209
Alexa (product), 176, 208–9
Alexander, Scott (pseudonym), 293
algorithms, 108, 124, 372
alpha, 114–15, 297–98, 305, 327
    expected, 114
    statistically significant, 298
Amazon (company), 43, 58, 89, 137–38, 147, 149, 182, 192
America (See United States of America)
American Affairs (publication), 343
American Business History Center, 271
American Economic Association, 252, 256
American Electric Power, 164
American Enterprise Institute, 189
American Institute for Economic Research, 246
Amish, 162
Anabaptists, 157, 160–63
analysis
    contingent claims, 115
    fundamental, 43
animals, 24, 49, 129, 131, 135, 137, 220–22, 224–25
    largest, 224
    small, 221
anthropic principle, 337
Anti-Communist Manifesto (book), 235
apes, 23, 296, 300
apocalypse, 36
    nuclear, 168
Apollo (spacecraft), 23
Apple (company), 43, 81, 138, 148–49, 192
Arcadia (concept), 53–54
Archimedes, 23
architecture, 9, 220, 227, 247, 323, 337
    financial, 333
    naval, 9, 247
    neural, 296
Argentina, 283, 338
Aristotle, 55, 300
Arizona State, 307
Armageddon, 167
Armstrong, Neil, 353
Arnott, Robert, 99
Aronson, Theodore, 91
ARPA, 188–89
Arrow, Kenneth, 113, 253
artificial intelligence (AI), 173, 175, 196, 207
    bioweapon, 183
    investment funds, 190
    missile system, 176
    software, 208
    stocks, 182
Asia, 6, 135, 272
Asness, Cliff, 99
asset allocation, 107
asset classes, 108, 111, 120, 258, 298, 308
assets, 28, 37, 96, 100, 114–16, 118–19, 121–22, 158, 256–58, 308
    bubbles, 96
    classes, 109
    liquid, 120
    managers, 292, 297
    non-tradeable, 121
    pricing studies, 126
    real, 100, 190
    return-generating, 120
    riskless, 114
    stranded, 227
    tradeable, 120
Athens, 61
    classical, 332
AT&T (company), 278, 311
authoritarianism, 239–40, 243
authorities, 101, 191
    central, 189, 191, 238

monetary, 255, 257
national, 342
public health, 341
automation, 33, 177, 180, 185
automobiles, 7, 39, 46-47, 84, 137, 140, 192–93, 204, 244
aviation, 184, 204

B

Babbage, Charles, 22
Babylon, 293
Bacon, Francis, 166
Bagehot, Walter, 96
Bangkok, 86
Bangladesh, 50
bankers, 81, 165
banking system, 94, 96
banks, central, 95–96, 98–99
Barclays Global Investors (company), 104, 298
Barnum, P.T., 200
Bastiat, Frédéric, 93, 95, 239, 261
Baum, Frank L., 98
Bayes, Rev. Thomas, 113, 118–20, 123, 292–95, 323–25
Bazacle (location in France), 330–31
Bell, Eric Temple, 166
Bell Northern Research, 217
Bell System, 198
Belyaev, Dmitry, 24
benefits
    employee, 166
    environmental, 41
    social, 182, 276
    technological, 19
Benz, Karl, 204
Berger, Pete, 125, 154, 273
Berggruen, Nicolas, 307–8
Berkeley, Calif., 105, 148
Berlin, Germany, 307
Berlin, Isaiah, 47, 317
Bernanke, Ben, 97–98
Berners-Lee, Tim, 189
Bernstein, Andrew, 235
Bernstein, Peter, 92, 115, 125, 142
Bernstein, William, 157
Bessembinder, Hendrik, 307–8
beta risk, 114
Bezos, Jeff, 78, 86
Bhansali, Vineer, 159
biology, 8, 17–18, 125, 131, 133, 136, 139, 142, 227, 303
    evolutionary, 130, 136, 138, 142
biophysics, 344
bitcoin, 158, 191, 204, 294

Black, Fischer, 113, 118, 125, 127
Black Americans, 245
Black-Litterman (model), 118, 126
Bland, Sandra, 363
Blank, Julius, 147
Boeing Company, 205, 311
Bogle, John C., 130
Boisguillebert, Sieur de (Pierre le Pesant), 269
Boissoneault, Lorraine, 357
bonds, 100–101, 118, 121, 129, 254, 257, 278, 332–33, 338
Bono. *See* Paul Hewson
Boolean logic, 23
Booth School of Business, 116
Borio, Claudio, 94
Boston, 4, 149, 282
Boston Dynamics (company), 212
Botswana, 73
Bourgeois Dignity (book), 5
Bourgeois Equality (book), 5
bourgeoisie, 3, 5, 10–16, 64, 277, 280, 282–83
    dignity of, 3, 5, 11, 13–15
Bourgeois Trilogy, The (books), 5, 283
Bourgeois Virtues, The (book), 5, 327
Boyer, John, 255
brain, 18, 27, 221, 291–301, 347
Brand, Stewart, 60, 148, 152
Braques, Georges, 307
Brazil, 71, 76, 222
    southern, 79
Breznitz, Daniel, 19
Brinson, Gary P., 330, 337, 371
Bristol (U.K. city), 167
Britain. *See* United Kingdom
Brookings Institution, 51, 236
Brooks, David, 277
Brown, Josh, 271
Brown, Patrick, 144
Brozen, Yale, 265
Brynjolfsson, Erik, 33, 42, 178
bubbles, 158, 182, 334
    cryptocurrency, 203
    dot-com, 163
    financial, 163
    tulip, 163, 329, 334
Buckley, William F., 167
Buffett, Warren, 78, 305–6, 326
buildings, 27, 53, 64, 81, 85, 108, 111, 177, 189–90, 210, 215, 219–31, 270, 283, 316, 323, 335
bull market, long, 182, 188, 306
Burj Khalifa (building), 222
Burma, 6

Burton, Edwin, 96
businesses, viii, 4, 9, 11, 21, 48, 76, 95, 105, 116, 130-, 134, 1367-40, 144, 148, 151–52, 154, 160, 164, 166, 169–70, 180, 198, 205, 210–11, 220, 225–27, 252, 270, 292, 317, 324, 326-327, 336, 349, 360
  big, 35, 48, 204, 212, 225
  industrial, 212
  profitable, 270
  venture-funded, 146
Byers, Brook, 147

C

Caesar, Julius, 333
CAFE (corporate average fuel economy), 39
Cai, Yong, 36
California, xii, 105, 109, 148, 152, 201, 224, 319, 342, 344, 347, 350, 371
  Southern, 342, 372
Cambridge University Press, 139
Canada, 62, 67, 217, 316, 335
cancer, 195, 294–95
Caneva, Duane, 347–48
capital, 12, 17, 37, 40, 52, 83, 95, 104–5, 141, 215, 267, 271, 313, 336
  accumulation, 3, 7, 17
  costs, 271
  destruction, 261
  financial, 42
  human, 11, 27, 42, 120–21
  private, 149
  social, 41–42
Capital Asset Pricing Model. *See* CAPM
Capital Ideas (book), 92, 115, 125
Capital Ideas Evolving (book), 92, 125
capitalism, 3, 9–12, 33, 40, 52, 63, 93–94, 105, 163, 184, 233, 235–47, 254, 265–67, 269, 271, 273, 282
  laissez-faire, 262
  liberal, 4
Capitalism and Freedom (book), 238, 254, 265
Capitalist Manifesto (book), 235, 237–38, 246, 271
capitalists, 7, 40, 52, 55, 61, 236, 263, 266–67, 273, 336
capitalization (stock market), 95, 203
CAPM (Capital Asset Pricing Model), 111, 113–16, 119, 127, 158
carbon, 70, 364
Carden, Art, 3–5, 7–12, 16
cars, See automobiles
Carson, Johnny, 212

cartels, 153
catastrophes, 86, 176, 183, 299
Catholics, 10, 159
Cato Institute, 10, 237, 263
Caufield, Frank, 147
Cavaliers (Brit. history), 61
CBS, 227
cell phones, 67, 80–81, 192, 194
Center for Research for Security Prices (CRSP), 116
Central Asia, 6
CFA Institute, 127, 312, 327, 351
CFA Institute Research Foundation, 19, 99, 126, 129, 159, 226, 256, 294
Chamberlain, Neville, 357–58
Chen, Yuyu, 36
Chicago, viii, 62, 107, 111–12, 116, 145, 166, 255–56, 259, 265, 273, 284–85, 294, 327, 347, 355, 371
Chicago Daily Tribune, 165
Churchill, Winston, 37, 357
cities, 76, 83, 144–45, 162, 222, 225, 239, 245, 272, 284–86, 332
citizens, 159, 161, 241
classes, social, 12–13, 60, 125, 277, 280, 282–83
Clean Air Act, 41
Clean Water Acts, 41
Cleveland (city), 8, 245
Clifford, Scott W., 298
climate, 59, 132, 136, 183
cloud (in computing), 109, 171, 187–217, 219
Cloud Revolution, The (book), 188, 197, 199–201, 203, 216
coal, 34, 83, 193, 244, 364
Cochrane, John, 102, 255–56
Coldiron, Kevin, 104–5
Cold War, 177
Coleman, Thomas, 98, 256, 294
Coleridge, Samuel Taylor, 277
commerce, 8–9, 11–12, 124, 209, 247, 341
commodities, price index of, 29, 103, 121
Commonfund Capital, 306
Commonwealth Edison, 165–66
communists, 64, 184, 235, 242, 245–46, 275–76, 336
companies, 21, 43, 77, 95, 136, 139–43, 145, 147–48, 150–55, 158, 164–66, 182, 188, 199, 226–27, 270, 311, 317, 330–31
competition, 6, 76–77, 132–33, 137, 139, 176, 282, 318, 333
Compton, Mary Ida, 99
computer scientists, 138, 148, 291, 305
Congress (U.S.), 204, 269, 323
convergence (in economics), 79, 130–32,

134, 136–38, 197
corporations, 48, 138, 225, 244, 266–67, 270, 330, 332, 338
Costello, Elvis, 267
COVID, 57, 62–63, 75, 97, 103, 341, 343–46, 348, 350–53
Cowen, Tyler, 105, 209, 247
Cowhey, Peter, 19
Cowles, Alfred, 126
Cowles Commission, 111, 126
Cox, Wendell, 285
Crapper, Thomas, 24
Cray, Seymour, 138
Cray-2 supercomputer, 23, 31, 192
CRB commodity price index, 103
Cronkite, Walter, 202
cryptocurrencies, 191, 201–2, 209, 256
Cugnot, Nicholas Joseph, 204
Cultural Revolution (China), 36
Cursitor-Eaton Asset Management, 146, 357
cyberattack, 227, 342

D

Daily Beast, 251
Daimler-Benz, 137
Dalton, Russell, 276, 326
Dana Point (Calif.), 276
DARPA (*see also* Defense Advanced Research Projects Agency), 178
Darwin, Charles, 125, 129–33, 135, 137, 142, 225, 230, 282, 296, 320
Davy, Sir Humphry, 20
Dawkins, Richard, 27
Dawson, William, 314
Dayton (Ohio), vii
Dean, Charity, 342–43, 346–47, 350, 352
decentralization, 190–91
Defense Advanced Research Projects Agency (DARPA), 178
De Finetti, Bruno, 127
DeLong, Bradford, 45–56
Delusions of Crowds, The (book), 157–69
dematerialization, 29–30, 32, 35, 37, 40, 42–43, 60, 192–93, 229–30
democracy, 12, 17, 184, 239, 282–83
Deneen, Patrick, 53, 246
Depp, Johnny, 304
DeRisi, Joe, 344, 348–49
Desmond, Matthew, 236
Detroit, 244–45, 284
Deuteronomy (Biblical), 166
Diamandis, Peter, 42
Diamond, Jared, 315
Dimson, Elroy, 99, 336

discounted cash flow (DCF), 124
diseases, 26, 63, 183, 324, 342, 345–47, 349, 352
 communicable, 352
 epidemic, 341
 infectious, 353
 mad cow, 168
 respiratory, 243
dividends, 104, 111, 141–42, 165, 270, 331
Divine Afflatus, The (essay), 46, 355
DNA, 131, 282, 340, 344, 349
doctors, 112, 124, 185, 195, 295, 312, 320, 324, 342, 348
Dodd, David, 142
Dominican Republic, 83–84
Doriot, Georges, 148
drugs, 178, 346
 addiction, 284
Dubai, 222
Dutch East India Company, 330
Dylan, Bob, 365

E

earnings (corporate), 60, 87, 140–41, 148, 158, 205, 217
East Africa, 81
East Asia, 6
East Coast (U.S.), 148
economic
 adjustments, 262
 agents, 101
 behavior, 138
 boom, 76, 175, 188, 200
 development, 72
 freedom, 10–13, 15, 239–40
 growth, 3, 7–8, 17, 28–30, 34, 42–43, 46, 50–51, 56, 80, 204, 209, 271
 historians, 8, 19, 157
 history, 45–46
 progress, 59, 65, 82
 reasoning, 56
 research, 16, 246
economics, xi, 16, 25, 34, 45, 56, 58, 89, 92, 112, 125, 129–31, 133, 138–39, 173, 209, 221, 251–52, 254–55, 258, 263, 267–68, 297, 326–27, 335–36, 340, 371
 behavioral, 291
 classical, 39, 124
 and evolution, 133
 free-market, 49, 253
 monetary, 95
 prescriptive, 268
economists, 43, 45, 51, 56, 96–99, 102, 125, 158, 178, 197, 205, 213, 216, 219, 228–29, 242, 244, 249, 251–53, 258, 262–

63, 267–69, 271–72, 277, 281, 295–96, 371
behavioral, 360
economy, 8, 17, 19, 28, 33, 45, 51, 67, 69, 76, 93, 95, 98, 129–31, 133, 146, 154–55, 160, 175, 177, 192, 197–99, 205, 209, 219, 225, 230, 242, 249, 255, 259, 261, 267, 269–71, 278, 280, 338
   advanced, 50, 60
   competitive, 154
   declining, 100
   developed, 286
   global, 78, 199
   growing, 41, 100–101
   mixed, 52
   open, 352
   planned, 240
ecosystem, 47, 59, 136–37, 198
Edison Electric (company), 311
Edison, Thomas, 20–21, 138, 164
Ediswan (company), 21
education, 3, 8, 28, 67, 75, 79, 142, 166, 267, 271, 273, 279, 292, 325
Egypt, 7, 240
Ehrlich, Paul, 33–34, 37
Eisenhower, 202
electricity, 18, 20, 27, 84, 86, 164, 177, 179, 208
electric utilities, 164, 210
electronics, 22–23, 174, 193, 205
elephants, 37, 219–31
Elizabeth I, Queen, 24
Ellington, Duke, 320
Emperor's New Mind, The (book), 337
Empire State Building, 190, 221–22
Emtage, Alan, 189
Encyclopedia Britannica, 31, 233, 278
energy, 18–19, 21, 28–30, 37–40, 43, 48, 59, 85–86, 164, 190, 193, 198–99, 208, 220, 228, 243, 296, 341
Engel, Louis, 116
engineers, 12, 19, 21, 72, 147, 180, 221, 297, 321–22, 327
engines, 85–86, 153, 171, 184, 207, 209
English Civil War, 13
ENIAC (computer), 23, 174
Enlightenment (historical period), 10, 64, 169, 246, 273, 291, 299
Enron, 368
environment, 33–35, 37, 40–41, 59–60, 69–70, 72–73, 82–84, 132–34, 194, 224, 243, 316–17, 326–27
Epstein, David, 315–25
equities, 42–43, 92, 99, 109, 122, 127, 130, 145, 226, 253, 257, 303, 307, 310, 317,
329, 332, 336
equity risk premium. *See* risk premium
Erdoğan, Tayyip, 103
Esquire, 149
Ethiopia, 79
Europe, 3, 7, 14, 19, 53, 63–64, 71, 94, 96, 162, 164, 215, 237, 245, 272, 277, 284, 333, 358
evolution, 17, 82, 129–34, 136, 138–39, 142, 296–97, 330, 337
Exelon (company), 165

F

Faber, Marc, 103
Facebook, 150, 184
factory system, 277
Fairchild Semiconductor, 146–49
Fallon, Jimmy, 212
Fama, Eugene, 253
famine, 36, 63, 100
farming, 49, 73, 76, 144, 279, 335
fascism, 184, 275–76
Federalist Papers, The, 4
Federal Reserve, 213–14, 281
Ferguson, Andrew, 6, 365–66
Ferguson, Niall, 5
feudalism, 149, 184, 275–80, 285–86
Fibonacci, 124, 126
Fifth Risk, The (book), 341–42
finance, x–xi, 89, 92, 96, 105, 111, 113–14, 124–27, 142, 201, 205, 253, 276–77, 279, 303, 326, 329, 332–36, 339, 371
   classical, 115
   decentralized, 190
financial
   advisors, xi
   analyst, 178
   archaeology, 339
   disasters, 166
   economist, 102, 118
   historian, 89
   journalists, 262
   markets, 92, 96, 126, 159, 338
   panics, 96, 159
   recklessness, 170
   writers, 89
fiscal deficits, 97
fiscal theory of the price level, 102, 255–56
Fisher, Irving, 126
Fisher, Lawrence, 111, 116
Fitzgerald, Scott, 54
Florida, Richard, 277
Folsom, Burton, 279
food, 18, 25, 76, 79, 177, 181, 224, 243, 277
Forbes, Steve, 104, 236, 344

Ford Foundation, viii, 371
Ford Motor Company, 137
Foster, Lauren, 313
Founders Fund, 149-51, 154-55
Foxx, Jimmie, 318
France, 67, 84, 330-32
French Revolution, 162
Friedman, Milton, 42, 52, 112, 238, 249-52, 254-60, 262-63, 265, 268
Frost, Robert, 365
Full Employment Act of 1946, 269
Fuller, Buckminster, 30, 32

G

Galileo, 110, 220, 222
GameStop, 158, 163
Ganem, Don, 348
Ganges Delta, 86
gasoline, 29, 103
Gates, Bill, 154, 219, 304-5
Gave, Charles, 146
Gavekal Group, 146
GDP (gross domestic product), 7-8, 34, 37-39, 73, 97, 102-3, 125, 178, 203, 267, 269, 272, 344
Geipel, Gary, 301
Genentech, 147-48
General Electric, 245
Generalists, 45, 200, 315-27, 340
General Motors, 85, 212, 278, 311
genes, 34, 131, 183, 315-16, 348-49
geography, 9, 247, 284, 286, 371
geolocation, 153, 195
Germany, 75, 79, 157, 159, 307, 336, 338, 356, 358
Gilbert, Sir Martin, 357
Gilded Age, 279
Gladwell, Malcolm, 317, 355-68
Glaeser, Edward, 35
Gleick, James, 315
global GDP, 37-38, 179, 203
globalization, 48, 77, 237
GMO (company), 102
GNP (Gross National Product), 269
gods, 9, 12, 92-93, 142, 155, 167, 169, 332
Goetzmann, William N., 99, 118, 124, 126, 253, 289, 329-40
gold, 109, 111, 113
Goldman, Jason G., 25, 179
Goldman Sachs, 179
Goldwater, Barry, 258
golf, 316, 319
Goodman, Rob, 23
Google, 138, 148-49, 174, 182, 227
Gordon, Robert J. (economist), 46-47

Gould, Joe, 362
Gould, Stephen Jay, 18
governments, 37, 39-41, 71, 87, 101, 191, 235, 239, 250-51, 261, 266, 338, 341-42, 351
Graham, Benjamin, 142, 152
Graham, Paul, 152
Graham Sumner, William, 93
Grant, James, 96
Grantham, Jeremy, 102-4
Great Depression, 62, 163-64, 197, 255, 269, 304, 306, 344
Great Mirror of Folly, The (book), 334
Greece, 54
Green, James, 167
Greenberg, Hank, 318
Greenspan, Alan, 143
Greenwich Village, (N.Y.), 362
Grinich, Victor, 147
Grossman, Gene, 34
Grove, Andy, 146-47
Gu, Baochang, 36

H

Haas Business School, 104-5
Hagstrom, Robert, 326
Hamilton, Alexander, 4
Hammurabi, 333
Hansen, Drew, 236
Harker, Patrick, 211
Harvard University, 36, 282, 304, 360, 368
Hawken School, vii
Hayek, Friedrich, 49, 52, 54, 97, 238, 250, 262
Hayes, Isaac, 304
health care system, 343
hedge funds, 150, 164, 317, 361
Henriksson, Roy D., 117, 126
Heterodox Academy, 317
Hewson, Paul, 148
Hillel, Rabbi, 293
Hilpman, Liz, viii
Hindenburg, Paul von, 357-58
Hiroshima, 86
Hitler, Adolf, 356-58, 366
Hoboken, New Jersey, 19, 94, 125-27, 160
Hoerni, Jean, 147
Holcombe, Russell, 306
Holdren, John, 33-34
Homer, Sidney, 96
Hong Kong, 6, 237, 241
Hoover, Gary, 271, 326
Horgan, John, 22
Housel, Morgan, 303-7, 309-14
houses, 18, 39, 86, 159, 208, 304, 308-9

Housman, A.E., 313
Huber-Mills Digital Power Report, 216
Huttenlocher, Daniel, 173–76
Hutton, Lyn, 306

I

Ibbotson, Roger, 92, 99–100, 111, 119, 121, 126, 129, 253, 296, 309–11, 320, 329–30, 337–38, 371
IBM Corporation, 141, 311, 317
Ilmanen, Antti, 99
Ilzetzki, Ethan, 182
immigration, 67, 71, 77, 149, 277, 284
income, 63, 73, 80, 104, 198, 270, 273, 279
   median family-of-four, 279
   national accounting, 268–69
   per capita, 73
   wage, 98
   working class, 60
index, of stock market, 308, 311, 336, 369
index funds, 43, 114, 141, 158, 297–98, 307–8, 372
India and Indians, 65, 70–71, 77, 129, 140–41, 237, 299
Indonesia, 76
Industrial Revolution, 3, 5, 13, 17, 33, 37, 46–47, 64, 171, 197, 333
industries
   automotive, 212
   glamour, 136, 138
   nuclear, 85, 175, 177, 193, 217, 342
   regulated, 312
   supercomputing, 138
   telecom, 278
inequality, 33, 50, 77, 93, 151, 277, 282
inflation, 97, 102, 129, 255–61, 279
   adjustment for, 178
   decreases in, 215, 261–62
   destructive, 261
   Great Inflation, 255, 263
   wage, 215
information, x, 104, 120, 123, 142, 155, 176, 198, 210, 231, 238, 275, 292–93, 322, 324, 330
infrastructure, 188–89, 268
innovation, 12, 17–28, 33, 40, 43, 49, 64, 80–81, 119, 153, 179, 196, 204
innovators, 113, 215, 268, 340
innovism (neologism), 8, 12
Institute for Quantitative Research in Finance, 276, 371
institutions, 6, 47, 155, 301, 310
Insull, Samuel, 157, 163–66
Intel Corporation, 147
intelligence, 174, 221

interest rates, viii, x, 11, 89, 92–97, 100–105, 158, 240, 256, 258, 292, 310, 320, 331, 333
   administered, 94
   central bank, 259
   compound, 333
   and inflation, 257, 260
   intermediate-and long-term, 101
   low, 94–95, 97, 103
   manipulated, 215
   negative, 98, 100, 159
   negative real, 101
   short-term, 96
   sky-high, 261
   ultra-low, 93
internet, 87, 146, 153, 178–79, 188–90, 194–96, 199, 209, 219
inventors, 21, 30, 144, 164, 194, 344
investing and investments, viii, xi, 7, 11, 89, 95, 100, 112, 124–25, 129, 131, 134, 136–38, 142–43, 147–48, 151–52, 155, 160, 163, 193, 199, 210, 219, 225, 230, 253–54, 266, 270, 295, 297–98, 304, 307, 309, 311, 317, 326–27, 335, 338, 368, 371
investment, benchmark, 138, 297–98
investment management, 89, 92, 116, 125–27, 130, 141, 146, 157, 160, 256–58, 297, 315, 372
investors, 4, 28, 42, 87, 92, 101, 107, 109, 111, 114–16, 118–20, 122–23, 125, 138–40, 142, 155–56, 158–60, 165–66, 169–70, 175, 182, 188, 190, 195, 199, 225, 230, 254, 257, 292, 295, 297–98, 305, 307–8, 312–13, 315, 326–27, 335, 338, 356, 361, 368
   angel, 150
   early, 361
   knowledgeable, 121
   lazy, 141
   long-term, 3, 241, 253
   optimizing, 119
   short-term, 253
   unleveraged, 306
   younger, 260
iPhone, 18, 23, 27, 32, 192, 242
Iran, 71, 282, 342
Ireland, 65–66
Islam, 65, 169
Israel, 139, 168, 196, 356
Italy, 65, 75, 151, 359

J

Jain, Suryaansh, 182
James, Lebron, 145

Japan, 3, 14, 67, 96, 237, 338
Jay, John, 4
Jesus, 9, 166
Jevons, William Stanley, 193, 195
Jews and Judaism, 11, 74, 166–68, 240, 255, 269, 293, 356–57
Joachim of Fiore, 166
jobs, viii, 73, 76, 109–10, 153, 166, 180, 182, 213, 215, 245, 257, 351
Jobs, Steve, 154
Johnson, Lyndon B., 258
Journal of Economic Perspectives, 252
Journal of Finance, 111, 124, 126–27, 336
Journal of Financial Economics, 127, 308
Journal of Investment Management, 127
Journal of Political Economy, 124, 126
Journal of Portfolio Management, 126–27, 253–54, 337
Journal of Retirement, 214, 281

K

Kahn, Ronald, 116, 126
Kahneman, Daniel, 291
Kalanick, Travis, 154
Kaplan, Lee A., 56
Katsuyama, Brad, 343
Kaufman, Beatrice, vii
Keats, John, 364
Kelly, Jesse, 235
Kelso, Louis, 235, 271
Kennedy, John F., 250, 258, 304
Kenya, 81, 86
Keynes, John Maynard, 52, 95, 97, 249–52, 262, 352
Khosla, Vinod, 143–44
Kindleberger, Charles, 142
Kissinger, Henry, 173–85
Kiyosaki, Robert, 235
Kleiner, Eugene, 146–47
Kleiner Perkins. Caufield & Byers (company), 147
Knox, Amanda, 358–59, 361
Kotkin, Joel, 275–86
Kotler, Steven, 42
Kristol, Irving, 266
Kroner, Kenneth F., 298
Krueger, Alan B., 34
Kuznets, Simon, 269

L

Labcorp, 349
Labio, Catherine, 334
labor, 3, 10, 21, 37, 45, 49, 53, 108, 211, 213–14, 251, 257, 282, 335

laissez faire, 4
Lakeside School, 305
Lam, Trevin, 119, 126
Landes, David, 6
language, 124, 174, 189, 272, 282, 318, 327, 335
Law, John, 163
Lebowitz, Fran, 300
LeCun, Yann, 184
Leeson, Peter, 273
Leibowitz, Martin L., 99, 116–17, 126
Lewis, Michael, 341–53
liabilities (financial), 103, 116–17, 257, 270, 331
liberals, 27, 247, 266, 299
libertarians, 4, 40, 249, 286
Lilliput, 222–23
linguists, 194, 291
LinkedIn, 58
Lintner, John, 113
Lippincott & Co, 30
Lipton, Eric, 343
Litterman, Robert, 109, 118–19, 125–26
Livermore, Jesse Lauriston, 163, 306, 309
Lohr, Steve, 193
Lomborg, Bjorn, 60, 82
Long Boom (U.S.), 45–55
Longfellow, Henry Wadsworth, 365
Lopes-Schleip, Priscilla, 316
Lorenz, Hendrik, 22
Lorie, James, 111, 116
Los Angeles, 145, 285
Louisiana, 86
Lovelace, Lady Ada, 22
Lowrey, Annie, 50
Low-tech innovation, 18, 23
Lucas, Robert, vii
Lyft (company), 154

M

MacArthur Foundation, 152, 348
machines, 23, 31, 33, 116, 123, 171, 199–217, 281, 361
Mackay, Charles, 157–58
Maclean, Norman, 347
macroeconomics, 52, 95, 252–53
Maddison Project Database, 73, 79
Madison, James, 4
Madoff, Bernie, 163, 334, 356, 361–63, 368
Malaysia, 6, 62
Mallaby, Sebastian, 143–51, 154–55, 220
Mamet, David, 240
management, 298
Manila, Philippines, 86
Mann Gulch fire, 346–47, 350

Mao Tse-Tung, 64
market economy, 50, 55, 238
market forces, 97–98
market portfolio, 114–15, 118, 121, 126
markets, 49, 52, 54–55, 63, 70–71, 93, 100–103, 113–16, 118–19, 121, 133, 138, 140, 158, 165, 196, 205, 211, 213, 225–26, 233, 237, 251, 253, 259, 266, 273, 306, 308–9, 311, 313, 326, 333, 335–36
Markopolos, Harry, 361–62
Markowitz, Harry, 107–19, 121–27, 327
Marsh, Paul, 336
Martin, Strother, 126, 368
Marx, Karl, 235, 253, 283
Massachusetts Institute of Technology, 174
materials (physical), 192–93, 199, 220, 229, 342
McAfee, Andrew, 29–30, 32–42, 192
McCaffrey, Paul, 100, 226
McCloskey, Deirdre, 3–5, 10, 16, 64, 74, 265, 277, 283, 327
McGraw-Hill, 160, 330, 338
mean-variance analysis, 112
mean-variance optimization, 107–11, 116–18, 120, 122, 124–25
Mecher, Carter, 343–47
Mehra, Rajnish, 99–100, 226
Mehrling, Perry, 113, 127
Mekong Delta, 86
Melvin, Michael, 109
Mencken, H.L., 45–46, 355
Mennonites, 162
Merrill Lynch (company), 116
MERS (disease), 346
Mexico and Mexican, 35, 70–71, 77–78, 348
Michael, George, 250
Michaud, Richard, 108–9, 117, 122, 127
Mills, Mark P., 171, 185, 188–90, 192–94, 196–202, 216, 330–31
Minnesota, 372
Mirzakhani, Maryam, 320
missile detection system, 175
Mississippi Delta, 86
Mitchell, Joseph, 362
modern portfolio theory (MPT), 111, 124–25, 253
Mokyr, Joel, 19
Monetary History of the United States (book), 255
monetary policy, 95, 97, 250, 255, 258
money, xi, 6, 11, 13, 21, 58, 62–63, 76, 78–79, 81–82, 85–86, 88–89, 95–96, 100–101, 123, 130, 138, 142–43, 149–50, 152, 155, 159, 165, 201–2, 219–20, 222, 236–38, 244, 246–47, 255–57, 271, 279–80, 298, 303–4, 306, 308, 314, 329–31, 333–35, 360–61, 363, 367–68
monopoly, 226
Montana, 346
Moore, Barrington, 282
Moore, Gordon, 146–47, 282–83
Morgenstern, Oskar, 138
Morningstar, 309–10, 371
Morocco, 243
Morton Thiokol (company), 320
Mossin, Jan, 113
Moulins de Bazacle. *See* Bazacle, France
Moulton, Lord, 112
Mozart, W. A., 26, 366
MPT. *See* modern portfolio theory
Mullainathan, Sendhil, 360
Munger, Charlie, 326
Murray, Charles, 277
Musk, Elon, 145, 150, 211, 215
Muslims, 72–73, 166–67, 169
MVO (see mean-variance optimization)
Myanmar, 6

N

Namibia, 73
Napier, John, 112
NASA, 320
Nasar, Sylvia, 138
NASDAQ, 142, 361
Nash
    John, 138
    Ogden, vii
Nashville, 285
National Cash Register, 154
National Geographic, 339
national income and product accounts, 269
National Lampoon, 103
nature, 40, 63, 136, 140, 243, 291, 299–300, 314, 325
Nazis, 174, 307
Netherlands, 329
Netscape (company), 148
Newsom, Gavin, 350
New Statesman, 251
Newsweek, 249, 252
Newton, Sir Isaac, 8, 20, 125
New York, viii, 27, 75, 105, 145, 147–48, 153, 160, 174, 240, 251, 279, 285, 326, 330, 338, 360–62
New Yorker, The, 362
New York Evening Mail, 355
New York Stock Exchange, 116, 333
New York Times, 193, 316, 343, 350
New York University, 184

Nguyen, Tuan, 194
Nichols, Tom, 148–49
Nigeria, 75
Nimoy, Leonard, 29
Nixon, Richard, 258–59
NJ, 19, 94, 125–27, 160, 336
Nobel Prizes, vii, 108, 113, 116, 125–26, 147, 176, 204, 252, 269, 372
Norberg, Johan, 233, 235–39, 241–47, 271
Nordhaus, William, 252, 267
Nordic Europe, 55
North Africa, 73, 124
North Korea, 177, 239, 342
Northwestern University, 216
Nosek, Luke, 154
Noyce, Robert, 146–49
nuclear
 energy or power, 59–60, 85
 physics, 8
 technology, 185
 war or weapon, 168, 175–76, 178, 342

O

Obama, Barack, 348, 353
Occam's Razor, 359
Ohio, 21, 162, 305
O'Keeffe, Georgia, 340
Old Testament, 92, 240
Oliver, Bryan, 256
Operation Warp Speed, 343
Oréal (company), 141–42
O'Toole, Peter, 250
Oxford, 131, 253–54, 337
Ozymandias (poem), 46

P

Pacific Ocean, 70
Packard Motor Company, 137
pandemic, 41, 58, 67, 75, 77, 100, 196, 276, 300, 341–53
 flu in 1918, 343, 346
Pareto principle, 150, 220
Paris, 165, 239
Parker Hannifin (company), 245
Pascal, Blaise, 25
Pasteur, Louis, 26
Patterson, James H., 154
PayPal, 150
Peking University, 36
Pennsylvania, ix, 174, 244, 269
Pennsylvania State University, 365
Peru, 79
Peterson, Jordan, 303
Pethokoukis, James, 189–90

Petrov, Stanislav, 176
Philippines, 6
Philosopher's Stone, 107–27
Pierobon, 196
Pinker, Steven, 10, 63–64, 133, 267, 272–73, 291–97, 299–301, 314
Plath, Sylvia, 364
Plexus Group, 372
Plöckinger, Othmar, 357
Poe, Edgar Allan, 229
Poincaré, Henri, 22
Polanyi, Karl, 49, 52, 54–55
policies
 anti-inflationary, 262
 central bank, 98
 easy-money, 103
 fiscal, 255
 foreign, 168
 nineteenth-century laissez-faire, 250
political economy, xi, 124, 126, 233, 250, 268
polytheistic religions, 169
Ponzi, Charles, 334, 361
Pooley, Gale, 10
population, 9, 24, 28–30, 34–36, 38, 51, 66–69, 71–74, 77, 79, 87, 98–99, 104, 117, 129, 131–32, 159, 169, 180–83, 214–15, 235–37, 276, 280, 283, 286, 294, 299, 345–46, 353, 365
populism, 41, 93
portfolio
 active equity, 130
 all-asset, 121
 bond, 257
 capitalization-weighted, 158
 efficient, 111, 114
 global, 336
 inefficient, 115
 managed, 43
 optimal, 108–9
 risky-asset, 119
 super-efficient, 121
 venture capital, 146
 world market wealth, 120, 126
portfolios, investment, 107–9, 111, 114–15, 119–23, 145, 151, 155, 164, 307–8
portfolio theory, 111–12, 124, 126, 253
Potemkin villages, 242
Potter, Brian, 221
Pouget, Sebastien, 331
poverty, 6, 9, 30, 34, 54, 69, 104, 229, 236–37, 244, 283
Powell, Jerome, 97
Prasad, Pulak, 129–31, 136–37, 139–42, 191, 230

Price, Richard, 294
Price of Time, The (book), 10, 89, 91–105
prices, 6, 13, 31, 39, 55, 70, 75, 81, 89, 92, 100, 103, 115, 141, 158, 164, 168, 182, 191, 193, 199, 237–39, 242, 255, 257, 269, 284, 294, 331, 333, 358
probability, 132, 220, 292–95, 298, 323–24
productivity, 28–29, 33, 76, 178–80, 182, 188, 196–97, 199, 203–4, 213, 215, 313
   agricultural, 76
   growth in, 93, 125, 179, 197–98, 204
   and wealth, 33, 188
Professor Sea Gull (character), 362
profits, 7, 10, 47, 136, 138, 160, 226, 266–68, 270–71, 313, 333
   corporate, 182
   decrease in, 137
   monopoly, 226
progress, vii, xi, 17, 19, 28, 30, 40, 51, 58, 63–65, 78, 80–81, 124–25, 153, 164, 176, 181, 192, 197, 199, 205, 235, 237, 266–67, 272–73, 299–301, 371
   angle of, 125
   incremental, 24
   material, 8
   medical, 59
   moral, 299
   technological, 8, 33, 42, 48, 154
Protestants, 159
Proverbs (Biblical), 312
Psychology of Money (book), 303
Public Broadcasting Service (PBS), 254, 256, 339
Putnam, Robert, 41

Q

Quantitative Research in Finance, 276, 371
Quantity Theory of Money, 255
Quantor Capital, 121
Quarterly Journal of Economics, 34

R

radio, 26, 31, 87, 227
railroads, 6–7, 40, 269, 311
RAND Corporation, 124
Raskin, Jef, 148
Read, Leonard, 61
Reagan, Ronald, 157, 167–68, 216, 251, 259, 262
real estate, 120–21, 152, 199, 210, 257, 270, 308, 329
reason (in philosphy), 99, 272–73
Reddit (website), 39, 152
Redfield, Robert, 53

Redford, Robert, 347
Redstone, Ilana, 317
religion, 11–12, 72, 157–69, 184, 332, 367
Remington, Frederic, 339
Renaissance (historical period), 11, 54, 63, 65, 124, 299, 329, 372
Republican, 258
resources, 6, 10–11, 17, 27, 29, 37–38, 43, 49, 63, 83, 85, 103, 140, 175, 178, 182, 238, 244, 246, 271
   master resource, 38
   scarce, 39, 246, 268
   waste of, 140
retirement, xi, 58, 98, 103, 109, 214, 270, 281, 311
return (on investment), 4, 8, 52, 100, 108–11, 113–14, 117, 119–22, 137–38, 145, 149, 158, 226, 240, 254, 256, 258, 271, 277, 297–98, 307–9, 331, 335
return, expected, 108, 111, 114–15, 122, 141, 305, 336
Reyburn, Wallace, 24
Ridley, Matt, 17–28, 92, 153
Rieves, Ralph, 372
risk, 42, 92–93, 95, 97, 107–8, 111, 114–15, 120–22, 130, 158, 177, 183, 191, 253–54, 257, 277, 292, 295, 341–43, 350, 361
   business, 92
   correlated, 112
   diversifiable, 114
   expected, 109
   medical, 92
   mortality, 92
   premium, 34, 60, 70, 92, 100, 119, 127, 308
Ritholtz Wealth Management, 311
RNA, 349
robber barons, 279
Roberts, Sheldon, 147
robots, 48–49, 171, 177, 201–17, 295
Rock, Arthur, 147, 150
Rockefeller, Laurance, 148
Rodrigues, Francisco, 223
Rodriguez, Alex, 318
Romans (ancient), 10, 12, 23, 26, 63, 124, 149, 332
Rome, 54, 61, 88
Rosenberg, David (economist), 103
Rothschild, Nathan Mayer, 78
Rowes, Barbara, 236
Russia, 25, 168, 177, 282, 335–36
Ruth, Babe, 318

S

Sacramento, 347

Saint Louis (U.S. city), 214, 281
Saint Louis, Federal Reserve Bank of, 272, 281
Salomon Brothers, 117
Salt Lake City, 285
Samuelson, Paul, 113, 117, 127, 249–54, 256, 258, 262–63, 267
San Diego (Calif.), 43, 62, 67, 105, 200, 231
Sandusky, Jerry, 365
San Francisco, 149, 284
  South, 105
Santa Barbara (Calif.), 342
SARS (disease), 345–46, 348–49
Saunders, Pete, 284
Savage, Jimmie, 112
SCADA (Supervisory Control and Data Acquisition), 48
Scandinavia, 329
Schmidt, Eric, 173–75
schools, 8, 61, 76, 222, 265, 272, 279, 305, 319, 342–43, 345
  engineering, 48
  grammar, 61
  private, 81, 305
Schumpeter, Joseph, 94
Schwartz, Anna, 255
Schwarzman College, 174
science, xi, 3, 6, 8, 12, 26–27, 34, 47, 74, 112–13, 139, 147, 174, 184, 220, 228, 272, 300, 317, 327, 340
  atmospheric, 161
  inexact, 312
  and technology, 27
Scientific American, 25
Seattle, 149, 305
securities
  global, 173
  investment, 107–8, 111, 118, 124–25, 142, 158, 170, 361
  trading of, 372
security analysis, 139, 142
Semper Augustus, 159
Sequoia Capital, 149–50
Seuss, Dr. (psuedonym), x
Sexauer, Stephen C., 105
Shakespeare, William, 24, 82, 320
Shannon, Claude, 22–23
Sharpe, William F., 113–14, 118, 121, 124–25, 127, 158
Shelley, Mary, 185
Shermer, Michael, 166
Shockley, William, 147
Shultz, George, 259
Siberia, 197
Siegel, Jeremy J., 98, 338

Siegel, Laurence B., x–xi, 3, 17, 19, 23, 29, 45–46, 57–58, 91, 95, 98–100, 107, 119, 121, 126, 129, 143, 157, 173, 181, 187, 201, 214, 217, 219, 226, 235, 249, 253–54, 265, 275, 281, 291, 298, 303, 315, 327, 329, 337–38, 341, 355, 371–72
Silicon Valley, 149–50
Sinclair, Upton, 281
Sinquefield, Rex, 111, 129
skills, 92, 239, 268, 297, 300, 304–5, 307, 315, 318
  developed, 11
  limited, 109
  motor, 212
  technical, 249
  traditional labor, 76
Slate Star Codex (former website), 293
slaves, 9, 25, 240, 334
Sloan School (MIT), 33
Smarr, Larry, 64, 138
Smil, Vaclav, 219–25, 228–29, 231
Smith, Adam, vii, 93, 238
Smith, Maynard, 139
Smith, Noah, 251
Smithsonian Institution, 357
socialist, 55, 251, 263, 276
societies
  advanced, 13
  free, 63, 238
  global, 29
  good, 55, 283
  mature, 94
  modern, 64
  neo-feudal, 286
  open, 352
  primitive, 53
  rich, 244
Solomon, King, 92
Solow, Robert, 204–5
Soni, Jimmy, 23
South Africa, 73
South America, 6
South Asia, 124
South Atlantic, 163, 334
South Korea, 52
South Pacific, 163, 334
South Sea Bubble, 163, 334
South Sea Company, 163, 334
Soviet Union, 7, 177, 250
Spain, 84, 331, 345–46
Spalding, John Lancaster, vii
Sparta, 61
Spelman College, ix
Spencer, Herbert, 132–33
spending, 116, 210–11, 258, 306

consumer, 257
  global capital, 210
Spitzer, Eliot, 361
Spock, Mr. (character), 29
Sports Illustrated, 319
Sri Lanka, 52, 241
Staggers Act, 40
Stalin, Joseph, 197
Standard & Poor's, 96, 104, 267, 270, 308
standards
  developed-country, 78
  global, 359
  historical, 51
standards of living, 10, 77, 242, 280–81
Stanford University, 147–48, 365, 372
Stanwick, David L., 62
Staunton, Mike, 336
Stegner, Wallace, 37
Stevenson, Adlai, 202
Stevenson, Robert Louis, 229
Stigler, George, 265
stocks, 100, 108, 114–16, 118, 121, 129, 136, 138,
    140, 142, 149, 155, 164–65, 182, 203,
    225, 227, 253–54, 257, 270, 286, 307,
    326, 330–31, 338, 368
  bubble, 182
  earliest, 332
  high-priced, 158
  small-capitalization, 225
Stoke Newington (town), 261
suicide, 163, 363–65
Sumerians, 333
Sumner, William Graham, 93
Sun Microsystems, 148
supply-demand-price mechanism, 39, 238
Swahili, 81
Swan, Sir Joseph, 20
Swift, Jonathan, 220, 222, 285
Swinkels, Laurens, 119, 126
Switch Inc, 189
Switzerland, 83, 95, 335
Sylla, Richard, 94, 96

T

Tafereel (see Great Mirror of Folly)
Taiwan, 52, 242, 344
Taleb, Nassim Nicholas, 72, 92–93, 142
Tasmania, 135–36, 224
taxes, 39, 41, 86, 153, 182, 215
Taylor rule, 101
technology
  benefits of, 18, 25–27, 34, 171, 179, 181–82,
    184, 190, 197–98, 204, 214, 216, 268
  financial, 332
  general-purpose, 178–79, 182, 353

medical, 365
  nuclear, 185
telecommunications, 46, 87, 153, 188, 197,
    227, 243, 339
Templeton, Sir John, 311
Tesla (company), 84, 215
Tetlock, Philip, 317
Thailand, 6
Thatcher, Margaret, 259, 262
theocracy, 184
Theory of Moral Sentiments, The (book),
    238
Thiel, Peter, 149–51, 154
Thoreau, Henry David, 251
Tijuana River, 70
TIPS bonds, 257
Tobin, James, 113–14, 118, 121, 126–27, 253
Toole, John Kennedy, 285
Touhy, Leigh Anne, 343
Toulouse, France, 330–31
Treasury bills, 114, 308
Troy, Tevi, 258
Trump, Donald, 251, 341, 343, 348
Tucker, Sir Paul, 96
Tufte, Edward, 323
Turing, Alan, 22
Turner, Brock, 365
Tversky, Amos, 291
Twitter (former company), 58, 148, 184

U

Uber (company), 153–54, 192, 195
Ukraine, 196
unemployment, 33, 180, 256, 260, 262, 269,
    271
Unimate (robot), 212
United Kingdom, 12, 21, 124, 250, 364
United Nations Environment Programme,
    84
United Nations Population Division, 72
United States of America, 3, 7, 9, 14, 37, 45,
    51, 53, 67, 70–71, 76–77, 79, 83, 86,
    96, 149, 163–65, 167, 179, 202, 210–11,
    214–15, 229, 235, 237, 242, 244, 250,
    252, 255, 270–72, 275–78, 281, 283–
    84, 329, 336, 339, 342–43, 345–46,
    350–53, 359
  capitalism in, 235
  cities, 71
  history of, 148, 164
  northeastern, 148–49
  western, 339
  workers in, 244
University of Bristol, 167
University of California, 48, 104–5, 276, 317

Irvine (UCI), 276
Los Angeles (UCLA), 372
San Francisco (UCSF), 348-49
University of Chicago, 42, 56, 64, 107, 111-12, 116, 255-56, 265, 273, 294, 327, 347, 355, 371
University of Illinois, 327
University of Pennsylvania, 174, 269
University of Southern California, 342, 372
University of Virginia, 96
University of Wisconsin, 372
utility, 30, 43, 153, 158, 209, 228-29, 292, 295

V

Valentine, Don, 149
van Gogh, Vincent, 320
Van Sloan, Edward, 185
Vasallo, Steve, 344
Venezuela, 52, 241, 283
venture capital, 143, 145-47, 149-51, 154-55, 220
venture capitalists, 143, 147, 151, 155, 197, 201
Verbiest, Ferdinand, 204
Veterans Affairs, 343
Viles, Jill, 315-16
Vinod Khosla, 143
Virginia, 96
Virochip, 344, 348
Vodafone (company), 81
Vonnegut, Kurt, 53
von Neumann, John, 22, 138

W

Wagner, Wayne H., x, 372
Wall Street Journal, 58, 258
Wapshott, Nicholas, 249-51, 258-59, 262
Waring, Barton M., 122, 127, 327
Waze (product), 32
Weijian, 237
Weimar Germany, 255
Welling, Kathryn M., 57-67, 69-88
Wells Fargo (company), 372
West, Geoffrey, 220, 230, 315
West Africa, 74, 346
Western Air Express (company), 204
Westinghouse (company), 311
White House, 259, 347-48

Whitman, Walt, 365
Whitney, J.H. "Jock," 148
Wikipedia, 21, 159, 181, 336-37
Wilde, Oscar, x
Wild West, 329
Will, George, 153
Wilshire Associates, 372
Wimbledon, 320
Wizard of Oz, the, 99
Wolfe, Tom, 149
Wolf of Wall Street, 334
Wolfram, Gary, 235
Wolverines (organization), 342-43, 346, 348
Wong, John, 6
Wood, Grant, 35
Woods
  Earl, 319
  Tiger, 318-20
Wordsworth, William, 311, 364
workers, 10, 28, 33, 76, 148, 178, 182, 244-45, 279
  developed-country, 242
  displaced old-economy, 261
  factory, 76
  gig, 277
World Bank, 35, 39, 69, 79, 104, 236-37
World Economic Forum, 182
World Health Organization, 343
World Trade Center, 190
World War I, 62, 338
World War II, 6, 62, 64, 76, 95, 124, 245, 269, 338
Wright Brothers, 47, 204

Y

Yale University, 219, 296, 323, 329, 334, 368
Yang, David Y., 36
Yardeni, Edward, 265-73
Y Combinator (company), 146, 151-52
Yeats, William Butler, 46
Young, Timothy G., 334

Z

Zahavi, Amotz, 139
Zimbabwe, 74
Zimmer, Robert, 265
Zweig, Jason, 58

About the Author

Laurence B. Siegel is the Gary P. Brinson Director of Research at the CFA Institute Research Foundation, economist and futurist at Vintage Quants LLC, and an independent consultant, writer, and speaker. In July 2009 he retired from The Ford Foundation, where he served as director of research in the Investment Division since 1994. From 1979 to 1994 he was a managing director of Ibbotson Associates (now Morningstar).

Larry's book, *Fewer, Richer, Greener: Prospects for Humanity in an Age of Abundance*, was published by Wiley in December 2019 and reached #1 in Economics and #1 in History on Amazon shortly after release. His first book of collected essays, *Unknown Knowns: On Economics, Investing, Progress, and Folly*, was published by Montesquieu Press in 2021. In addition, he has written, co-authored, or edited a large number of journal articles, magazine articles, and CFA Institute Research Foundation monographs. He serves on the board of directors of the Q Group (Institute for Quantitative Research in Finance) and other organizations.

Larry received his BA in urban geography from the University of Chicago in 1975, and his MBA in finance from Chicago Booth in 1977. He lives in Wilmette, Illinois and Del Mar, California. His web site is http://www.larrysiegel.org

About the Editor

Wayne Wagner's support for Larry Siegel began with Wayne's serving as the Research Committee Chairman of the CFA Institute Research Foundation. Wayne's career has spanned the history of capital market theory since his Wells Fargo days, when he created the operating algorithms for the very first index funds. He was a founding partner at Wilshire Associates, where he became an investment manager for the state of Minnesota's $1.3 billion Wilshire 5000 Index Fund. As a co-founder of Plexus Group, he specialized in institutional transaction cost consulting.

Wayne is the Editor of *The Complete Guide to Securities Transactions: Enhancing Investment Performance and Controlling Costs* (Wiley, 1969) and co-editor with Ralph Rieves of *Investment Management: Meeting the Noble Challenges of Funding Pensions, Deficits and Growth* (Wiley, 2009.) He was also the co-author of *MILLIONAIRE, The Best Explanation of How an Index Fund Can Turn Your Lunch Money Into a Fortune* (Renaissance Books, 2000.)

Wayne is a graduate of the University of Wisconsin Business School and holds a master's degree from Stanford University's Department of Statistics/Management Science. He taught courses in investment management and securities trading at UCLA and the University of Southern California.

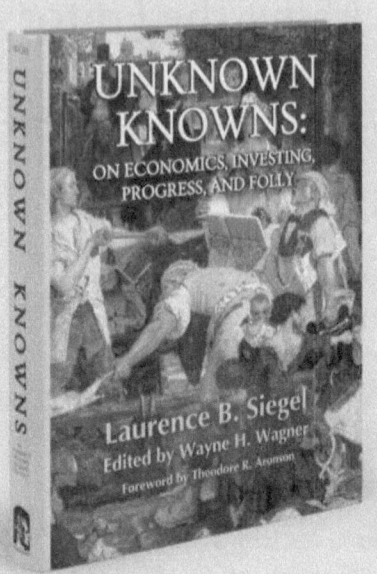

Available on amazon.com

"Siegel rewards the reader with many an 'aha' moment, as he turns the rock around to a different side than the one we usually look at. His erudite wit is entertaining and will hold your attention."

— *M. Barton Waring*
Chief Investment Officer for Strategy and Policy, Emeritus, Barclays Global Investors (retired)

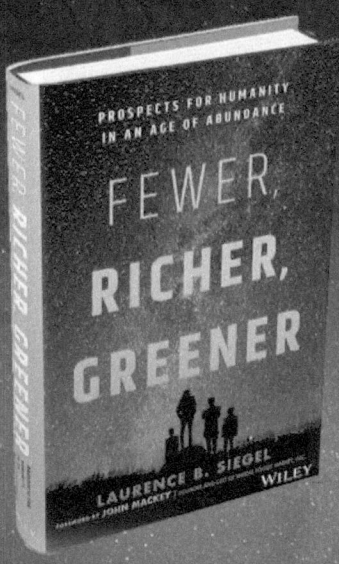

CHANGE YOUR PERSPECTIVE ON LIFE

Available on

"The many young people who seem to share a gloomy view of the future should read the new book by Laurence B. Siegel"

**Jason Zweig
The Wall Street Journal**

"As the twenty-teens draw to a close, may I wish everybody a Happy New Decade, and recommend a book that convincingly argues in great detail that it will be one."

**Matt Ridley
Author of *The Rational Optimist***

FewerRicherGreener.com

www.ingramcontent.com/pod-product-compliance
Lightning Source LLC
Chambersburg PA
CBHW022041200426
43209CB00072B/1920/J